The Rough Guide
Chronicle

China

Rough Guides online

www.roughguides.com

credits

Text editor: Orla Duane
Rough Guides series editor: Mark Ellingham
Production: Michelle Draycott and Helen Prior
Cartography: Maxine Repath and Ed Wright
Proofreading: Russell Walton

publishing information

This edition published October 2002 by
Rough Guides Ltd, 62–70 Shorts Gardens, London, WC2H 9AH

distributed by the Penguin group

Penguin Books Ltd, 80 Strand, London WC2R ORL
Penguin Putnam, Inc, 375 Hudson Street, New York 10014, USA
Penguin Books Australia Ltd, 487 Maroondah Highway, PO Box
257, Ringwood, Victoria 3134, Australia
Penguin Books Canada Ltd, 10 Alcorn Avenue,
Toronto, Ontario M4V 1E4, Canada
Penguin Books (NZ) Ltd, 182–190 Wairau Road,
Auckland 10, New Zealand

Typeset to an original design by Henry Iles
Picture research by Eleanor Hill of Lovely

Printed in Spain by Graphy Cems

© Justin Wintle, 2002
480 pages includes index

A catalogue record for this book is
available from the British Library.
ISBN 1-85828-764-2

The Rough Guide
Chronicle

China

by
Justin Wintle

Chronicles series editor
Justin Wintle

for Kimiko Tezuka-Wintle

notes and acknowledgements

Wherever appropriate, quotations are reproduced by kind permission of the publisher; sources are as follows:

p.23 Adapted from the translation of James Legge as found in Clae Waltham, *Shu Ching: Book of History* (Allen & Unwin); pp.27, 58 *Mencius* (Penguin); p.34 *Cambridge History of Ancient China* (Cambridge University Press); p.39 Confucius, *The Analects* (Penguin); p.43 Sunzi, *The Art of War* (Oxford University Press); p.50 Lao Tzu, *Tao Te Ching* (Penguin); p.82 Arthur Waley, *One Hundred and Seventy Chinese Poems* (Constable & Robinson); p.86 Burton Watson, *Ssu-ma Ch'ien: Grand Historian of China* (Columbia University Press); p.07 Adapted from material contained in Michael Loewe, *Everyday Life in Early Imperial China* (Batsford; Putnam's); p.99 Hans Bielenstein, *The Bureaucracy of Han Times* (Cambridge University Press); p.102 *The Classic of Mountains and Seas* (Penguin); p.141 Woodbridge Bingham, *The Founding of the T'ang Dynasty* (Baltimore; Octagon); p.165 Pauline Yu, *The Poetry of Wang Wei: New Translations and Commentary* (Indiana University Press); p.190 C.P. Fitzgerald, *China: A Short Cultural History* (Westview Press; Holt, Reinhart & Winston); p.205 Robert Temple, *The Genius of China: 3000 Years of Science, Discovery and Invention* (Prion); p.224 Marco Polo, *The Travels* (Penguin); p.276 Sven Hedin, *Jehol City of Emperors* (Kegan Paul); p.301 Arthur Waley, *The Opium War: Through Chinese Eyes* (Stanford University Press); p.308 Chien Yu-wen, *The Taiping Revolutionary Movement* (Yale); pp.324, 328, 337, 341 Pei-Kai Cheng and Michael Lestz (eds.) with Jonathan Spence, *The Search for Modern China: A Documentary Collection* (W.W. Norton); p.335 *The Revolutionary Army: A Chinese Nationalist Tract of 1903* (Mouton & Co); p.390 Zhisui Li, *The Private Life of Chairman Mao* (Random House); p.393 *The New York Times*; pp.395, 414 Foreign Languages Press, Beijing; p.398 Anhua Gao, *To the Edge of the Sky* (Viking)

contents

introduction

What we now know as China began to emerge four to five thousand years ago, in the fertile flatlands of the middle Yellow River. In the second millennium BC first the shadowy Xia, then the Shang, and finally the cultivated Zhou dynasty created an integrated, expansive kingdom that spread north, east and south, swallowing up smaller, now mainly forgotten states and peoples. Then in 221 BC the semi-alien Qin, coming from the Wei River valley in the west, forged the 'empire' itself, centred on the same heartland.

In due course, the territories ruled from the 'dragon throne' stretched from Mongolia to Vietnam, and from Korea to the Pamir Mountains. But for the 'Han' Chinese (as the dominant people often call themselves) lengthening frontiers were a continuous challenge. Successive waves of 'barbarian' troublemakers from the north and west threatened the divine order at the centre. As China prospered, so its expanding borders demanded protection. At times, the effort proved too much. In the 13th century China was itself conquered by the Mongols, and in the 17th by the longer-lasting Manchu Qing. Indeed, if we judge Marxism-Leninism to be an alien intrusion, then for the last eight hundred years China has only been self-governed during the Ming dynasty (1368–1644) and the war-torn early 20th century.

More persuasively, it is claimed that Chinese communism, for all its anti-imperialist rhetoric, has in fact restored the 'Middle Kingdom' (the Chinese empire), ruling through a bureaucracy reminiscent of the Confucian mandarins who managed China's affairs for almost 2000 years. Like its imperial antecedents, the Beijing politburo also rules a vast territory. Officially, 91 percent of an equally vast population (at

1.3 billion the world's largest) are Han Chinese. The remaining nine or ten percent – made up of Tibetans, Uigurs, Yao and a host of other minorities – together comprise a population that exceeds the combined totals of Italy and Spain.

Separatism within its borders has been another persistent theme in China's history. Even the Han themselves are prone to division, as recurrent stand-offs between north and south testify – not to mention other pulls such as Sichuan and Yunnan. But the commanding contemporary example of internal discontent must be Tibet. While the oppression of the Tibetan people is widely condemned, what is less understood is how, historically, Tibet personifies the central dilemma of the Chinese imperium. Tibet's western borders, once secured, are eminently defensible; the western borders of China proper without Tibet are far less so.

That China still constitutes an empire is self-evident. Whether Han or otherwise, its people are subject to an authoritarian regime that owes its existence to past conquest and continuing force. Genuinely democratic institutions are few and far between, either on the peripheries, or in the heartlands. China is still recovering from Mao Zedong's experiment in iconoclastic totalitarianism and as long as the Communist Party cherishes the notion of a nation organically unified under its own direction, Mao's legend as the 'Great Helmsman' cannot be casually dismissed.

Pragmatically, the line officially promulgated by the People's Republic is that Mao's policies were 30 percent wrong, but 70 percent right. By such legerdemain, from the late 1970s, Deng Xiaoping sponsored economic reform. But as the miserable showdown in Tiananmen Square demonstrated in 1989, political reform remains largely off-limits. At one end of the contemporary spectrum are government-approved, as also government-unapproved, millionaires; at the other, in both town and countryside, is a distressed underclass that can no longer rely on state socialism for basic life-support, but whose grievances, however acute, are, without representative institutions, politically insignificant.

China at the beginning of the 21st century, therefore, is not so very different from China at the beginning of the 19th, 16th, 12th or the 8th. It continues to abide by its own political traditions. Yet away from politics, China reveals another facade. While its historic high culture, as expressed in its art and literature, is predictably idiosyncratic, when it comes to its material culture there is far more of a continental, even global, homogeneity.

In this respect, the key engine has been the steppe corridor, leading out of the Yellow River basin through Gansu, and linking the Pacific to the Mediterranean. From the 1st century this became known as the Silk Road, enabling a patchy, but mutually enriching commodity exchange between East and West. But as archeology increasingly demonstrates, the same steppe highway functioned as Eurasia's umbilical throughout pre-history, serving as a conduit for primary technological transfer: the wheel, horsepower, metallurgy, and before those the woman-based industrial art of weaving. In its early stages, such transfer was mainly West–East, or rather it radiated west and east from around the Black Sea region. Later, however, it became East–West. As well as silk, the Chinese gave us printing, gunpowder, the magnetic compass, the stern-rudder – not to mention peaches and ice cream.

Today, it is broadly accepted that Chinese material culture during the Tang and Song dynasties was more advanced than anywhere else on the planet, and that for many centuries western Eurasia was a net beneficiary of Chinese innovation. Perhaps though, in the wider chronology, the precise order and rate of exchange is secondary to the sense of a shared human endeavour, underpinned by shared capacities to which different centres of civilization contribute at different times, both as makers and as users.

The Chinese then are our collaborators, far more than potential competitors or enemies. Like ourselves, they have marched on foreign soils, though no Chinese gunboat has ever approached a European or American shore in anger. It should also be recalled how, from the 17th century onwards, it was not some wild horde issuing from the Gobi or Taklamakan desert that unhinged the complex equilibrium of Chinese civilization, but our own venal and often brutal ancestry.

note

Given China's vast history, much has necessarily been omitted here. The rich histories of Macau, Hong Kong and Taiwan, for example – except where they impinge directly on the story of the 'mainland' – have been deliberately excluded. This is not to deny their participation in the Chinese experience, only to acknowledge that they would benefit from an entirely separate volume. The 'books' section at the back of this chronicle is intended as a guide to more comprehensive study.

The Pin-yin method in transcribing Chinese names and words into their English equivalents, devised in 1954, has been chosen in preference to the older, more cumbersome Wade-Giles method. Pin-yin romanization sounds pretty much as it reads – always allowing for the considerable variations in Chinese dialect – with the following glaring exceptions: c (as in Cai) reads as *ts* (= Tsai); q (as in Qin) reads as *ch* (= Chin); and x (as in Xia) reads as *hs* (= Hsia). Z is the most problematic, giving a sound between *dz* and *ts*, while zh wavers between *dj* and *ch* (as in Chan). In a handful of cases, an older form is given in parentheses (as well as in the Index as a cross-reference) where it still regularly occurs in English usage (eg Peking, Canton and Taoism for Beijing, Guangzhou and Daoism), but only on first appearance. Taiwanese Chinese, however, still prefer Wade-Giles, so Chiang Kaishek is retained at the expense of Jiang Jieshi. As regards the names of provinces, no attempt has been made to supply historical variants. Down the centuries new provinces have come and gone, as have other kinds of administrative territory. Here, unless specified, only modern provincial names are used to help identify towns, cities and birthplaces.

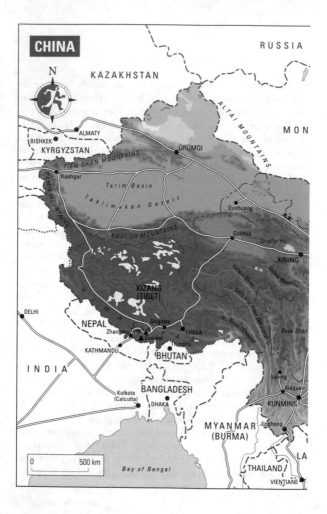

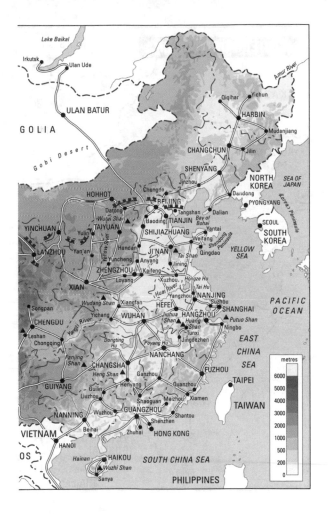

CONTEMPORARY CHINA

RUSSIA

KAZAKHSTAN

KYRGYZSTAN

MON

Ürümqi

XINJIANG

QINGHAI

Xining

XIZANG (TIBET)

SICHUAN

Lhasa

NEPAL

BHUTAN

INDIA

BANGLADESH

Kunming

YUNNAN

MYANMAR
(BURMA)

LAOS

*Bay of
Bengal*

THAILAND

1
Pre-imperial China

Up to 221 BC

n 221 BC the **Qin** (Chin), one among several 'Chinese'
kingdoms, conquered its rivals and established a unified
empire that survived, though not uninterruptedly, until
1912. Yet the Qin were not the first dynasty to govern a
sizeable territory in the heartlands of China. In the second
millennium BC the **Shang** created a compact, but powerful,
state in the middle reaches of the Yellow River. This was
succeeded in the mid-11th century BC by the **Zhou**
(Chou). Before either of these, there is a growing body of
evidence confirming a proto-dynasty known as the **Xia**.

All three archaic dynasties were theocratic: the ruler, as well
as overseeing defence and the daily business of government,
performed important religious rites. Only a king could commune with the state's founding ancestors and something of
this survived into imperial times. The long succession of
Chinese emperors were individually known as 'The **Son of
Heaven**' (*Tianzi*). They sat 'facing south' on their thrones,
living icons at the apex of an elaborate hierarchy. **Mao
Zedong**, too, in the 20th century, achieved, in his own lifetime, quasi-divine status, his enlarged portrait presiding over
Tiananmen Square in Beijing, its back to the north.

The theocratic element, however, is but one among many
themes that inform, nourish and ultimately bind the uniquely
continuous and unfinished theatre of China's history. In the
pre-imperial period other perennials were established. Of these
the most significant was Chinese as a **written language**, a

non-phonetic mnemonic sign system that acquired aesthetic as well as practical values. Through it, government could communicate edicts and instructions regardless of dialect or even tongue – an essential asset given the levels of mutual incomprehension among a people as ethnically diverse as China's inhabitants. By the same means a common high-culture literature was enabled. By the time of the first emperor, **Qin Shihuangdi**, the texts upon which Chinese thought would dwell for the next two thousand years were already written.

Much of this literature was utilitarian. Not only the **Confucians**, but also the many rivals of Confucius sought answers to the same questions: What is the moral nature of man? How best should man be governed? Out of this centuries-long debate, and out of the circumstances of the times, emerged a class of educated officials: the 'mandarinate' that, however elitist in its prejudices, at its best supplied China with a disinterested management, at local as well as central level.

Conversely, the pre-imperial period was rich in metaphysical speculation. **Shamanism**, **astrology** and **numerology** flourished. Again, in as far as China can boast an indigenous, yet globally recognized, religion, then the name for this is Daoism. But **Daoism**, the most eclectic offspring of the ancient foment, was also, in its own way, practical in its concerns. It sought alignment with nature, and non-alignment with the pretensions of power and power-holders.

Survival has often meant survival in the face of government. Either people have abided by the land, or developed their considerable talents as craftsmen and artisans. As an evolving **material culture**, China's ingenuity was arguably unrivalled until the European industrial revolution. The ancient Chinese may not have been the first to work bronze, but from around 1400 BC their bronze artefacts became world-class. They also developed excellence in jade, ceramics, lacquerware, silk, cuisine and mechanics. From early on, with the growth of planned cities, theirs was a consumer society.

The Shang Dynasty and before: until c.1045 BC

To study Chinese history is also to study Chinese historians. From Former Han times onwards, each dynasty compiled a history of its predecessor. The full set of 26 official histories is unparalleled as a rich and unbroken narrative of the government of any one people. The last, the **Qing shi gao**, in 534 chapters, was completed in 1927. The most famous, however, remains the first – the **Shiji**, written around 100 BC by **Sima Qian**. Not only did Sima construct a record of the Qin, whom the Han had replaced, but he sought to present the whole story of China from its origins. Into his book he inserted a series of well-established, but unsubstantiated, legends about a founding 'Yellow Emperor' and other mythical figures.

In giving credence to these, Sima had a specific political purpose. In his view, as in the view of others, rulers were entitled to govern by the 'Mandate of Heaven' (*Tian ming*). If they misgoverned, then that licence was forfeit. The **Yellow Emperor** and his successors, including Yu (the supposed founder of Xia) not only invented all the essentials of civilisation, but provided a model government. As a result of human corruption, however, this divinely instituted order soon collapsed, and thus began the familiar 'dynastic cycle'. A new regime comes to power, but sooner or later loses the divine right to govern, at which point it is replaced by another that does enjoy the Mandate. And this transferability of the Mandate, Sima suggests, is the underlying principle of history.

Thus, according to Sima, first the Xia were thrown out by the Shang, then the Shang by the Zhou (Chou). In the same manner, to secure the legitimacy of the Han emperors, he had to demonstrate the unworthiness of the Qin. In so doing he deliberately demonized them, much as Shakespeare, pandering to Tudor self-esteem, demonized Richard III. And subsequent dynastic histories, though impressively assembled, adopted a similar strategy, making them less than 100 percent reliable as evidence.

Sima embodied two further biases: the idea of history as being properly the history of the court; and the paramountcy of that people conventionally known as the **'Han' Chinese**. Even in the 18th century, when scholars took a more critical approach toward the 'classics', the flavour of Chinese historiography changed little. And when, from early on in the 20th century, Chinese historians turned to the Western science of archeology, they did so to confirm what they already knew. The sites investigated were sites suggested by traditional texts.

Today, the picture is quite different. Partly on account of provincial pride and provincial chauvinism, partly through the growing influence of Western research techniques, including carbon-dating and dendrochronology (tree-ring dating), and partly through sheer accidents of discovery, archaeology is transforming our understanding of China's protracted gestation. It is already clear that, three or four thousand years ago, China was multicentred and multicultural; remained that way until the beginning of the imperial era; and at times reverted to the same condition. It just happened that the society that initially evolved along the **Yellow River**, the 'cradle' of Chinese civilization, was the one that kept records and gradually engulfed all others.

Sima was scarcely the first of China's Yellow River chroniclers. He worked within an established tradition, drawing on, amongst other sources, the **Shu jing**, or 'Book of Documents', compiled in the 9th and 8th centuries BC. Yet in one respect, archeology is at least beginning to vindicate

Sima's somewhat battered reputation. Excavation of Shang remains at Anyang and elsewhere does indeed point to a polity of real, if foreboding magnificence, unmatched elsewhere in China at the time.

c.2m BC *Homo habilis*, mankind's common ancestor, trifurcates into an African, an Asian and a European type. Only the African variety will mutate into *homo sapiens sapiens*, through an intermediate stage of *homo sapiens*.

c.800,000 BC The era of the **great ice ages** begins. Recurring every 100,000 years, these have a decisive impact on the evolution and spread patterns of many species (including hominids) throughout the Eurasian landmass, as well as on the latter's physical characteristics.

For **China**, an important consequence of meteorological upheaval will be the accretion of mineral-rich **loess deposits**, washed from the Mongolian steppes into the Yellow and Huai river basins. Such alluvia will reach a hundred metres deep in places. But loess also contributes to the formation of a vast and unstable flood plain north and south of the Yellow River.

Soon a tool-making hominid (discovered in 1965), with half the cranial capacity of modern man, *Sinanthropus lantienensis*, appears at Lantian, modern Shaanxi province.

c.600,000 BC Microlithic evidence indicates the presence of hominids at Yuanmo (modern Yunnan province) in China's far southwest.

c.500,000 BC The era of **Peking Man** (*Sinanthropus pekinensis*), so called after the discovery by the Swedish paleontologist J G Anderson of bone remains within a complex of caves at Zhoukoudian, outside Beijing, from 1918 onwards. Intact skulls indicate a cranial capacity roughly two-thirds that of modern humans. Peking Man, uses fire, makes stone implements and may be capable of

Loess and Millet

From early on, unusually high population densities were achieved in northern China, particularly either side of the middle reaches of the Yellow River, in an area that came to be known as the **Zhongyuan**. The first reason for this is the presence there of vast quantities of **loess** – an exceptionally fertile alluvial sediment. Being highly porous, loess easily absorbs nitrogen from the air while allowing minerals in its substrata to surface. A second reason was the choice of millet as a staple crop by China's Neolithic farmers. Less digestible than rice or wheat, millet is a hardier plant, able to withstand climatic variations. Farmers were therefore able to grow significantly more food than they, or their dependents, required, thus releasing labour for such enterprises as the **Shang tombs**, the **Great Wall**, the **Grand Canal** and the early proliferation of cities, all of which required huge levels of manpower to build. Such fertility also pre-empted reliance upon draught and manure animals, explaining the prevalence of chickens, ducks and pigs as the main providers of meat.

But while it has been calculated that Chinese agriculture was six to seven times more productive than its Roman equivalent, the loess deposits have not been all good news. Because loess dehydrates quickly, any prolonged absence of rainfall leads to famine. When there is too much rain, the structural instability of loess creates severe flooding. Down the ages, many millions of Chinese have died as a consequence of these hazards, and to this day natural catastrophe remains a political liability.

speech. He is not a direct ancestor of the Chinese, as was formerly supposed, however, but a variety of *homo erectus*, related to, and perhaps descended from, similar but much older remains found in Java. In Europe a secondary lineage of *homo habilis* evolves into Neanderthal Man, also sometimes labelled *homo sapiens*, but untraced in Asia. Further human remains unearthed at Sjara-osso-gol (Inner Mongolia) and Kehe (near the Yellow River) confirm the spread of *homo habilis* in China at this time.

c.60,000 BC Having evolved in Africa c.100,000 BC, *homo sapiens sapiens* arrives in China, either along the steppe corridor that connects the Black Sea to modern Gansu province, or by sea. Heralding the extinction of 'Peking Man' and his *homo habilis* descendants, *homo sapiens sapiens* brings with him several primary technological skills. These include cooking by fire, the manufacture of relatively advanced stone and doubtless wooden implements, rudimentary house-building and perhaps pottery.

c.30,000 BC Of various humanoid species worldwide, only *homo sapiens sapiens* survives.

c.16,000 BC During the last **great ice age** sea-levels drop to the extent that Hainan, Taiwan and Japan are, for three or four thousand years, joined to mainland China.

c.8000 BC As the last of the ice ages recedes and a warmer climate prevails, *homo sapiens sapiens* begins devising a sedentary lifestyle, replacing hunter-gathering with husbandry and agriculture – the **Neolithic Revolution**. In China, wheat and soya-bean are the first plants to be domesticated, in the north. The first animal to be domesticated may be the water-buffalo, in the extreme southwest.

c.7000 BC A steadily increasing diversity of artefacts recovered by archeologists from many different parts of China in the 20th century indicates a diffusion of 'primitive' stone and pottery civilization.

c.6000–5000 BC Millet and wheat are widely cultivated in the Yellow River region and other northern centres. Further south, maize and rice are grown, the latter perhaps introduced from Southeast Asia. Dogs and pigs are domesticated. Evidence also suggests the gradual emergence of textile manufacture, using hemp, as a major activity among the proto-Chinese.

c.5000–3000 BC Several distinct Neolithic 'cultures' – generally named after the sites of their initial archeological discovery, and distinguished by their individual styles of **pottery** – emerge in different parts of China: 'Xinle' in the far northeast; 'Dawenkou', on and around the Shandong peninsula; 'Hemudu' and 'Majiabang' at the mouth of Yangzi; 'Dapenkeng' in the south and southeast; 'Dalongtan' in Yunnan; 'Majia' to the west; and 'Yangshao' in southern Shanxi and Shaanxi. The excavation of a **Yangshao** site at Banpo in Shanxi reveals a habitation of some 50,000 square metres surrounded by a ditch, with a central 'longhouse' measuring 20 by 12.5 metres, and pottery kilns and a cemetery placed outside the perimeter. Banpo's inhabitants eat millet. Red and black Yangshao pottery – characterized by fish motifs represented by increasingly abstract linear and geometric patterns – are distributed over a wide area, suggesting a local cultural hegemony. The large-headed, thin-bodied Chinese dragon first makes its appearance as a common motif in pottery, with possible shamanic implications. It is during this period, too, that the first **jade** artefacts and shallow **burial chambers** are found.

c.3500 BC A new and highly distinctive late-Neolithic culture, known as **Longshan** (first detected at Changziyai in 1932), emerges on and around the Shandong peninsula. Longshan pottery is notable for its clear use of the potter's wheel; its black, lustrous finish; its avoidance of surface ornamentation; and, above all, for the shapes of its vessels, many of which – but especially the tripodal drinking cups and jugs (*ding* and *gui*) – will later be replicated in Shang ritual bronzes. Indeed, 'mainstream' Chinese bronze-ware can be seen as an extension of Longshan ceramics, once the latter had collided with, and been modified by, the decorative traditions of the Yangshao and other Neolithic cultures to the east of Shandong.

An earthenware Neolithic burial jar c.2000–1700 BC painted in colours, found in Yangshao, Gansu province.

Other features of Longshan culture will also prove significant. These include the practice of 'burning' **divinatory scapulae** (shoulder-blades, usually of oxen) and **turtle shells** (plastron) to create 'cracks' that can then be 'read' as either favourable or unfavourable omens; and the presence of **jade carvings** incised with animal forms for ritual use. Longshan settlements further reveal the habit of burying objects of inherent, as well as ritual, value along with their richer owners' bodies in wooden chambers in stepped burial pits. This increasingly lavish style of entombment and funerary furnishings will spread across China and survive into the imperial era, providing historians with a continuous record of a people's material progress. Of equal significance, the presence so early on of widely differentiated degrees of individual wealth indicates a society that is as unequal as it is productive.

Jade

From the mid-Neolithic **jade** was central to Chinese manufacture, and, increasingly, Chinese beliefs, to the extent that it becomes appropriate to think in terms of a widely diffused jade culture. As a mineral, jade occurs in two forms: **jadeite** and **nephrite**, scattered in small pockets across the world. But while jade artefacts are found at archeological sites across China from around 5000 BC, several puzzles endure. First, significant jade deposits are unknown in China's heartlands. Nephrite had to be brought from the Tarim Basin, and jadeite from Burma. This has led some commentators to posit an established trading system from perhaps the fourth millenium BC. **Longshan culture**, in particular, exhibits stylized jade pieces of some sophistication. Second, it is unclear how a medium as hard as jade was carved at a time when such modern tools as the industrial diamond were unknown. If abrasives were used, their identity is obscure. Third, the emergence of jade's character as a magical stone is not easily dated. While early jades consist of such practical items as axeheads and blades, by Shang and Zhou times, jade is associated with longevity, even immortality. Circular jade *bi* were ritual conduits between earth and heaven, and funerary jade pieces were employed to 'stop' the nine orifices of a corpse. Nor were the musical properties of jade ignored, adding to its mystique. Spectacularly, by early imperial times, the dead were sometimes buried in jade suits, made up of many thousands of jade platelets, supposedly to prevent decay. By then, jade was already associated with the strong male principle of *yang*, and later an imaginary 'Jade Emperor' was worshipped as a supreme deity.

c.3000 BC As temperatures climb, **sea-levels** rise to between five and ten metres above their modern norm. Human settlements migrate inland as many parts of eastern China are inundated, accelerating perhaps the confluence of Longshan and Yanshao cultures. Although the waters soon recede, it will be 3000 years before China's coastline assumes its present contours.

c.2600 BC The **Yellow River** alters course, now exiting into the Yellow Sea south of the Shandong peninsula, instead of into the Bay of Baohai. Throughout history, the volatility of the Yellow and some other rivers will play havoc with China's economy.

c.2500 BC **Stamped-earth** (*hangtu*) construction for towns, cities and fortifications is widely practised throughout China, further indicating effective mechanisms for regional cultural and technological exchange. *Hangtu* involves compacting soil, usually with up-ended logs or beams, into a hard base which is then used as a platform upon which to erect wooden edifices, or built up using the same process to form walls and ramparts. Its appearance, especially in the north of China, denotes considerable manpower resources.

c.2000 BC The Yellow River reverts to its northern course. The first evidence of Chinese **metalwork**, consisting of coarse copper with traces of tin and zinc, appears at Qijia, and subsequently several hundred other related sites in Gansu province, suggesting that the principle of metallurgy seeps into China through the steppe corridor from its chronological origins in the Black Sea area – a hypothesis supported by the discovery, in 1994, of **Caucasian corpses** preserved at Loulan, at the eastern end of the Tarim Basin. Not only are the bodies of these Neolithic wanderers well-preserved, so, too, is their clothing, some of it rendered in a patterned plaid twill associated with the Anatolian Celtic peoples. Simple looms are perhaps among the technologies that travel westwards across the Eurasian

Chinese Mythology

The Chinese have several **creation myths**. In the best-known the universe was created by **Pan Gu**, who separated earth (weak, anarchic, dark, cold, lunar, female, *yin*) from heaven (strong, ordered, light, hot, solar, male, *yang*), and whose body parts later metamorphosed into the stars, planets, satellites, rivers, mountains, winds, precious metals, living creatures, etc. The exception was mankind, which evolved, or devolved, from parasites infesting Pan Gu's bodily cavities. The Pan Gu story, however, failed to become centrally embedded in any organized religion. More importunate are the legends surrounding the **'Five Sage Rulers'**. First among these was *Huangdi*, the 'Yellow Emperor', conceivably an actual personage alive c.2500 BC. He and his fellow successor sages – Zhuan Xiu, Ku, Yao and Shun – invented all the arts and skills necessary for civilized survival. Shun is particularly revered by Confucians for having chosen his successor, Yu, on merit; and Yu (the putative founder of the Xia dynasty) is revered for his prowess in flood control. But these were earthly figures.

Alongside the Sages, any number of gods and spirits were

landmass. Such transmissions, however, are likely to be trans-generational – the outcome of slow migrations rather than the purposeful exploitation of established land-routes. Conversely, the **silkworm** is first domesticated in China at about this time, giving rise to an indisputably indigenous fabric industry.

c.1800 BC **Bronze artefacts**, dating from around this period and later, and of markedly different styles and manufacture, are found at sites across China, including Sichuan and Jiangxi, and not just the Yellow River region. Some evidence suggests, however, that China's bronze culture originates in the Zhongyuan, or northern central plain, from where it diffuses to other centres, to be adapted according to local needs and design values.

thought to exist, an animistic pantheon perpetuated in folklore and in the more arcane teachings of **Daoism**. By Shang times, a supreme ancestral deity had emerged: **Di**, sometimes called *Shangdi*; and in Zhou times *Di* was displaced by **Tian**, or 'Heaven', a distinctly abstract and moral dispensation. Yet while the concept of *Tian* and its impersonal wishes – focused on the well-being of China and the Chinese – has survived into the present as a political metaphor, 'Heaven' has rarely, if ever, satisfied the spiritual longings of the Chinese. For this reason, China has periodically been receptive to more-demotic imported belief systems, notably **Buddhism**. Conversely, ancestor-worship and ancestor-appeasement have featured throughout recorded Chinese history, accentuating the status of family and clan. The late pre-imperial period also spawned – as well as the speculative philosophies of the cyclical 'Five Elements' or 'Phases' (fire, water, metal, wood and earth) and of *yin-yang* itself – such cults as 'the Queen Mother of the West' (*Xi Wang Mu*) and her eastern counterpart, the Blessed Isle of Penglai, where a perpetual 'Jade Fountain' dispenses the ultimate elixir.

c.1700 BC Excavations of pre-Shang foundations below major Shang remains at the key sites of Erlitou and Erli-gang (Zhengzhou) suggest a well-developed forerunner state located in the same territories later ruled by the Shang. It is likely that such earlier cities belonged to the **Xia**, a dynasty that leaves no written records, but whose existence is attested by China's early historians, and whose ancestors the Shang acknowledge in their later divinatory bone inscriptions. If the Xia do exist, then they may be credited with passing on to the Shang a potent synthesis of northern Chinese cultural traditions.

During this period, cowrie shells are used as an exchange medium, the first known **money** in China.

Chinese Bronzes

Bronze was used by the ancient Chinese, from around 1800 BC, to manufacture many artefacts, including weapons, farming implements, tools, buckles, hairpins and, in the Yangzi region, bells and drums. That bronze production became a major state industry is evidenced by the existence at Shang Anyang of a **royal foundry** measuring 10,000 metres. The bronzes most prized by collectors – for their peculiarly 'impersonal' quality as well as their craftsmanship – are the ritual vessels cast by the Shang, and subsequently the Zhou. Only later was bronze used in China to depict the human form.

Early bronze-ware was highly stylized, deploying a variety of motif derived from previous ceramic ornamentation. One such constituent is the *taotie*, a mythical animal with large eyes that became the static points around which other design elements moved and flourished. **Dragons** were also represented in the maze-like surfaces of many pieces,

Ding (Late Shang) ritual tripod bronze vessel, 12th century BC.

hidden among interlocking *leiwen*, or rectilinear spirals. Yet the design of such vessels – used to offer wine and food to gods and ancestors – was never static. During the Shang, five distinct phases have been identified, moving from the less to the more figurative. During the Zhou, something like a free-for-all developed, with designers 'rediscovering' past patterns, so that as an art form Chinese bronzes become 'self-referential'. If this was sophisticated, so too was the technology. The Shang pioneered casting bronze from **clay moulds** cut into segments — quite different from the 'lost-wax' methods of early west Asian and European bronzes. The inside surfaces of these segments were incised to produce dramatically varying levels of relief on the finished article. From late Shang onwards, bronzes were also embellished with written Chinese. Yet as a class, the ritual vessels, in particular, never quite shook free from their origins in an even older ceramics, so that when we look at a *ding* or a *gui* we are looking at something that goes back not just three, but four, even five thousand years.

An assortment of finely worked Shang and Zhou dynasty bronze ritual vessels demonstrating the different styles.

c.1580 BC Probable inception of the **Shang dynasty** – a line of 29 kings (*wang*) who, for the next 500 years, will rule over a small, but strategically paramount, state in the Zhongyuan. The same kingdom may or may not have been taken over directly from the Xia. Based on ancestor-worship, the Shang polity advances many of the core components of early Chinese civilization: a useable **calender** based on astronomical observation, with sixty-day cycles divided into ten-day weeks; a hierarchical society codified in a system of **rites** in which the king himself assumes the role of intermediary between the living and the dead; the development of a labour-intensive **bronze industry** geared to manufacturing ceremonial artefacts; an effective and disciplined administration that can be characterized as a **rudimentary bureaucracy**, the more so after the introduction of the most striking aspect of the Shang legacy, **written Chinese**. Shang rule also witnesses the emergence of a quasi-professionalized Chinese military, made more effective by Shang metallurgical capabilities and the adaptation of the **chariot**, borrowed from peoples living beyond its northwestern fringes.

Through force of arms, the Shang are able to introduce a **tribute system**, turning surrounding kingdoms into vassal states. Yet the Shang is also a death culture. Its many and imposing subterranean tombs, created by a great expenditure of manpower, will be filled with the bodies of human **sacrificial victims**, some of them slaves, others not.

According to legend, the Shang dynastic family originated from a village of the same name. Its founder, Xie, is said to have been conceived after his mother swallowed an egg dropped by a blackbird.

c.1500 BC From their own records, it is known the Shang kings moved their capital several times. Excavations begun in 1958 reveal a substantial city at **Erlitou**, on the southern bank of the Yellow River. Artefacts recovered from Erlitou include crude bronzes, but little jade. Although at this stage the Shang may be technologically more advanced than their rivals, there is little reason to suppose they enjoy political pre-eminence.

c.1400 BC A very different picture of Shang's standing emerges from excavations undertaken from 1952 onwards at **Zhengzhou**, further east along the Yellow River's southern bank. At **Erligang**, within the Zhengzhou precinct, archeologists have uncovered a city whose ten-metre-high, twenty-metre-deep walls stretch over seven kilometres, enclosing an area of more than three square kilometres, which in turn contains a raised stamped-earth platform measuring a hundred metres square. Nothing of comparable magnitude belonging to the same period has been detected elsewhere in east Asia, and it is calculated that to build Erligang would have taken 12,000 men ten years. Outside the city walls **bone workshops** and two **bronze foundries** are found. The wealth implicit in such facilities is reflected in the vastly superior bronzes found at Zhengzhou and related sites. Not only are they up to ten times larger than their antecedents, but their craftsmanship is far superior. Jade objects too occur in greater abundance. In retrospect, it seems that at Erligang the Shang achieve the height of their power, creating a **regional hegemony** in central China. Contemporaneous bronzes found elsewhere in China (including south of the Yangzi River) are either imported from Erligang, or manufactured by local foundries under Shang control.

c.1300 BC Already, Shang's hegemony may be compromised. The bronze record suggests that – having learned bronze-making from the Shang – a number of emergent or re-emergent states use the same technology for their own ends, without licence from the Shang. Some of these newly **competing states** are possibly ruled by sub-lineages of the Shang themselves. As bronze culture diffuses, it

is notable that wholly distinctive styles emerge in places far removed from the Yellow River. Notable finds include idiosyncratic artefacts (among them bells and great drums) from **Xingan** (Jiangsi province), first unearthed in 1989, and from a spectacularly well-furnished burial pit at **Sanxingdui**, in Sichuan. Bronze objects recovered from the latter site include – as well as outsize masks – a life-size human figure that exhibits an unprecedented exoticism. That China at this stage is moving toward a greater, not a lesser, plurality of cultures is confirmed by other finds in the far north. Strangely, however, very little surfaces in the Wei river valley, the western enclave from which the Shang's eventual conquerors will emerge. It is during the 13th century that **lacquer varnishing** originates in China.

The life-sized, highly stylized human or possibly divine figure crafted in bronze unearthed at Sanxingdui in Sichuan in 1986.

c.1250 BC The founding of a new Shang capital at **Anyang** (Henan province) north of the Yellow River by Pan Geng marks a revival of Shang fortunes after a period of presumed contraction. The Shang bronze industry takes on a renewed dynamism, but far greater significance is the first unambiguous appearance of a **Chinese script** in the form of **inscribed oracle bones**, recovered from storage pits outside Anyang from 1899 onwards. Many of the 4000-odd characters employed, although 'archaic', are recognizably 'Chinese'. By involving the written word at the heart of state ritual in an enduring medium, the Shang deploy a skill they themselves perceive as an essential prop to theocratic power.

A further strong feature of late Shang culture, manifest in a 24km site outside Anyang, is the imposing scale of its **royal tombs**. These exhibit complexes of adjacent sacrificial pits sometimes containing hundreds of human, as well as animal, victims, boarded burial chambers sunk in shafts between ten and twelve metres deep, double coffins, and long ramparts providing access. Although the tombs will be systematically looted after the collapse of the Shang dynasty, surviving remains include **chariot burials**, with sacrificed charioteers and horses, reflecting a significant augmentation of Shang military capacity as well as the import of an alien technology, most probably from a people on the Mongolian steppes. Like the city of Anyang itself, the tombs are labour-intensive in their construction. Yet the sheer number of **human sacrifices** recovered not only from among the tombs, but also from Anyang's foundations, suggest a surfeit of manpower. It is assumed the late Shang made slaves of prisoners-of-war. In all probability theirs is a raider state.

c.1200 BC Lady Hao, chief consort of the 21st Shang monarch Wu Ding, is buried in a royal tomb. This will escape looting, providing archeologists with an unmatched

Dragon-bone Inscriptions

In 1899 AD, during a malaria epidemic in Henan, some conmen, pandering to a superstition that powdered dragon-bone provides a cure-all, began peddling bones they had found at Xiaotun, near Anyang. It was soon noticed, however, that the same bones were incised with written characters. Thus was discovered the earliest unambiguous evidence of the Chinese script, dating back to 1200 BC. The bones were divinatory scapulae and turtle plastrons of the Shang court, directed at the otherworld of the dead, and buried outside the Shang capital. Since then, some 200,000 have been excavated, yielding an incomparable, if fragmentary, insight into archaic custom.

The inscriptions were added after the bones had been fired, and their 'crackings' interpreted. Although only half the 4000 characters used have been deciphered, it is clear that the inscriptions relate to a multitude of activities for which prognostications were deemed necessary: harvests, military campaigns, the taking of prisoners, sacrifices, hunting expeditions, marriages, pregnancies, dreams, floods, tribute payments, building programmes and health checks among them. The bones were also used to provide weather forecasts, and each is dated, according to the prevailing calendrical system. They reveal that concubinage was already established among China's early rulers, and that it was deemed propitious to make offerings to distant Xia as well as Shang ancestors – compelling hard evidence that the Xia did in fact exist.

A scapula incised with early Chinese calligraphy, one among many thousands found at Anyang.

hoard of **funerary furnishings**. As well as a full set of ritual bronzes, these include two ivories and jade pieces dating back to before 2000 BC. Already the Chinese are collectors.

c.1185 BC Wu Ding dies. Much admired by posterity, he is credited with consolidating Shang power at Anyang. Although the date of Wu Ding's accession is not known with certainty, it is during his reign that Chinese writing first appears in the form of bone inscriptions. It is also recorded that he fought protracted wars against the non-Chinese Tufang and Guofang peoples, the first specific reference to hostile '**barbarians**' on China's northern borders.

c.1066 BC Chang, leader of the **Zhou** people residing in the **Wei river valley**, is imprisoned by the Shang. While the reasons for Chang's arrest are unknown, the seeds of the Shang's overthrow are perhaps contained in this episode.

c.1059 BC Chang is released, and returns to the Zhou capital **Zongzhou** (near modern Xian). Shortly, he becomes king of his people, taking the reign-name **Wen** ('Cultured').

c.1053 BC King Wen of Zhou launches an attack on the small kingdom of **Li**, in southern Shanxi. A Li army is defeated on Shang territory. Despite protestations from the Shang ruler **Di Xin**, Zhou forces mount a campaign against **Yu**, another Shang vassal state. In a third sortie, the Zhou clash directly with Shang forces at **Mengjin Ford** on the Yellow River. Further manoeuvres are curtailed by Wen's death.

c.1047 BC Wen's wars against the Shang are resumed by his son **King Wu**. Wu advances to the Mengjin Ford, where he is met by '800 Lords of Shang'. He withdraws without engaging the enemy.

Spoken Chinese, Written Chinese

Today, Chinese is the first language of more people than any other. As a lingua franca, only English can claim to be its rival. Further, literacy rates among the Chinese are close to those of the 'first world'. Yet these bald assertions conceal formidable complexities. While Chinese is a member of the broad 'Sino-Tibetan' language group, inside China there are at least seven major dialects, among them **Mandarin, Cantonese** and **Shanghainese** – a barrier to internal face-to-face communication that has only been partially overcome by the promulgation of a 'modern standard Chinese' (*Putonghua*) post-1949. Nor is the historic diffusion of a broadly common language among China's culturally and ethnically diverse subjects understood. Yet despite these circumstances, a common written language does prevail.

On paper, dialect is not an issue. Primarily, **Chinese characters** signify meaning, not pronunciation. They can be used, in theory, to record the speech and thoughts of any language. Various terms are employed to characterize written Chinese, none of them quite satisfactory: pictographic, hieroglyphic, zodiagraphic, logographic, etc. Part of the problem is that the first examples of Chinese script, contained in the Shang **'dragon bone' inscriptions**, embody a relatively advanced mnemonic script. Already we find compound characters in which semantic and phonetic determinants compete.

For the contemporary child learning to write Chinese, there is no easy short-cut to memorizing thousands of complex symbols. There is no alphabet as such. Yet despite its obvious drawbacks, written Chinese has been a mainstay of Chinese culture, as also of Chinese politics. The adoption of a non-phonetic script enabled successive governments, whether monarchic, imperial or republican, to assert control, and successive generations of writers and thinkers to partake of a single enterprise.

c.1045 BC Wu returns to Shang territory with a larger army, reputedly numbering 45,000 men and 300 chariots. He advances toward Anyang, but is met by the main Shang force at **Muye**. The Shang are routed. Di Xin, the 29th and last Shang king, on hearing the outcome of battle, commits suicide by fire, and Wu enters Anyang to found a new dynasty. Many Shang nobles are removed to the Wei valley and executed. Others pledge their support and service to the new master. Only Di Xin's son, **Wu Geng**, offers continuing resistance.

From this point onwards, Chinese historians will highlight the personal shortcomings of Di Xin, including extreme debauchery and cruelty (he literally made mincemeat of his critics), in order to underscore the virtue of the early Zhou, downplaying any notion that the **Zhou conquest** is an opportunistic strike against a temporarily mismanaged Shang polity whose influence has contracted to a bare 25-mile radius around Anyang.

> " Heaven and earth are the parents of all creatures; and of all creatures man is the best endowed. Among men the most intelligent and most sincere may become a great ruler; and a great ruler is the parent of his people. But now the King of Shang has no regard for Heaven, and spreads disasters among his subjects. Lost to drink and lust, he practices cruel tyranny. Not just offenders are punished, but also their relatives. He has made great offices hereditary. He has built innumerable palaces, towers, lodges, gardens, lakes and indulged every other extravagance, all at the expense of you, the myriad people. The faithful and the virtuous he has burned and roasted. Pregnant women have been torn apart. Seeing all this, High Heaven is stirred to anger, and charged my father King Wen to enact its wrath. But he died before he could complete his work. "
>
> Wu, ruler of Zhou, addressing his followers at Mengjin Ford, from the *Shu Jing*

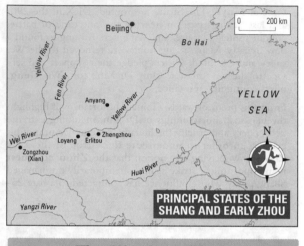

PRINCIPAL STATES OF THE
SHANG AND EARLY ZHOU

The Western Zhou
(Chou) c.1054–771 BC

With the **Zhou**, Chinese history steps up a gear. From now on, a continuous political narrative can be constructed, pre-dating the founding of Rome by about three centuries. The Zhou acquired a territory perhaps ten times greater than the Shang, with evidence of Zhou supremacy being found in areas as far removed from their Wei River capital Zongzhou as **Gansu**, **Shandong** and **Lioaning**. Yet what impresses historians is the extent to which the Zhou were the inheritors of established traditions. They did indeed supplant the Shang, but in supplanting preserved more than they destroyed – perhaps because even at this stage there was a rudimentary **pan-Chinese culture**, at least in the north, so that the supremacy of any one particular dynastic house was a matter of personnel more than of kind. If China was still a 'myriad of kingdoms', then such kingdoms seem broadly compatible in their social structures, values and purposes.

On the basis of available material and written evidence, the Zhou adopted wholesale – before modifying – Shang practice in ancestor worship, in patrilineal succession, in a theocratic style of rule, in bone divination, in social stratification, in bronze and jade work, in ceramics, in building, in design generally, and, as crucially as any of these, in military hardware. The Zhou used the chariot, as well as knives and arrows. They spoke, and quickly learned to write, the same language. All of which begs the question: just who were the Zhou? A replacement people, or a replacement house?

At the court dynastic level, and relative to the Shang, we know too much, not too little. Whatever the true authorship of the 'Confucian Classics', we are burdened by them with an image of the early Zhou royals, and in particular the **Duke of Zhou**, as paragons of Chinese rule. What is not transmitted is any sense of how far down – once the decisive Shang–Zhou battles had been fought – the Zhou take-over permeated. We know that the ruling family's relatives and supporters were rewarded with sizeable 'feudal' grants of land and demesne; but we do not know to what extent humbler subjects were affected by the supposedly momentous power-struggle that had taken place. Did the House of Zhou merely, by military means, transfer and expand their operational base, or was the Zhou conquest the triumph of one nation over another?

Several theories have been advanced. In legend, **Jiang Yuan** became pregnant after treading on the footprint of the great god Di during the reign of the mythical King Yao. Her son, **Hai Ji**, 'Lord of the Millet', was founder of the house of Zhou. Both Shanxi and Shaanxi provinces have claimed the Zhou for their own. One view has it that they originally inhabited an area of the Fen River, a tributary of the upper middle Yellow River and running parallel to it. According to this theory, they migrated, or perhaps fled, into the Wei River valley after falling out with their Shang overlords. Another theory says they had subsisted in the Wei River all along. A third posits the notion that they may have established an earlier kingdom elsewhere, either in Gansu or Sichuan. What is certain is that by the beginning of the 11th century BC the Zhou – whether as a distinct people or an aristocratic clan – were firmly ensconced at **Zongzhou**, **Qishan** and other Wei River sites.

It is also known that the Zhou had close links with the westerly **Jiang** people. Many members of the Zhou elite took Jiang wives. Since the Jiang are classified as 'barbarians' by the Chinese, it is conceivable the Zhou themselves were barbarian. Whatever the case, the Zhou swiftly sloughed off any taint of outlandishness once they had erupted into the Zhongyuan. In particular, they developed the presence of music and dance in court ritual, a borrowing perhaps from the southern Chinese. They did, however, for close on four hundred years, retain their principal capital at Zongzhou – hence the appellation 'Western Zhou'.

c.1043 BC The Zhou King Wu dies, triggering a fiercely contested succession crisis. Wu's younger brother, Zhou Gong Dan, always known as the **Duke of Zhou**, moves quickly to have Wu's son (King **Ting Cheng**) enthroned, in order to perpetuate the Shang and possibly Xia custom of patrilineal descent, but also perhaps to secure a regency for himself. Three of the Duke's brothers, Guanshu Xian, Caishu Du and Huoshu Chu, deplore this outcome and join forces with the overthrown Shang king's son Wu Geng.

In the civil war that follows (called the **Second Eastern Campaign**) Guanshu Xian and Wu Geng are killed. Caishu Du is captured and exiled. Because several surrounding polities are drawn into the conflict, the Duke of Zhou is able to impose the authority of the new Zhou state on a much augmented territory, stretching to the Yellow Sea in the east and the Liao river in the north. Loyal Zhou princes are rewarded with state-sized fiefdoms, creating an unprecedentedly large federation of states. In particular, Zhou subordinate kingdoms are created at Yan, Jin, Wey, Qi and Lu. In the long run, as lineal connections dilute, the cohesion of this federation will falter.

It is at about this time that **rice alcohol** is first distilled in China.

c.1035 BC The Duke of Zhou is confronted by his former ally and half-brother, **Shao Gong Shi**. The immediate cause of contretemps is the Duke's decision to build a new 'eastern capital' at **Chengzhou** (modern Loyang). When it transpires he intends to transfer the whole apparatus of government to Chengzhou, Lord Shao's faction voices its opposition. According to the *Shu ji* ('Book of Documents') the argument turns into a debate about the nature of the *Tian ming* (Mandate of Heaven). Shao and his followers take the absolutist line that the Mandate cannot be

> ❝ The Duke of Zhou sought to combine the achievements of the Three Dynasties and the administrations of the Four Kings. Whenever there was anything he could not quite understand, he would tilt his head back and reflect, if need be through the night as well as the day. If he was fortunate enough to find the answer, he would sit up to await the dawn. ❞
>
> *Mencius*, IV.20, trans. D.C. Lau

questioned, even that the King is himself divine. The Duke of Zhou – prone to appointing commoners to senior positions – argues in favour of a 'meritocracy'. Heaven's blessing cannot be guaranteed, only earned. When Shao wins the debate the Duke of Zhou is shunted off to retirement in Chengzhou, and the capital remains at Zongzhou. So ends the first recorded and possibly most consequential ideological dispute in Chinese history. Although the Duke of Zhou is bested, in the long-term his interpretation of the Mandate as a means of containing absolute power will become integral to Chinese political culture.

The Yijing (I Ching)

Although for a while the Zhou continued to 'consult the bones', scapulamancy disappeared within a century of their conquest. In its place a new form emerged, to become the basis of the *Yijing*: divination by **yarrow** (milfoil) stalk. Yarrow stalks are either broken or unbroken, negative or positive. In the first instance, the permutations of a group of three yield eight possibilities. In the second, an 'upper' and a 'lower' trigram are combined in **hexagrams**, yielding 64 permutations. Each of these is then assigned an 'interpretation' – a cryptic verse couplet sometimes called the 'judgement', according to its overall preponderance of negative and positive. But judgement is speculative. The *Yijing* does not say 'This will happen'; rather it says 'This may happen if...' Further, a second casting of stalks, providing a new hexagram, is read against the first, so that some positive lines 'change' to negative, and vice versa.

Out of these procedures, pitting a plus/minus **binary matrix** against a semi-articulated metaphysics, flows a semantic system of immense interpretive range and ambiguity made all the more potent in the 4th or 3rd century BC when the 'positive-negative' dualism was augmented by the even richer dichotomies of

c.1005 BC Death of King Cheng. His final testament instructs: 'Make pliable those distant, and make capable those near.' Backed by the now elderly Lord Shao, Cheng's son Zhao takes the throne as Zhou Wang (ie Zhou King) **Kang**.

c.1000 BC As scapulamancy (see p.20) dies out, divinatory inscriptions appear on Zhou bronze artefacts. Increasingly **inscribed bronze vessels** will be distributed by the king to acknowledge lineal connections between court and nobility, and to reward officials. Bronze **bell-sets**, a southern inspiration, become a regular feature of northern finds. The **four-horse chariot** makes its debut in China as Chinese chariot wheels develop inclined spokes (dishing).

yin-yang. In this and other ways, the legendary 'Book of Changes' has itself been subject to change.

While yarrow-stalk divination may date back to before 2000 BC, it was first written down as the now lost manual *Zhou yi*, around 900 BC.

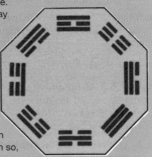

Since then, layer upon layer of added material, including the expository 'Ten Wings', have accreted around a core text, making the version that has come down to us inextricably mongrel. Even so, no less a figure than Carl Jung described *Yijing* as 'a monument to Chinese thought'. Others dismiss it as florid portentology. Like the Tarot pack, however, it offers contemporary users space and concepts with which to weigh the implications – abstract as well as personal – of decision-making: a concentration, not an abandonment, of mind.

The Chinese also pioneer shaft-and-collar harnessing to replace the yoke, for greater manoeuverability. Meanwhile, **mummies** exhumed from the Tarim Basin, among them 'Cherchen Man' and 'Cherchen Woman', indicate the presence of oasis-hopping Caucasoid settlements in modern Xinjiang.

c.978 BC Death of King Kang. Surviving records indicate little hint of disturbance during his reign, widely regarded by the Chinese as a second golden age.

c.977 BC After a mandatory two-year mourning period, Kang's son assumes power as **King Zhao**. Much of Zhao's reign is spent combating a military threat posed on Zhou's southern borders by the emergent state of **Chu**.

c.957 BC War against Chu culminates in a series of crippling defeats for the Zhou, who 'lose six armies' in the vicinity of the Han river. Zhao is killed, and the Zhou suffer a permanent dent to their prestige.

c.956 BC Accession of **King Mu**, credited with commissioning China's first systematic **legal code**. To reward his expanding corps of officials, Mu dismantles several larger feudal estates, creating resentment among the Zhou aristocracy.

c.943 BC Although Mu defeats the **Quan Rong** – one among several troublesome northern tribes – those states and peoples bordering the Zhou federation are prepared to challenge Zhou authority.

In the same year, the 'barbarian' **Xu Rong**, invade Zhou territory from the east, briefly capturing Chengzhou. From this point, 'western' Zhou bronzes, previously abundant throughout the federation, are increasingly restricted to the Wei river area. Such bronzes also undergo a fundamental change. The greatly increased size of state offertory vessels marks a shift from secluded ritual to **state ceremony**, presided over by specialist officials. Such theatricality is emphasized by stylistic changes. Animal motifs all but disappear from surface ornamentation, replaced by ridging, grooving and banding.

c.918 BC Mu is succeeded by King Gong.

c.899 BC Gong is succeeded by King Yih.

c.873 BC Yih is succeeded by King Xiao.

c.865 BC Xiao is succeeded by King Yi.

c.862 BC Ai Gong, the 'local' king of Qi, is allegedly boiled alive in a cauldron by King Yi. Although no explanation for this episode survives, it reflects growing tensions between the Zhou court and its **feudatory states**.

c.859 BC The northern Rong attack the Zhou capital, but are repelled.

c.858 BC The southern state of Chu resumes hostilities, attacking the small but strategic vassal state of E. The Zhou military, organized into eight 'armies of the west' (Wei valley) and six 'armies of the east' (Chengzhou) is able to fend off Chu aggression.

c.857 BC Yi dies. The accession of **King Li**, young and weak, heralds a century of Zhou decline, and strengthening among the lineal states.

To the south, the kingdom of **Yi** follows Chu's example by staging raids in the Luo River valley. The first satirical poems in Chinese appear, prompted by Li's over-dependence upon a single minister, Rong Yi Gong.

c.843 BC Attacks along the southern frontiers are compounded by attacks by 'western belligerents'.

842 BC Li's problems are brought to a head when an internal rebellion erupts – the **first date** in Chinese history that can be pinpointed in the Western calender, thanks to the accuracy of Zhou astronomical records. Whether the revolt Li faces is a 'peasant uprising' or a conspiracy among feudal magnates remains in dispute, but Li is forced into exile at Linfen in the Fen valley. His son Jing narrowly escapes death at the hands of a lynch-mob when Li's minister **Shao Gong He** offers up his son instead. For the next fourteen years, the kingdom of Zhou will be governed by a council presided over by Shao Gong He himself.

828 BC King Li dies in exile. Jing succeeds as **King Xuan**. His 46-year reign marks a partial recovery of Zhou fortunes. Even so, a new threat to stability manifests in the bellicosity of the **Xianyuan** 'western barbarians'.

823 BC Xuan campaigns successfully against the Xianyuan.

821 BC To counter Chu and Yi expansionism Xuan orders his armies southwards as far as the Huai River.

816–15 BC Xuan scores further victories against the Xianyuan, but is unable to resolve succession disputes in the dependencies of Wey, Lu and Qi. Away from the capital Zongzhou local rebellions become commonplace.

806 BC The dependent state of **Zheng** is created by Zheng Huan, a chief minister and younger brother of King Xuan, to provide a buffer against 'eastern barbarians'.

782 BC Perhaps assassinated, Xuan is succeeded by his dissolute son **King You**.

780 BC In the view of early Chinese historians, a spate of natural disasters portends a withdrawal of the Mandate of Heaven. The area around Zongzhou is devastated by earthquakes. The Wei, Luo and Jing rivers run dry. Solar and lunar eclipses occur in the same year.

You, meanwhile, becomes infatuated with the concubine, **Bao Si**. He divorces his queen, daughter of the Duke of Shen, and deposes their son as heir apparent. Incensed,

Shen joins forces against You with the **Quan Rong**, or 'dog barbarians', the same perhaps as the Xianyuan.

Documents and Songs

As well as the *Yijing*, two other 'classics' – once thought to have been edited by Confucius – can, in part, be dated to the Western Zhou. The *Shi jing* ('Book of Songs') contains 305 odes and poems. Of these, 145 may safely be ascribed to the period immediately following the Zhou conquest. Among them are liturgical hymns recited to the accompaniment of music. Overall, the collection is greatly varied, in both form and content, and includes love poems, praise poems and harvest songs.

By contrast, the *Shu jing* (Book of Documents) was an exercise in state propaganda. Consisting mainly of speeches and debates occurring at key junctures during the Xia, Shang and Western Zhou dynasties, it adumbrates the doctrine of a transferable mandate. 'Heaven's favour is not easily sustained,' says the Duke of Zhou. 'Men forfeit it because they cannot uphold the reverence and brilliant virtues of their ancestors.' Conversely, responsible rulers, like King Mu, 'tremble with anxiety as though treading on a tiger's tail or walking on spring ice'. But exactly how old is the *Shu jing*? Once the bible of Confucian historians and bureaucrats, its authenticity has been challenged. Yet textual analysis shows that while many chapters must have been fabricated at least in the Spring & Autumn period, if not later, some at least are near-contemporaneous with the events they describe.

Whether the *Shu jing* is to be regarded as a version of history foisted *post hoc* by scholars determined to perpetuate an ultimately accountable monarchical system, or whether such scholars' doctrines were inspired by an original *Shu jing* is very nearly immaterial. The values espoused by the Duke of Zhou and other ancient worthies – including promotion on the basis of merit, and the commutation of corporeal punishment to fines among the wealthy – simply became part and parcel of mandarin orthodoxy.

771 BC Encouraged by dissident nobles, The Quan Rong sack Zongzhou. Those fleeing the onslaught bury their bulkier valuables. These recently unearthed 'treasure hoards' show that the Zhou possess 'sets' of ritual bronzes much larger in both size and type than the Shang, and that such 'southern' artefacts as bells and drums have established themselves in the 'northern' repertoire.

You is killed, and Bao Si placed under arrest. Although the Court of Zhou will shortly be reconstituted at Chengzhou (Loyang), and Yuan's son enthroned as King Ping, the period of the **Western Zhou** draws to an abrupt close.

The Eastern Zhou: The Spring & Autumn Period and the Warring States: 771–221 BC

The Western Zhou regime – in its heyday regarded by Chinese scholars as a touchstone of good governance – collapsed under pressure, unable to support a greatly increased client population in its capital Zongzhou, to combat unruly tribes impinging on its frontiers, or to control the ambitions of its own aristocratic under-kings. In its place arose a **multitude** of states large and small, initially numbering above a hundred. China became a land of contending courts, whose differences were expressed through increasingly fickle alliances and ferocious wars, until one by one the weaker states were swallowed up by the stronger, and just a handful were left to contend the ultimate prize.

On paper, this meant half a millennium of anarchy. But half a millennium is a long time, and China a vast territory. Paradoxically, this era of prolonged confusion was also one of sustained enrichment as each state sought and exploited any means to gain an edge over its rivals. Like modern corporations, the courts watched each other closely, borrowing and adapting policies, technologies and even personnel. For the skilled and the clever, China became a land of opportunity. As rural areas became more heavily regulated, something like a **market economy** took root. Even territorially, China expanded. The Yangzi River kingdoms of the south – which had hitherto pursued a separate existence – now became enmeshed in the real-politik of Zhongyuan inter-state acrimony. In the north, too, individual states expanded, pacifying outlying barbarian tribes, or embarking on programmes of land reclamation.

The same multitude of courts and kingdoms, of clans and adventurers, was productive in a cultural way. Towns and cities hosted rival styles of craftsmanship, and rival schools of thought. Out of this melange issued **Confucius**, **Laozi**, **Mozi**, **Mencius**, **Shang Yang** and a host of others, including the steely-eyed military theorist **Sunzi**. Concurrently, Chinese technology took huge strides forward. The first great walls were built, and the first canals.

Yet through it all – until within striking distance of the founding of the empire, and to the puzzlement of historians – the Zhou endured: a small and hopelessly enfeebled state, confined to Loyang and its immediate environs. Though perhaps the survival of Zhou, in its 'eastern' incarnation, is not such a mystery after all. Given the theocratic nature of ancient Chinese rule, China needed a papacy. The Kings of Zhou, dressed in elaborate costumes, and supported by gifts from the contentious polities surrounding it, went on performing the rituals, perpetuating (albeit dimly) the notion of a divinely ordered succession. Enough, however, for the eventually triumphant Qin to need to get rid of Zhou, in order to fully assert the Mandate of Heaven.

770 BC Beginning of the **Spring & Autumn Period**, named after the alternative title of the important 'Chronicles of Lu' (*Lu Chunqin*), sometimes ascribed to Confucius. This will last until 481 BC. After a brief succession wrangle, **King Ping** is enthroned at Chengzhou/Loyang, the 'eastern capital' originally built by the Duke of Zhou. But although an unbroken line of **'eastern' Zhou** monarchs survives until 256 BC, their impact on Chinese politics is limited by the indifference and autonomy of its supposedly suzerain states. Loyang, however, becomes an important centre for the preservation of ritual.

With the collapse of the Western Zhou, 148 separate polities spring to life – or rather openly assert what may already be a de facto autonomy. Some are no more than small city states; others extend over much greater territory. Nearly all, though, are outcrops of **Zhou feudalism** – estates originally granted to Zhou family members or other high-rankling nobles. Even at this stage, a clear pecking order among the many states is apparent. Fifteen are pre-eminent: Qi, Jin, Chu, Lu, Cao, Zheng, Song, Xu, Chen, Wey, Yan, Cai, Wu, Yue and Qin. Of these only Chu, Wu and Yue in the south cannot be derived from Zhou lineages. Scattered around and among these states are a number of 'non-Chinese' tribal peoples, referred to as 'barbarians', subsisting by their own custom. These include the Man, Yi, Rong and Di.

c.730 BC Among the rivalrous states, **Zheng** achieves temporary pre-eminence. Its ruler, **Zhuang Gong** (r. 743–701 BC), successfully contains Rong insurgency and establishes a hegemony over his neighbours.

King Ping of Zhou attempts to create an alliance against Zheng, but when this fails, he is forced by Zhuang to exchange hostages – a humiliating affront to his supposed suzerainty.

714 BC Zheng state suffers renewed incursions by the northern Rong.

707 BC King Huan of Zhou resuscitates Ping's strategy against Zheng. A new alliance is formed with the states of Chen, Wey and Cai. Its army, however, is defeated by Zhuang Gong. Huan, 'the Son of Heaven' is wounded in the shoulder – a further humiliation that marks the eclipse of Zhou participation in active politics. Zhuang Gong – making the most of his military prestige – brings the states of Qi, Lu, Song and Wey under Zheng control.

706 BC Qi state suffers incursions by the northern Rong.

701 BC The death of Zhuang Gong initiates a succession crisis in Zheng state. Civil war rages for twenty years. Qi, Lu, Song and Wey recover their independence. As Zheng loses its pre-eminence, **Qi** emerges as the strongest polity in the north, **Chu** the strongest in the south.

c.700 BC From early on in the 7th century BC, altars to the gods of the soil and of grain become widespread. The protein- and vitamin-rich **soya bean**, cultivated in the northeast, makes its re-appearance as a staple in the diet.

685 BC **Huan Gong** accedes as the ruler of Qi. Building on Zheng Zhuang's exercise in hegemony, Huan will formalize the **'Ba system'**: by mutual consent the ruler of one state, usually the most powerful, will act as 'Ba', or **hegemon** (lord of lords), in order to resolve disputes between other rulers and reduce levels of interstate conflict. This arrangement works well intermittently, and contains the northwards expansionism of Chu. Huan also raises **dykes** along the lower Yellow River to control flooding and improve agricultural yields.

Qi's power is based on several factors, later copied by other states: its leadership; its expanding population; its control of important trade routes; its possession of Shandong's salt flats; and its abandonment of feudal institutions in favour of a more meritocratic style of administration. Qi is divided up into fifteen *xiang* by Huan, with two of his 'ministers' being given charge over five *xiang* each. Military and corvee duties are reorganized on a district basis, strengthening the ties between state and soldiery, and enabling more efficient mobilization.

676 BC Accession of **Xian Gong** – a descendant of the early Zhou King Wen – as ruler of the northerly state of **Jin**. During his reign, Jin annexes sixteen smaller surrounding states.

670 BC Chu occupies the 'northern' state of Sui. The ruler of Chu, Cheng, challenges the authority of the *Ba* by reaffirming his use of the title *wang* (king).

667 BC Huan Gong convenes a conference attended by the rulers of Song, Zheng and Cheng, and is formally 'elected' Ba, a title already acknowledged by King Hui of Zhou.

664 BC Huan enhances his leadership of the Zhou states by assisting Yan repel Rong incursions.

662 BC When the small city-state of Xing is attacked by the 'barbarian' Chi Di, Huan intervenes to ensure the security of what are now called the Hua Xia people.

660 BC When the Chi Di attack Wey, killing its ruler, and Chu launches raids of its own, Huan again co-ordinates effective multistate countermeasures.

Some Sayings of Confucius

'What worry have you, gentlemen, about the loss of office? The Empire has long been without the Way. Heaven is about to use your master as the wooden tongue for a bell.' (*Analects* III.24)

'I am a fortunate man. Whenever I make a mistake, other people are sure to notice it.' (VII. 31)

'The common people can be made to follow a path, but not to understand it.' (VIII.9)

'While standing by a river the Master said, 'What passes away is, perhaps, like this. Day and night it never lets up.' (IX.17)

'If for a single day a man could return to the observance of the rites through overcoming himself, then the whole Empire would consider benevolence to be his.' (XII.1)

'When names are not correct, what is said will not sound reasonable; when what is said does not sound reasonable, affairs will not culminate in success; when affairs do not culminate in success, rites and music will not flourish; when rites and music do not flourish, punishments will not fit the crimes; when punishments do not fit the crimes, the common people will not know where to put hand and foot.' (XIII.3)

'If by the age of forty a man is still disliked there is no hope for him.' (XII.26)

Trans. by D.C. Lau

659 BC As Chi Di forces capture Xing, Huan takes personal command of an army composed of Qi, Song and Cao troops. The Chi Di are defeated and Xing reconstituted, only now with a permanent Qi garrison.

656 BC In his last active campaign, Huan leads a coalition army against Chu, after Chu – determined to master the Huai River area – seizes Cai. Cai is taken again by Huan, who compels the ruler of Chu to attend an interstate conference at **Shaoling**, setting a precedent for the wider application of the *Ba*-system.

651 BC Another conference at **Kuiqiu**, under Huan's aegis, discusses social priorities. Rulers of the Zhou states agree to common policies. These include: the death sentence for the 'unfilial'; protection of a wife's status in the face of a rival concubine; the rewarding of merit in the service of the state; and the abolition of hereditary offices. While these nostrums remain most honoured in their breach, they indicate the growth of **non-feudal values**. At the same conference, standards are set for the construction of inter-state irrigation works.

c.650 BC The **northern Rong** people are replaced as a threat by the **Di**.

645 BC Death of minister **Guan Zhong**, the architect of many of Huan Gong's reforms.

643 BC Death of Huan Gong. A disputed succession heralds the temporary waning of Qi power.

639 BC In Lu, the chief minister Zang Wenzhong ends the practice of punishing shamans unable to make rain. Irrigation and relief programmes are instigated instead.

636 BC Accession of **Wen Gong**, son of Xian Gong, as the ruler of **Jin**. Soon to assume the title *Ba*, Wen will establish the primacy of Jin 'for three generations', and draw Chu and the western Wei River state of Qin into the 'eastern Zhou' fold.

635 BC Wen Gong's standing is enhanced when King Zhang of Zhou is driven from his palace by his brother Zhao. Wen swiftly restores Zhang, and is rewarded with estates lying close to the Zhou capital Loyang.

633 BC **Chu's** armies attack the state of **Song**. Jin Wen Gong orders counterattacks on the Chu dependencies of Cai and Wei.

632 BC A Jin-led Zhou coalition that includes the states of Song, Qi and Qin, inflicts a heavy defeat on Chu in battle at **Chengpu**. At an interstate conference held immediately afterwards, the title *Ba* is formally conferred upon Wen by King Xiang of Zhou. Although seven states swear loyalty to the throne, rivalry between states continues. A mini 'warring states' period ensues.

627 BC A **Qin** army is defeated by Jin after Qin attempts to annex the state of Zheng.

625 BC Jin forces invade Qin.

624 BC Jin's armies are repulsed by Qin, which now joins Jin, Qi and Chu as one of the **'big four'** states.

c.600 BC During the 6th century BC the **iron age** arrives in China from western Asia. The first states to develop iron weapons are Wu and Yue in the south, where the iron ploughshare makes its first appearance.

In bronze-casting, the **pattern block** (used to repeatedly impress identical patterns on the inside of clay moulds) enables the mass production of ornamented pieces. The west Asian 'lost wax' method for casting is also introduced.

Tea is first used in China, initially as a medicine. Other plants and herbs are exploited for their therapeutic benefits.

598 BC In a reversal of previous outcomes, Jin is heavily defeated by Chu at the **Battle of Mi**.

589 BC As Qi attempts to restore its hegemony by occupying Lu and Wey, Jin responds strongly, defeating Qi in a series of engagements.

583 BC Jin undermines Chu power in the south by sending assistance to the smaller, emergent state of **Wu**, also at war with its southern neighbour **Yue**.

580 BC The new ruler of Jin, Li Gong, persuades Qi and Qin to form an alliance against Chu. The ensuing campaign, however, is inconclusive.

579 BC The small, but commercially powerful, state of **Song** persuades Jin, Qi, Qin and Chu to abandon warfare and abide by existing frontiers.

575 BC Skirmishing resumes between Chu and the northern states.

574 BC Chu suffers a major defeat at the hands of Jin and its

allies. Shortly afterwards, Li Gong is assassinated by his own ministers after attempting to dismiss then. Jin prestige is maintained by Li's son, who assumes power as **Dao Gong** and is quickly recognized as *Ba* by Qi, Qin and other lesser states.

562 BC The hereditary ruler of **Lu** is ousted by his own ministers, the **'Three Huan'**, who divide the spoils and establish their own lineages. Similar usurpations will be repeated in other states, notably Qi and Jin.

551 BC Probable birth of **Confucius** (in *pin-yin*, Kong Fuzi, 'Master Kong').

c.550 BC **Metal money** appears for the first time, in the form of miniature bronze spades.

A unit of 'spade' money cast in bronze with a hole for threading.

546 BC At the urging of Song and Zhang, a major interstate conference is held at **Shengqin**. The independence of Qi and Qin is recognized by Jin, while smaller states submit to 'satellite' status vis-à-vis Jin and Chu. Tributes are fixed, and chariot quotas are agreed. As a result of this comprehensive north–south peace pact, there will be no fighting between Jin and Chu for forty years. The south, however, will continue to be disrupted by hostilities as Chu, Wu and Yue each seek control of the fertile Yangzi delta.

541 BC Jin ends a century of sporadic border fighting by finally pacifying the 'barbarian' **Di** people.

532 BC In **Qi**, factional in-fighting is resolved when one ministerial clan, the **Tian**, annihilates its rivals.

518 BC In the south, according to legend, an army of Wu defeats an army of Chu when the ruler of Wu commands 3000 of his front-line men to slit their own throats in full view of the enemy. Terrified, the Chu soldiers flee.

507 BC A Jin army is defeated by the **Xianyu**, heralding a fresh wave of northern barbarians.

506 BC Its armies commanded by **Sunzi** (Sun Wu), Wu stages a concerted campaign against Chu, which is defeated five times; but Wu is prevented from pressing home its advantage by Yue.

496 BC King He of Wu invades Yue, but is killed in battle.

> **"** When campaigning, be swift as the wind; in leisurely march, majestic as the forest; in raiding and plundering, like fire; in standing, firm as the mountains. As unfathomable as the clouds, move like a thunderbolt. **"**
>
> Sunzi, *The Art of War*, vii.13, trans. Samuel B. Griffith

Confucius c.551–479 BC

When **Confucius** died, few except his immediate disciples mourned. Fewer still foresaw that future generations would hold him in awe as China's greatest thinker. Yet so it came about – in part the invention of successive generations of bureaucrats, who discovered in his transmitted conservatism a philosophy overwhelmingly attuned to their own needs and fears. Out of this was born the legend of the **Confucian classics**. To his pen were ascribed – with varying degrees of falsity – the *Shu ji*, the *Shi ji*, the *Chunqin,* the *Liji* ('Records of Ritual'), even the *Yi jing*; whereas in fact, hardly anything Confucius himself wrote survives. His philosophy, or an abstract of it, has been preserved in the ***Lun yu* ('Analects')**, compiled by his followers.

493 BC Yue is defeated and subjugated by **King Fuchai of Wu**, avenging his father's death.

486 BC His sights set on becoming *Ba*, Fuchai begins building a canal to link the south directly to the north – a grandiose project that will take 100 years to complete, and later form part of the **Grand Canal**.

485 BC Wu attacks and defeats Qi. Faced by Wu aggression, Ding Gong of Jin gives up his claim to the paramount leadership of the northern states. When Dao Gong of Qi

Here, Confucius emerges both as a provider and an arbiter of opinion and taste. He tells his intimates what it is right to think, and what is wrong. But as subtly seductive as his reasoning often is, he seldom engages in hard analysis. Rather, he is a man who knows the truth, but sees no need to explain anything *ab initio*. Sincerely follow the correct behavioural forms (*li*), at every level of society, and a well-ordered society will follow. A ruler must be benign as well as wise, or at least wisely counselled. Children must be filial, fathers strong, wives compliant, elder brothers accorded respect. Outside the family, relations should be conducted on the basis of consideration and reciprocation. Thus are enshrined the enduring values of Chinese social relations.

But all this, as Confucius acknowledges, is easier said than done, and one way of reading the *Analects* is to see it as a Jeremiad – a bitter, even geriatric, lament for the collapse of the same values. Repeatedly, he invokes the long-dead Duke of Zhou as a model of right conduct. Such despair almost certainly flows from the disappointments of Confucius's own career. The child of a family that had known better times, he was raised in the small state of Lu by his mother. He aspired to great office, but held only minor posts, and spent much time in other states, either as an exile, or looking for employment. Only when he returned to Lu was his poorly remunerated status as a licensed teacher secured.

dies, his heir is murdered by the head of the ministerial Tian clan, which now usurps power while allowing a legitimate puppet ruler to occupy the Qi throne.

482 BC At an interstate summit held at **Huangchi**, members agree to elect King Fuchai as *Ba*, marking the zenith of **Wu power**. Fearing a takeover of the whole of the south, **King Gonjian** of **Yue** resolves to undo Wu supremacy, vowing to spend twenty years rebuilding and training his army.

Conventionally, the usurpation of power in Qi by the Tian, and the temporary transfer of hegemony from the north to the south brings the **Spring & Autumn Period** to an end. What follows (481–221 BC) is most often called **The Warring States**. But although there is a move toward greater dependence on 'ministers' by rulers, and escalation in the scale of warfare – made possible by administrative reforms designed to maximize individual states' ability to

Sunzi (Sun-Tzu) and *The Art of War*

The *Sunzi*, always known as 'The Art of War', is probably more widely admired than any other military treatise. Its thirteen chapters, composed of crisp apothegms, enunciate decidedly modern precepts. 'All warfare is based on deception' runs one verse. 'To defeat the enemy without fighting is the epitome of skill' runs another. And again, 'Numbers alone confer no advantage'. But it is the *Sunzi*'s overall grasp of how the different components of warfare interact that has earned its reputation. Conceding that war is inherently fluid, that as 'water has no constant form, so war has no constant circumstance', it avoids discussion of specific weapons and tactics. Instead, it stresses the importance of intelligence, espionage, psychology, morale, training, timing, and familiarity with terrain and weather conditions. Overall its message is 'Attack the enemy's strategy first, his troops second' – a point not lost on Mao Zedong in the 20th century.

Its eponymous and putative author, aka **Sun Wu** of Qi, commanded the armies of Wu at the close of the 6th century BC; but because *Sunzi* mentions crossbows, the text we have cannot date from before the mid-5th century BC. It was therefore probably adapted from Sun's own writings. Little else is known about him, although an apocryphal story tells how he won the king of Wu's respect by beheading his two favourite concubines. King He asked Sun to demonstrate his training techniques, using 180 'beautiful women'. Sun appointed the favourites as 'officers', and ordered their deaths when they disobeyed his commands.

raise armies – there is no compelling reason to favour any one intermediate date as being climactic for the whole period between 771 and 221 BC.

Laozi (Lao Tzu)

Whereas conventional wisdom credits **Laozi** (aka Li Er Dan), with the creation of **Daoism**, the truth is more likely to have been the other way round: Daoism created Laozi. The word means simply 'Old Man' or 'Old Master'. The book named in his honour – and sometimes called the *Dao te jing* ('Treatise on the Way and Virtue') – has been shown to be a compendium by several hands of the late 4th or early 3rd century BC. Doubts have even been raised as to whether the *Laozi* was in fact antecedent to the second Daoist classic, the also eponymous *Zhuangzi* (see p.57). Conversely, textual evidence reveals that individual verses may predate Laozi's supposed contemporaneity with Confucius, confirming the notion that Daoism was long in the offing before being transmuted first into a distinct philosophical school, and then, in imperial times, into a semi-organized religion.

Quite possibly, the author of the *Laozi* himself was invented in order to add authenticity to ideas that may have been derived by its actual authors from texts that are now lost. According to legends regurgitated by **Sima Qian**, Laozi was born in Chu and served as Librarian at the court of Zhou before fleeing to the wilderness to become the archetypal Chinese sage hermit. Around 501 BC, he allegedly met **Confucius**, reproving the younger man for his ambition and arrogance. In contrast to Confucian philosophy, the *Dao te jing* has little truck with the 'rites', family values, or with the presumed benefits of education. Instead of constant exertion for the public good, Laozi commends **personal inaction** (*rang*) and attunement with the 'Way', the guiding and ultimately nameless principle of all that is, as the fittest means for surviving a hostile world. These precepts have inspired commentators to variously discover in Laozi a garbled phenomenology, a masterpiece of mysticism, a blueprint for escapism, and a manifesto for ecologically correct naturism.

479 BC Death of **Confucius**, outlived by his putative older contemporary **Laozi**, the 'father of **Daoism**'.

473 BC Eleven years ahead of schedule, **Gonjian** of Yue begins his campaigns against Wu.

470 BC Gonjian captures the Wu capital and asserts the supremacy of **Yue**. King Fuchai hangs himself. At a hastily convened summit, the *Ba*-ship is conferred upon Gonjian, but he is the last to hold it.

453 BC The state of **Jin** disintegrates as power is usurped by ministers. Out of the old state three new states, each with its own lineage of rulers, are formed: **Wei**, **Zhao** and **Hann**. While Wei will become the strongest of the three, Zhao to the north protects its autonomy by pioneering the use of **cavalry** on Chinese soil.

c.450 BC Invention by the Chinese of the **crossbow**.

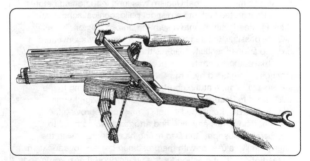

Reconstruction of the precision-made trigger mechanism of a 5th-century Chinese crossbow.

441 BC The state of **Qin**, thus far confined to the Wei River basin, and easily defended against easterly aggressors by blocking the Hangdu Pass, begins its century-long campaigns against Shu, Ba and other yet more peripheral polities to its south. The successful outcome of these will secure for Qin the great 'grain basket' of **Sichuan**, a vital resource for combating the encroachments of barbarian peoples to its north. The same resource, with its access to previously untapped manpower, will also furnish Qin the wherewithal to make a bid for power over China as a whole.

c.430 BC Large-scale integrated **irrigation projects** – significantly increasing agricultural yields – are constructed in the Ye district of **Wei**, where perhaps for the first time officials' salaries are paid in grain.

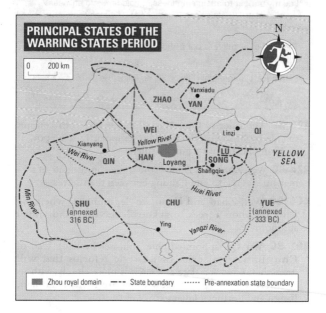

PRINCIPAL STATES OF THE WARRING STATES PERIOD

0   200 km

N

ZHAO

Yanxiadu

YAN

WEI

Linzi

QI

Xianyang

Yellow River

LU

YELLOW SEA

Wei River

QIN

HAN

Loyang

SONG

Shangqiu

Huai River

Min River

SHU
(annexed 316 BC)

CHU

YUE
(annexed 333 BC)

Ying

Yangzi River

▨ Zhou royal domain   --- State boundary   ⋯⋯ Pre-annexation state boundary

Some Sayings of Laozi

"The nameless was the beginning of heaven and earth;/The named was the mother of the myriad creatures." Lao Tzu I.2

"Do that which consists in taking no action, and order will prevail." III.10

"It is because it does not contend that it is never at fault." VIII.22

"Favour and grace are things that startle;/ High rank is, like one's body, a source of great trouble." XIII.30

"I do my utmost to attain emptiness;/ I hold firmly to stillness./ The myriad creatures all rise together / And I watch their return." XVI.37

"The best of all rulers is but a shadowy presence to his subject." XVII.39

"Exterminate learning and there will no longer be worries." XX.44

Lao Tzu, *Tao Te Ching*, trans. D.C. Lau

425 BC The ruler of Qin, Huai Gong, is forced to commit suicide by his own officials, who temporarily seize power, replacing Huai with a puppet ruler.

424 BC Wei, Zhao and Hann – the three constituents of former Jin – agree to end fighting between themselves.

403 BC Wei, Zhao and Hann are 'legitimized' when the King of Zhou agrees to acknowledge their individual autonomy.

401 BC **Wu Qi**, appointed chief minister by King Dao of **Chu**, initiates a series of Jin-style reforms that will strengthen Chu as a state and align it more closely with its northern counterparts. New cities are built in Hunan, Jiangsi and northern Guangxi.

385 BC The Qin prince **Xian** returns to the state of **Qin**, following years of exile, and reclaims power on behalf of his lineal house. A raft of reforms introduced by Xian – some of them based on similar reforms already undertaken in Wei – include the abolition of human sacrifice and curtailment of 'elite' funerals.

383 BC The state of Zhao makes war against Wey. Wey appeals to Wei for help. When Wei then attacks Zhao, Zhao enlists the support of Chu. The ensuing **war of contagion** threatens to engulf the whole of China.

380 BC Chu's armies, advancing north, effectively rescue Zhao from Wei's hegemonic ambitions – a campaign that is followed by a ten-year war between Chu and Jin.

377 BC The 'barbarian' **Xianyu** set up **Zhongshen**, an independent but Sinicised state bordering Zhao. This survives as an autonomous entity until 295 BC.

375 BC Xian strengthens his absolutist control over **Qin** by introducing the *xian* (county) as a basic administrative unit, and by instituting the registration of all households in mutually responsible groups of five.

366 BC Qin inflicts a heavy defeat on the combined armies of Hann and Wei.

364 BC Wei is again defeated by Qin at **Shimen**. At the end of the day, some 60,000 heads are collected. The state of Wei, however, is spared conquest by the intervention of its competitor Zhao.

362 BC Qin establishes a presence east of the Hangdu Pass by attacking Wei.

361 BC Xian of Qin is succeeded by his son **Xiao Gong**, who – with the help of his chief minister **Shang Yang** – will complete his father's reforms, creating the strongest of the increasingly centralized 'warring states'. The pressure

Of Wars and Cities

Between the years 771 and 221 BC, warfare escalated across China, and with it an **arms race**. In the 5th century BC, the bronze-triggered crossbow was introduced, capable of piercing a man's skull at two hundred paces; and also cavalry. Such advances saw off the chariot as an effective instrument of battle. Yet neither replaced the value of massed (and expendable) infantry, armed with knives, swords and halberds. As the contest hotted up, so armies grew. By the end, Qin had an estimated million troops in the field. Such forces required elaborate logistics. Hence, as the Chinese countryside was ravaged, so too was it transformed.

The relentless demand for ever greater supplies of grain and soldiery led governments to take close interest in every hectare of land under their rule. But the same process, generating greatly increased levels of wealth and economic activity, fuelled a dramatic growth in the number and size of cities, inside which new classes of subject incubated: ministerial families and their

on Wei is maintained, to the extent that the ruler of Wei, **Hui Hou**, relocates his capital at Daliang, south of the Yellow River.

356 BC Hui, having revitalized **Wei**, compels the rulers of Hann, Wey, Lu and Song to pay him homage.

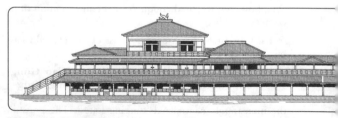

Drawing Philip Winton. From *Chronicles of the Chinese Emperors* by Ann

hangers-on; merchants and artisans, specialising in new commodities and new services; and the *shi*, or scholar-gentry, whose administrative skills were highly prized by the state.

At its height, **Linzi**, the capital of Qi, contained a population of perhaps 750,000. Emporiums, gambling dens, dog-racing, music-halls and brothels abounded. Common artefacts, including funerary furnishings, also underwent a profound alteration. *We shang yu shi* became the watchword of every medium: 'decoration overpowering substance'. In architecture, terraced pavilions and raised mausoleums became a symbol of opulence among the ruling class. But such cities had also to be defended against enemies. They were built therefore as grids, with broad intersecting avenues doubling as sight-lines and troop-runs, locked in by high, thick walls. These latter marked the boundaries between urban and rural life, inaugurating a deep and characteristic fissure within Chinese society. Far from levelling China, 500 years of internecine war stratified it.

In Qin, Shang Yang introduces a stern tariff of punishments for those transgressing a clearly defined legal code. He urges that those reporting on the misdemeanours of neighbours should be rewarded equally to those killing enemies in battle, and that those who do not kill enemies in battle should receive punishment.

THAMES & HUDSON

Paludan, published by Thames & Hudson Ltd., London.

353 BC Wei's expansion is checked by **Qi** during a year of interstate feuding. Qi fields four separate armies, and Wei suffers a heavy defeat at Guiling.

350 BC The Qin capital is relocated at **Xianyang** (modern Xian), just south of the Wei River.

In Zhongshen, defensive walls are built against the **Xiongnu**, nomadic raider-pastoralists making their first appearance on China's borders. Considered the eastern wing of the Huns, the Xiongnu drive sheep, hoard gold and silver, carry advanced iron weapons, and fight on horseback.

348 BC Shang Yang tightens Qin's control of manpower resources by replacing household taxation with capitation.

344 BC Hai Hou of Wei becomes the first of the original 'Zhou states' rulers to assume the title *wang*, or 'king'. While this is perceived as a snub toward the King of Zhou, Hai also seeks parity with the 'kings' of the southern non-Zhou states.

341 BC The decline of Wei and reascendency of Qi is underlined as the former is again heavily defeated by the latter at **Maling**. Immediately afterwards, however, the two states form an alliance against Qin in the west.

338 BC Death of Xiao, ruler of Qin. Dissidents seize the opportunity to turn on Shang Yang, who is forced to flee Xianyang. Refused hospitality by an inn-keeper for not carrying the right permit, he retreats toward his family estates in Wei, but is captured and torn apart by chariots.

334 BC Chu finally overruns Yue, and takes undisputed control of the lower **Yangzi**. The ruler of Qi, Wei Hou – following the example of the ruler of Wei – also declares himself 'king'.

At the Qi capital Linzi, the **Jixia Academy** is founded to promote political philosophy. The Mohist philosopher Hui Shi – best known for his paradox that 'a wheel never touches the ground' – establishes himself as the Academy's leading light; but its more famous member will be **Mencius**.

325 BC Huiwen Hou of Qin declares himself 'king'. Within two years all other remaining Chinese rulers follow suit.

318 BC A detachment of **Xiongnu** cavalry is enlisted in a broad alliance against Qin.

314 BC The state of Qin completes a programme of pacification against hostile peoples on its own western and northern borders.

312 BC Wars between two temporary alliances – Qin, Wei and Hann, on the one hand, and Chu and Qi on the other – are fought. A strategic victory is gained by Qin at **Danyang**, rendering Chu militarily insignificant from this time onwards. Qin gains control of the Hanzhong region, securing access to its Sichuanese colonies Ba and Shu.

c.300 BC As silk and bamboo become the preferred media, and the brush the preferred implement for writing, **Chinese calligraphy** becomes markedly more fluid and expressive.

300 BC Accession of King Min as the nominal ruler of **Qi**. His court is dominated by the warlord **Tian Wen**, who, anxious to assert Qi supremacy over Qin, revives the alliance with Wei and Hann. Tian becomes 'first minister' of this coalition, but will be dismissed by Min when Qin responds by creating its own alliance with Zhao, which shortly annexes Zhongshan.

298 BC Qi and its allies advance against Qin, but are held at the Hangdu Pass. Concurrently, Qin begins building defensive walls to its north and west. Designed to contain the 'barbarian threat', these will later be incorporated into

The Hundred Schools

The Warring States period spawned a profusion of intellectual activity, especially in the related fields of political theory and ethics. Those who came after Confucius were known from early imperial times as the 'Hundred Schools' – a soubriquet Mao Zedong aped when he launched his 'Hundred Flowers' movement of 1956. The most renowned philosopher was **Mozi** (c.480–390 BC), father of the 'Mohist' school, which celebrated the supposed frugality and fraternity of the archaic Xia. An engineer by training, he deplored war and distrusted ritual as being wasteful of resources. Good men, he thought, were defined by their abilities, not their sentiments. With more difficulty, he advocated rational altruism, or 'impartial caring', as a realizable human potential.

Mencius (Mengzi, c.382–300 BC) pursued a similar line by insisting on the innate goodness of man. If human nature was not benevolent, he argued, then it would be incapable of recognizing instances of good. What mattered was education. Being well taught is of more value than being well-governed. But like

the **Great Wall**. In Zhao, the accession of King Huiwen heralds a period of reform and military assertion.

295 BC Qi forces its way through the Hangdu Pass and obliges Qin to surrender territories previously captured from Wei and Hann. Qin bolsters its strength by throwing a wood-and-stone bridge across the Wei River near Xian, enabling swifter internal transport and communications.

294 BC Qi King Min, determined to annex the state of Song, agrees peace terms with Qin.

293 BC As interstate warfare again becomes endemic, a reputed 240,000 men are killed as Qin defeats the combined forces of Wei and Hann.

Confucius he considered virtue to be its own reward, and he developed the Master's ideas to the extent that he is regarded as China's 'second thinker'. In particular, he extended the notion that rulers should serve the people, and not vice versa.

Confucianism was also thrown a lifeline by **Xunzi** (c.310–215 BC). Unlike Mencius, he thought man's nature tends toward evil. Nonetheless, he vigorously opposed the Mohists, proposing instead that even if Confucius's system was misguided, it was in everybody's interests to adopt it. Xunzi's stature, however, is largely retrospective. In his lifetime, his was but one voice among many. Notably **Zhuangzi** (365–280 BC) – who famously asked 'Do I dream that I am a butterfly, or does the butterfly dream that it is I?' – furnished a core text of **Daoism**, to stand beside the *Laozi*. *Yin-yang* thinking came into its own, and there was a galaxy of other, now forgotten, thinkers.

In the short-term, however, it was the **Legalists** (see p.60) – usually excluded from the 'Hundred Schools' – who, under the aegis of Qin power, swept aside all others. Only during Han times did the Confucians emerge as venerated sages.

288 BC The rapprochement between Qi and Qin is seemingly sealed when their two rulers declare themselves 'Eastern Emperor' and 'Western Emperor' – the first time the term *Di* is assumed by human rulers. Almost immediately, however, King Min is 'persuaded' by Su Qin (acting for King Hui of Yan) that Qin, and not Zhao, poses the greater threat to Qi.

287 BC **Qi** completes its conquest of **Song**. The exiled former chief minister of Qi, Tian Wen, persuades Qin, Wei and Zhao to create an alliance against his former master.

284 BC Tian Wen's anti-Qi strategy is brought to fruition as Qi is attacked from the north by Yan, and from the west by

Some Sayings of Mencius

"If the mulberry is planted in every homestead of five mu of land, then those who are fifty can wear silk; if chickens, pigs and dogs do not miss their breeding season, then those who are seventy can eat meat; if each lot of a hundred mu is not deprived of labour during the busy season, then families with several mouths to feed will not go hungry. Exercise due care over the education provided by village schools, and discipline the people by teaching them duties proper to sons and younger brothers, and those whose heads have turned grey will not be carrying loads on the roads."

Mencius, I.7 trans. D.C. Lau

"Suppose we have here a piece of uncut jade. Even if its value is equivalent to 10,000 yi of gold, you will have to entrust its cutting to a jade-cutter. But when it comes to the government of your state, you say, 'Just put aside what you have learned and do as I tell you.' In what way is this different from teaching the jade-cutter his job?"

Advice to King Xuan of Qi, ibid I.9

"The gentleman's virtue is like wind; the virtue of the people is like grass. Let the wind sweep over the grass and the grass is sure to bend."

Ibid III.2

Qin, Hann, Wei and Zhao. King Min is killed, and the power of Qi effectively crippled. Territory is ceded by Qi to Zhao, which now embarks on a programme of territorial expansion.

279 BC Tian Dan re-establishes a much weakened Qi state.

278 BC Qin inflicts further defeats on Chu, forcing Chu to contract south of the Yangzi River.

273 BC Qin inflicts a reputed 150,000 casualties on the armies of Wei.

269 BC The state of **Zhao** challenges Qin for supremacy in northern China by defeating it in battle. In response, King Zhao of Qin (r. 306–251) turns to **Fan Sui**, who advocates a policy of 'alliance with those who are distant, and attacks against those who are near'.

266 BC Fan Sui is appointed chief minister of Qin as other ministers are purged. He proposes the conquest of China as the only solution to end perennial interstate warfare.

265 BC In accordance with Fan Sui's strategy, Qin creates an alliance with Qi to attack Hann.

263 BC Qin forces, commanded by Bo Qi, begin a three-year campaign against Zhao.

260 BC King Xiaocheng of **Zhao** replaces his commander Lian Po with Zhao Kuo. Zhao immediately launches a large offensive against Qin. Bo Qi, grasping Zhao Kuo's tactics, lures him on, then attacks his flanks while cutting his supply lines. For 46 days, Zhao Kuo is surrounded at **Changping**, then killed in Bo Qi's culminating counterassault. The starving Zhao army surrenders. Reputedly, 400,000 Zhao troops are buried alive. While Changping eliminates the last of Qin's serious rivals, victory is quickly sullied by factional rivalry between Fan Sui and Bo Qi, who is forced to retire and commits suicide.

> ❝ The Legalists are very strict and of small mercy. But they have correctly defined the distinctions between lord and subject and between superior and inferior, and these distinctions cannot be changed. ❞
>
> Sima Tan, father to Sima Qian, in an essay found amongst his papers, c.120 AD

Shang Yang Legalism

If Confucius is the acknowledged master of Chinese political thought, **Shang Yang** is its evil genius. The **Book of Shang**, compiled by later followers, sets out the system of authoritarian rule that Shang instituted in Qin in the middle of the 4th century BC as Duke Xiao's chief minister, and which propelled Qin onto centre stage. 'In a well-ordered nation,' Shang urged, 'punishment is endemic, reward scarce.' Individually, his measures may not have been uniformly original – **Guan Zhong** (d. 642 BC) and **Shen Buhai** (d. 337 BC), chief ministers of Qi and Hann respectively, can fairly claim authorship for many of them – but as a package, they constituted a form of totalitarianism.

Households and groups of households were made collectively responsible for their members' behaviour. For a subject, going to war should seem preferable to receiving the attentions of the state's law-enforcers. Moreover, all subjects, from the highest to the low, were expected to pull their weight on behalf of the state, and were ranked in seventeen grades accordingly. Nobody was spared military and corvee duties. Encoded, these and other strictures acquired the name 'Legalism' – the rule of law, in a narrow absolutist sense.

Shang Yang himself, however, would not have recognized the term. Only after his death did it gain currency, and a distinctive 'school' of Legalist philosophers emerge. Of these, **Han Feizi** – writing in the 3rd century BC, and famed for his advice that any book not written by a Legalist should be destroyed – was the most prominent. Although Legalism was formally discredited soon after the collapse of the Qin dynasty, its no-nonsense solutions to the problems of government endured.

258 BC Fan Sui is himself dismissed, then executed, when a Qin army is defeated by a remnant Zhao force.

257 BC A permanent pontoon bridge is constructed by the Qin at the point of confluence between the Wei and Yellow rivers.

250 BC King Zhao of Qin is succeeded by Xiaowen.

249 BC Xiaowen is succeeded by Zhuangxiang.

246 BC Zhaungxiang dies, and is succeeded by his young son **Zheng**, the future 'First Emperor'. Zheng's mother **Zhao Ji** and the merchant **Lu Buwei** – sometimes reputed Zheng's real father – become his regents. In the Wei River valley, a newly constructed canal system brings an additional 200,000 hectares under cultivation.

238 BC Zhao Ji and Lu Buwei are disgraced for smuggling a man disguised as a eunuch into the palace. King Zheng assumes full control over Qin, and appoints **Li Si**, an admirer of Shang Yang Legalism, as his chief minister. Swaths of subjects are press-ganged into military service, or to work on state projects.

In Sichuan, the Qin governor **Li Bing** oversees construction of still-surviving earthworks designed to control and exploit the Min River.

230 BC Zheng unleashes the final campaigns of the Warring States period. Mixing intelligence and brutality, he reduces what remains of China's polycentrism. No force can withstand his well-drilled armies; and on principle all prisoners-of-war are put to the sword. In the opening manoeuvres Hann becomes the first state to capitulate.

228 BC Zhao is occupied by Qin and dismantled as a state.

225 BC Wei is occupied by Qin.

223 BC Chu is occupied by Qin.

222 BC Yan is occupied by Qin.

221 BC With the voluntary surrender of Qi, Zheng achieves his ambition. The whole of China is at his feet. In the idiom of Sima Qian, 'the silkworm devoured the mulberry leaf'. He returns to Xianyang and, in a deliberate evocation of the Yellow Emperor, proclaims himself **Shihuangdi**, or **'First Emperor'**, intending that his directly descended successors should be known as 'Second Emperor', 'Third Emperor', and so on, in an unlimited series.

2
The Early Empire

221 BC–220 AD

The protean confusion of the Spring & Autumn and Warring States periods yielded to the draconian, all conquering state of **Qin** (Ch'in), culminating in King Zheng's assumption in 221 BC of the title **Shihuangdi**, First August Emperor, and the founding of the 'Chinese' empire. Elsewhere, the civilizations of Egypt and Greece were in steep decline, and the emergent state of Rome barely controlled the Italian peninsula. In the same year, Hannibal assumed command of the north African Carthaginian army: a brilliant tactician whose subsequent campaigns all but smothered the Roman empire at its republican birth. Yet within fifteen years, by the end of 207 BC, the scene had changed dramatically in both theatres. Hannibal's dreams of a European kingdom lay smashed at Metaurus, and the Qin regime was in tatters.

These developments were wide apart and unconnected. Nor would there be, for many centuries, any accurate mutual awareness of events as they unfolded at the extremities of the Eurasian landmass. Even so, it is curious that the close of the 3rd century BC proved, in hindsight, climactic for Europe and East Asia alike. If, as a result of its first Punic victories, Rome was born again, then so too the prospect of a return to internecine strife among contending centres of power brought China swiftly to heel. Instead of renewed fragmentation, the **Han dynasty** created order and stability; and in so doing, impressed a form and style of government that, with significant adaptations and hiatuses, endured for 21 centuries.

The principal engine of the empire's longevity was an overarching **administration** that depended for its efficacy as much on the measurable performance of its middle managers, as on its leaders' flair, or lack of it. What the Han achieved was a regulated meritocracy whose elaborate hierarchy offered sufficient scope for all but the most ambitious individuals among China's privileged classes.

In reality, the Han compact was synthetic: that is, it blended sometimes disparate elements from what had gone before. The teachings of **Confucius** were adapted to at least some of the principles of **Qin Legalism**. The same compact was also vulnerable in its inflexibility. The story of the first four dynasties – the Qin, Former Han, Wang Mang (Xin) and Later Han – is very much the story of holes within a system, or systems, sometimes imperfectly applied. Added to this, was the threat of a new and more lethal type of 'barbarian' on China's northern and northwestern borders: the **Xiongnu.**

Sometimes called the 'Eastern Huns', the Xiongnu belonged among the marauding nomads who, for 1600 years, caused havoc everywhere by their dominance of the steppe corridor. Neither hunter-gatherers nor agriculturalists, they drove sheep and cattle on horseback, and by the same means eyed the spoils of the more settled communities on their peripheries. In time, their western counterparts, the Huns, overthrew Rome. Often it seemed China would experience a similar fate.

The Qin and Former (Western) Han Dynasties: 221 BC–9 AD

Qin Shihuangdi swept to victory over China riding the tiger of the Legalist revolution, wielding greater authority than any other man on earth since Alexander. His energy and determination seem phenomenal. But his success brought with it the familiar problems of triumphant absolutism. He did not know when or how to ease off. Instead, he dragooned the Chinese people into programmes of

Imaginary portrait of Qin Shihuangdi from a 19th-century Korean album, but derived from a Ming dynasty portrait.

formidable labour: a network of imperial roads, a new imperial city, the first 'Great Wall', and an underground tomb for himself, big enough to house an entire army.

Such projects were completed with breathtaking speed – within less than ten years of Shihuangdi's accession. But impressive as the results were, the cost was inordinately high. Taxation, whether in kind or specie, or as corvee, was burdensome in the extreme. And the First Emperor failed to secure a smooth transition of power within the regime he had created. His son, **Er Shi**, was unfit to rule, and power passed to **Zhao Gao**, the first of many overmighty eunuchs to impress themselves on Chinese history.

Rebellion spread quickly. Among the aggrieved were those 'nobles' who had lost their patrimony, and an oppressed peasantry. Shihuangdi had levelled society, but in no sense was his government egalitarian. Remarkably, however, one man, **Liu Bang**, prevented China from permanently reverting to a collection of hostile kingdoms. Assuming the dynastic title 'Han', he and his successors installed an internally accountable bureaucratic government that balanced and sometimes checked the power of the court.

The same dynasty broadly contained the Xiongnu threat, and extended China's frontiers, especially to the west and to the south. But although within a century the bureaucracy was staffed by self-professed Confucians – to the extent that in its idealized form imperial government came to be seen as an inherently Confucian undertaking – the **Former Han** retained many Legalist practices. A tariff of harsh punishments remained in place, and the new regime also engaged in massive public works, albeit at a more leisurely, bearable pace. Feudalism, too, was partially restored by the granting of both hereditary and non-hereditary fiefdoms, so that while the principle of office by appointment was applied across the empire, there re-emerged a potentially troublesome aristocracy.

The First Emperor 259–210 BC

The boy destined to become China's **First Emperor** became first the king of Qin in 246 BC. Aged 13, he had necessarily to submit to the regency of his mother Zhao Ji and her associate Lu Buwei. Their disgrace in 238 BC, however, enabled **Zheng** to fully assume the reins of power. With meticulous planning, and the help of his Legalist chief minister **Li Si**, he set about finally subduing China's 'warring states' – a task achieved by a decade of uncompromising warfare. Militarily, no quarter was given. Defeated armies were systematically slaughtered. Victory secured, Shihuangdi summoned all high-born families and their retinues to Xianyang. There he housed them in 270 palaces, modelled on those of the vanquished states he had for the most part destroyed. His own **'A-fang' palace**, meanwhile, was on a scale hitherto unknown, as was the **Terracotta Army** (pp.72–73) created for his tomb.

Yet no extravagance could satisfy the First Emperor's megalomania, nor any security arrangement allay his paranoia. Following two assassination attempts, disclosure of his whereabouts became punishable by death. Much of his reign was spent as a fugitive in his own apartments, obsessed with gaining actual immortality – a fixation that hastened his death in 210 BC. Described by his follower Wei Liao as having 'the proboscis of a hornet' and 'the voice of a jackal', Shihuangdi was castigated by Han historians as a callous tyrant. Among most Chinese, he is accorded begrudging respect for having forged the empire; and Mao Zedong, Shihuangdi's equal as a strongman, admiringly studied his methods.

221 BC As the **empire** is inaugurated an estimated million men begin construction of a new capital, **Xianyang**, close to modern Xian. Simultaneously, work commences on 4700 miles of new roads. Three-lane **highways**, lined with trees, and provided with staging posts at regular intervals, greatly hasten the distribution of imperial decrees. Axle-widths of chariots and carts are standardized to fit fixed-gauge ruts. All **weights**, **measures** and written Chinese are also standardized.

The empire, meanwhile, is divided into 36 administrative units, known as **commanderies** (*jun*), governed by salaried appointees answerable directly to the throne. Each

The Great Wall

Zigzagging between **Shanhaiguan** on the Yellow Sea and **Jiayuguan** at the edge of the Tarim Basin, China's premier icon joins points 2700km apart. Measuring 50ft at its highest, five horsemen can ride abreast along its rampart. Its primary purpose was defence, defining the boundary between the civilized world of the Han Chinese, and the uncivilized world of nomadic 'barbarians', but with the opening of the silk and other trading routes it also enabled officials to monitor and tax incoming and outgoing merchandise.

The Wall is studded with over two thousand watchtowers, each within sight of the next, and with larger fortifications that served as barracks for rapid-deployment forces. At night, beacons lit at preordained times reassured those manning the Wall that its security had not been breached. But although the concept of an unbroken defensive line across the whole of the northern frontier was Qin Shihuangdi's, it was not the creation of a single generation, nor even a single era. Segments of the Wall had been raised during the **Warring States Period**, while those parts seen today are the fruit of a restoration undertaken during the **Ming Dynasty** (see pp.227–261), when the original stamped-earth construction, consuming many thousands of mainly conscript lives, was modified with stone and brick overlay.

Further, maintaining the Wall was a huge logistical operation. Troops manning it had to be fed, paid and armed. One solution – first practised by the Qin – was to make grants of nearby agricultural land to soldiers on permanent garrison duty, so that the Wall also became a kind of colony. It was never self-sufficient, however, and frequently fell into disrepair.

commandery is subdivided into counties. The Qin practice of making groups of five and ten households collectively responsible for each other's behaviour is extended across China, as is a system of 'twenty grades', defining the rank of every subject. Hereditary titles are abolished, scholars

ROBERT HARD NG

The Great Wall of China as it snakes across the Chinese landscape, built by Qin Shihuangdi, but restored in Ming times.

and merchants accorded only lowly status. All households and their occupants are registered. All men are required to perform military and labour duties.

Shihuangdi also institutes worship of the **Four Di** as a state religion, with one 'high god' for each of the empire's 'four corners'.

219 BC Reviving a custom dating back to Shang times, Shihuangdi ascends **Mount Tai**, one of China's 'four scared mountains', in order to 'commune with the gods'. Following an attempt on his life by a blind musician wielding a lead harp, the emperor begins exhibiting an obsessional interest in cults and practices associated with longevity and immortality. As shamans and soothsayers become regular visitors to his A-fang palace, supervised teams of virgin youths are sent eastwards in search of the mythical **Isle of Penglai**.

218 BC A further attempt on the emperor's life is foiled when the would-be assassin attacks the wrong carriage during an imperial tour of inspection.

214 BC Shihuangdi orders General Ming Tian to create what will become the **Great Wall** out of existing defences against the **Xiongnu** and other northern barbarians.

213 BC In an attempt to suppress every possible source of dissent, Shihuangdi orders a general **burning of books** throughout the empire. Only some Legalist texts, agricultural manuals and the *Yijing* are exempted. Copies of all outlawed texts are, however, kept at the Imperial Library in Xianyang, and many scholars conceal what is forbidden rather than see it destroyed. A number of ancient texts are lost for good.

212 BC In order to discourage rebellion, the walls of many provincial cities are razed. According to Sima Qian, 460 scholars are buried alive for refusing to surrender their books. Others are sent to work on the Great Wall.

210 BC Shihuangdi dies of a fever contracted in high summer during a journey to the eastern shores, probably undertaken as a personal search for Penglai. His death, however, is concealed by his chief minister **Li Si**, who explains the odours emanating from the cart conveying the First Emperor's corpse as the smell of dead fish. Li forges, first of all, an edict ordering the designated heir apparent Fu Su to commit suicide, then, reaching Xianyang, Shihuangdi's will, designating a younger son, Hu Hai, as his rightful heir.

Hu Hai is duly enthroned as the **Emperor Er Shi**. Dissolute by nature, Er Shi falls under the spell of Zhao Gao, a court eunuch. Zhao orders a purge of ministers and officials, many of them close to Li Si. Ten princesses are dismembered. Taxation, conscription and punishment all increase.

209 BC Isolated at court, Li Si is first disgraced, then executed, nominally by imperial edict, but in fact by Zhao Gao, who takes over his post as Grand Chancellor. As a multiplicity of factions – some in government, others not – begin scheming for the restitution of the separate states, many officials flee Xianyang. The empire is plunged first into intrigue, then open warfare.

208 BC **Chen She**, a Yangzi valley peasant, refuses conscription. As news of his revolt spreads across China many thousands of others repeat his action. Soon the countryside is awash with disruptive peasant bands. Local government disintegrates as local officials decline to support the court.

207 BC In central China, **Liu Bang**, a minor official of peasant stock, and one-time brigand, creates a sizeable following and joins forces with the main 'anti-Qin' army led by **Xiang Yu**, an aristocrat from the former state of Chu.

The Terracotta Army

Just some of the thousands of life-sized and differentiated terracotta soldiers found near Xian.

So recent is the discovery of Qin Shihuangdi's astonishing 'Terracotta Army' that archeologists and historians are still grappling with its implications. In 1974 workmen digging a well at Lintong, outside Xian, uncovered some life-sized 'baked earth' warriors. Unwittingly,

In Xianyang, Zhao Gao sets up a personal dictatorship as the emperor's mental health is called into question. To confuse Er Shi further, Zhao instructs his courtiers to call a stag a horse. Sensing subterfuge, Er Shi attempts to have the eunuch removed. Zhao invests the palace with his own troops, forcing the emperor to commit suicide.

In his place, Er Shi's nephew **Ziying** is enthroned, but only as the King of Qin. He succeeds, however, in having Zhao Gao murdered.

they had stumbled upon a vast necropolis, lying beneath an artificial hill or tumulus. Since then, over 7000 such figures, as well as bronze chariots and horses, have been excavated, contained in three great pits measuring five acres. More extraordinary still is that each soldier has been individualized. No two faces are the same. Rather, **mass-produced common parts** – arms, legs, torsos, heads – have been covered by layers of finer clay, sculpted before being fired. A variety of ethnic types is plainly visible. Quite possibly, the First Emperor's best-loved troops sat for their portraits. The figures, all facing east as Shihuangdi's armies originally faced east in their conquest of China – are arrayed in serried ranks, protected by pillars and a ceiling of plaster and woven mats. Around them lie real metal armaments of the highest quality. Further still, a **copper vault** inlaid with pearls, and 'rivers' once filled with mercury, suggest a deliberate attempt to represent nothing less than an entire cosmos. Not surprisingly, the whole assemblage is called the 'eighth wonder of the world'. Just as wondrous are the resources that must have been expended: the materials, the kilns, the craftsmen, the millions of man-hours, all to satisfy one man's hubris. For the Terracotta Army was not designed to be seen, except by ancestral spirits. And there is more to come. Shihuangdi's burial chamber has yet to be unearthed.

Six weeks later, Liu Bang – having accepted the title King of Han – enters Xianying. In return for the court's surrender, he spares Ziying's life. A month later, Xiang Yu sacks the capital and executes every member of the Qin royal family. Among other buildings, the Imperial Library is destroyed. At loggerheads with his former ally, Liu Bang withdraws to Sichuan, to raise a new army.

In the far south, a Chinese army led by Trieu Da annexes

the weak kingdom of **Nam Viet** (the northern part of modern Vietnam), and so instigates the perplexed 'Older-Younger Brother' relationship that will haunt Sino-Vietnamese relations until the present day. Taking advantage of its disarray, Trieu renounces his allegiance to the Xianying court and launches the first of many 'Vietnamese rebellions'.

206 BC Xiang Yu – attempting to create a federation of states under his own imperial tutelage – is opposed by those he wants to become vassal kings.

205 BC **Liu Bang** emerges as Xiang's most effective foe, and is therefore able to rally support around him. But fighting between the two leaders, engulfing much of China, continues another three years.

The Xiongnu begin to conduct raids deep into the Yellow River Valley.

202 BC Liu Bang finally outflanks and defeats Xiang's armies. His followers urge him to assume the imperial title. After 'three refusals', Liu accepts. His enthronement as the Emperor Gaodi inaugurates the 'Han' (in fact Liu) dynasty, which, in the first instance, will rule China for 211 years, as the 'Former' or 'Western' Han. Although a southerner, Gaodi shows his respect for tradition by siting his capital at Changan ('Forever Safe') at modern Xian, close to Xianyang, and by taking a northerner, Lu Hou, as his empress. He continues the Qin dynasty's sectioning of China into gubernatorial commanderies, but rewards some of his relatives and followers with hereditary 'feudal' domains or 'kingships'.

Gaodi's government is organized into a pyramidical administration, headed by three 'grand' ministries, with nine further ministries beneath them. Policy, however, continues to be determined by imperial decree, and the code of punishments (including amputation and castration) remains severe. Collective household responsibility and the state worship of the four Di are retained, although a fifth Di is added for the 'centre', echoing the prevalent philosophy of the 'Five Elements'. Shihuangdi's highways are maintained and extended. On one occasion a relay of imperial riders covers 575 kilometres in 24 hours. The tax burden is lightened on all social classes except merchants, who become taxed more heavily, and are subjected to other restrictions: they and their families are barred from public office and forbidden to wear silk or travel in wheeled vehicles. Despite these measures, and the deliberate frugality of the early Han court, trade soon flourishes in China's cities.

201 BC To counter the **Xiongnu**, and to impress upon his subjects his valour as a commander, Gaodi leads an army to the north, but the campaign almost ends in disaster when Gaodi is trapped for seven days by Xiongnu forces inside the walls of Pingcheng city. Elsewhere in China, pockets of resistance to the restitution of the empire persist, and much of Gaodi's reign will be spent attempting to eliminate them.

200 BC Surviving records show that at this time China is divided into ten **kingdoms** and fifteen **commanderies**. In time, however, the kingdoms will be subdivided by inheritance, and the number of commanderies greatly increased as the Han emperors progressively pursue a policy of dismantling larger estates.

198 BC After further inconclusive campaigns, Gaodi and the **Xiongnu** agree a **truce**. In effect, the Xiongnu leader (or *shanyu*) is bought off with annual 'gifts', and the promise of a Chinese princess.

196 BC In a major recruitment drive for an expanding bureaucracy, Gaodi decrees that all high-ranking officials must, upon pain of dismissal, recommend men of probity and talent (the 'filially pious and incorrupt') for office.

The Emperor Gaodi 247–195 BC

The founder of the **Han dynasty** has long enjoyed the special affection of the Chinese people. The historian Sima Qian wrote of his rule: 'It removed the harsh corners of the Qin code and retreated to an easy roundness, whittled away the embellishments and achieved simplicity.' As a commoner who had achieved no more than minor office before he joined the anti-Qin rebellion, however, **Liu Bang** was beholden to the Qin bureaucracy once he had attained the throne. Nor could he hope to govern without the support of the aristocracy. As a means of consolidating his power he awarded kingships to nine of his brothers and nephews, and created 150 marquisates for lesser followers. Gaodi's empire, therefore, was a tripartite federation. One-third was given over to others, one-third governed as commanderies, with only one-third remaining as his personal domain.

What little is known about his character suggests an energetic, capable leader who knew when to compromise and delegate authority. Although he never lost his bluntness of manner, nor an appetite for alcohol, he took care to establish the dignity of his office. Confucian ministers were ordered to design fresh rituals for the court. In other respects, too, he adapted quickly to high position. In his hectic seven-year reign he promoted at least four major concubines, by whom he had eight sons and one daughter.

195 BC Gaodi is killed by an arrow while fighting against the King of Huianan. He is succeeded by his son Liu Ying, known as the **Emperor Huidi**. As Huidi is a minor, actual power is assumed by his mother, the forceful Dowager-empress **Lu Hou**. Together with other members of the Liu family, Lu focuses attention on expanding the empire's frontiers in the west and south. While little comes of such military adventures initially, Huidi appears in public inaugurating shrines to his father's memory in several cities. Taxes in kind are reduced to one-fifteenth of agricultural produce.

194 BC Construction of Changan begins in earnest, on a north–south 'yang-yin' axis. Each of its four walls will have three gates, and designated areas are set aside as marketplaces trading in specific commodities. Outside Changan, an imperial garden will stock rare zoological and botanical specimens.

191 BC Huidi personally rescinds the edict of 213 BC ordering the burning of proscribed books.

188 BC The death of Huidi without an official heir prompts **Lu Hou** to arrange, in quick succession, the enthronement of Shaodi Hong and Shaodi Kong, sons of imperial concubines. Formally assuming the title Regent, she becomes China's ruler until her own death.

Changan's walls are finally completed. Built of stamped earth, they measure eight metres high and, at their top, twelve metres wide. The export of female livestock and metalware to 'the people of the south' is prohibited.

187 BC Wang Ling, a Confucian, becomes the first **'Grand Tutor'** appointed by and to the court. Although this highly remunerated post will often fall vacant, it nonetheless plays a significant role in consolidating **Confucian values** at the heart of government.

180 BC Following her death, members of Lu Hou's family attempt to seize power. The Liu family and two ministers originally appointed by Gaodi respond vigorously, and the Lu faction is removed from court.

The Emperor Gaodi's fifth son, Liu Heng (b. 202 BC), is enthroned as the Emperor Wendi. During his reign Confucianism continues to establish itself as the principle philosophy associated with government, although Daoism is also promoted by his empress Dou.

175 BC Wendi is forced to licence the **private minting** of copper coins after imperial finances are destabilized by a shortage of species. Attempts to recapture the imperial monopoly on currency production include an issue of 'skin money' – pieces of the hide of a rare stag maintained in Changan's royal pleasure park.

168 BC As the empire's monetary system recovers, agricultural **taxes in kind** are reduced to one-thirtieth, providing a boost to economic activity.

At **Dujiang Weir** (Sichuan), China's first known human stone statue is erected. Representing the 3rd century BC hydraulic engineer Li Bing (see p.78), it also functions as a flood and drought warning, depending on whether the water level rises above its shoulders or falls below its calves.

-166 BC A Xiongnu horde breaks through China's 'western passes' and is only defeated a short distance outside Changan.

165 BC Although many appointments continue to be made by recommendation, the **written examination** is introduced for those seeking to enter the bureaucracy.

157 BC The Emperor Wendi is succeeded by his fifth son Liu Qi, the Emperor Jingdi. During his reign the Xiongnu are held at bay, and China continues to prosper.

154 BC An attempted putsch by some of the emperor's feudal vassals – known as the **Rebellion of the Seven Kingdoms** – is foiled. As a result, the number of 'kings' is greatly reduced. Although the throne continues to reward family and followers with the grant of lands, the title *hou* (marquis) is henceforward preferred to *wang* (king).

145 BC In a further curtailment of **feudal power**, the court assumes responsibility for the appointment of all senior officials within the various kingdoms, dukedoms and marquisates.

141 BC Jingdi is succeeded by his eldest son Liu Che, the

Emperor Wudi. Wudi's reign – the third longest in Chinese history – is marked by a surge in imperial confidence. Many **new territories** are added, while Changan's perimeter walls are extended to fifteen kilometres, making it the largest city in the world.

The bronze industry revives, and underground **burial chambers** are increasingly surmounted by impressive mausoleums. Stone sculpture becomes commonplace.

139 BC **Zhang Qian**, an imperial envoy, embarks on a twelve-year exploration of the **'far west'**. Although his mission is to report on military and diplomatic opportunities vis-à-vis the Xiongnu, Tibetans and other hostile 'barbarians', it will also have a lasting cultural impact. Using routes already known to long-haul traders, Zhang travels as far as **Bactria**, beyond the Pamir mountains. As well as Indian and Turkic cultures, he encounters outposts of the **Graeco-Roman world**, and returns to Changan with the walnut and the grape.

136 BC In a revival of 'pre-imperial' learning, a court-sponsored **study group** under the direction of the Grand Master of Ceremonies is established. Five 'erudits' are commissioned to furnish acceptable versions of **five prescribed texts**: the Book of Documents, the Book of Songs, the *Yi jing*, the *Chunqiu* (Spring & Autumn Annals) and a compendium of the *Li* (rites and etiquette). Although Confucius's name is associated with each of these, and an imperial edict confers upon Confucianism the status of an official cult, neither his Analects nor Mencius is yet accorded the status of an approved 'classic'.

135 BC Following the death of his grandmother the Dowager-empress Dou, Wudi embarks on programmes of grandiosity and exuberance. **Conquest** rather than defence becomes the preferred solution to China's border problems. Temporarily, the **Xiongnu** are driven back into the **Gobi**

Sculpture of flying horse from 2nd century AD.

Desert. In the southeast, modern **Zhejiang** and **Fujian** are brought fully under Chinese control for the first time.

134 BC In an act of self-glorification, Wudi introduces hyperbolic **reign titles** – for example 'New Beginning' and 'Vast Imperial Power' – to mark five- or six-year segments of his rule.

132 BC **Torrential rains** in western China cause heavy flooding in the central plains. Dikes breached along the **Yellow River** will not be repaired for twenty years.

131 BC A **canal** (one day to become part of the **Grand Canal system**) linking Changan to the Yellow River, is completed, cutting the Wei River journey time by half.

80 Chapter Two ▶ 221 BC–220 AD

The Emperor Wudi 157–87 BC

Although **Wudi** acceded to the throne in 141 BC, it was not until the death of his grandmother in 135 BC that the greatest of the Han emperors came fully into his own. Thereafter, his despotic personality – mixing vision with vanity – developed swiftly. For 48 years he dominated not just China, but all East Asia as the empire doubled in size. Turning the tables on the Xiongnu and other troublesome barbarians, his armies marched into and across the Tarim Basin, creating new commanderies as they went. Areas within modern Vietnam and Korea were annexed.

Yet even though Wudi means 'Martial Emperor' – and all emperors are known by their 'temple names' bestowed after their deaths – Wudi himself was not a military figure. He preferred instead to strengthen his rule from the centre. To this end, he forged a palace secretariat that offset the prestige of the bureaucracy, undermined the aristocracy by sometimes confiscating their estates, and promoted the lowborn to high office. But the salt and iron monopolies instituted during his reign were fiscally necessary expedients, and too much depended on Wudi's forceful temperament. Five of his Grand Chancellors were executed, and well before his own death Wudi exhibited the same obsessive preoccupation with longevity as had affected Qin Shihuangdi. To the chagrin of his Confucian advisors, the court was once again filled with sorcerers, soothsayers and alchemists.

130 BC Concerned about his **immortality**, Wudi begins welcoming shamans and soothsayers to his court. In the same year, he orders every commandery and kingdom to send two men of outstanding ability to Changan as candidates for senior office.

127 BC Wudi decrees that feudal estates should be divided equally among a holder's sons.

126 BC A real-value copper coinage is minted by imperial edict, to stabilize prices. Such **Wuzhu coins** will still be in use during the Tang dynasty.

124 BC An Imperial Academy (the *Taixue*) is founded and endowed with a campus outside the walls of Changan. Initial enrolment is less than fifty students, but will rise to 3000 by 8 BC, and to 30,000 by the 2nd century AD as it assumes the character of a Confucian finishing school for the 'sons of gentlemen'. Wudi also establishes provincial feeder schools.

121 BC In a bid to regulate China's troublesome **northern borders**, 'dependent states' are created among tribal peoples willing to acknowledge Han suzerainty. Local rulers

> " They fought south of the Castle,
> They died in the moors and were not buried.
> Their flesh was the food of crows.
> 'Tell the crows we are not afraid;
> We have died in the moors and cannot be buried.
> Crows, how can our bodies escape you?'
> The waters flowed deep,
> And the rushes in the pool were dark.
> The riders fought and were slain:
> Their horses wander neighing.
> By the bridge there was a house.
> Was it south, was it north?
> The harvest was never gathered.
> How can we give you your offerings?
> You served your Prince faithfully,
> Though all in vain.
> I think of you, faithful soldiers;
> Your service shall not be forgotten.
> For in the morning you went out to battle
> And at night you did not return. "
>
> Anon, 'Fighting South of the Castle', c.124 BC. trans. Arthur Waley

are given Chinese seals of office. As such peoples are themselves subject to Xiongnu and Tibetan predation, however, the long-term benefits of these arrangements are limited.

120 BC Wudi restores the **state monopoly** in **minting coins**, which are now issued as *qian* or 'cash'. Each coin has a square hole in its centre, to facilitate its storage on cord, and to save metal in its manufacture.

At about this time, the **Great Wall** is extended as far as **Dunhuang**, partly to separate the Xiongnu and Tibetans, but also to provide protection for several hundred thousand Han settlers and the emergent **Silk Road** trading route.

119 BC Campaigns against the **Xiongnu** climax in 'comprehensive' victory, earning China respite for a generation and more. Nonetheless, to defray the expense of these and other military ventures, Wudi approves the creation of **state monopolies** in **salt** and **iron** (foundries as well as mines), in effect creating nationalized industries. While these intermittently bolster imperial revenues for centuries to come, they encourage a slippage in quality control vis-à-vis iron production, and the emergence of a salt black-market.

Having returned from the far west, **Zhang Qian** sets off on a second expedition that will take him to northern **India**.

117 BC **Huo Qubing**, the outstanding general of Wudi's later campaigns, dies. His tomb, in the form of a 'magic mountain', is adorned with notable statuary.

115 BC Building on the success of the salt and iron monopolies, the government takes control of copper and bronze production.

114 BC The *Yuefu*, **'Bureau of Music'**, is established by imperial edict, to stage state performances, and to collect poems set to music. An imperial cult of *Hou tu* (**'Lord of the Earth'**) is promulgated throughout the empire.

113 BC Promulgation of the imperial cult of *Tai yi* (**'Grand Unity'**).

111 BC The southern kingdom of **Nanyue** – covering parts of Guangdong and Guanxi – is annexed to Han rule as a major expeditionary force is dispatched to restore Han control over **Nam Viet**, now called Qiao Qi.

110 BC Wudi ascends **Mount Tai** to conduct traditional sacred rites. About this time, **Zhao Guo**, a middling official, introduces **'ridge and furrow' farming**, enhancing grain yields across the northern plains.

109 BC Wudi personally oversees work-gangs repairing Yellow River **flood defences**. As men labour the emperor recites poetry.

108 BC Han commanderies are established in northern Korea, in Yunnan and on the island of Hainan.

106 BC To curb corruption and embezzlement, an **inspectorate** is instituted to furnish the Grand Council with an annual audit of the administration of each commandery and kingdom. In the first instance, thirteen special commissioners (aka shepherds, and clad in specially embroidered garments) are sent out to review thirteen provinces, as well as the area immediately surrounding the capital.

104 BC In the wake of **Zhang Qian**'s western missions, **Li Guanli** leads an expeditionary force into the **Tarim Basin**. In four-years' campaigning he will reach the Sogdian kingdom of **Ferghana**. But while some mainly Turkic peoples are brought within the Han fold, Li's costly actions encourage the growth of mountain rebel groups. His campaigns, however, contribute to the emergence of the **Silk Road** as a significant land route for trade between China, the Middle East and Europe.

100 BC Commanderies are established among the **Qiang**, or 'eastern' Tibetan peoples. **Dunhuang** is strongly fortified as the highway between it and Changan is made 'safe', and Chinese garrisons are established in **Ferghana**, to ensure a steady supply of **war-horses**. As a consequence, Dunhuang becomes a major entrepot on the Silk Road.

About this time, alfalfa is first imported from the west, and the traditional sixty-day cycle of the **Chinese calender** is replaced with 30- and 29-day months. **Sundials** become popular, and a rudimentary **water-clock** is developed.

99 BC An army of 5000, led by **Li Ling** suffers defeat as the **Xiongnu** resume their fighting.

98 BC Wudi attempts to make **alcohol** production a **state monopoly**, but his edict is widely ignored.

91 BC As Wudi grows senile, a **succession crisis** erupts. For five days, two factions – one consisting of members of the royal Liu family, the other centred on the **Empress Wei** and her relatives – resort to armed combat in and around Changan. When the Liu triumph, Wei and her son (the heir apparent Liu Jiu) are forced to commit suicide. Her family is exterminated.

As imperial finances falter, the government issues promissory notes (a forerunner of **paper money**) and authorises the sale of imperial titles.

90 BC Li Ling is again defeated by a Xiongnu army. The 'Grand Historian' **Sima Qian**, author of the *Shiji*, dies.

87 BC Wudi dies two days after nominating his 8-year-old son Liu Fuling as his heir (the **Emperor Zhaodi**) and appointing **He Guang** (d. 68 BC) as Regent. The stepbrother of the Empress Wei, He Guang uses his position to accumulate a wealth greater than the emperor's. During Zhaodi's reign, expensive military campaigns are avoided, taxes lightened and the code of punishments ameliorated – all policies recommended by his Confucian advisers.

Sima Qian c.145–90 BC

Sometimes compared to Herodotus, **Sima Qian** is read for his wryly fluent style as much as for his apparent factuality. Divided into 130 chapters, the *Shiji* tells the story of China from its mythic origins up until Sima's own lifetime. As well as a sequential narrative, it offers short treatises on chosen themes, and brief biographies of individual figures – anticipating Plutarch by 150 years.

But the *Shiji* is more than a compendium of often arcane knowledge. Sima seeks to establish a cyclical and moral understanding of events, into which is incorporated the theory of the **Mandate of Heaven**. The governance of man is, like other observable phenomena, necessarily subject to decay. Thus Sima characterizes the Xia dynasty as the rule of good faith lapsing into mere rusticity; the Shang as piety dwindling into superstition; and the Zhou as refinement degenerating into theatricality.

It is the Qin dynasty, and its abuse of power, however, that draws Sima's sharpest contempt. By contrast, the Han dynasty is lauded, even though Sima himself suffered cruelly at its hands. He was castrated – 'the palace punishment' – for supporting Li Ling after Li had lost an army against the Xiongnu. Yet this did not deter the man employed as a court astronomer from privately completing the book begun by his father, Sima Tan. 'How can I, his son, dare to neglect his will?' he wrote. In due course, the *Shiji* became the model for the great series of officially commissioned 'dynastic histories', instigating a tradition whereby the faults of each dynasty are emphasized by its successor.

> **❝** I delight in reading the Shiji and am never without it on my table. I read it and sigh, I break into song, I weep or I laugh. Ah, the men of his day looked upon Sima Qian's work as so much trash. How little they realised that, a hundred generations later, there would be men who, reading it, would sigh, or sing, weep and laugh. **❞**
>
> Rai Sanyo, Reading the Shiji, c.1810

81 BC Unusually, a conference of sixty officials is convened at Changan to openly discuss the pros and cons of the salt and iron monopolies. This 'synod' (aka **'The salt and iron debates'**) quickly engages in a wide-ranging policy review. Opinion polarizes between two groups: **'Progressives'**, and conservative **'Reformers'**, representing the **'orthodox' Confucian view**. The latter win the argument, launching vigorous attacks on opulence and ostentation in private as well as public life, on corruption among officials, and the decline of agricultural values. But while this victory sets the seal on **Han expansionism**, it is seen by some later commentators as heralding the economic stagnation that caused the decay of the Former Han dynasty.

74 BC Zhaodi dies aged 22, possibly the result of foul play. His immediate successor is Liu He, the debauched grandson of Wudi by his consort Li.

> ❝ In times gone by men served their parents with their whole hearts and attended their funerals with untempered grief. So also our sacred leaders constructed rules to contain the excesses of such feelings. Today however sons render neither the love nor the obedience due to their living parents. But when the parent dies, there is unseemly competition to be seen to honour the dead. To conceal their want of grief and enhance their reputations they spare no expense staging a funeral and providing costly furnishings for the grave. In this way they hope to outshine their peers, to the extent that ordinary citizens, emulating the fashion of the rich, frequently ruin themselves. ❞
>
> From the concluding report of the 81 BC 'salt and iron debates'.

Within four weeks, however, Liu He is ousted by the Council of Ministers and replaced by Liu Bingyi, the **Emperor Xuandi**, another grandson of Wudi by the Empress Wei. Snatched from Changan during the factional conflict of 91 BC, he has been raised as a commoner, and shares the **Reformers'** distaste for extravagance.

71 BC Xuandi's wife, the Empress Xu, is poisoned by a senior concubine, who becomes the Empress Huo.

60 BC The office of **Protector-General** is instituted to regulate relations with the peoples of **Central Asia**.

59 BC The **salaries** of middle and lower officials are raised fifty percent in an endeavour to remove the principal cause of bureaucratic corruption.

51 BC The leader of the southern **Xiongnu** peoples is received by Xuandi in Changan. While the shanyu is able to extract economic concessions in return for pledges not to launch further attacks against China's frontiers, the court gains a strategic victory by exploiting differences between the southern and northern Xiongnu (who remain hostile toward China). Meanwhile, in order to ascertain the authenticity and correct interpretation of Confucian and other texts, a working party of scholars is convened at the **'Pavilion of the Stone Canal'**.

49 BC Xuandi is succeeded by his son, the **Emperor Yuandi**. Yuandi continues his father's economies. During his reign many state-funded shrines are closed, and banquets are outlawed.

36 BC 145 reputedly **Roman soldiers** are captured in Gansu. Possibly survivors of the Battle of Carrhae, they are given Chinese wives and land to farm.

33 BC Yuandi is succeeded by the **Emperor Chengdi**, a womanizer and gambler. The responsibilities of government are undertaken instead by his mother **Wang**. Like previous dowager-empresses Wang exploits her power to raise members of her family to high office.

31 BC The imperial **cult of _Tian_** (Heaven) is established at altars in Changan and other cities. The emperor's title as the 'Son of Heaven' is officially promulgated.

18 BC Infatuated with a low-born concubine, **Zhao Feiyan**, Chengdi deposes his empress Xu. Feiyan becomes empress. Two sons of Chengdi by other concubines are put to death.

7 BC Chengdi is succeeded by his nephew Liu Xin, the Emperor Aidi, aged 17. As Aidi succumbs to the homosexual advances of the courtier Dong Xian, the Dowager-empress Wang continues to wield real power.

Contemporaneous sources record that the court employs 829 musicians, while 3000 slaves are at work in the imperial kitchens. Imperial finances are undermined by the retention of revenues by larger landowners.

3 BC Encouraged by Wang, worship of the **'Queen Mother of the West'** (_Xiwangmu_) spreads rapidly across China. According to myth, she governs the cosmos from a fastness in the **Tianshan** (Mountains of Heaven), and is able to bestow immortality.

1 BC Following the sudden death of Aidi, Wang seizes the imperial seals and elevates her nephew **Wang Mang** to the rank of acting Regent. Yuandi's 8-year-old grandson, Liu Jizi, is enthroned as the **Emperor Pingdi**, and immediately married to Wang Mang's daughter.

AD 1 China at this time is sectioned into 83 commanderies and twenty reduced 'kingdoms' and has a population of about **58 million**.

7 The boy-emperor Pingdi dies and is succeeded by the 2-year-old **Emperor Ruzi**.

8 **Wang Mang**'s regency is confirmed by imperial edict.

Material Culture of the Former Han

Although **bronzes** continued to be cast throughout the Han period, there was a diminution in both their number and their quality. Iron and steel (which China produced centuries before Europe) were preferred for the manufacture of heavy-duty items, including swords. But **jade-work**, **ceramics** and, especially in Sichuan, **lacquerware** continued to flourish. The Former Han also added to the Chinese material repertoire by **introducing earthenware modelling**, **painting** and **stone statuary**.

As with the pre-imperial times, the most important archeological finds have come about as the result of burial excavation. In 1990 the tomb of the **Emperor Jingdi** and his empress **Wang** revealed a second 'terracotta army'; some 40,000 figurines assembled in battle order. These, however, are miniatures, as are many

ROBERT HARDING

Prince Liu Sheng's jade burial suit designed to offer complete protection against corporeal decay

other Former Han objects – among them modelled houses, farm buildings, animals and carts, yielding an especially intimate portrait of Former Han society.

That the same society relished luxury is evidenced from two other tombs. At Mawangdui (Changsha) the body of **Lady Dai** is finely preserved in a swaddling of twenty silks. Buried with her were over 200 lacquer and ceramic vessels, including cosmetic boxes, 48 bamboo suitcases and, in an antechamber, a full Chinese dinner of seven different meats. In her son's tomb nearby a library of books was discovered, inscribed on bamboo strips, some of them previously presumed lost. Just as impressive is the tomb of **Liu Sheng**, a Han prince, and his wife **Dou Wan**: a series of chambers including a washroom hollowed out of limestone cliffs at Mancheng (Hebei), excavated from 1968. Among thousands of objects recovered was a jade suit, enclosing Liu's body.

9 Realizing they have been outmanoeuvred by the Wang, the **Liu** family attempt revolt. Wang Mang, claiming that the Liu have forfeited the Mandate of Heaven, declares himself Emperor. The lives of Ruzi and other Liu are, however, spared.

Wang Mang (9–23 AD) and the Later Han Dynasty (25–220 AD)

In order to justify his usurpation, **Wang Mang** touted the ideals of the archaic Zhou dynasty. Like Qin Shihuangdi, however, he sought to bolster the throne by expunging the power of the feudal aristocracy. By simple fiat, he confiscated their lands, or attempted to. But the failure of an ambitious package of currency reforms and the onset of a concatenation of natural disasters quickly put paid to his Xin or 'New' dynasty. Even before he had time to groom an heir, Wang was cut down.

Briefly, China reverted to civil war as different factions jockeyed for control, until the prize was again secured by the **Liu family**. But capable as he was, the **Emperor Guangwudi** could not govern without the support of the feudal lords, many belonging to his own clan. Thus, the resumption of Han rule was essentially a continuation of the Former Han polity. Court politics swiftly fell prey to the machinations of eunuchs, concubines, dowager-empresses and their followers. Nor can it be said that any of Guangwudi's successor emperors (with the exception of Mingdi 57–75 AD) displayed the strength of character to check the forces of decay that seemed to be always knocking on the door.

The wonder of the Later Han is that they lasted as long as they did. For historians, the conundrum has been to determine at what point terminal rot set in. Was it the **Revolt of the Yellow Turbans** in 184, or the massacre of the **eunuchs** in 189? Or was it at some point during the preceding century? The history of the court makes desultory reading. For two hundred years the empire was held together by the bureaucracy, whose Confucian character was confirmed by the re-founding of the **Imperial Academy**, and by the emergence of a clearly defined body of Confucian classics which furnished the curriculum for civil service examinations.

It was also during the Later Han that **Daoism** developed into something like a nationwide religion, and that **Buddhism** made its debut in China. Culturally, there was diversity of a kind not seen since the Warring States Period. Of equal significance was a shift of people and resources southwards, drawn to the hugely fertile **Yangzi delta**. But it wasn't just economic opportunism that caused this migration. There was also the ongoing threat from the northern barbarians, who on several occasions penetrated the central plains.

These incursions, while falling short of full-scale invasion, best explain the eventual Han unravelment. Although there was a standing army, it had to be deployed too often against not just the Xiongnu, but also the Wuhuan, Qiang and other smaller, but equally restless, peoples. To meet such threats, military authority was invested in the commanders and feudal lords of the border areas. Almost unnoticed, and as imperial revenues dwindled, actual power ebbed away from the centre, making it so much the more susceptible to other kinds of calamity.

9 Having seized the throne, **Wang Mang** justifies his usurpation by invoking the values of the archaic **Zhou dynasty**. In order to undermine the surviving Han aristocracy, he 'nationalizes' all land, outlaws the private sale of slaves, and declares an imperial 'monopoly' in gold, offering copper in exchange. He also decrees that Chinese exports must be paid for in gold – a move that will constrain the **Roman emperor Tiberius** to ban the import of **Chinese silks**.

In a further reform of the domestic economy, Wang introduces a new **currency** in 28 denominations, made of cowrie shell, gold and silver, as well as copper. He also commissions Liu Xin to compile a catalogue of **'approved' books**. Of the 677 titles listed, only a quarter will survive into modern times.

23 After fourteen years, Wang Mang has little to show for his monetary reforms. Instead, an unusual proliferation of **natural disasters** – including constant flooding in the Yellow River area – has created pandemic disruption and unrest. Wang's reign ends when he is hacked to death by a soldier in

Changan, and his head stoned by onlookers in a marketplace.

As aristocratic factions vie for power, disorder is compounded by the eruption of the **Red Eyebrows peasants' revolt** in the eastern Yellow River region. The Red Eyebrows (so-called on account of the red paint daubed on their faces) are the product of want and famine, as are a similar group called the **'Green Woodsmen'** in Hubei. For a while they join forces with the **Liu faction**, but when the Liu are unable to agree who should become Emperor, the alliance dissolves. The Red Eyebrows set fire to Changan and pillage its outlying royal mausoleums.

25 Twenty-year-old **Liu Xiu** – a capable commander and wealthy southern descendant of the Emperor Jingdi – breaks the deadlock in the north and is enthroned. As the **Emperor Guangwudi**, he inaugurates the **Later Han Dynasty** (aka the **Eastern Han**) because its capital will be sited at **Loyang**. To buttress support, he takes a northerner, **Guo Shentong**, as his empress. It takes Guangwudi a decade, however, to eliminate rival claimants. To assuage and reward his closer male relatives, he makes grants of 'feudal' territories. He revives the imperial monopolies in salt and iron, but reduces agricultural taxes in kind. By buying up grain in times of plenty, storing it in **state granaries**, and redistributing it in times of need, Guangwudi stabilizes food prices and reduces popular discontent.

In the wake of the Red Eyebrows' destruction of the Imperial Library at Changan, Guangwudi orders copies of surviving books from across China to be deposited at Loyang; and he institutes over a hundred provincial colleges to train and prepare civil servants. During his reign, admittance to the bureaucracy by **formal examination in Confucian texts** becomes more widely (though still not exclusively) instituted. State policy, however, is determined by an **'inner cabinet'** composed mainly of Guangwudi's blood relatives.

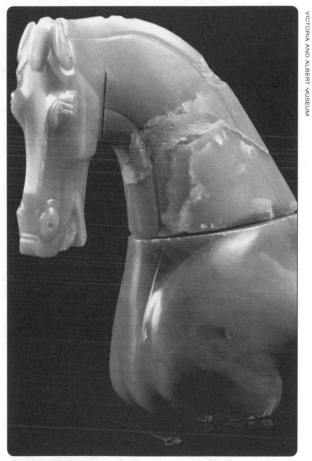

Head and partial torso of a horse in green jade from the later Han dynasty.

29 The **Imperial Academy** reopens outside the walls of Loyang.

31 The invention of a **water-powered bellows** for use in iron foundries paves the way for the world's first production of steel.

36 The defeat of rebel forces in **Sichuan** completes Guangwudi's reunification of the empire.

39 A major revolt breaks out in **Vietnam**. Led by the two **Trung Sisters**, this is supported by all landowners as well as feudal tenants. For four years Vietnamese self-rule is asserted.

41 Guangwudi replaces the Empress Guo with his southern concubine **Yin Lihua**, by whom he already has five sons.

43 The revolt in **Vietnam** is broken by Ma Yuan. In despair, the Trung sisters drown themselves.

49 The troublesome **Wuhuan**, dwelling in the far northeast (Manchuria), are brought within the Chinese pale.

54 Death of **Ban Biao**, a leading poet and prose writer, and the head of an important literary family that includes his son **Ban Gu** and his daughter **Ban Zhao**, author of

> ❝ I see silken clothes, if you can call them clothes at all, that in no degree afford protection either to the body or to the modesty of the wearer, and clad in which no woman could honestly swear she is not naked. These are imported at great expense from nations unknown even to commerce in order that our married women may not be able to show more of their persons to their paramours in a bedroom than they do on a street. ❞
>
> Seneca, fulminating against the effects of Chinese silk on Roman society, *De Beneficiis*, Bk VII

'Lessons for Women' (*Nujie*), counselling compliance toward men, but also advocating female education.

56 Guangwudi ascends **Mount Tai** and makes ritual offerings to *Tian* ('Heaven').

The Han Bureaucracy

The administrative apparatus evolved by the early empire was its greatest legacy. It survived until 1912, and elements of it are traced in the modern Communist Party. In essence, a pyramid-structure was headed by three great officers, known after 8 BC as the **'Three Excellencies'**: the Grand Chancellor, responsible for finance; the Grand Secretary, responsible for the bureaucracy itself and for justice; and a Grand Commander, responsible for 'defence'. Below these were **nine ministers**, and below them, in a carefully graded hierarchy, any number of lesser offices. Thus, there existed a 'Prefect of Flinty-hoofed Horses', a 'Prefect of the Long Lanes' and a 'Grand Prolonger of Autumn', as well as such bodies as the 'Foremen Clerks of the Orchid Terrace' and 'Gentlemen Rapid As Tigers'. Between them, these appointees ran the daily affairs of the capital, the imperial domains, and the empire at large. And the same system was replicated in each feudal kingdom, commandery and prefecture as well as in the households of the empress and the royal princes and princesses.

As this extended bureaucracy grew, and was colonized by Confucians, so it took on a life of its own. Although it never enjoyed an absolute monopoly on literacy, it performed some, at least, of the cultural functions of the medieval Catholic Church, guarding its interests and elaborate rituals jealously. Even as an **examination-based meritocracy**, its doors were seldom more than half open. Moreover, because it also controlled the means of propaganda – including the wording of imperial edicts – it became adept at avoiding censure. When trouble flared, it was never the bureaucrats' fault. Even if periodically widespread corruption is discounted, the question can still be asked: did the bureaucracy exist to serve the state, or the state to support the bureaucracy?

57 Guangwudi is succeeded by Liu Yang, the **Emperor Mingdi**, his eldest son by Yin Lihua. Cruel as he is, Mingdi consolidates the restoration of Han rule in a more flamboyant manner than his father. Loyang becomes a place of visible wealth, attracting foreign traders. But although Mingdi and his wife the **Empress Ma** revel in the trappings of power, he retains the respect of senior officials, among them the outstanding general **Ban Chao**, who is immediately given the responsibility of containing the resurgent northern **Xiongnu**.

60 As extravagant **public works** again become a feature of Chinese life, construction of the emperor's 'Northern Palace' is halted by a mutiny of conscripted labourers.

65 The gathering of a group of **Buddhist monks** and worshippers at **Pencheng** is the first recorded instance of **Buddhism** on Chinese soil. It is probable, however, that Buddhist contacts between China and India have been accumulating for several decades via western trading routes.

69 Under the supervision of the engineer **Wang Jing**, work begins on a new system of dykes and water-gates along 400 kilometres of the Yellow River.

71 Mingdi orders the arrest of more than 500 officials suspected of plotting rebellion. They are summarily flogged to death.

72 Mingdi becomes the first emperor to visit the shrine of Confucius at Qufu. Given a commandery in the Yangzi delta as a reward for his hydraulic projects on the Yellow River, engineer Wang Jing promotes silk production and the use of the ox-drawn plough in the area around Nanjing.

73 **Ban Chao** begins a three-year campaign that will restore Chinese authority in the **Tarim Basin**.

> **"** There existed no written constitution in Han China, and the wielding of power was based on custom. The emperor shared power with the officials, and the officials shared it with each other. Expressed in lofty terms, this meant that the sovereign should subordinate his own interests and private feelings to the welfare of the state, that he needed the assistance of wisely chosen officials, that loyal officers should criticize the shortcomings of the sovereign, that he should accept such remonstrances, that officials should not be guided by self-interest, and that faithful advisers were a priceless treasure for an enlightened sovereign. Reality was different, and harmonious relations between the throne and officialdom were relatively rare. Decisions came out of conflict. **"**
>
> Hans Bielenstein, *The Bureaucracy of Han Times* (1980)

74 Mingdi orders an offensive against the northern Xiongnu to curb the westwards spread of their influence and activities.

75 Following his death, and to the satisfaction of his Confucian ministerism, Mingdi is buried by his own command, not in a costly new mausoleum, but in his mother's tomb. He is succeeded by his son Liu Da, the **Emperor Zhangdi**. In the west, the kingdoms of **Karashahr** and **Kurcha**, in league with the **northern Xiongnu**, inflict crushing defeats on Han forces.

79 As the Northern Xiongnu are checked, a conference of scholars is convened at the White Tiger Hall in Loyang to discuss how the **'classics'** should best be interpreted. **Commentaries** on the classics become an integral part of Chinese literature from this point onwards.

84 Flogging and torture are banned as a means of conducting investigations into criminal cases.

88 Zhangdi dies and is succeeded by the **Emperor Hedi**, his 9-year-old son by a concubine, and the first in a line of boy-emperors. The **Dowager-empress Dou** (Zangdi's wife) and her brother General **Dou Xian** assume power as regents, marking a return to influence of 'consort families'.

89 Fifteen-years' warfare culminate in a comprehensive victory by Chinese over **Xiongnu** forces, and Han power is once more established in central Asia.

c. 90 The **wheelbarrow** is invented by the Chinese as a means of bringing produce to market by small farmers.

The Classic of Mountains and Seas

Written by various hands between the 3rd century BC and the early 2nd century AD, *The Classic of Mountains and Seas* defies genre classification. For the modern reader, its eighteen sections are a curious mix of fable, folklore and natural history. Purporting to give an account of the fringes of the Chinese world, it offers mythical, zoological, anthropological, topographical and medicinal snapshots. As well as the 'four seas' that supposedly bound earth under heaven, over 5000 mountains are referred to individually, inhabited by a startling assortment of chimeras: birds with horns, horses with dragon-heads, dogs with human faces, and so on, all imbued with magical powers. But alongside this Borgesian bestiary there are, among the chapters written during Han times, unflattering descriptions of semi-feral tribes: the 'Egg Folk', for example, or the 'Mushroom People', so called because of their dwarfish stature. Yet just how much is fiction, and how much fact? For all its immense surface charm, *The Classic of Mountains and Seas* makes no disclaimers. Rather, it attaches credence to every kind of peculiarity, reinforcing a deep-seated belief that outside the ordered Chinese community all is monstrosity and chaos.

91 Emperor Hedi, now 12 years old, and tiring of his grandmother's control, attempts to assert his independence by intriguing with his eunuchs. He fails initially, but from this time onwards eunuch power steadily increases.

Following victories against the Xiongnu, **Ban Chao** is made Protector General of the Western Regions. He establishes a permanent base at **Kucha**, and his troops advance as far as the **Caspian Sea**. An envoy dispatched to Rome reaches **Mesopotamia** before turning back.

92 The effects of a particularly vicious eight-year cycle of **floods** and **drought**, made worse by plagues of **locust**, are successfully palliated by granary-based government **relief programmes**.

The poet **Ban Gu** dies before completing the *Han Shu* (or second standard dynastic history) begun by his father Ban Biao (see p.96). The work, however, will be completed by his sister **Ban Zhao**.

102 The death of General **Ban Chao** presages a weakening of China's hold over Central Asia.

105 'Proto-paper' – a compound of hemp, linen and tree-bark invented by **Cai Lun** (d. 121) – is given recognition. As a writing medium its immediate advantage over silk is its low manufacturing cost, but paper will not be widely used in China until the 3rd century. It will reach Korea and Japan in the 7th century, and Europe in the 12th.

106 Hedi is succeeded by his 1-year-old son, the **Emperor Shangdi**, following the intervention of Hedi's wife the **Dowager-empress Deng**. The boy dies in September, and is succeeded by his 12-year-old cousin and grandson of Zhangdi Lin Yu, the **Emperor Andi**. Although Andi will live another nineteen years, the court rapidly succumbs to the machinations of his consort the **Empress Yan** and her relatives.

From The Classic of Mountains and Seas

"There is a bird on this mountain which looks like an owl, but it has human hands. It makes a noise like a hen quail. Its name is the crimsonowl. Its name comes from its call: 'Joo'. Wherever it appears numerous officers will be banished from that district." I.ii

"Three hundred and fifty leagues further west is a mountain called Mount Jade. This is where Queen Mother of the West lives. In appearance, Queen Mother of the West looks like a human, but she has a leopard's tail and the fangs of a tigress, and she is good at whistling. She wears a victory crown on her tangled hair. She presides over the Catastrophes from the Sky and the Five Destructive Forces." II.iii

"The River Gain contains many swordfish which look like sudden-fish but have scarlet scales. They make a noise like a human bawling. If you eat them, you won't have smelly armpits." III.ii

"The country of Deepseteyes lies to the east of there. Its people go about with one hand raised." VIII

"There is Mount Divinepower, This is where Shaman Whole, Shaman Reach, Shaman Share, Shaman Robust, Shaman Motherinlaw, Shaman Real, Shaman Rite, Shaman Pushaway, Shaman Takeleave and Shaman Birdnet ascend to the sky and come down from Mount Divinepower. This is where the hundred drugs are to be found." XVI

From *The Classic of Mountains and Seas*.
Trans. Anne Birrell

107 Insurgency in the western and northwestern commanderies prompts a successful campaign against the **Qiang** people; but faced with the expense of this and similar operations, ministers begin urging that it would be cost-effective to withdraw from **Central Asia** altogether.

A 'fact-finding' embassy of chieftains from **Japan** visits the imperial court, inaugurating the long process of the Sinification of Japanese culture and politics.

120 An embassy to the Chinese court from the **Kingdom of Shan** portends the spread of Chinese cultural influence into **Southeast Asia** beyond Nam Viet.

Material Culture of the Later Han

Whatever the fiscal problems facing government, archeology indicates that Later Han society was robustly prosperous. Although none of its **wooden architecture** survives, pictorial records show the full fruition of building techniques that subsequently spread throughout East Asia. Now, on traditional stamped earth platforms, multistorey timber-framed palaces and houses were erected. If these have vanished, the **stone sculptures** that are a particular feature of Later Han have not. To the 1st century AD is owed the abiding 'spirit road': avenues leading up to the entrances of royal and other major tombs lined with statues of guardian animals and humans. Compared to Greece or Rome, stone carving may have come late to China, but the medium was quickly mastered. Later Han tombs evolved internally too. Shaft tombs as repositories of actual treasures all but disappeared. In their place – whether underground, or enclosed in raised tumuli – simulacra of dwellings appeared. The walls of such apartments were often constructed of brick, and the bricks used stamped with pictorial motifs. **Funeral furnishings** reflect life-style as much as naked wealth. But the outstanding Later Han survival is the shrine-tomb of **Wu Liang**, from the 2nd century AD. Wu, who oversaw completion of the work, was a scholar with pronounced political views. A series of two-dimensional stone relief carvings – some of them depicting myth, others real personages – make clear that Chinese craftsmen and artists were already proficient at creating form and content on essentially flat, uncurved surfaces.

121 **Xu Shen** completes his *Shu wen*, the first surviving **dictionary** of Chinese words containing 9353 distinct characters and recognized as an outstanding philological achievement.

122 A troupe of **Roman jugglers** arrives in Loyang, apparently having entered China via a 'southern' land-route.

125 In May the Emperor Andi is succeeded by an infant known only as the **Emperor Shaodi**, unacknowledged in official histories.

In December Shaodi is murdered by eunuchs who install Andi's 10-year-old son Liu Bao, the **Emperor Shundi**, on the throne. Shandi's marriage to **Liang Na** will restore the influence of the 'northern clans' to court life.

Zhang Heng (78–139) comes to imperial notice when – by using **water-power** to rotate an **armillary sphere** of his own design – he improves annotation of the movements of heavenly bodies.

132 **Zhang Heng**'s reputation is enhanced by his invention of a form of **seismograph** for detecting earthquakes in different parts of the empire. His instruments are installed on the *Ling tai* ('spiritual terrace') inside Loyang. In the four years remaining to him, he introduces **grid-cartography**, and calculates π at 3.162.

135 An imperial edict allows **eunuchs** to pass on any **titles** and **estates** awarded them to adopted sons.

140 Repudiating their allegiance to the empire, the **Southern Xiongnu** enter an alliance with **Tibetan** and **Wuhuan** chieftains and attempt an invasion of the Wei River valley. Although this rebellion is repulsed, it raises the prospect of an **anti-Han league** stretching from the west to the northeast.

Daoism

It was during the Later Han that **Daoism** emerged as a distinctive socioreligious phenomenon in Chinese life. From 100 AD Laozi (see p.47) was widely venerated as a deity, with many shines erected for his worship. The first definably Daoist community – consisting of priests and laity, and called the 'Five Pecks of Rice' sect – was founded in the Hanzhong area of Sichuan in 142 by **Zhang Daoling**. Money was considered unclean, as were those gods whose rites required offerings of meat. Illness was a sign of moral infirmity. But if Zhang's appointment of a body of elders (or 'libationers') was the first step toward a Daoist church, elsewhere in China Daoism continued as a portmanteau belief-system disseminated by mendicant wise men and their disciples.

Attracting a growing number of adherents, it slowly synthesized an open-ended assortment of beliefs and superstitions. Although **Laozi** and **Zhuangxi** were its acknowledged masters, Daoism's philosophy incorporated such cults as the Queen Mother of the West, as well as *yin-yang*, the Five Elements (earth, fire, wood, air and water), alchemy, herbal medicine and macrobiotics. The health and longevity of the individual, not of the family or society, were Daoism's primary concerns. If all individuals embraced the same goals, then government would become superfluous. As such, Daosim was, supremely, an outlook on life centred on a speculative curiosity about the natural world. As a storehouse of ideas largely jettisoned by the emergent statist philosophy of Confucianism, it developed a populist appeal that could be manipulated politically during times of unrest – the Yellow Turban uprising of 184 being a case in point. Yet it is just Daoism's distaste for organizational structures that has ensured its survival. Offering its opponents scant target, Daoism became, and remains, a potent fertilizer for Chinese poetry and art.

144 Shundi is succeeded by his 1-year-old son, the **Emperor Chongdi**.

145 After surviving five months, Chongdi dies and is succeeded by a 3-year-old great-grandson of Zhangdi, the **Emperor Zhidi**.

146 Having survived sixteen months, Zhidi also dies, and is replaced by another of Zhangdi's great-grandsons, the 14-year-old **Emperor Huandi**, known as 'the first of the bad emperors' on account of the harsh social and fiscal policies initiated during his reign. The **Dowager-empress Liang Na** immediately marries Huandi to her younger sister, Liang Nuying, and appoints her kinsman **Liang Ji** as **regent**. Although Huandi will enjoy the throne for 22 years, he will never take charge of government. Uncomfortable with Confucian officials, he is drawn toward **Daoism** – another reason perhaps for the unfortunate soubriquet bestowed upon him by court historians.

It is decreed that the sons of all senior officials should attend the **Imperial Academy**. Although enrolment soon reaches 30,000, relatively few such 'students' will sit the imperial examinations.

148 The first known translation of **Buddhist texts** from Sanskrit into Chinese is undertaken by **An Shigao**, a missionary from the Caspian Sea area.

150 The hostile **Xianbi** people begin making their presence felt in (modern) Manchuria.

153 A series of powerful **earthquakes** is followed by a plague of **locusts**. Fearing he has earned Heaven's disapproval, Huandi becomes a recluse, leaving the exercise of his authority to his **eunuchs**.

159 The death of the empress **Liang Nuying** prompts Huandi to conspire with five eunuchs to rid his court of the all-powerful Liang family. Despite protests by as many as 30,000 students, the eunuchs are themselves empowered, particularly with the appointment of **Shan Chao** as 'General of Chariots and Cavalry'.

166 At Huandi's instigation, imperial sacrifices are offered to Laozi, and to the Buddha. While this reflects the extent to which Daoism and Buddhism have penetrated even the ·highest reaches of Chinese society, it also shows that the two belief systems are as yet non-rivalrous.

Traders from the Roman Empire, claiming to represent Marcus Aurelius, reach southern China.

168 Following the death of Huandi, another great-grandson is enthroned, the 12-year-old **Emperor Lingdi**. Huandi's widow the **Dowager-empress Dou** secures the appointment of her relative **Dou Xian** as regent. Immediately, he conspires to massacre the court eunuchs en masse. His plot discovered, Lingdi orders his suicide under eunuch pressure.

With the eunuchs firmly in control of the palace once more, all imperial revenues are directed to the emperor's 'personal' exchequer, known as the **Hall of 10,000 Gold Pieces**. Offices of state are offered for sale on a scale previously unknown, and those already holding office obliged to pay 'fees'.

175–83 Following intense debate among scholars, 'correct' versions of the **Confucian classics** are inscribed on fifty-odd stone tablets at the **Imperial Academy**. While the purpose is to provide authoritative texts for all to see, copies of the classics made by students filling the incised characters with ink, and then pressing over them with silk or paper, are considered forerunners of **print**.

178 Lingdi undermines the bureaucracy's already damaged integrity by decreeing a tax on all grants of office, and on all promotions.

181 At the climax of a long-running palace feud, Lingdi's senior concubine **Wang** is poisoned by his consort the **Empress He**.

The Yellow Turbans

Popular uprising that is also the eruption of a militant cult dependent on a charismatic leader, and induced by high levels of famine, is a recurrent theme in Chinese history. The greatest 'messianic' revolt was the pseudo-Christian Taiping Rebellion of the mid-19th century. In Han times, the **Yellow Turbans** (*Huang-jin*) offer another striking example. In 184 – driven by a Utopian vision supplied by Zhang Jue, and claiming to follow the taiping dao, or 'way of great peace' – they threatened to bring down the imperial government. **Laozi** was worshipped as a saviour, although of equal influence was the now lost *Taiping jing*, 'Book of Great Peace'. Yellow was chosen in honour of the mythical founder of the Chinese nation, the Yellow Emperor. Thirty-six *fang* ('adepts') were placed in command of 36 districts. 'Holy water' was offered as a remedy for every sickness. Those who did not recover were deemed morally corrupt. Zhang Jue, however, also co-ordinated his planned rebellion with a group of court eunuchs. Mobilizing an army of perhaps 300,000 peasants, he terrorized the area between the Yellow and Huai rivers.

Although minor Yellow Turban uprisings continued sporadically for a decade after Zhang's death, by 186 it was militarily a broken vessel. Overall, the movement lacked the resources to gain its objectives, although communist historians, in particular, have hailed it as an early manifestation of Chinese people power. That it was also a symptom of Daoism's greatly increased rural appeal is supported by the parallel emergence of the less militant **'Five Pecks of Rice'** sect in Sichuan. But while the two cults shared some ideological and organizational traits, no firm evidence has yet been produced to link them politically.

184 Harsh government and deteriorating public finances create a climate of unrest. When the Yellow River bursts its banks, a major peasant uprising, the **Revolt of the Yellow Turbans**, breaks out. Starting near the **Shandong peninsula**, the Yellow Turban movement quickly assumes the character of an insurrection against the Han dynasty. Their ranks swollen by hundreds of thousands made homeless by natural catastrophe, the Yellow Turbans first ravage the countryside, then march on **Loyang**.

In **Sichuan**, the Daoist **'Five Pecks of Rice'** sect – so called after the measure of grain due to the sect's leadership, and founded by **Zhang Daoling** in 142 – claims the emperor has forfeited the 'Mandate of Heaven'.

The Yellow Turbans are defeated, and their leaders executed by a coalition of imperial forces led by **Cao Cao**, the adopted son of a eunuch.

In the northwest, meanwhile, the **Qiang** begin 27 years of uninterrupted insurgency against the Han Chinese.

185 **Warlordism** spreads through the empire as the government is unable to recruit troops sufficient to its needs.

187 In the northeast, the previously pacified **Wuhuan** revolt.

189 Lingdi's death provokes an acute succession crisis as his consort, the Empress He, and the Dowager-empress Deng contest which of two sons should succeed. After reaching an 'understanding' with the eunuchs, He enthrones her own son, the officially unrecognized **Emperor Shandi**. Thwarted, Deng enlists the support of a western 'warlord', **Dong Zhuo**. Dong marches on Loyang, and puts 2000 eunuchs to the sword. Much of the capital, including the Imperial Library, is destroyed.

Shandi flees Loyang. When he attempts to re-enter the capital disguised as a peasant, he is seized and executed. After interfactional negotiations, it is agreed his brother Liu Xie should become Emperor. But although **Xiandi** rules for 31 years, he is Emperor in name only. Denied the support of either eunuchs or aristocrats, he becomes Dong Zhuo's puppet.

Concubines and Eunuchs

Concubinage and eunuchry were commonplace throughout the ancient world. Every hereditary ruler wanted a son to succeed him, and what better way to ensure direct male succession than a plurality of 'wives'. Yet the larger the harem, the greater the risk that conception might occur away from the royal bedchamber. Only by employing **eunuchs** to guard and administer his **concubines**, could a ruler presume their 'purity' remained intact.

In China, eunuchs and concubines appear in the earliest written records, but it was during the early empire that their role expanded into politics. Like the bureaucracy, the harem was graded. Famously, **Guangwudi** cut such grades back from fourteen to just three: 'Honoured Lady', 'Beautiful Lady' and 'Chosen Lady'. The number of concubines, however, did not diminish. By the early 1st century there were some 3000, housed in special quarters known as the 'side-court'. They were mainly girls of good families, hand-picked for imperial service, and lavishly maintained. If they had the emperor's ear, they could advance members of their families – hence their fathers' willingness to enter them for harem duty.

But 3000 concubines demanded an equivalent number of eunuchs. Called the 'regular palace attendants', they too sought preferment, and in Later Han times especially, the emperors found other uses for them, chiefly as a buffer against both the bureaucracy and the factions attached to empresses and dowager-empresses. By 175 the eunuchs ran the court. Predictably, the decay of the Later Han was laid at their door by Confucian historians. Recent commentators argue, however, that the eunuchry was a necessary, albeit insufficient, tool in the emperors' long struggle against their own emasculation.

190 The capital is returned from Loyang to Changan.

192 Cao Cao, the destroyer of the Yellow Turbans, ousts and murders Dong Zhuo, then obliges Xiandi to marry his daughter, the **Empress Cao**. Consolidating his command over northern China, he is credited with instituting the

'**Nine Grades**', a new kind of ranking system, based partly on 'moral character', within the bureaucracy. Southern China eludes his grasp.

208 Cao Cao marches on the **Yangzi** in an attempt to overcome the rebellious Sun family, but his forces are repelled at the **Battle of Chibi**.

215 Courting popular sentiment, Cao Cao ennobles **Zhang Lu**, the leader of the Daoist 'Five Pecks of Rice' sect.

220 When Cao Cao dies, his son **Cao Pi** usurps the throne, but only as 'Emperor of the Wei Dynasty'. Xiandi abdicates, to die a natural death fourteen years later.

3
The Disunity

220–589

In the immediate aftermath of the last Han emperor's displacement by **Cao Pi**, three discrete and competing states emerged: Wei, in the north, Shu in the southwest, and Wu in the southeast. But the longest surviving of the **Three Kingdoms** lasted less than sixty years. Although the Western Jin briefly reunified the empire, a more serious partition lay ahead. Early in the 4th century the **Xiongnu** crashed through the Great Wall and established themselves in China's traditional heartlands, seizing control of the Yellow and Huai River plains. Only south of the Yangzi did the Chinese continue to rule themselves; only in this region, according to conventional Chinese histories, was the essence preserved, under the aegis of the successive **Six Dynasties**: the remnant Western Jin, the Eastern Jin, the Song, the Qi, the Liang and finally the Chen.

There was also a succession of dynasties in the north. The Xiongnu were themselves overrun by the Turkic **Toba** people, who founded the impressive dynastic kingdom of Northern Wei in 386. The Toba, however, were torn between retaining their own customs and becoming 'Chinese'. In due course, their kingdom split in two, the Western and Eastern Wei; and these in turn transmuted into the Northern Qi and the Northern Zhou.

To complicate matters further, there were, again in the north, the **Sixteen Kingdoms**: smaller states, most of them based in and around lone cities that managed to sustain an independence of sorts in the face of Xiongnu and Toba dominance. Yet it would be wrong to compare this 'Period of Disunity' with the Warring States period of pre-imperial times. China may have become fragmented, but the fragments were for the most part far larger than before. The southern imperium of the Six Dynasties, with its capital at **Nanjing**, may only have been approximately half the size of the Han empire, but still its territory and its population, of perhaps 30 million, were sizeable enough.

Nor was warfare endemic. Although tensions between north and south habitually boiled over into armed conflict, large areas of China, particularly in the south, were at peace for generations. And it was in these circumstances that a cultural transformation occurred. As the Confucian bureaucracy, temporarily at least, weakened its hold, often giving way to personal patronage, so **Daoism** came properly into its own. But not just Daoism. Although **Buddhism** had arrived in China during the first century, it was only now that it became embedded in the Chinese mind – until the advent of Marxism-Leninism in the 20th century the only non-Chinese creed to have directly engaged a majority of Han Chinese.

Various reasons have been advanced for the acceptance of Buddhism among a people long conditioned to a sense of their own cultural superiority. Of crucial significance was Buddhism's theocratic appeal to the 'barbarian' rulers who had seized northern China. An alien ruler could prove his worth by turning the 'great wheel of existence'. So at least it was that the formative influx of Buddhist doctrine entered China by the **Silk Road** and other northerly routes, connecting with India and Central Asia.

That the Buddhist surge spread rapidly to the south was partly due to a migration of Buddhist converts, motivated by economic as well as political reasons; but it was also due to the simple fact that throughout disunity the Chinese retained a cohesive identity. Ideas and individuals passed freely across new internal frontiers. Thus, the empire that **Yang Jian** reconstituted in 589 was both a natural return to something that had existed before, and qualitatively different from the empire that had dissolved in 220. The Middle Kingdom's partial conquest by outsiders was a blow to Chinese pride, but not an altogether unenlightened blow.

Principal Dynasties of the Disunity of 220–589

Three Kingdoms
Wei 220–254
Shu 221–263
Wu 222–280

Five Northern Dynasties
Northern Wei 386–535
West Wei 535–556
East Wei 534–550
North Qi 550–577
Northern Zhou 557–580

Six Dynasties
Western Jin 265–316
Eastern Jin 317–419
Song 420–478
Qi 479–501
Liang 502–556
Chen 557–589

220 In the north, **Cao Pi**, newly enthroned as the Emperor Wendi of Wei, consolidates the first of the **Three Kingdoms**. Both Loyang and Changan are retained as capitals. Elsewhere in China, contending factions vie for power and territory.

221 **Liu Bei**, an erstwhile mercenary, secures the southwest and creates the **kingdom of Shu**, styling himself the Emperor Xuande. His capital is sited at Chengdu (Sichuan).

222 The warlord **Sun Quan** forces the rest of southern and southeastern China into submission, creates the **kingdom of Wu**, the third of the Three Kingdoms centred on the Yangzi delta region, and styles himself the Emperor Wudi.

223 Death of Xuande (Liu Bei). Succession passes smoothly to his son **Hou Zhu**, who will rule **Shu** for forty years.

226 Wendi (Cao Pi) is succeeded by **Mingdi**, who will rule **Wei** for twelve years. During his reign local rebellions and incursions by **northern tribes** constantly threaten Wei's stability.

240 **Shaodi** succeeds Mingdi in the Kingdom of **Wei**, but is unable to fully restore order. Tribal incursions continue.

248 In **Vietnam**, the standard of **revolt** is raised by Trieu Thi Thanh, famous for her ivory shoes and golden hairpins. But within six months her rebels are crushed by an army dispatched from Wu.

249 Death of the philosopher **Wang Bi** (b. 226), remembered for his conviction that *wu* (non-existence) forms the underlying principle of all things.

252 **Feidi** succeeds Wudi as the ruler of **Wu**.

253 **Gao Gui Xiang Gong** succeeds Shaodi in the kingdom of Wei. Attacks by northern tribes intensify.

The Romance of the Three Kingdoms

Although the protracted dissolution of the Han empire forms a sorry passage in Chinese history, the same period inspired a literary masterpiece sometimes compared, for its scope and brilliance, to Homer and Shakespeare. The *Sanguozhi tongsu yanyi* (conventionally translated as 'The Romance of the Three Kingdoms'), was written in the 15th century, probably by **Luo Guanzhong**. A prose epic in 105 chapters, it combines history with dramatic storytelling, and was described by the Qing dynasty scholar Zang Yuecheng as 'seven parts fact, three parts fiction'.

Omens and magic are embedded in a densely populated narrative that is picaresque as well as courtly, covering the years 168–280. Its unifying theme, however, is political, reflected in an opening statement that encapsulates the theory of the 'dynastic cycle': 'The empire, long divided, must unite; long united, must divide'. Three strangers – **Liu Bei, Lord Guan** (a soldier of fortune, later revered as Guandi, God of War) and **Zhang Fei** (a butcher) – take a blood oath during the Yellow Turban revolt to preserve the throne. The villain of the piece is **Cao Pi**. Yet his usurpation of 220 paves the way for Liu Bei to set up the rival kingdom of Shu. 'The empire belongs to no one man but to all in the empire: he who has virtue may possess it.' Only after the three heroes are long dead is their goal fully realized, with reunification under the Jin. In between is a feast of intrigue and cunning warfare. Among many stories told is the celebrated 'empty city stratagem'. **Zhuge Liang**, fighting for Wu against Wei, finds himself trapped at Xicheng without sufficient troops. When he opens the city gates and appears nonchalantly playing his zither on the battlements the enemy believes he has set a trap and withdraws.

258 In **Wu**, **Jingdi** succeeds Feidi.

260 **Yuandi** succeeds Gao Gui Xiang Gong as ruler of **Wei**. A natural **militarist**, Yuandi endeavours to contain the northern tribes while attempting to expand Wei southwards.

About this time **Huangfu Mi** compiles a practical treatise on **acupuncture** and **moxibustion**, both established practices in Chinese medicine.

Seven Sages of the Bamboo Grove

Straddling the last years of the kingdom of Wei and the first years of the Western Jin there emerged in the north a coterie of Daoists known as the **Seven Sages of the Bamboo Grove**. Their twin purpose was to preserve the 'pure' tradition of the early Daoist masters in opposition to the movement's takeover by alchemists and other practitioners of the occult; and to bear witness against both the formalism of Confucianism, and the political unruliness of the times. Their leader, **Xi Kang**, was executed on the orders of Sima Zhao, father of the first Western Jin emperor, for 'showing disrespect'. The others included **Shan Tao**, an erstwhile minister; **Yuan Ji** and **Yuan Xian**, celebrated musicians who were also uncle and nephew; and the scholars **Wang Rong** and **Xiang Xin**. But the best-known of the group was the poet **Liu Ling**. He travelled about in a cart pulled by a deer attended by two servants: one carrying wine, the other a spade. Should the poet die suddenly, the latter was instructed, then he was to be buried immediately. It was also Liu who defined the Seven Sages's creed, when he pronounced that 'the affairs of the world are so much duckweed in a river'. Although they failed to change the world whilst they lived, posterity has assigned them an honoured place in China's dissident folklore.

262 **Yuandi** swiftly reduces the Kingdom of **Shu**, which ceases to exist as a separate state from this point onwards.

264 Just as Yuandi is within sight of his objectives, he is ousted by one of his own generals, the forceful **Sima Yuan**, who wrests control of the expanded **Wei** kingdom. As the Emperor Wudi, he sets up the **Western Jin**, the first of the

Six Dynasties, and continues Yuandi's quest to reunify the whole of China. As smaller states fall into his hands, he revives the bureaucratic infrastructure. **Pei Xiu**, an eminent **cartographer**, is appointed Minister of Public Works, and a pontoon bridge is built across the Yellow River.

In **Wu**, Jingdi is succeeded by Sun Quan's licentious grandson **Modi**.

280 The era of the Three Kingdoms closes when **Wu** falls to the **Western Jin**. Modi's Nanjing harem is found to contain some 5000 concubines. But although China is formally reunified, failure to restore imperial revenues hampers Jin Wudi's attempts at consolidation.

Xiongnu horsemen raid the Yellow River basin, and little is done to curb either the military or the economic power of China's **grandees**. By distributing large estates among his 25 sons, Wudi adds to his successors' and China's long-term problems – the more so as the peasantry is now conditioned to enlistment in 'private' armies.

286 The Buddhist **Lotus Sutra** is translated for the first time into Chinese.

289 Wudi is succeeded by his weak son **Huidi**. Two rival princes enlist the help of the northern Xiongnu to oust him. Over the next seventeen years, Huidi is almost constantly on the run as China slips once more into anarchy – a passage sometimes known as the **War of the Eight Princes**.

304 The **Xiongnu** establish footholds in the Yellow River plains as a result of their support for Jin Huidi's brothers. Almost at once their own leaders begin quarrelling amongst themselves. Thus begins an era of instability in the north known as the **Sixteen Kingdoms**: a succession of relatively small states lasting 135 years.

306 Huidi is finally toppled by his two brothers, one of whom, Huaidi, becomes the third Western Jin emperor. Huaidi swiftly discovers, however, that his Xiongnu helpers are unwilling to return to their homelands. He is taken captive almost immediately and is only released after paying a heavy ransom.

311 The **Xiongnu** sack **Loyang**, destroying the Imperial Library. Their leader, a convert to **Buddhism**, is known only by his Chinese name **Shi Le** (d. 333).

313 As barbarian incursions escalate, Huaidi is succeeded by his cousin **Mindi**, a grandson of Wudi.

316 The largest **Xiongnu army** to date sweeps into the Wei River valley and sacks **Changan**. Mindi is taken prisoner and executed, signalling the end of the Western Jin dynasty. There follows an exodus of the nobility to the south, leaving Shi Le in control of the northern plains. The Xiongnu, however, find themselves under attack from other equally aggressive peoples, including the **Qiang** and the first outriders of the **Turkic hordes**, known generically as the **Tartars**. Because of the mountainous terrain of the Yangzi region, unsuited to mounted fighting, the Xiongnu will not expand further southwards. China becomes partitioned as a result.

317 The Jin court reassembles at Nanjing. Refugees from the north bring with them their wealth and cultural treasures. Some also bring their Buddhist faith, acquired via the Silk Road. The Jin dynasty is revived when a minor prince is enthroned, the Emperor Yuandi. But although Yuandi is regarded as the founder of a new dynasty – the Eastern Jin, second of the Six Dynasties – policy is determined by magnates and grandees. The bureaucracy remains intact, but with a reduced remit. The tenor of southern society will become progressively eclectic. As overland routes to southeast Asia and India are developed to compensate for the loss of their northern counterparts, so a new kind of exoticism pervades 'Chinese' culture. The arts and scholarship flourish, as does commerce, although the economy remains relatively decentralized.

322 The Eastern Jin emperor **Yuandi** is succeeded by **Mingdi**.

325 Mingdi is succeeded by Chengdi.

342 Chengdi is succeeded by Kangdi.

343 Kangdi is succeeded by the relatively assertive Emperor Mudi.

347 The **Eastern Jin** recover a large area of **Sichuan**, formerly part of the kingdom of Shu, from mainly Tibetan 'barbarians'.

356 Just as in the north the Xiongnu are increasingly obliged to look to their own backs, **Loyang** is captured by the **'southern' Chinese**.

361 The death of Jin Mudi, succeeded by **Aidi**, puts a halt to southern expansionism.

364 **Loyang** is recaptured by the **Xiongnu**.

365 Aidi is succeeded by **Hai Xi Gong**. **Wang Xizhi** (b. 306), a Daoist poet famed for a calligraphy reflective of the subtleties of nature, dies in the same year.

366 Construction of the first of the **Thousand Buddha caves** begins at **Dunhuang** (see p.186).

370 Hai Xi Gong is succeeded by **Jian Wendi**.

372 Jin Jian Wendi is succeeded by Xiao Wudi.

383 The **Xiongnu** – having adapted to the sedentary lifestyle of the Yellow River plains, but now harried from the north by the **Toba** (aka the **Tabgach**) – attempt an invasion of the Yangzi valley area, but are repulsed by armies of Eastern Jin.

Buddhism

By 600 AD an estimated ninety percent of China's population subscribed to Buddhist beliefs and practices. Such a statistic, however, even if accurate, requires qualification. The advent of **Buddhism** scarcely led to an abandonment of existing beliefs. Rather, it became part of a syncretic outlook that continued to develop Daoist and Confucian concepts. For most Chinese there was, and is, no contradiction in following different paths simultaneously. Nor are those paths wholly distinct. If sometimes acrimonious competition arose between exclusively dedicated Buddhist and Daoist sects, the two owed much to each other.

Buddhism was able to permeate the Chinese mind just because it shared the Daoist tendency to negate the significance of the immediate world and its exigencies. Conversely Buddhism's organizational strength – its elaboration of a monastic code and structure – provided Daoism with a model for its own progress as a church. Further, it was a particular kind of Buddhism that took root in Chinese soil: **Mahayana**, or the 'Greater Vehicle', as opposed to **Hinayana**, the 'Lesser Vehicle'.

386 Weakened by their failed assault on the south, the Xiongnu suffer defeat at the hands of the **Toba**, who now create the dynastic kingdom of **Northern Wei** under the leadership of Toba Gui, centred on **Shanxi** province. The Toba are of Turkic stock, with ancestral homelands in **Mongolia**. Although the Sixteen Kingdoms will continue another 53 years, Northern Wei emerges as the **dominant state** in the north, due largely to its creation of a disciplined economy unbeholden to any feudal aristocracy. What remains of the northern Chinese intelligentsia is recruited into government service as the Toba, relatively few in number, themselves become increasingly Sinicized.

In the south **agrarian unrest** sets in, both in Sichuan and along the eastern seaboard. As peasant and pirate gangs

In the great ferment of Buddhist ideas affecting central and western Asia in the centuries before the advent of Islam, the figure of the Buddha himself, however iconic, was by no means paramount. While Hinayana claimed to preserve the teachings of a human figure who, by dint of self-denial, attained 'enlightenment'– and through enlightenment 'nirvana', or release from the karmic cycle of suffering and rebirth – Mahayana was less stringent. It preached universal salvation and the transferability of 'merit' earned by good works. The historic Buddha, an Indian prince living in the 5th century BC, was but one in a series of divine bodhisattvas. The last would be the **Maitreya**, or 'Laughing Buddha', who would reconcile earth and heaven. Until Maitreya, the known cosmogony, with all its gods, goddesses and demons, held good. But if this doctrine hosted a politically destabilizing millenarianism, Buddhism in China also stimulated communal self-help. **Monastic wealth** provided capital for local projects – a new bridge here, a new grain mill there – outside of centrally controlled government spending.

proliferate, so the power of generals sent to quell them is augmented.

396 Xiao Wudi is succeeded by **Andi**. In the north, **Toba Gui** of Northern Wei assumes the title of Emperor.

398 Toba Gui orders a permanent capital to be built at **Pingcheng** (modern Datong, Shanxi) to house a hitherto mobile court.

c. 400 In **Changan**, the Indian monk **Kumarajiva** sets new standards for the Chinese translation of Buddhist texts.

406 Death of **Gu Kaizhi**, a painter of the Nanjing court renowned for the sensitivity of his **portraits**. Copies of his work made during the Tang dynasty survive into the present.

Kumarajiva 344–413

The early spread of **Buddhism** in China was sponsored by many of its northern rulers whose ethnic loyalties lay beyond its frontiers. No better example of such cultural importation exists than the career of the monk **Kumarajiva**. His father, having held high office in India, had moved to the independent Tarim oasis town of Kucha by the time his son was born, specifically to live in an established Buddhist community. Ten percent of Kucha's population was monasticized, and Kumarajiva was entered into a monastery at the age of seven.

Although brought up to speak Tokharian, he displayed an aptitude for Sanskrit while learning Chinese perhaps from passing merchants. In 383 this led to his kidnap by the ruler of Liangzhou, a small kingdom in Gansu where he was set to work preparing Chinese translations of Sanskrit texts. In 401 he was transferred to **Changan**, at the request of another more powerful ruler. There, he assembled a team of scholars who between them rendered 39 Buddhist texts into Chinese.

The standard of translation surpassed anything that had gone before. Instead of using Daoist approximations for esoteric concepts unknown to the Chinese, Kumarajiva converted Sanskrit terms into 'loan-words', so that Chinese Buddhism from this point enjoyed its own specialist vocabulary. Of equal importance, the texts selected by Kumarajiva belonged to the 'Greater Vehicle' or **Mahayana school**. Although he had been raised a Hinayanist, he converted to what was still a relatively new school as a young man while visiting other Buddhist centres, notably Khotan: a biographical detail that had a profound impact on the emergent character of Chinese Buddhism.

414 The scholar-monk Fa Xian returns from a fifteen-year journey to India, bringing with him Sanskrit texts that, when translated, will become seminal to Chinese Buddhism.

418 Andi is succeeded by **Gongdi**.

419 An army of the **Northern Wei** crosses the Yangzi and lays siege to Nanjing. In the ensuing turmoil Gongdi abdicates, bringing to an end the Eastern Jin dynasty. The throne is usurped by **Liu Yu**, an enterprising general who has risen through the ranks from humble origins.

420 Having repulsed the Northern Wei, Liu is proclaimed Emperor, thus inaugurating the **Song**, the **third** of the **Six Dynasties**. As the Emperor Wudi he goes on the offensive against the Toba and other non-Han peoples north of the Yangzi, reclaiming some previously abandoned territories.

Fa Xian fl. 399–420

While monks from the west brought Buddhist teachings to China, the same journey was made in reverse by some Chinese devotees. The most eminent of these was Sehi, a Shanxi scholar who adopted the name 'Fa Xian', meaning 'The Splendour of Religious Law'. Setting out in 399 to gather Sanskrit texts that had been but poorly translated, if at all, he crossed the Taklamakan desert to Khotan, then the Pamirs. Arriving in India in 402, he spent several years exploring major Buddhist sites, including Bodh Gaya and Benares. Next, having elected to return home via the southern sea route, he journeyed on to Sri Lanka, already a thriving centre of Buddhist scholarship. After another two years, he set sail for Guangzhou. Narrowly escaping death twice during ferocious storms, he eventually landed on the Shandong peninsula. Warmly welcomed at the court of the Eastern Jin, he devoted the rest of his life to a body of Buddhist translations that subsequently became part of the 'Chinese canon', and to writing an account of his journeys. It is the latter (*Foguoji*, or '**Record of the Buddhist Kingdoms**') for which he is chiefly known today. But of equal significance was his contribution to the evolution of monastic life in medieval China. Several of the scrolls he brought back dealt specifically with the rules and regulations governing the proper conduct of monks.

422 Song Wudi is succeeded by his son Liu Yifu, the **Emperor Ying Yang Wang**.

423 Ying Yang Wang is succeeded by his brother Liu Yilong, the **Emperor Wendi**. Like his father Wudi, Wendi rules autocratically, and the 'southern empire' enjoys a period of prosperous stability. To check the burgeoning influence of Daoists and Buddhists the *shi* (scholar-gentry) are recruited into government, effecting a restoration of **Confucian values**.

424 **Loyang** falls to the **Northern Wei**. Under Toba rule it again becomes a flourishing commercial city, with designated quarters for traders from central Asia and other alien territories.

435 To contain **Buddhism** further, **Wendi** conducts an **inquiry** into the behaviour of monks and nuns. Exempt from taxation, many monasteries have been generously endowed by landowners whose peasants have then been enrolled as 'religious'. Wendi decrees that new temples may only be built, or new Buddha images cast, under imperial licence. But although the effects of these actions are keenly felt in Nanjing and other cities, Wendi's edicts fail to penetrate the countryside.

439 135 years of tribal warfare known as the **Sixteen Kingdoms** are finally ended by **Northern Wei**'s **pacification** of the north.

442 The patronage of **Daoist cults** by the **Northern Wei** court reflects the extent to which its Toba leadership is willing to adopt Chinese custom.

444 The Daoist ascendancy in **Northern Wei** is advanced when the emperor is persuaded to launch a persecution of **Buddhists**. Many monks flee to the south.

450 Northern Wei, launching a military campaign against the south, reaches the walls of Nanjing. Song Wendi rejects

Barbarians

China was vulnerable to aggressors on its northern and western frontiers. During the 4th century first the Hunnish **Xiongnu**, then the Turkic **Toba** mounted successful invasions. At the heart of such threats was the inherent volatility of Central Asia, a region dominated by nomadic tribes, and sensitive to relatively minor changes in climate and demography. Repeatedly mass migrations created chain reactions, the effects of which reverberated throughout Eurasia. Thus the Xiongnu and Toba irruptions were regional manifestations of a much wider upheaval that propelled the 'White' Huns, the Vandals and the Goths westwards, swallowing up the Indian Gupta as well as the Roman empire. Only with the emergence of the Russian empire, and its Soviet successor, did stability in Central Asia become a possibility.

For China, the consequences of a 2000-year siege were formative as well as traumatic. They account for an intensely xenophobic, even supremacist, mindset: against the odds China did survive. They have also led to an ambiguous foreign policy. The 'barbarian' threat could be contained either by outright conquest, or by diplomatic means allied to a credible defence. Both were tried, and both intermittently failed. However often Chinese armies battled their way to the Pamirs, or however many concessions were made to tribal leaders, peace was seldom vouchsafed for more than a generation. More usually, a compromise between defensive and offensive strategies was pursued, giving rise to the **'tribute' system** (see p.240). But whatever the preferred solution, its *sine qua non* was strong government at the centre. In this way, China's penchant for authoritarian rule was reinforced by the unremitting hostility of its changeable neighbours.

an offer of 'complementary' royal weddings, however. Their supply lines cut, the Northern Wei are forced to retreat.

451 Wendi sends a **revenge force** north, but this in turn is defeated.

453 Wendi is succeeded by his licentious son the Emperor Xiao Wudi.

460 At **Yungang**, near the Northern Wei capital Datong, construction begins on a massive Buddhist **cave temple** complex. 50,000 rock sculptures combine Chinese with Indian themes.

464 Xiao Wudi is succeeded by his son Liu Ye, who is killed within a year and succeeded by **Mingdi**, eleventh son of Song Wendi. A patron of **Buddhism**, Mingdi will become renowned for his obesity and fondness for poisoning: during a seven-year reign he dispatches 33 relatives, including his wife and three brothers.

465 The **Dowager-empress Feng**, of mixed Toba and Chinese blood, begins a 25-year regency over **Northern Wei** during which a traditional **Chinese-style bureaucracy** is rehabilitated and many new Buddhist monasteries are created.

472 Mingdi abdicates in favour of his unstable adopted son, **Cang Wu** (aka Feidi).

476 Cang Wu is murdered after firing arrows at a target pinned to the stomach of a sleeping minister. He is succeeded by his half-brother **Shundi**.

479 Shundi is assassinated and usurped by **Xiao Daocheng**, a fervent Buddhist. As the **Emperor Gaodi** he establishes the **Qi**, the fourth of the **Six Dynasties**.

482 Gaodi is succeeded by his capable son Wudi.

485 As in the south, so in the **north** the growth of Buddhist monasteries and other religious foundations diminishes imperial revenues. In sweeping reforms designed to bolster imperial finances the **equal field** system is instituted.

490 Death of the Northern Wei **Dowager-empress Feng**.

The Equal Field System

All dynastic governments depended upon the grain and labour that could be exacted from China's peasantry. During the Han dynasty the reluctance of aristocratic landholders to hand over what was due to the state eroded royal power. In the 4th and 5th centuries the growth of monastic estates, both Buddhist and Daoist, further undermined royal revenues. As monks were exempt from taxes, many landowners compelled their peasant tenants into holy orders. Northern Wei's solution was to assert control of smallholdings. By decree, fixed-acreage lots were granted to peasant farmers on a lifetime basis. When the peasant died, his 'equal field' reverted to the state. Conversely, 'mulberry tree land' was granted in perpetuity, in recognition of the time required to develop a silk orchard. In return, equal field tenants had to pay a part of their produce as tax, and render corvee labour. Other stipulations granted half-shares to boys when they reached the age of eleven, and exempted men over seventy from all forms of taxation. Women, slaves and cows were granted proportionately smaller lots. Rationalizing practices instituted by Qin Shihuangdi and Wang Mang, and retained by the Tang dynasty, the equal field system later won the admiration of communist planners aware that real security of tenure countermands the interests of a centralized coercive polity.

493 Death of **Qi Wudi**. Both his immediate successors, the princes Yulin and Hailing, are murdered by their uncle **Xiao Luan**.

494 Xiao Luan becomes the **Emperor Mingdi**. The **Northern Wei** emperor **Xiaowen**, continuing Feng's policy of Sinicization, moves his capital from Datong to **Loyang**. New building works include the creation of a second Buddhist cave complex comparable to Yungang at **Longmen**.

Xiaowen decrees that all his subjects should adopt Chinese names, wear Chinese dress and speak the Chinese language.

Giant Maitreya Buddha statue, carved in the Longmen caves and said to be modelled on the empress Wu Zetian.

Such measures are intended to undermine the power of outlying Toba leaders as well as to promote the possibility of a pan-Chinese imperium.

496 **Toba traditionalists** launch the first of several **rebellions** against Xiaowen.

498 Qi Mingdi is succeeded by his adolescent son **Dong Hunhou**, known as the 'Marquis of Eastern Fatuousness'.

499 The death of **Xiaowen** of the Northern Wei dynasty heralds the beginning of its disintegration.

500 Dong Hunhou is assassinated to make way for a supposedly feeble younger brother, the **Emperor Hedi**. **Xiao Yan**, a rich landowner, is appointed regent.

About this time the *Wenxin diaolong* ('The Literary Mind and the Carving of Dragons') is written, an anonymous treatise on **literary criticism**; the **abacus** is also invented.

501 Seizing control, the youthful Song **Hedi** decrees the death of his tutors and arranges the murder of Xiao Yan's brother. Xiao retaliates by besieging **Nanjing**. An estimated 80,000 are starved to death. Hedi is assassinated, and his head, coated in wax, sent as a token of **surrender** to Xiao.

502 Xiao Yan becomes Emperor, establishing the **Liang**, the fifth of the **Six Dynasties**. A poet-scholar as well as capable commander, Liang **Wudi** promotes both Buddhism and Confucianism during his generally peaceable 47-year reign. New **academies** for the study of the classics are opened, with obligatory attendance by the sons of the nobility.

517 Liang Wudi orders the **closure of Daoist temples** as Buddhist monasteries multiply in the **south**.

523 An Indianesque **pagoda** erected at **Dengfeng** monastery in Henan is the oldest surviving all-brick building in China.

527 **Liang Wudi** makes the first of three **abdications** in order to retire to a Buddhist monastery outside Nanjing. The emperor's devotion to Buddhist principles is such that he bans the sacrifice of live animals during traditional ancestral rites.

528 Amid increasing turbulence in Northern Wei, **Loyang** is stormed by **Turkic tribesmen**. A boy-emperor, a dowager-empress and 2000 courtiers are killed.

529 Liang Wudi is enticed back into public life from the second of his retreats when members of his administration agree to pay over a **ransom** used to promote **Buddhist projects**.

535 Following partisan opposition to its policies of Siniciza-tion and increased insurgency on its northern borders, the ailing dynastic kingdom of Northern Wei divides into the **Eastern** and **Western Wei**. While the former continues to be governed from Loyang by a Chinese-style court, the latter reverts to Toba custom.

542 In upper Vietnam a revolt led by **Ly Bon**, a Chinese official, is crushed by Liang forces.

546 The Indian monk **Paramartha** introduces **yoga** to southern China.

547 During the last of Wudi's monastic retreats, his ministers launch unsuccessful attacks against the two northern **Wei kingdoms**. Some **southern provinces** are lost in a coun-terattack.

548 Wudi's third son **Xiao Gang** – impatient of his father's pacifism, and egged on by the northern warlord **Hou Jing** – stages a rebellion during which **Nanjing** is besieged, with severe loss of life.

550 Xiao Gang is enthroned following his father's death. Within a few months, however, he is murdered by **Hou**

Jing. In the north, the Eastern Wei dynasty is replaced by the **Northern Qi**.

Around this time **silk** is manufactured for the first time outside China, in **Byzantium** – the result perhaps of industrial espionage perpetrated by **itinerant monks**.

551 Another of Liang Wudi's sons is enthroned as the Emperor Yu Zhang Wang, but is murdered by his Daoist brother Xiao Yi, who becomes the **Emperor Yuandi**. Yuandi kills **Hou Jing**, pieces of whose body are thrown to the starving citizens of Nanjing.

554 Yuandi abdicates in favour of his ninth son, the 13-year-old **Emperor Jingdi**. As Yuandi prepares to leave Nanjing, he sets fire to the Imperial Library, incinerating an estimated 200,000 books.

555 In **Northern Qi** all **Daoists** are ordered to become **Buddhists**. After four are executed for disobedience, most 'convert'.

556 **Liang Jingdi** is assassinated on the orders of the landowning militarist Chen Baxian who, as the **Emperor Wudi**, establishes the last of the **Six Dynasties**.

557 Overcome by the scale of administrative problems confronting him, Chen Wudi enters a monastery. In the north, **the Western Wei** dynasty is replaced by the **Northern Zhou**.

559 Chen Wudi is succeeded by his nephew, the **Emperor Wendi**.

566 Wendi is succeeded by his teenage son the **Emperor Lin Hai Wang**.

568 Lin Hai Wang is deposed by his uncle, a capable commander who becomes the **Emperor Xuandi**.

573 **Xuandi** achieves territorial gains at the expense of the **north**.

577 **Northern Zhou** defeats and subjugates **Northern Qi**. But although Northern Zhou can now fairly claim to rule the whole of northern China, in the wake of this 'victory' smaller breakaway kingdoms are formed.

580 The forceful emperor of **Northern Zhou** dies suddenly and is replaced by his mentally unstable son. The new emperor orders his wife to commit suicide, but she is spared after the intercession of her mother. The young empress's father, **Yang Jian**, master of the feudal fief of Sui and an outstanding commander, intervenes directly. Moving his troops into Loyang he forces his son-in-law to appoint him **regent**.

581 As the emperor of Northern Zhou is deposed, **Yang Jian** establishes the **Sui imperial dynasty**, ordering a new capital to be built at **Changan**. Swiftly, he eliminates his remaining rivals in the Yellow and Huai River valleys.

582 Chen Xuandi is succeeded by his eldest son, the febrile and sybaritic **Hou Zhu**. As the new emperor withdraws to his concubines' quarters, government of the southern imperium passes into the hands of eunuchs. Almost immediately, **Yang Jian** appears with an army outside **Nanjing**. The city is stormed, and Hou Zhu is discovered cowering behind two women. Expediently, Yang Jian allows him to live out his natural term.

583 Yang Jian establishes **four state granaries** to ensure food supplies for Changan, and to be used publicly during famines.

584 Yang begins a programme of **canal restoration** in the north.

589 The death of **Chen Hou Zhu** removes the final obstacle to Yang Jian's ambition. The **pan-Chinese Sui Dynasty** is inaugurated.

4

Imperial Restoration: The Sui and Tang Dynasties and the Second Disunity

589–960

Midway through the 6th century, the restitution of the empire must have seemed no more probable than midway through the 5th or 4th centuries. Indeed, the longer disunity continued, the more likely China would permanently fragment. While the south did more to preserve the culture and institutions of the Han empire, in the north intermarriage between Chinese aristocrats and the families of assorted tribal chieftains produced rulers of mixed blood and unpredictable loyalties. This in turn generated fresh territorial divisions, in the first instance between the Western and Eastern Wei, then between the Northern Zhou and Northern Qi. And yet, almost fortuitously, the empire did reconvene. Following what was little more than a family squabble, **Yang Jian** seized control of Northern Zhou soon after its subjugation of Northern Qi, and then pressed home his military superiority over an ailing regime in Nanjing. Out of these circumstances emerged first the short-lived **Sui dynasty** (589–618), and then, more famously, the **Tang** (618–907).

The Sui Dynasty
589–618

As the **Emperor Wendi**, Yang Jian rebuilt the Chinese imperium, blending Han and non-Han principles and practices. Disbanding the private armies of his allies and of those he had either overcome or who surrendered voluntarily, he used the **'equal field system'** developed by the Northern Wei to resettle soldiers as peasant farmers. Some he posted to the Great Wall, which he began urgently to repair. China's existing canals too were refurbished, although it befell his son to oversee construction of the enduring Grand Canal. He reformed local government, and at all levels recruited officials for their skills, not their family connections. He revived the imperial examination system, and promulgated a basic and universal **code of law** which, although now lost, seems to have been more humane than the arbitrary provisions of many of his 'barbarian' predecessors in the north.

Yang also reorganized **imperial government** into three departments: **State Affairs** (*Shangshu sheng*); **Imperial Secretariat** (*Zhongshu sheng*); and **Chancellery** (*Menxia sheng*). While this tripartite structure broadly followed the administrative dispositions of the Later Han emperors, he shrewdly excluded the military from the innermost councils of state. By such means, Yang created a strong, centralized polity that looked set to survive. A generation later, however, the Sui dynasty was on its knees. Wendi's succesor, the overly ambitious **Emperor Yangdi**, squandered his patrimony on ruinous campaigns against the kingdoms that then comprised Korea. By 616, as floods and famine crippled the Yellow River plains, warlords and rebellious peasants once more dictated terms.

In the event, the born-again empire was rescued by another strongman, **Li Yuan**, the **Duke of Tang**. The dynasty Li founded was destined to become China's most prestigious, at

> With a hundred victories in a hundred battles we advance the ten Buddhist virtues. The implements of war are as incense and flowers offered to the Buddha, our worldly domains indistinguishable from his kingdom.
>
> Edict issued by Yang Jian, 581

least in its early manifestation. Because of this, and the prejudices of Tang historians, the very real achievements of the Sui have been overshadowed. But by any reasonable reckoning, Yang Jian was one of China's great makers.

589 As the **Emperor Wendi**, Yang Jian establishes the Sui Dynasty that rules the whole of China, keeping Changan as his capital. To ensure the loyalty of the south, he exempts its people from taxation for ten years. While his efforts to create a bureaucracy capable of managing an empire continue, Wendi emerges as an energetic promoter of **Buddhism**. During his reign some 4000 Buddhist shrines will be built, and many thousand Buddha images commissioned.

597 Koguryo, one of three **Korean** kingdoms (the others being Paekche and Silla) refuses to render 'traditional' tribute and launches a raid against northeastern China. **Wendi**'s punitive expedition is indecisive.

600 Shotoku Taishi, the **Japanese regent**, sends the first of four 'constitutional' **fact-finding missions** to Changan. Others follow in 607, 608 and 610. But while Japan's adoption of the Chinese imperial system dates from these emissaries, Japan does not become a tribute-paying state.

Emperor Wendi (Yang Jian) 541–604

Had the Sui dynasty lasted longer, its founder would be more widely regarded as one of China's foremost emperors. Born into a 'high' family of mixed Chinese-Turkic blood, **Yang Jian** was raised by a Buddhist nun. At the age of 14, he joined the Northern Zhou army and rose rapidly to the rank of commander. As the **Emperor Wendi** he combined diplomacy and vision to furnish the reconstituted empire with a solid and enduring foundation. Among his reforms was the 'rule of avoidance', whereby officials were barred from serving in their own prefectures.

At Changan he built a new capital, larger than any previous capital, and initiated improvements to China's existing inland waterways that in the reign of his son produced the Grand Canal.

But as important as any of these initiatives was the style of his rule. Particularly after 601, he espoused the theocratic ideals of **chakravartin kingship**: the Buddhist ruler as an incarnation of a moral, as well as a political, absolute. In private, he was prone to ferocious ill-temper, provoked perhaps by his wife, the Empress Wenxian, who thought nothing of eliminating a favourite concubine. But after her death in 602, Wendi became progressively morose, ridden, it is said, by remorse for his own acts of violence. Inevitably, his Tang biographers focused on these late imbalances of character. They also deplored his barbarian ancestry, forgetting that the Tang themselves were cross-bred.

601 Emulating the 3rd century BC Indian emperor **Asoka**, Wendi orders the building of **Buddhist stupas**, containing holy relics, across **China**.

604 Wendi is succeeded by his second son, the **Emperor Yangdi**, reputed to have hastened his father's demise from a wasting illness. Best known for implementing the **Grand Canal**, Yangdi continues many of Wendi's policies, including the expansion of the bureaucracy and building of **Buddhist temples**.

The Grand Canal

By the 6th century, the fertility of the northern loess deposits was already in decline. The readoption of **Changan** in the Wei River valley as the imperial capital, therefore, posed formidable problems of supply. In order to feed its several hundred thousand inhabitants, grain had to be transported from across the empire. From the beginning of his reign, the first Sui emperor set about repairing and extending existing waterways. It was his son **Yangdi**, however, who created the **Grand Canal**, a project rivalling the Great Wall in magnitude. To provide an unbroken inland transport between the Yellow and Yangzi river almost astronomic levels of manpower were applied. By 610 new stretches of canal joined not only Loyang to Yangzhou, but also Yangzhou to Hangzhou, south of the Yangzi delta. Another section, extending to a terminal in the northeast close to modern Beijing, was also laid, to supply armies Yangdi hoped would conquer Korea.

In the long-term, the Grand Canal became a vital conduit for the empire's expanding economy. As well as officials, troops and grain all manner of merchandise could be moved along its 2000 kilometres. But in the short-term it contributed to dynastic collapse. The exactions imposed by Yangdi during its construction – in the form of conscripted labour and requisitioning of resources – helped foment unrest. Worse, to appease his vanity, Yangdi also commissioned a costly '**dragon fleet**' for use on the Canal. According to his Tang detractors, this stretched sixty miles prow to stern and required 80,000 men to pull. The royal barge itself – a four-decked floating palace – contained decorated cabins for 120 concubines as well as a lavish throne-room.

605 Lin Fang, having been sent to quell a revolt in northern **Vietnam**, occupies the southerly kingdom of **Champa**.

607 Yangdi's chief minister Bin Ji reforms the bureaucracy and reorganizes many prefectures as **commanderies**.

Two **higher degrees** are added to the imperial examination system. Work begins on costly alternative **royal palaces** at **Loyang** and **Yangzhou**. In **Shanxi**, mass labour is levied to strengthen the Great Wall against Turkic aggressors.

608 **Qiang Zhun**, the Secretary for Imperial Colonies, heads a two-year exploratory mission to **Southeast Asia**. Relations are established with the kingdom of **Songkla** on the Kra isthmus.

609 Campaiging in the west, **Yangdi** re-establishes Chinese control over **Dunhuang**.

In December he hosts a gathering of Turkic and other 'tribal' leaders in Changan. A census puts China's registered population at **50 million**.

610 As a major fissure develops within the Turkic peoples, the Khan of the **western Turks** refuses to acknowledge Chinese suzerainty. **Yangdi** proclaims his support for the **eastern Khan**.

The **Grand Canal** is extended southwards as far as **Hangzhou**, and northwards as far as modern **Beijing**.

611 With the completion of the northern section of the Grand Canal, **Yangdi** assembles an army to attack **Koguryo**, but the campaign is postponed when the **Yellow River floods**. Bandit groups establish bases in the water margins.

612 When the Khan of the **eastern Turks** overcomes the **western Turks**, the western Khan flees to **Changan**, bringing with him 10,000 horsemen. Yangdi agrees to protect him, and uses the Khan's cavalry in his **Korean campaign**. **Koguryo**, however, resists stubbornly, and the imperial army is forced to retreat.

As the year ends, there is **drought and pestilence** in Shandong and Hubei.

613 Launching a second **Korean campaign**, Yangdi attacks Koguryo townships east of the **Liang river**. Despite initial victories, the offensive is undermined by **domestic unrest**, stirred by high levels of taxation and other exactions. The most serious revolt is led by **Yang Xuangan**, President of the Board of Rites. Only by deploying crack units is Yangdi able to contain him. But although Yang is captured and executed, other rebellions hatch, disrupting imperial supplies.

> ❝ At this time the people abandoned their family homesteads to assemble within the fortifications of walled towns. There was nothing to provide for themselves. Although what was in the granaries and the storehouses was still very plentiful, the minor officials all feared the regulations and none dared to assume the responsibility of distribution of provisions for public relief. As a result there was increased distress. At first everyone peeled the bark off trees in order to eat it. Gradually they went so far as to eat the leaves. When bark and trees were all exhausted they then boiled earth. Some pounded straw to powder and ate it. After this men then ate each other. ❞
>
> from the *Sui-shu* (official dynastic history of Sui, written under Tang supervision)

614 Internal strife notwithstanding, **Yangdi** launches a **third Korean campaign**, and reaches Koguryo's capital **Pyongyang**. When Koguryo's king still refuses tribute, the Chinese army withdraws, its supply lines overstretched.

615 **Yangdi** convenes a second gathering of tribal chieftains in Changan, but this is less well attended than in 609. Meanwhile, a **folk prophecy** that the Sui will be vanquished by a man called **Li**, gains currency. Two rebel leaders, Li Hun and Li Min, are executed.

In September, during an inspection of the **Great Wall**, Yangdi is surprised by a 100,000-strong eastern **Turkic army**, and is besieged at **Yenmen** (Shanxi) for five weeks.

616 Rebellion breaks out at **Taiyuan** (upper Shanxi), supported by the **eastern Khan**. The rebels are convincingly repulsed by Yangdi's 'loyal' general **Li Yuan**, the Duke of **Tang**. In August, however, **Yangdi** abandons Changan, fleeing in his royal barge down the **Grand Canal**.

In the same year, the world's oldest surviving stone **spandrel bridge** is completed at **Anyi**, also on the Grand Canal.

BRIDGEINK

The main 37.5 metre arch of the Anyi spandrel bridge on the Grand Canal. One thousand one-tonne stones were used to complete the project.

Emperor Yangdi 580–618

Stereotyped as a 'last bad emperor' whose megalomania wrecked a dynasty, **Yangdi** came close to achieving greatness. Strongly associated with the **south** – where he was Viceroy between 591 and 600 – he deliberately appointed southerners as ministers to heal the wounds of the north–south partition. By building an alternative capital at **Loyang** he also sought to minimize the influence of the northwestern aristocracy on government. Nor was Yangdi's creation of the **Grand Canal** anything other than an undertaking of the greatest potential benefit. Militarily, too, he was strong, at least initially, when he succeeded in containing the **eastern Turks**. It was when he turned his attention to the seemingly lesser challenge of subjugating **Korea** that his rule faltered. Yet even these disastrous campaigns might have been forgotten had they not coincided with a cycle of **floods** and **famine** in the **Yellow River plains**. Like other emperors he ran into foul weather – a factor sometimes undervalued by Western historians keen to distance themselves from the Chinese superstition linking natural disasters with the withdrawal of Heaven's Mandate.

617 Turmoil prevails throughout China as government disintegrates. Both **aristocratic factions** and **peasant bands** seize control locally. The Yellow River again breaks its banks. Yangdi's authority is restricted to **Hunan** and **Shanxi**, where **Li Yuan** endeavours to uphold imperial rule.

Encouraged by his teenage son **Li Shimin**, many officials and *hao-shi* (**'brave gentlemen'**) flock to Li Yuan's side, urging him to accept the title of Emperor. The issue is forced when a further **Turkic invasion** threatens, and forces dispatched by Li are defeated. Yangdi summons Li to his fugitive court. Knowing that Yangdi is fearful of his name, and therefore suspecting a trap, Li refuses. Instead, Li Shimin raises a force known as the **Righteous Army**.

Li Yuan, meanwhile, comes to terms with the eastern Khan, promising him rich rewards in return for horses and other materiel. In July **Li Yuan** disavows his allegiance to **Yangdi**.

In August **Tang** forces march on **Changan**. The state granaries are opened for the needy. With the help of **Turkic cavalry** Li Shimin breaks into the **Wei River valley**, defeating a Sui army at **Yinma Springs**.

In December Changan falls to the Tang army, now 200,000 strong. But instead of proclaiming himself Emperor, Li Yuan enthrones a 6-year-old grandson of Wendi, the **Emperor Gongdi**.

618 The **Tang** consolidate their position in the north and capture **Loyang**.

In April **Yangdi** is **assassinated** in Chengdu, strangled by the son of a previously disgraced minister. This persuades **Li Yuan** to take the final step. Gongdi is deposed, and Li – after customarily refusing the throne three times – is proclaimed emperor on June 18.

The early Tang Dynasty 618-763

Thanks to the first Tang emperors, but particularly **Taizong** (**Li Shimin**), 'China' became a fixture on the global map instead of a vanished chimera. Its frontiers extended beyond the limits achieved by the Han, and **Changan** developed into a dazzling cosmopolitan city the like of which had not been seen since Aurelian Rome. Indian, Central Asian and Middle Eastern traders mingled in its streets with the expositors of a score of different esoteric religions – Christian Nestorians, Manicheans, Zoroastrians and early Moslems among them. In the empire at large, poets, painters, sculptors, ceramicists and musicians scaled new heights of expressive sensitivity.

The result was an outward-looking pluralistic culture confident of its accrued strengths, be they Confucian, Daoist or Buddhist. The key, however, lay in the dynasty's powers of patronage. Instead of land the aristocracy was given generous stipends. It was also required to reside in the capital. Everything revolved around the **court**, and the favours of the court: banishment to an outlying commandery was as much a psychological as a physical punishment.

Yet behind the palpably glamorous facade of the early Tang – sustained by a reinvigorated bureaucracy – lurked familiar problems. On the one hand was the perennial conundrum of how to manage a vast population of diversifying pursuits and backgrounds cast across a huge, differentiated and unstable terrain. On the other was the bellicosity of China's northerly and westerly neighbours.

In the **An Lushan rebellion** of 755 these adverse factors coalesced. A too-capable barbarian mercenary general turned on the centre, riding the tiger of domestic discontent. Although Changan weathered the storm, the Tang compact was lastingly blighted. The aristocracy regained control of collecting taxes as the 'equal field system' collapsed. Imperial revenues ruptured.

In retrospect, the Tang placed too great a faith in their own talents as imperial rulers. As the pitiful decline of the once-great **Emperor Xuanzong** exemplifies, any system of government dependent upon the principle of hereditary at the top is bound to fail. Yet for almost a century and a half, the facts belied the prognosis. The early Tang were exceptional, as was the **Empress Wu**, who could claim no blood relationship.

618 As the **Tang Dynasty** is inaugurated, the lives of surviving members of the Sui clan are spared. Continuing pockets of resistance, however, will take **Emperor Gaozu** (Li Yuan) and his son **Li Shimin** six years to overcome.

Gaozu broadly retains and restores the institutions and instruments established by Sui Wendi, including the **equal field system** of land tenancy. The bureaucracy is further

The Emperors Gaozu 565–635 and Taizong 600–649

Not least among the second Tang emperor **Taizong**'s triumphs was his creation of the **History Commission**, a body of professional chroniclers detailed to compose a narrative of the Sui dynasty and the preceding Disunity that, whilst purporting objectivity, propagandized on behalf of the Tang. But in his pursuit of personal glory, Taizong went a step beyond the usual distortions of dynastic history-making, belittling the achievements of his own father, **Gaozu**.

Accordingly, it was **Li Shimin** who masterminded not only **Li Yuan**'s bid for the throne, but also the brilliant military campaigns that eliminated his rivals. Yet when those campaigns commenced, Li Shimin was a youth of 17, and it was not to him that opponents of Sui Yangdi flocked. Once this bias is allowed, however, and it is acknowledged that the regime created by the Tang depended on perpetuating the institutions of the ousted Sui, it can be seen that Li Yuan and Li Shimin were a remarkable duo, with different, but complementary, strengths.

If Gaozu was the more cautious, shrewder man, he was also an effective commander. As a servant of the Sui, he secured a military reputation against both Turkic aggressors and peasant insurgents, and it was this that furnished a platform for the successful **Tang revolt**. Similarly, if on the evidence of campaigns conducted after becoming Emperor, Taizong was indeed one of China's outstanding warriors, he also displayed a genius for

expanded, although Gaozu also nurtures a **reformed aristocracy**. His reign sees a continuing **migration** of Han Chinese of all classes to the south, drawn by the greater economic opportunities of the Yangzi, and its safety from the incursions of **northern tribes**. The extreme south and southwest remain only partly pacified, and it becomes Tang practice to 'exile' disgraced officials to remote commanderies.

CORBIS

A Qing dynasty idealized portrait of the emperor Taizong.

PIERRE COLOMBEL/CORBIS

administration. More than any other emperor, it was he who put the **imperial examinations** at the heart of government. In this, too, Taizong led from the front, through an exemplary **calligraphy** that, as a model for others, survived a thousand years. Where father and son diverged was in their religion. While Gaozu adhered to Daoist beliefs, claiming Laozi as an ancestor, Taizong reverted to the **Buddhism** of his mixed-blood forebears, mindful of the political advantages of chakravartin kingship.

624 The **Tang Legal Code** – a systematic body of laws and regulations – is promulgated. Revised at twenty-year intervals, this not only furnishes the basic law of the later **Song** and **Ming** dynasties, but will be copied by such other east Asian states as **Japan**, **Korea** and **Vietnam**. Gaozu indicates a personal preference for **Daoism**, but this has little impact on policy.

626 **Li Shimin** stages a **coup** against his elder brother **Li Jiancheng**, the heir apparent, who dies amidst a hail of arrows. Li Shimin next persuades **Gaozu** to abdicate in his favour. As the **Emperor Taizong**, he becomes the most widely admired Chinese emperor of any dynasty. Already famed as a soldier, he quickly demonstrates an equal aptitude for government. Expanding the empire's frontiers, he institutes daily meetings of an enlarged **cabinet**, comprising, as well as chief ministers, special **advisers** (*zaixiang*). But while Taizong promotes Confucian virtues within the bureaucracy, he reverses his father's penchant for Daoism by vigorously embracing **Buddhism**.

An 18th-century facsimile of an imperial edict urging virtue and obedience issued

629 **Taizong** orders a ban on unauthorized foreign travel. Despite this, **Xuan Zang** sets out on a sixteen-year trip to India.

630 Having vanquished the **eastern Turks**, Taizong turns his attention against the **western Turks**. Reasserting Chinese control over the **Tarim Basin**, his campaigns mark the beginning of a **conquest** that will carry Chinese arms beyond the **Pamirs**.

634 As the kingdom of **Tibet** takes shape, Taizong presents the Tibetan king with a **Chinese bride**, his own adopted daughter **Wencheng**, and a **peace treaty** is concluded. As Tibet accumulates strength, however, the ability to counterattack it from its rear becomes a strategic objective of Taizong's campaigns.

635 The **Nestorian** monk **Alopen** arrives in **Changan** and is permitted to open the first **Christian church** of any denomination in China.

by the emperor Taizong and written in his own hand.

The Nestorians

The first **Christians** in China belonged to the **Nestorian sect** that had its origins in the 3rd century, when a group of theologians advanced the concept of Christ's dual nature: he was divine, but also human, and his two beings were separate. Excommunicated by successive Christian councils, the Nestorians moved eastwards, founding communities in modern Syria and Iran. In 635 a monk called **Alopen** was granted an audience with Taizong, who was moved to declare: 'After examining his doctrines we find them profound and pacific. After studying his principles we find they stress what is good and important.' Such an affirmation did not amount to a conversion, but Alopen was allowed to stay.

Subsequently, the Nestorian faith spread to many Chinese cities. Unlike Judaism, Zoroastrianism and Manicheanism, it recruited at least some native Chinese, including members of the nobility. In 845, however, Nestorianism suffered eclipse as a result of a generalized religious persecution. But in 1625 a stele was discovered in the ruins of Changan. This, the **Nestorian Tablet**, cut in 781, recounted Alopen's mission, and provided Jesuits with 'evidence' that Christianity had an historic place in Chinese society.

636 The **death** of Taizong's empress **Wende** triggers a sustained **succession crisis** as their eldest son and heir apparent, the lame **Li Chengqian**, develops a fixation about his **Turkic ancestry**. Living in a tent, and wearing Turkish garments, he becomes the object of **ridicule**. When he is discovered plotting against another royal prince he is killed, and Taizong's ninth son, **Li Zhi**, is proclaimed heir.

638 A **Persian Sassanid** embassy is received in Changan, but denied its request for support against the militant spread of **Islam**. Some delegates remain in China to found a **Zoroastrian** community.

642 The **Sassanid empire** falls to the Muslim **Umayyad Caliphate**.

The Tang Imperium

In its idealized form, **Tang rule** was sustained by five pillars: the revitalized bureaucracy; the equal field system; a code of laws applicable throughout the empire; a framework to contain and exploit the aristocracy; and a professional army. The **Legal Code** promulgated in 624 – probably modelled on the antecedent code of Sui Wendi – provided magistrates with an unequivocal statement of what constituted a misdemeanour, and how it should be punished.

As regards the **aristocracy**, the Tang's *coup de grace* was to separate it from patronal estates. Aristocrats were rescheduled into nine ranks, from 'First Class Prince' at the top, to simple lord at the bottom. Each rank was allotted a fixed stipend based on the taxes receivable from between 300 and 10,000 commoner families; but no authority was given over such families, or their land. With each succeeding generation a noble family slipped one rank, so that, unless promotion was won through imperial service, after ten generations the highest family was reduced to commonality. Conversely, entry into the nine-grade system was used to reward outstanding officials. The remit of the aristocracy was also curbed by army reforms.

The early Tang developed a mixed **professional-militia system** outlined by the Sui. Under Taizong, a total of 600 *fu-ping* militia units were formed, consisting of between 800 and 1200 men. Militiamen, exempted from taxes, might serve either on short-term secondments to the capital, or at border garrisons, or in their own provinces. They were overseen by a professional corps of officers, rotated around the empire to preclude the possibility of their forming personal power bases. The Tang also maintained a standing force, the elite **'Northern Army'**, barracked outside the capital. These and related measures were costly, but for 150 years they paid for themselves by enabling the empire to expand commercially as well as territorially, without the distractions of internal revolt.

643 The first of four embassies from **Byzantium** arrives in **Changan**. Others follow in 667, 701 and 719. Like the Sassanids, they seek Chinese help against **Islam**, but succour is consistently refused.

645 Despite Taizong's successes on the northern and western frontiers, **Korea** remains intractable. A Chinese army is defeated by the kingdom of **Silla**. **Xuan Zang** returns from India bringing with him 657 **Sanskrit manuscripts**, as well as **Buddha relics**. Welcomed by Taizong, his exploits will later be embellished in the popular novel *Journey to the West* (see p.250).

649 **Taizong** dies while preparing a Korean campaign. He is succeeded by Li Zhi, the insipid **Emperor Gaozong**. Aged 21, Gaozong is soon dominated by the most formidable woman in Chinese history, **Wu Zetian**. One of his father's concubines, Wu becomes Gaozong's consort.

651 The **Moslem Arabs**, having overcome the Sassanids, send their own envoy to **Changan**.

655 To the chagrin of Gaozong's empress **Wang**, Wu Xetian gives birth. But Wu, disappointed to have produced a girl, smothers her, then lays the blame on Wang.

Wang is **murdered**, and **Wu** becomes **Empress**. With equal ruthlessness, she eliminates other rivals, persuading Gaozong to promote her allies.

656 **Wu** gives birth to the future **Emperor Zhongzhong**.

657 The **western Turks** are decisively **defeated** at **Issykkul**.

660 **Gaozong** being incapacitated by a stroke, **Wu** assumes full power. Ruling China for 45 years, she pursues an expansionist policy. Immediately, she launches a fresh **campaign in the west** that will secure control of the **Ili Valley** as well as territories beyond the Pamirs within ten years.

666 **Wu** leads a group of women up **Mount Tai** to conduct rites previously performed only by men.

668 As Wu's western campaigns near completion, she orders fresh **campaigns in the east**. Within eight years the kingdoms of **Korea** are reduced to vassal status.

673 A colossal **statue** of the **Maitreya Buddha** in the Longmen Caves outside Loyang is commissioned by **Wu**, its features said to resemble her own.

680 The crown prince **Li Hong** is **poisoned** and other royal princes exiled as Wu plots for the succession of **Li Zhe**, the emperor's seventh son, and her own third.

Chan (Zen) Buddhism

Zen Buddhism evolved in China in the 6th and 7th centuries as **Chan Buddhism**. Its central tenet was that inside every individual is a Buddha essence which, unlocked, produces immediate 'enlightenment'(*wu* in Chinese, *satori* in Japanese). Chan disregarded other elements of Buddhism, such as merit-making, scriptural studies and belief in karma, or rebirth. Enlightenment was to be achieved by arduous self-discipline imparted through prolonged personal contact with a Chan master.

In Chan tradition, its philosophy was brought to northern China circa 516 by a south Indian prince called **Boddhidharma**, the patriarch of the Yogic Dhyana sect. Among many stories attaching to Boddhidharma is his navigation of the Yangzi perched on a reed, and nine years spent in Loyang contemplating a blank wall. Whatever the basis of these legends, there began a Chinese succession of patriarchs. The sect splintered in the 8th century, giving rise to the two main Japanese schools, **Rinzai** and **Soto**. In China, Chan continued to attract followers until Ming times. It owed as much to native Daoist practices as to Indian philosophy, making Zen's many millions of contemporary adherents worldwide part-followers of an ancient Chinese path.

In **Korea**, resistance to Chinese suzerainty begins in the southern kingdom of **Silla**.

681 **Flooding** in the **Yellow River** plains encourages further **migration** to the south.

682 Pestilence strikes Changan and Loyang as the first known instances of **bubonic plague** occur in China, introduced from central Asia along the **Silk Road**.

683 On Gaozong's death the throne passes to 27-year-old Li Zhe, the **Emperor Zhongzhong**.

684 A **power-struggle** develops between Zhongzhong's empress **Wei**, and Dowager-empress **Wu**. With the emperor in her thrall, Wei ensures the appointment of her own father as Chief Minister. Swiftly marshalling her followers – among them a hardcore of officials – Wu has the emperor himself charged with treason. After a bare six months, Zhongzhong is deposed and banished together with Wei. In his place, Wu enthrones her youngest son, the 22-year-old **Emperor Ruizong**, whom she keeps confined to the Inner Palace, ruling in his stead.

685 **Xue Huaiyi**, Wu's close companion, is appointed **abbot** of the White Horse temple, an important **Buddhist shrine**. He soon 'discovers' an ancient text foretelling the reincarnation of the **Maitreya Buddha** as a woman who will rule all mankind. Wu orders statues of Laozi's **'Sage Mother'** to be erected in Daoist temples.

688 At great expense, Wu orders the building of the *Ming tang*, or 'Hall of Light', a supreme shrine to 'Heaven'.

690 Ruizong is persuaded by Wu to **abdicate**. **Wu** herself is proclaimed **'Emperor'**, the only woman to sit in her own right on the Dragon Throne. To safeguard her position, she encourages informers to come directly to the palace.

Empress Wu (625–706)

Wu Zetian entered imperial service as a junior concubine at the age of 12. When Emperor Taizong died in 649, she should have 'retired' to a nunnery; instead she became first the Emperor Gaozong's favourite concubine, then his empress. The principal obstacles to her progress – the Empress Wang and another concubine Xiao – were not only killed by Wu, but allegedly mutilated. Before being tossed into either a river or a vat of wine, their arms and legs were sawn off. From 660 Wu's authority was supreme.

Although throughout her ascendency Changan witnessed many executions, suicides and banishments, the empress was consistent in her policies. Ridding government of a controlling clique of aristocrats, she systematically promoted able men of lesser birth; and while without exception she struck fear into her adversaries – not least through her network of spies and informers – she carefully groomed her populist image as a '**Sage Mother**'. Nor did she use her powers to advance members of her own family. But like all despots, she had scant sense of her advancing frailty. In the end it was her ill judged infatuation with the Zhang brothers that wrought her downfall. Dethroned in February 705, she died, a broken octogenarian, the following December. Among the grotesque details added to her biography was an addiction to aphrodisiacs. This, said the chroniclers, caused Empress Wu to sprout supernumerary teeth and eyebrows.

694 As **Wu** proclaims herself an incarnation of the **Maitreya Buddha**, surviving members of the **Tang family** are **imprisoned** in Loyang.

Manicheanism – an amalgam of Christian and Zoroastrian beliefs founded by the Persian prophet Mani – enters China. Within three years, Manichean temples are dedicated in **Changan** and other cities.

695 At about this time, the first **Moslem immigrants** settle in modern **Gansu**. Moslem traders also establish themselves in Changan, Guangzhou and other cities.

696 **Chinese armies** are defeated in two engagements: one against **Tibet**, the other, in the northeast, against the **Khitan**, a nomadic people from the Amur and Sungari valleys. Expanding into upper **Manchuria**, the Khitan rapidly become a serious problem for Chinese frontier security.

697 **Wu** purges her administration of high-born officials whose loyalty is suspect. Some are executed, others exiled to remote prefectures. Sons of the condemned are barred from office. The court itself, however, slips into disarray as the ageing empress takes the young **Zhang brothers** as her lovers.

705 The **Zhang** are murdered by officials anxious to halt the degeneracy of the court. Within hours, **Wu** abdicates, and the former **Emperor Zhongzhong** is restored to the throne. But while actual power is assumed by Zhongzhong's forceful consort the **Empress Wei**, a rival faction forms around the former emperor **Ruizong**, orchestrated by his sister and Wu's daughter, **Princess Taiping**.

710 **Zhonhzhong** dies suddenly, aged 44, probably poisoned by **Wei**, who conceals his death until their 15-year-old son **Chong Mao** can be enthroned. Within a few days, the boy emperor is toppled by **Princess Taiping**. **Ruizong** is recalled as Emperor and Wei's family purged.

712 Set on becoming dowager-empress *manquée*, **Princess Taiping** attempts to remove the heir apparent, Li Longji. Swayed by the appearance of a comet, **Ruizong abdicates**, so that his son's reign can commence.

Under **Emperor Xuanzong** domestic tranquillity prevails. While he works to restore the prestige of the **Confucian bureaucracy**, he trims down its size and reduces the stipends of royal and other hangers-on. He energetically promotes **Daoism**, ordering a copy of the Dao teaching to be kept in every household. Conversely, measures are taken to curb the growth of **Buddhist monasteries**.

713 Finally outmanoeuvred by Xuanzong, Princess Taiping kills herself. The emperor prohibits members of the royal family from holding office, restricts them to their palace quarters and forbids access by outsiders. He further orders government inspectorates to be unified into a single body with authority to probe all corners of the empire.

As **Islam** wages **holy war** in central Asia, destroying, among other things, Buddhist kingdoms in (modern) **Afghanistan**, Caliph Walid dispatches envoys to **Changan**. China agrees not to intervene on condition its own borders remain inviolate.

714 An **attempted invasion** of the Yellow River plains by **Tibet** is repulsed.

720 **Xuanzong** moves against a group of soothsayers surrounding his brother **Prince Fan**, although Fan himself is pardoned for consorting with outsiders.

724 Xuanzong's empress **Wang** is demoted for failing to produce an heir. Declining to take a second wife, the emperor spends more time amongst his concubines.

In a major crackdown against tax evasion 'illegal' **migrants** to the south are persuaded to register their households in return for a five-year exemption from dues.

725 **Wei Bin**, brother-in-law to Xuanzong's own brother Prince Ye, is beaten to death for 'dealing in prophecies'.

732 Victories are gained over the **Khitan** and the smaller **Xi** people. But while the Xi people are persuaded to incorporate themselves within the empire, the Khitan merely "withdraw" deeper northeast.

733 **Kotukan**, leader of the **Khitan**, defeats a Chinese army, killing its commander. **Zhang Shougui**, previously victorious against the Tibetans, is sent to restore order in the northeast. Amongst his younger officers is **An Lushan**, a brilliant soldier of mixed Sogdian and Turkic blood.

734 The **Khitan** are brought temporarily within the Chinese pale as Kotukan is defeated by **Zhang Shougui**.

735 The **Khitan** and **Xi** combine to fend off an attack by **Turkic** marauders.

736 The **Khitan** and **Xi** declare their **independence**. A Chinese army led recklessly by **An Lushan** is routed. Faced with execution by his commander, An pleads: 'The barbarians remain hostile, yet still you want to kill a brave officer. Is this the depth of your strategy?' He is pardoned, but **demoted**.

Wearying of the cares of government, Xuanzong appoints **Li Linfu** as his **chief minister**. Li rapidly emerges as the champion of the **aristocracy**, fomenting a rivalry with the **bureaucratic meritocracy** in the 'outer court'.

737 **Zhang Shougui** pacifies the northeast with victories against the **Khitan**.

739 **Zhang** is **disgraced** after attempting to cover up for a subordinate. The independent kingdom of **Nanzhao** is established in modern **Yunnan**, in the far southwest.

740 As fighting again breaks out in the northeast, **Khitan** and **Xi** forces are defeated by a royal general, **Li Shichi**. Amongst his field commanders is **An Lushan**, newly restored to favour.

741 **Xuanzong** becomes obsessed with **Yang Guifei**, a talented Sichuanese married to one of his many sons. Yang deserts her husband and, posing as a Daoist priestess, enters the palace. As the emperor's infatuation deepens, Yang persuades him to promote members of her family. Led by her cousin **Yang Guozhong** (the military governor of

Changan

The Tang empire reached its zenith during the reign of **Xuanzong**. No other capital in the world was larger, busier or more cosmopolitan than **Changan**. Like other Chinese cities it was built on the grid system. Its high stamped-earth walls – studded with drum-towers from which the intervals of the day were beaten – enclosed an 80km rectangle, divided east and west by a great boulevard, 150 metres wide. At its northern end were administrative buildings and the imperial palace. Below these, each half of Changan contained a great market, one trading in 'foreign' goods, the other in domestic produce. On the western side lived the ordinary people: merchants, artisans and tradesmen; on the eastern side, the establishment – the nobility, officials, and their servants. Inside Changan's warren of intersecting streets and lanes could be found every kind of activity. The area around the eastern market especially was notorious for its brothels. While by night the two societies of Changan were segregated, by day they intermingled. Men and women paraded in their finery down the central corridor. Everywhere, too, were shrines, temples and monasteries – some Buddhist, some Daoist, others belonging to 'barbarian' religions. Of an estimated two million inhabitants, fully one-third were foreign. But Changan suffered two disadvantages. Its brilliant architecture was made of wood, and geographically it was badly sited. Attacked, the city easily burned; and at peace, the efforts to keep it fed were necessarily prodigious. By 900 it had been reduced to an empty wasteland, and no future dynastic house thought to return.

Sichuan), these form a **clique** against **Li Linfu**. As **Li Shichi** is recalled to Changan, to become joint chief minister, **An Lushan** is appointed Deputy Commander in the northeast.

Li Linfu d. 752

From 736, the Emperor Xuanzong entrusted the affairs of state to **Li Linfu**. As his name suggests, Li was a member of the imperial family, and earned the enmity of the scholar-gentry by appointing fellow aristocrats to senior office. Lampooned for his want of learning, Li was nonetheless a high-octane performer: as an administrator; as a master of intrigue; as a creature of near-infallible political instinct; and as a smooth-talker well able to ingratiate himself upon those whose support he needed. Where his critics were right was in their characterization of Li as a self-server. Personally corrupt, he ruled China for sixteen years as a virtual dictator, impervious to its deeper interests. By making Changan a place of festering intrigue, and by promoting the seemingly biddable **An Lushan** to high command, he set in place forces that, after his death, caused havoc.

742 In the northeast, **An Lushan** is promoted **Military Governor** of **Pinglu** province.

744 Chinese authority is imposed in the **Lake Balkash** area of the far west. As the western Turkic empire finally disintegrates, the **Uighur** people first make their presence felt along the **Orkhon river**. After being feted as a 'Grand General' in the capital, and gaining the confidence of Yang Guifei, **An Lushan** is appointed **Military Governor** of **Youzhou** city.

745 **An Lushan** crushes a combined **Khitan/Xi revolt**, after their leaders murder their **Chinese brides**.

746 **Li Linfu** overcomes factional opposition by exposing the 'treason' of his fellow chief minister **Li Shichi**, who is driven out of Changan, then **murdered**.

747 Chinese forces cross the **Hindu Kush** to attack **Tibet** from the west.

In Changan, Li Linfu, preferring the 'simple soldier' to

court politicians, appoints **An Lushan** as President of the Censorate. Other ethnic generals are promoted to military governorships. An remains in the northeast, however, where a court begins to assemble around him.

750 Chinese arms are carried into **Transoxiana** against the **Islamicized Abbassids**.

In the northeast, **An Lushan** gains further victories over the **Khitan**, and is made a **prince**.

At about this time, the population of **Changan** reaches 2,000,000, twice the size of **Byzantium**. 26 other cities in the empire boast populations of 500,000 or more, and the population for the whole of China climbs to **70 million**.

751 In perhaps the most decisive engagement of the era, **Chinese forces** led by a Korean mercenary are **defeated** by a **Moslem confederacy** at the **Battle of Talas River**. Never again will a Chinese army venture beyond the Pamirs. The Tang lose control of the **Tarim Basin** and major entrepots on the **Silk Road**, reducing court revenues.

Adopted by **Yang Guifei** as her 'son', **An Lushan** launches a fresh campaign against the **Khitan**, but when **Xi mercenaries** turn coat midway through battle his army is badly mauled. By blaming and immediately executing two subordinates, An escapes censure.

752 Intense factional infighting between **Li Linfu** and **Yang Guozong** ends with Li's death. Yang becomes **Chief Minister** and purges Li's followers. Li himself is posthumously stripped of his titles and reinterred as a commoner.

An Lushan keeps a low profile – but in the face of Yang's hostility, and encouraged by a growing band of disaffected officials and northern aristocrats – realizes his best hope of survival depends on his continued command of the northeast.

Emperor Xuanzong
(aka Ming Huang) 685–762

While **Xuanzong** took China to the limits of its 'medieval' potential, no other episode in its 2000-year dynastic history has seized the Chinese imagination more than the pitiful denouement of a once glorious reign. Fleeing Changan, the emperor was compelled by mutinous soldiers to order the death of his beloved and effervescent concubine **Yang Guifei** – a sacrifice summarized by Bai Juyi as 'the everlasting wrong' in a poem of the same title. But scrutiny of the facts suggests a less romantic scenario.

At the time of An Lushan's rebellion, Xuanzong was 70. Yang was a good 25 years younger, and had used her position, in the way of all aspiring concubines, to further her family's ends. Nonetheless, Bai's poem has been followed by countless other romances, many of them stage plays – fittingly perhaps, as Xuanzong is credited the first imperial patron of Chinese drama. That his reign was also gilded by some of China's finest poets has likewise tended to obscure the realities. While as a younger man Xuanzong was an effective ruler – maximizing revenues, expanding China's borders and instituting administrative reforms – overall the seeds of his dynasty's decay can be found in the means he employed. Praised for trusting his ministers, it was the most powerful of them, **Li Linfu**, who did most to restore the influence of a querulous aristocracy. It was also Li who appointed 'barbarian' generals to restore order along progressively fractious frontiers.

754 The 'outer court' resists **Emperor Xuanzong**'s proposal that **An Lushan** be made an equal Chief Minister on the grounds of his illiteracy.

755 After three-years' uneasy stand-off with Yang Guozong, **An Lushan** marches south from Youzhou. His immediate pretext is an invitation to a royal wedding, which An suspects is a trap. He puts **Kaifeng**'s population to the sword, then captures **Loyang**. As he approaches Changan, **Xuanzong** flees toward Sichuan with **Yang Guifei** and close members of both their families. Blaming An Lushan's rebellion on his concubine, his military escort first murder **Yang Guozong**, then demand her death as well. Xuanzong orders a eunuch to strangle Yang Guifei with silk in a pagoda in Ma Wei. Abdicating in favour of his son Li Yu (**Emperor Suzong**) Xuanzong resumes his flight, at length arriving at **Chengdu**.

Changan, meanwhile, falls to **An Lushan**. Across northern China, local leaders and military governors express dissatisfaction with his coup by either voicing support for the house of Tang, or by setting up their own independent commands. For eight years **civil war** plagues the **Yellow River** plains.

757 As factions develop within his army, **An Lushan** is murdered in January by one of his officers.

In December, with the help of **Uighur mercenaries**, **Changan** is recaptured by **Suzong**. The rebels, however, do not lay down their arms, but split into two forces, one led by An's son, the other by a subordinate general. Suzong adopts a strategy of compromise, making peace individually with lords and commanders in return for **concessions** that include the power to collect taxes in their own 'estates'.

759 Suzong reimposes the imperial **salt monopoly**, in abeyance since Han times.

762 Suzong is succeeded by his eldest son, **Emperor Daizong**. Along the Yangzi, **peasant unrest** erupts as China's warring factions increase **taxes**. Overall, however, the An Lushan Rebellion shows signs of collapse as Daizong continues his father's policies of compromise and non-recrimination.

An Lushan 703–757

The **An Lushan Rebellion** of 755–763 was the climactic episode of the Tang era. Before this time, the dynasty was strong, centralized and confident. Afterwards, it was weak, decentralized, and prey to opportunists. Not surprisingly, An has been vilified by Chinese historians, the more so since he was a 'pure' barbarian. But uncertainty surrounds the motives of his revolt. An was the son of a noted Sogdian general from the Gobi desert. Either because his father was killed in battle, or because Sogdians lost favour with their Turkic overlords, An joined a general exodus of Sogdians to Manchuria as a teenager. Almost immediately, he entered the Chinese military, which was then recruiting Turkic 'deserters'. His promotion was rapid, his only liability a hot-headedness in battle that sometimes led him to squander troops. In Changan, however, as his star rose, he was caricatured as an illiterate buffoon. Yet nothing in his early and mid-career casts a shadow on his loyalty to the empire. He was a genuine intimate of the **Emperor Xuanzong**. It was only when Yang Guozong threatened to destroy him that An turned his army on Changan. Whether he had an ulterior motive is uncertain. Did he simply wish to make himself safe? Did he covet the throne? Whatever the case, the support he attracted indicates a much broader dissatisfaction with the prevailing regime than is usually allowed.

763 As the last of **An Lushan**'s generals are defeated and killed, a greatly weakened and structurally altered empire returns to **peace**.

The later Tang Dynasty (763–907) and Second Disunity (907–960)

The An Lushan Rebellion was a turning-point not just in the fortunes of the Tang dynasty, but also in the evolution of the empire. In stark terms, it exposed the divisions between the 'inner' and 'outer' courts, and also between an inner and an outer China. Unless the throne maintained a purposeful and costly watch over the peripheries, then sooner or later the peripheries would impinge on the centre. If the immediate occasion of the barbarian general's rise to power was his ability to contain the **Khitan**, it was only by enlisting the mercenary help of the **Uighurs** that the Tang managed to save themselves. But what they saved was a pale shadow of their former amplitude. The provinces had fallen into the hands of military governors, and there they stayed.

These new grandees – some of them Chinese, others not – quickly took it into their heads that their fiefdoms should become hereditary. Since they now had the authority to collect taxes, they could hold the government to ransom. Some flatly refused to hand over any imperial revenues. With the collapse of the equal field system, the Tang's tax-base was reduced by as much as seventy percent. Only the revived **salt monopoly** prevented utter bankruptcy.

In retrospect, it is a moot question who did more damage to the Tang regime: **An Lushan** and his fellow non-Chinese generals, or chief minister **Li Linfu**, the champion of the aristocratic party. But what was also now lacking was a strong presence on the throne itself. After the rebellion, only **Xianzong** (805–820) rose above a ruck of mediocrity as the palace progressively succumbed to eunuch machinations.

During the 9th century, the **eunuchs** formed their own palace council. Through this they exerted control over the succession, and therefore over the empire. Nor was a contracting and lacklustre bureaucracy able to withstand adversity. Almost alone the Confucian scholar **Han Yu** opposed the tide. The only aspect of his critique that struck a resonance with those who governed, however, was his condemnation of **Buddhism**. In the mid-century was launched a damaging religious persecution. While Buddhism survived, other minority faiths did not, and Tang society, while remaining multiethnic, became less multicultural.

In 907 the dynasty finally disintegrated. The north returned to the plague of civil war, as one commander after another wrestled for advantage. In the south, too, power devolved among a number of separate 'kingdoms'. But just as the south had come through the An Lushan rebellion unscathed, so now it remained relatively at peace, attracting yet more immigrants. **Chengdu**, in particular, became a refuge for scholars and artists. Overall, the balance of the population had shifted – summarized perhaps in the final sacking of Changan. From this point onwards, the Wei River valley – the sacred 'land within the passes' – was relegated to a minor role in Chinese affairs.

763 A **Tibetan army** occupies **Changan** for two weeks in the autumn. In the southwest, **Nanzhao** launches **incursions** into Chinese territory. Although both attacks are repulsed, similar episodes recur almost annually until 777. Tibet gains control of the **Gansu corridor**. More interested in the mysteries of **Buddhism**, the **Emperor**

Han Yu 768–824

Under the Tang, **Confucianism** often had to play second fiddle to Daoism and Buddhism, but in **Han Yu**, a Henanese scholar-official, China's ancient philosophy of 'moral realism' found an articulate champion. In 819, when Xianzong proposed exhibiting the Buddha's finger-bone as a holy relic in Changan, Han risked all by issuing a scathing attack on **Buddhism** in a memorial to the throne. Buddha, he wrote, 'was merely a barbarian from the western kingdoms who recognized neither the loyalty that binds a subject to his ruler, nor the obedience due from a son to his father'. For this he was banished to Guangzhong. Recalled by Muzong, he courageously faced down an eastern revolt by appearing undefended before the rebels and arguing the case for restraint. Equally opposed to 'Daoist inaction', Han Yu is prized for his clear, purposeful, no-nonsense essays. His writings, as well as fuelling the religious persecution of the 840s, inspired the **Neo-Confucian revival** of the 11th and 12th centuries.

Daizong allows the western frontiers to slip from China's grasp.

779 **Daizong** is succeeded by his son, the **Emperor Dezong**. Although he regains the allegiance of **Nanzhao**, Dezong is unable to curb the powers of **regional commanders**. Nor does his policy of placing supposedly loyal **eunuchs** in command of his own army prove an unqualified triumph. Taking advantage of their expanded authority, the eunuchs bully the Changan populace, and **bribery** is institutionalized.

781 A succession of **provincial revolts** by **military governors** will continue five years. At issue is the right of governors to pass on their titles and powers to their sons.

795 The **Uighurs**, though vulnerable to Tibetan belligerence, begin posing at the least an economic threat through their ability to apply a tourniquet to the Silk Road.

805 **Dezong** is succeeded by his disabled son, the **Emperor Shunzong**. Within the year, Shunzong abdicates in favour of his own son, the **Emperor Xianzong**. By taking personal command of his army, by insisting on **merit** as the yardstick of imperial appointment, and by limiting the influence of the **eunuchs**, Xianzong restores imperial respect.

814 **Regional revolts** again proliferate in reaction to Xianzong's reforms, but the emperor prevails.

819 The **Confucian** scholar **Han Yu** characterizes **Buddhism** as an agent of moral, political and economic decline.

820 **Xianzong** is assassinated by two **eunuchs**. He is succeeded by his dissipated son, **Muzong**.

824 **Muzong**, killed playing polo, is succeeded by his son, the **Emperor Jinzong**, a youth addicted to concubines and esoteric gurus.

827 Assassinated by his **eunuchs**, Jinzong is replaced by his more serious, but also more pliable, half-brother, the **Emperor Wenzong**.

830 When **Wenzong** dies aged 30, the **eunuchs** again determine the **succession**, enthroning his 16-year-old brother, the **Emperor Wuzong**. Two other candidates and their mothers are murdered.

At the Imperial Academy the **Nine Classics** (including the Confucian Analects) are engraved on 228 **stone tablets**. These survive virtually unblemished into the present.

842 An imperial decree ordering monks and nuns to either pay taxes or return to their villages marks the beginning of a campaign not only against **Buddhism**, but against all religions other than Daoism. As much as forty percent of China's wealth and land is controlled by Buddhist institutions, many of them fronts for provincial grandees.

Tang Poets

'Nowhere,' asserts the *Princeton Encyclopedia of Poetry and Poetics*, 'has poetry been more widely or continuously esteemed and practised than in China'. From Tang times onwards, those sitting the imperial examinations were required to compose verses on prescribed topics. Many emperors also wrote poetry, and 'singing girls' – the Chinese prototype of Japanese *geisha* – adjusted their tariff according to their ability to recite ballads. In the poetry that has survived, from earlier periods as well as the Tang, there is often an assured virtuosity. Rigid metres, rhyme, assonance, alliteration, onomatopoeia and tonal pitching produce a poetry of startling musical compactness, although in the long run, ultrademanding rules smothered creativity. But, under the Tang, the obverse held true. Competing cultural values inspired China's greatest poetry. Of 3000-odd known Tang poets, four are habitually singled out. **Li Bai** (Li Po, 701–762) most conforms to the Western stereotype of the romantic artist, and is therefore deemed the most 'accessible'. A Sichuanese Daoist, he chose a life of constant wandering. **Du Fu** (713–770) kept himself gainfully employed until falling foul of the An Lushan rebellion. The most disciplined of the four, he is hailed as the 'scholar's poet' for his acutely expressive reticence. The older **Wang Wei** (699–761), also famous as a painter, composed haunting Buddhist ruminations on the landscape surrounding his retreat outside Changan. In marked contrast, **Bai Juyi** (772–846) espoused an overtly public role, declaring that 'the duty of literature is to be of use to the writer's generation'. Yet Bai's reputation rests less on his high-minded satires than on his lighter pieces, including the ever-popular 'Everlasting Wrong'.

843 The court persecutes **Manicheaism**, popular among **Uighurs**. Seventy nuns are murdered in their cells, and all Uighurs living on Chinese soil are forced to adopt **Chinese custom**.

844 Many smaller **Buddhist monasteries** close as monks and nuns aged under 50 are ordered to return to their lay occupations.

845 Hundreds more Buddhist monasteries are dismantled as tens of thousands of monks and nuns are laicized. Countless holy images are destroyed or melted down. Only one temple per city is allowed to remain open. Heavier proscriptions are issued against **Nestorians**, **Zoroastrians** and **Jews**.

846 **Wuzong** poisons himself whilst experimenting with chemical elixirs. Ignoring his sons, the **eunuchs** arrange for the accession of Xianzong's thirteenth son, the second Tang emperor to be known as **Xuanzong**. He annuls the previous year's prohibitions against **Buddhism**, but Nestorian, Zoroastrian and Manichean churches remain outlawed.

849 **Tibet** ceases to be a regional power following the extinction of its royal house. China is temporarily able to consolidate its western frontiers.

855 A woman alchemist, known only as **Geng**, is the first recorded individual to distil **camphor**.

858 **Nanzhao** launches forays into **Sichuan** and **Vietnam**.

859 **Xuanzong** dies after taking a **Daoist elixir** and is succeeded by his eldest son, the febrile **Emperor Yizong**. An extravagant patron of **Buddhist temples**, Yizong allows the influence of both **eunuchs** and **military governors** to grow during his reign.

868 An **army** garrisoned in the **southwest** mutinies over pay and conditions and marches 'home', looting several cities on its way. Reaching **Jiangsu** it forms the nucleus of a sixteen-year rebellion.

873 **Yizong** is succeeded by his fifth son, the **Emperor Xizong**. A mere boy, Xizong falls immediately under the baneful influence of the chief eunuch, **Tian Lingzi**.

874 The government does little to assuage widespread famine. As **Tian Lingzi** and fellow eunuchs think only of self-enrichment, and tax-levels are raised, China becomes pitted with both **warlord** and **popular revolts**.

In Jiangsu, **Huang Zhao** – a failed civil service candidate – assumes the leadership of the **mutineers** of 868, creating the largest and most mobile of the late Tang insurgencies.

875 **Huang** leads his rebel force southwards across the **Yangzi**.

879 **Huang**'s rebels sack **Guangzhou**. Over 100,000 foreign residents, including Arab, Indian and Southeast Asian merchants, are massacred.

881 Having recrossed the Yangzi, **Huang** storms **Changan**. As the capital is razed, **Xizong** takes flight.

884 **Huang Zhao's rebellion** finally **crushed**, Xizong re-enters Changan, but no attempt is made to rebuild the city.

888 **Xizong** is succeeded by his 21-year-old brother, the **Emperor Zhaozong**. Like Xizong, Zhaozong can lead only a fugitive existence, the symbolic property of his eunuch entourage.

904 The court is captured, and **Zhaozong assassinated** by **Zhu Wen**, a former general in Huang Zhao's rebel army. Zhu enthrones Zhaozong's 12-year-old son, the **Emperor Aidi**, as his puppet.

907 **Zhu** deposes **Aidi** and proclaims himself Emperor, initiating the **Later Liang Dynasty**. As the **Emperor Taizu**, Zhu's rule is restricted to the central area of northern China. Elsewhere, government passes into the hands of local commanders and chieftains. There follows the **Second Disunity**, known also as the period of the **Five Dynasties and Ten Kingdoms**.

Tang Art

Buddhism brought with it a potent stimulus to China's arts, most obviously apparent in the numinous carved Buddhas at the **Longmen Caves** and other sites. It also introduced the Indianesque pagoda, and a diffused Hellenism. Painting, too, in the form of murals adorning temples, palaces and tombs, was influenced by China's exposure to Central Asia. Given that the Tang boasted at least some nomadic blood, not surprisingly the horse features strongly in much Tang work. Yet such 'foreign' influences account

ESKENAZI, LTD., LONDON

An earthenware figurine of a court lady decorated with red, green, black and cream pigments from the Tang period.

for only half of the story. In their quest for grandeur, the Tang emperors built themselves vast Han-style mausoleums. Enough remains of these for us to know that the likes of Taizong and Wu

Zetian were entombed on a scale hitherto unknown.

The genius of the Tang, however, is located in the millions of **figurines** buried, again Han-style, with less prominent but still wealthy subjects. Alongside servants, grooms, dancers, matrons and slaves are camels as well as the ubiquitous horse, all designed to ensure an equal comfort in the afterlife. As these are unearthed, so Tang fads and fashions are brought back to life. Many such pieces exhibit surreal vitality and grace. And as though to underline that this was the golden age of Chinese ceramics, two new techniques emerged. Some figurines are either part or wholly glazed. Where this is done in three colours, the prized result is known as **sancai**. Then, from about 700, the Chinese mastered **porcelain**. An advanced iron industry meant they were used to working with kiln

A glazed clay wine pot, with copper band on an irregular mouth rim – a typical example of 'Tang White' porcelain c.9th century.

temperatures of the necessary 1400° centigrade, and proto-porcelain is known from earlier times. But scratch-resistant, semi-diaphanous '**Tang white**' was not just a technological accomplishment: it set a fresh benchmark in aesthetics.

The Five Dynasties

Later Liang 907–923
Later Tang 923–935
Later Jin 936–947
Later Han 947–948
Later Zhou 951–960

911 **Taizu** is murdered by his son, who becomes the Liang emperor **Modi**.

916 **Abaoji**, ruler of the **Khitan**, proclaims himself Emperor of a dynasty known as the **Liao**, after the river supposed to be the Khitan ancestral homeland.

923 Modi is overthrown by the son of a Turkic general who establishes the **Later Tang dynasty**, of which he becomes the first emperor, **Zhuanzong**. The 'northern empire' is expanded as previously surrendered territories are reclaimed, except in the northeast. There, territory is conceded to the Khitan in return for military assistance.

926 Zhuanzong is succeeded by **Minzong**, the second emperor of the Later Tang. **Abaoji** also dies. In the name of one of his sons, his widow, **Empress Chunqin**, will rule **Khitan Liao** until 947.

934 Minzong is succeeded by **Feidi**.

935 Feidi is overthrown by another Turkic warlord, who, as the **Emperor Gaozu**, establishes the **Later Jin dynasty**.

938 Led by **Chunqin**, a Khitan army seizes sixteen Chinese prefectures around **Yangzhou**, close to modern Beijing. In **Vietnam**, a rebellion led by **Ngo Quyen** ousts Chinese rule.

939 Attempting to regain **Vietnam**, a southern Chinese force is outwitted at the battle of **Bach Dang River** when

The Ten Kingdoms

The 'Ten Kingdoms' consisted of eight states in the south that broke away from imperial rule either in, or after, 907, and two 'barbarian' states in the north whose lands included Chinese territory. The first of the barbarian states was the **Khitan** kingdom, formalized as the **Liao dynastic empire** in 916. The second belonged to the **Tangut**, a Tibetan people who accrued a kingdom in modern Gansu, formalized as the **Xi Xia 'empire'** in 1038. The Song dynasty – although it reunified the empire from 960 onwards – was unable to reduce either. The eight kingdoms of the south, ruled by Chinese houses, were: **Wu** (907–937); **Nan Tang** (937–975); **Nan Ping** (907–963); **Chu** (927–951); **Former** (907–925) and **Later Shu** (934–965); **Min** (909–944); **Nan Han** (907–971); and **Wu-yue** (907–978), where 'Nan' simply means 'southern'. Those that were not absorbed by each other were absorbed, in due course, by the Song. The three most powerful were **Shu** (Sichuan); **Nan Tang** (Hunan); and **Wu-yue** (controlling the Yangzi delta and much of China's lower eastern coast).

stakes driven into the tidal riverbed impale the invading flotilla.

944 **Gaozu** is succeeded by **Chudi**, the second emperor of the Later Jin.

946 Under Chunqin's direction, five permanent capital cities are established in the **Khitan Liao** empire, and a Chinese form of administration adopted.

947 In a third Turkic coup, **Chudi** is overthrown by the founder of the **Later Han dynasty**, the **Emperor Gaozu**.

948 **Gaozu** is succeeded by his son **Yindi**.

951 **Yindi** is ousted by **Taizu**, founder emperor of the **Later Zhou dynasty**.

Footbinding

The exclusively Chinese practice of 'binding' a female's feet from the age of four or five – to produce a supposedly sexually attractive 'lily foot' – perhaps originated during the **Second Disunity**. Strips of wet cloth were wrapped around the child's feet. As these dried, the bone collapsed. One theory suggests **footbinding** was intended to produce lookalikes of slender dancers. But while it added an inch or two to a woman's height, its burden was social rather than aesthetic. Such women were unable to move quickly. Unfit for most types of employment, they became a 'chattel', the status symbol of their male 'owners'. Accordingly, footbinding spread through China's bourgeoisie from the 11th century onwards. Peasant women, however, were spared the ordeal, as were minorities. Not until the Republican Revolution of 1912 did footbinding become unfashionable; and it was only finally outlawed by the communist regime of 1949.

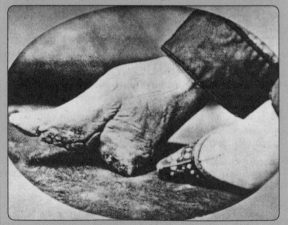

The final outcome of footbinding, hideous to the modern sensibility, but somehow attractive to the medieval Chinese male.

954 **Taizu** is succeeded by **Shizong**.

960 **Shizong**'s death causes panic among his commanders when it is realized that succession by his infant son will mean rule by an unwelcome dowager-empress. The throne is offered instead to a Chinese general, **Zhao Kuangyin**, founder of the pan-Chinese **Song Dynasty**.

The Khitan

Also known as the Khitai, from which derived 'Cathay', the medieval European name for China, the **Khitan** posed a persistent threat to the northern and northeastern frontiers. As a people, they have been characterized as proto-Mongol. They grazed horse and sheep, ate millet, smelted iron and lived in mobile tent cities. Related to the **Toba**, their chieftains convened every three years to elect an overall khan. The dominant Khitan clan, however, were the **Yelu**, and their leader, **Abaoji**, established a hereditary kingship from around 907. As his state expanded, so its raids on Chinese territory escalated, and by 940 it controlled sixteen prefectures inside the Great Wall. But while the Khitan also ruled over much greater areas of Manchuria and Mongolia, to rule their Chinese subjects they devised a historically significant 'dual-government' system. Steppe custom was maintained among Khitanese subjects, but Chinese institutions were adopted for those living in Chinese territory. In due course, the Khitan lost their military edge, and became vulnerable to the next group of nomadic invaders: the Jürchen.

5
The Song Dynasty
960–1279

The Song dynasty defused the destructive potential of aristocrats and hereditary commanders by ruling through a reinvigorated, expanded and well-rewarded central bureaucracy. At the outset of his reign, **Song Taizu** persuaded his rival generals to abandon their armies in the interests of national reconciliation. Simultaneously, he established an enlarged **Grand Council** of ministers and advisers whose decisions were arrived at, if not by voting, then at least by consensus. In a sense, China became a meritocratic oligarchy over which the emperor presided as chairman. It also became a great deal more middle-class. Under Song rule, the empire achieved an unprecedented **diffusion of wealth**. The capital, whether at Kaifeng or Hangzhou, was but one among many centres of trade participating in what has been called the first commercial revolution. The introduction of **paper money** backed by specie contributed to a credit environment in which commodities could be moved freely in bulk and over long distances to the likeliest markets.

As significant, was the innovation that made paper money possible: **printing**. The publication of texts new and old, with print-runs stretching to sometimes hundreds of thousands, meant that the administrative class was culturally homogenized. If, in the future, the printed word became a two-edged sword for governments, under the Song – as male literacy rates reached as high as ten percent – it served to unite, rather than fragment, the effective elements of society. Ideological conflict, as in the face-off between 'conservatives' and 'reformers' from the mid-11th century onwards, did not spill over outside the ranks of the governing class. Nor was it attended by violence.

While well-off families broke the taboos that separated public service from mercantile activity, they took pains to groom selected male offspring for success in the **imperial examinations**. But the same examinations – now based on an established canon of thirteen 'Confucian' texts – were, hypothetically at least, open to the people at large, through a system of provincial and prefectural schools and colleges. Rural clan associations and urban trades guilds could raise sufficient funds to enter their own candidates.

The society that emerged was scarcely egalitarian, but it was one of opportunity. In those parts of the countryside well-connected to the cities by roads and canals, farming families diversified their crops and manufactured **handicrafts**. The best and the brightest could hope to prosper, whatever their background. As such, the multiskilled civilization promoted by the Song was unrivalled anywhere on the planet in the pre-democratic era – an assessment borne out by its cultural and technological attainments. Several centuries before the European Renaissance, **Chinese painters** achieved a virtuosity that may still astonish. In **Zhu Xi**, the period sported a philosopher equal to the ancients. Su Song's celebrated **water-clock** of 1090 synthesized an array of advanced mechanical procedures. Famously, the age of the Song was also the age of the **magnetic compass**, and of **gunpowder**.

Militarily, however, the Song were weak. Theirs was a contracted empire, shorn of the horse-breeding pastures needed to repel the mounted cavalries of successive northern warrior peoples. First the **Khitan**, then the **Jürchen** marauded through the Yellow River plains. Similarly, in the northwest, the Song were unable to vanquish the emergent Tangut-Tibetan kingdom of **Xi Xia**. In 1127 – having for eighty years endeavoured to buy off their aggressors – the Song conceded defeat, withdrawing to a line south of the Huai River.

Half of China was forfeit. The **Southern Song**, as the surviving regime is called, continued the policies of their predecessors. While reunification remained a goal, trade and culture finally mattered more than arms. The Song dynasty blossomed anew. There was even a perceived advantage to the revised status quo. The Jürchen Jin conquest furnished a buffer against whatever else might spring from beyond the now dilapidated Great Wall. But what was not foretold was the awesome ferocity of a new breed of steppe warrior: the **Mongols**.

960 Zhao Kuangyin, founder of the Song Dynasty, begins a sixteen-year reign as the **Emperor Taizu**. At an extraordinary banquet, he persuades his rival generals to surrender their commands, offering them pensions and 'wives' from the ranks of his family. Members of the Northern Zhou dynastic family are pardoned. Taizu re-employs former officials, but away from their accustomed turf. All but three of the eight **southern kingdoms** are persuaded to renounce their independence. The **Confucian bureaucracy** is restored and extended, to become the mainspring of Song government. The regulatory **Board of Censors** is given wide powers to root out corruption. As the army is reformed, military governors are replaced by salaried civilians. **Kaifeng**, to the east of Loyang on the Yellow River, is chosen as a capital.

971 Military pressure brings the southern kingdom of **Nan Han** back into the imperial fold. The **Buddhist canon** –

a massive compilation of texts seminal to Chinese Buddhism – is printed.

973 Unwilling to jeopardize the empire by allowing the succession to pass to a minor, Taizu nominates his brother **Zhao Guangyi** as his heir.

975 The southern kingdom of **Nan Tang** surrenders to the Song. When its king asks to continue as a feudal vassal, Taizu responds: 'What crime has the land south of the river committed that it should remain apart from the empire?'

976 Zhao Guangyi accedes to the throne. An accomplished poet and calligrapher, **Emperor Taizong** continues to strengthen the bureaucracy by raising officials' salaries. The role of eunuchs, concubines and dowager-empresses is curbed by a new **palace code**.

Zhang Sixin – constructing a water-driven **mechanical clock** – invents the chain-drive, and substitutes mercury for water to prevent freezing in winter.

978 The southern kingdom of **Wu-yue** renounces its independence.

979 When the kingdom of **Northern Han** in Shanxi is defeated in battle, Taizong completes the process of reunification. His government sets about replacing debased coinages with a **standard currency** based on the traditional 'string' of 1000 copper 'cash'.

The emperor is less successful in a campaign against the **Khitan Liao** empire in the northwest. His army defeated, himself struck by an arrow, Taizong escapes in a cart.

982 The Tibetan-Tangut kingdom of **Xi Xia** consolidates its hold over the northwest.

983 The *Taiping yulan* – an imperially sponsored **universal encyclopedia** – is published under the aegis of its editor

Print

Few would contest that **printing** is China's greatest single contribution to world civilization. It came about slowly, however. In the sense that printing simply means repeatedly impressing a word or an image onto a permanent medium, then many ancient civilizations discovered the print principle through such artefacts as coins and seals. In China, however, the idea of printing whole texts was enabled by the invention of **paper** during the **Han dynasty**. While 'proto-paper' may have evolved as a clothing supplement, by the 2nd century AD, its quality was sufficient for scholars and officials to write on it. Even so, the oldest surviving example of a printed text is a Buddhist charm impressed on silk, circa 750. It was in the following century that printing in the conventional sense took off. Using ink and paper, Chinese students made rubbings of the Confucian classics incised in stone at the Imperial Academy from 833. The oldest surviving text to be properly printed on paper is the **'Diamond Sutra' scroll** of 868, recovered from the **Dunhuang Caves** in 1907 (see p.186).

Not only were Chinese characters carved into wood-blocks, but so, too, was a frontispiece illustration. Thereafter, printed books appear in ever greater profusion, creating an appetite for learning that underpinned government by an educated clerisy. It is to the Song dynasty also that we owe the invention of **moveable type**, by **Bi Sheng** in 1041. Introduced into Europe by Johann Gutenburg in 1458 – almost certainly as a result of diffused transmission from China – moveable type became the mainstay of mass-communication in the West and was only finally eclipsed as a dominant print technology by the advent of computerized typesetting in the 1980s. But whereas moveable type intrinsically suited phonetic alphabets, it was less suited to Chinese. A standard Chinese font consists of many thousands of individual characters. Although the computer screen has made compositing Chinese less physically cumbersome, print continues to fuel arguments against the retention of an ideographic script.

Li Fang. Printed by wood-block, it contains 1000 chapters giving information on 5000 subjects arranged in 55 categories.

986 After another Chinese army is heavily defeated, Taizong turns to diplomacy as his preferred solution to the Khitan problem.

995 Following a domestic feud between the senior males in Taizong's family, his third son **Zhao Dechang** becomes heir apparent. His eldest son is demoted to the status of a commoner.

998 Zhao Dechang accedes as the **Emperor Zhenzong**. To foster a sense of mystique around his throne, Zhenzong revives imperial sacrificial rites and colludes in the fabrication of prophetic documents conferring 'divine' approval on the Song dynasty. During his reign a new strain of rice allowing for a double harvest is introduced from Southeast Asia into the Yangzi region.

1004 When the **Khitan** launch a surprise attack on the Yellow River plains the court flees to Chengdu. Zhenzhong is able to regroup, and retakes Kaifeng. By the terms of a treaty concluded at Shunyuan, the emperor concedes parity between his own and the Liao Empire. Annual tribute paid to the Khitan is fixed at 100,000 ounces of silver and 200,000 rolls of silk. The economic burden of such payments represents only a fraction of otherwise necessary military expenditure, and is further alleviated by the Khitan's readiness to buy Chinese luxuries, stimulating economic growth.

1007 Faced by a shortage of copper coinage, merchants in Chengdu begin issuing **paper money** secured against its equivalent value in iron.

1009 Completion of the *Wenyuan yinghua*, a voluminous printed anthology of Chinese literature.

1020 The population of China reaches an estimated **100 million**, two-thirds of whom live below the Huai river.

1022 Zhenzhong is succeeded by his sixth son, the 13-year-old **Emperor Renzong**. Dowager-empress **Liu**, the third of Zhenzhong's five consorts, is appointed regent by the Council of State.

1024 Establishing a Bureau of Exchange Medium, the government takes over the printing of paper money in Chengdu. Although first limited to Sichuan, it will spread throughout China.

Paper Money

Paper money depended on two inventions which were also Chinese: paper itself, and printing. Although printed credit notes (called 'flying money') were used during the Tang period, **paper money proper** (ie promissory notes backed by metal reserves equivalent to the value of the notes issued) was a Song innovation. Because copper – heavy, and relatively low-valued – was the traditional exchange medium, larger transactions were cumbersome. To guard against forgery, notes were soon printed using three colours, later on six. Such notes were valid for three years. At the end of their term, they could be replaced, but only at a discount, so that from the beginning, paper money had a built-in inflationary mechanism. By 1126 the Song – running an economy up to ten times larger than the Tang – had issued notes worth 70 million 'strings' of copper cash. Whether these were consistently backed by adequate reserves is doubtful. The decision by the **Yuan dynasty** to use only paper currency was influenced by the short-term benefits of printing money. The idea caught on rapidly in the Far East however, Japan and Korea being among those nations to adopt it. But Europe had to wait until 1661, when the lead was taken by Sweden.

The Dunhuang Caves

Remote **Dunhuang**, sometimes known as the 'Jade Gate', occupied a vital pass at the lower end of the Gansu corridor connecting China to Central Asia. But as well as being a strategic commandery during the course of the first millennium, Dunhuang developed into a wealthy entrepôt and an important centre of Buddhist learning, attracting visitors from all directions. In 900 one in ten of its inhabitants were monks or nuns. Some followed the Mahayana school, others Tibetan and Tantric sects. Regularly, armies marched through Dunhuang, or fought outside its walls. Further away, and untroubled by conflict, were the **'Thousand Buddha Caves'**.

Around 1035 these shrines, cut into an imposing cliff, were abandoned, perhaps through fear of a Moslem invasion. But before this happened over **13,000 scrolls** were sealed behind a wall. In 1900, a local holy-man called **Wang** found this library. Seven years later, in return for four silver horse-shoes, he sold 7000 scrolls to the British archeologist **Sir Auriel Stein**. Thus was transacted one of the foremost finds relating not just to China, but to the region as a whole. While many of the scrolls were Buddhist sutras hitherto believed lost, and written in a diversity of languages, some had been inscribed on the backs of other documents, among them contracts and charters, giving a unique insight into social habits of the times. And if this were not enough, the icons and frescoes inside the caves had survived largely unscathed.

1028 Xi Xia is formalized as an autonomous empire with its own written language.

1033 On the death of the dowager-empress, **Renzong** assumes control of the court. He divorces his empress Guo in favour of Cao. While his forty-year reign will be remembered as a period of great commercial growth, Renzong's government takes care to fortify its northern cities against the Khitan and other raiders.

c.1035 At **Dunhuang**, on the edge of the Tarim Basin, a complex of Buddhist cave-shrines is abandoned.

1038 Xi Xia begins harassing the Chinese empire through the western passes.

A catalogue of the **Imperial Library**, listing 80,000 manuscripts and printed books, is completed.

1041 The invention of **moveable type** is credited to **Bi Sheng**. By being re useable, his clay-baked characters herald a revolution in printing that will spread worldwide.

1044 Xi Xia concludes peace terms with China. By conceding his vassal status its king is rewarded with an annual tribute of 130,00 rolls of silk, 50,000 ounces of silver and 280,000 ounces of tea. Learning of this, the Khitan renegotiate their tribute at 300,000 rolls of silk and 200,000 ounces of silver.

To guard against further extortion, the imperial army is expanded to 1.25 million men. The cost of this provides a sharp brake on Song economic growth, and engenders a lasting polarization of opinion within the bureaucracy. As taxes climb and smallholders are driven into debt, larger estates re-emerge. While '**reformers**' (aka 'classicists'), led by **Wang Anshi**, urge measures in favour of the lower classes, '**conservatives**' (aka 'historicists') adopt a *laissez-faire* line.

1054 A stellar explosion in Taurus, creating the **Crab Nebula**, is observed by astronomers in China and Japan, but nowhere else.

1055 The 67-metre-high earthquake-proof **Timber Pagoda** in Shanxi is erected by the Liao emperor Daozong as a memorial to his father. The oldest surviving wooden structure in China, it combines Khitanese with Chinese features.

1061 Ouyang Xiu's *Xin Tang shu* ('New History of the Tang'), covering the period 403–959, is completed.

1064 Renzong is succeeded by Zhao Shu, a grandson of Taizu. Too ill to govern, **Emperor Yingzong** hands over power to the Dowager-empress Cao, a favourite of the conservatives. As inflation weakens the economy, Xi Xia resumes hostilities.

1067 Yingzong is succeeded by his 19-year-old son, the **Emperor Shenzong**. To restrict the military uses of **gunpowder** to the imperial army Shenzong outlaws the sale of saltpetre and sulphur.

Wang Anshi 1021–1086

Wang Anshi was the leader of a radical faction that favoured root-and-branch solutions to underlying problems. Coming to power in 1068, he was staunchly supported by the Emperor Shenzong. Although dismissed in 1076, the throne upheld his policies for another fifteen years. Wang's **'New Laws'** were designed to make China's resources yield interlocking economic, social and military benefits. At the heart of government was a cumbersome **system of taxation** in kind. Each year, vast amounts of grain and silk were transported to the capital, at considerable cost to provincial administrations, only to be re-sold at below-market prices. The real burden, however, fell on the rural population.

As city-dwellers grew rich, the outlying peasantry remained poor, obliged not only to surrender a proportion of its produce, but also to perform corvee labour on 'public' projects, often during harvest-time. To purchase seed, farmers fell foul of moneylenders. In a law called the **'equalisation of loss'**, Wang set up an intraprovincial tax accountancy that allowed grain to move directly to the neediest areas, and for tax and corvee duties to be remitted in cash. His law of **'Young Shoots'**

1068 Shenzong retires the Dowager-empress Cao, and dismisses 'conservative' ministers. Wang Anshi is appointed chief councillor. While his radical measures to succour the poor are resented by the establishment, they bolster imperial revenues.

Entry into the civil service is reorganized on the basis of triennial **examinations** held at three levels: provincial, state and imperial. Unlike Wang's other reforms, this will endure as the definitive structure for bureaucratic recruitment.

1071 An imperial census reveals that **Changsha**, the centre of the copper industry, is China's most populous city.

provided farmers with low-interest state loans. State pawn shops were opened alongside those in the 'private' sector. Profits on non-essential goods were limited to twenty percent of their 'real' value, and the price of essential commodities was fixed.

Wang also took steps to strengthen the army. Collective household responsibility was revived, not only to control crime, but to furnish a quota of trained soldiers. Called **'tithing'**, the purpose of this was to replace the empire's dependence on mercenaries with an effective **national militia**. For these and other measures, Wang earned the hatred of the the conservatives. Led by **Sima Guang**, they slandered both his person and his policies, making it difficult to assess the latter's effectiveness. He has been held responsible, by some, for the Song's vulnerability to the Jürchen. For others, he was a socialist champion of the empire's oppressed. Wang himself, though, was probably more concerned with reinstating values prevalent during Han and even Qin times. Despite the Song's 'commercial revolution', China's backbone remained agrarian. A contented peasantry was the means, not the object, of imperial rule.

1076 Wang Anshi is relieved of his responsibilities after his arrogance incurs imperial displeasure. Other reforming officials remain in place.

1078 China produces an estimated 115,000 tonnes of **iron**, mainly from deposits in the east. In Kaifeng, thousands are employed in state-run foundries.

1084 **Sima Guang** (1019–1086), the leader of the **conservative faction**, completes his *Zichi tongjian* ('Comprehensive Mirror for Aid in Government'), based in part of the Ouyang Xiu's *Xin Tang shu* of 1061. Unlike Ouyang, he questions the assumptions underlying the writing of 'standard' dynastic histories. By reviewing rival interpretations of common events, he aims to discourage the imperial appetite for reforms whose outcomes may be similarly ambiguous.

> ❝ The conservatives criticised the new laws not because they were bad, but because they were new. The methods of the past, the way of the ancestors, were right simply because they were traditional. New policies were wrong because they did not conform to these ancient patterns. That is the burden of Sima Guang's frequent memorials of complaint. When he was asked whether, in fact, one of the New Laws was not operating well in Shaanxi province, he replied that although he was himself a native of that province he did not know how the laws worked, but that as the old laws had meant much hardship for the people, it was evident that the new laws must be still more oppressive. This was the mentality with which Wang Anshi had to contend. ❞
>
> C.P. Fitzgerald, *China: A Short Cultural History* (1935)

A reconstructed model of Su Song's elaborate water clock, perhaps the single most complex machine of its time.

Huizong 1082–1135

Unlike most modern rulers, many Chinese emperors took a close interest in the arts, as patrons and as sometimes accomplished practitioners. In both respects, **Huizong** outshone the rest. The academy he founded in 1104, the *Xuanhe hua pa*, attracted painters from across the empire. Alongside this, he expanded the imperial art collection, open to select members of the public, into a gallery that would stand comparison with any contemporary equivalent, and he commissioned perhaps the world's first **Encyclopedia of Art**, a catalogue of artists' works and their biographies stretching back to the 3rd century. In his own **paintings** – studies of exotic birds and plants, and vignettes from court life – he practised beautifully what he sought of others: that the eye should copy what it sees, with detailed realism, but also with an empathy for form and colour.

The same aesthetic informed his **calligraphy**. Known as 'slender gold', its chill elegance can affect even those who have no knowledge of the Chinese script. It was perhaps an expression of his despair with politics, and the seemingly endless quarrels between conservatives and reformists. Both parties must have wished he would take more interest in the empire. When the Jin seized Kaifeng, he abdicated, assuming the Daoist title 'Master of Learning and the Way'. But this could not prevent his capture. Bundled off to Manchuria as a political trophy, Huizong died in captivity nine years later.

1085 The throne passes to Shenzong's 9-year-old son, the **Emperor Zhezong**. Dowager-empress **Gao**, widow of Emperor Yingzong, and a supporter of the conservative faction, is appointed regent.

1086 Gao dismisses reformist officials and repeals Wang Anshi's New Laws. Sima Guang is appointed senior minister.

1090 Su Song builds a 30ft-high **clock tower** surmounted by an armillary ring at Kaifeng, the most advanced piece of

The astonishing delicacy of the emperor Huizong in his incarnation as an artist is here reflected in a composition known as Quarrelling Birds.

machinery in the world. Its water-powered mechanism keeps accurate measure not only of diurnal time, but also of the movements of known celestial bodies.

1093 Zhezong ousts conservative and reinstates reformist ministers following the death of Dowager-empress Gao.

1094 Zhezong's senior minister **Cai Jing** reimposes Wang Anshi's New Laws; but such is the prevailing conservatism of the provincial bureaucracy that restitution is only partially fulfilled.

1101 Dying childless, Zhezong is succeeded by Shenzong's eleventh son, the **Emperor Huizong**. A talented painter,

The Jürchen

Indigenous to the **Amur River** valley, the forest-dwelling **Jürchen** had by the early 12th century been resettled by their Khitan overlords on the Liaoning peninsula. Unlike the Khitan, they were hunter-farmers rather than pastoral nomads, and lived in fixed wooden dwellings. The dominant Jürchen clan were the **Wanyan**, and it was their leader, **Akuta**, who instigated the revolt of 1115 that led first to Jürchen independence, then to the conquest of northern China. According to legend, Akuta rebelled when the Liao emperor ordered him to dance before the Khitan throne. From the outset, the Jürchen were strongly disposed toward Chinese custom. Indeed, the Khitan had already distinguished between 'cooked' and 'uncooked' Jürchen – those who did and didn't 'live like the Chinese'. Despite some Jürchen cultural recidivism, the new **'Jin' dynasty** (aka 'Kin', or gold) adopted a fully Chinese-style administration, at least in its Chinese territories. Eventually overwhelmed by the Mongols, the Jürchen Jin bequeathed three legacies: a style of theatre that mixed prose and verse; Beijing as a capital city; and, through their distant descendants, the Manchu Qing dynasty.

poet and calligrapher, and a prodigious augmenter of the imperial art collections, Huizong is unsuited to rule an empire that, during the course of his reign, faces economic and military crises.

1104 Huizong establishes an **Academy of Painting** at Kaifeng, while personally instructing court artists in the 'correct' style of realist representation.

1115 As the Khitan Liao empire weakens, the minority **Jürchen** people revolt and, under the leadership of **Akuta**, establish their own **Jin** dynastic kingdom in eastern Liaoning.

1116 Akuta seizes control of the Liao River itself, the traditional Khitan homeland.

1120 The Jürchen and the Song form an alliance against the Khitan.

1123 With Chinese help, Akuta captures the Khitan's 'southern' capital **Yanjing** (modern **Beijing**) and its surrounding territory. He persuades many ethnic Chinese officials to serve under him by adopting the Khitan dual-government system. Later in the year he dies.

1125 Akuta's brother completes the Jürchen conquest of the Khitan empire. Many Khitan flee to Turkestan, to establish the **Western Liao empire**. There they are converted to **Nestorianism**, later giving rise to the legend of **Prester John**: the Christian king ordained by God to rid Eurasia of the Mongols.

In northern China, the Song-Jürchen alliance collapses as Huizong's ministers meddle in an internal Jürchen rebellion. The Jürchen attack Yellow River cities, including Kaifeng. Huizong abdicates in favour of his son, the emperor **Qinzong**, and temporarily abandons the capital. The Jürchen fail to gain a decisive victory, and the court returns to its capital.

Song Painting

If the Tang dynasty was the golden age of Chinese poetry, the **Song** is widely urged as the golden age of Chinese painting. In its favour are three circumstances: the bald fact that few

Detail from the Spring Festival scroll of Zhang Zeduan showing one of the gatehouses in the walls of Kaifeng city.

paintings survive from earlier periods; a perceived decline into mannered formalism among painters of subsequent eras; and the undisputed excellence of much Song work that has survived. Particularly in **Song landscapes** favouring wild mountains and deep gorges that dwarf human figures into inconsequentiality, Chinese pictorial art attains its quintessence. Rhythm, vitality and refined feeling are combined almost as a matter of course.

Of equal importance, is the presence of a **'conscious'** **brushwork**, the object as well as the means of expression. This belies the social provenance of the artists themselves. The 'writing brush', the *sine qua non* of Chinese calligraphy, was introduced probably at the end of the 3rd century BC. To move from brushing a word to brushing an object or a scene was, for a scholar-gentleman, a seamless progression. Virtually all Song artists known to us were members of the administrative class. Yet it would be wrong to characterize their work as a secular hobby. Not only was the emphasis on nature a symptom of a diffused Daoist sensibility, but a man of talent could turn professional.

There was a particular demand for **'scroll paintings'**: landscapes that unfurled horizontally, taking the viewer on a journey of discovery. Of these, two brilliant examples are extant. One, by **Xia Gui**, dating from the early 13th century, depicts the upper and middle reaches of the Yangzi. The earlier *Qingming* scroll of **Zhang Zeduan** is an exuberant celebration of city life. Over five metres long, the 'Spring Festival on the River' leads the viewer across a bridge on Kaifeng's outskirts to the very heart of a teeming metropolis. All of life is there, in its streets, its markets, its shops and its tea-houses, and the thousands of figures who fill these spaces. Like the contemporaneous Bayeaux Tapestry, such panoramas are historically illuminating. Unlike the Bayeaux Tapestry, they are not cartoons.

1126 The Jürchen renew their attacks on the northern plains. As **Kaifeng** falls, 3000 members of the imperial family (including Huizong and Qinzong) are captured, bringing to an end the retrospectively named **Northern Song Dynasty**. Over 6000 paintings in the imperial art collection are destroyed. Those courtiers and officials who can flee southwards, joining an exodus perhaps numbering millions. The Jürchen Jin, however, retain **Yanjing** as their capital.

1127 Having escaped Kaifeng, **Zhou Gao** – Huizong's peculiarly able ninth son – proclaims himself Emperor in the Yangzi delta, thus founding the **Southern Song Dynasty**. As the **Emperor Gaozong**, he makes rebuilding the army his priority, despite some southern landowners' unwillingness to contribute taxes. For eight years, Gaozong is harried by Jin forces, but he uses the Yangzi's network of canals and waterways to outmanoeuvre his pursuers.

1129 Hangzhou and Ningbo are sacked by Jin forces.

1135 The death of the second Jin emperor impedes the campaign against Gaozong, who establishes his capital at **Hangzhou**.

1141 A treaty between the Jin and Song courts asserts the vassal status of the latter. Gaozong agrees to pay an annual tribute of 250,000 ounces of silver and 250,00 rolls of silk. With peace thus secured, Gaozong concentrates on rebuilding his state along the same lines as the Northern Song. He takes personal command of the bureaucracy, scrutinizing local as well as central appointments. New academies are opened, each containing shrines to **Confucius** and other sage masters. Amongst Gaozong's ministers, however, a rift develops between those wishing to reconquer the north, and those who accept the status quo.

1147 In the face of incursions by a new tribal grouping, the **Mongols**, the Jürchen withdraw from their ancestral homelands along the Amur River in the far northeast.

1150 Seizing power over the Jin empire, the **Prince of Hailing** instals a broadly 'Chinese' system of government in the north.

1153 In Hangzhou, the war party among Gaozong's officials is encouraged by a revival of Khitan strength. As the

Maritime China

After 1126 the Song empire may have been territorially reduced, but it continued to thrive commercially, due largely to its **maritime enterprise**. As the southern ports expanded, so too did China's **merchant navy**. While Chinese shipbuilders learned much from Arab and other visiting seafarers, it was their own accrued skills that gave their junks an edge on the high seas. Not only were they the largest vessels afloat – able to carry up to 600 tonnes of merchandise – but they were amongst the most efficient, incorporating several Chinese innovations.

The naturally magnetic loadstone had been known to geomancers from around the 4th century BC, but from the 10th century AD the first steel-needle **magnetic compasses** were made – an invaluable navigational aid away from sight of land. Junks were also fitted with stern-rudders, and their hulls divided into watertight compartments – both inventions harking back to the Later Han. But perhaps the greatest advantages of the junk were above-deck. The Chinese were the first to build **multi-masted ships**. From the 2nd century they had grasped the principle of fore-and-aft rigs deployed in conjunction with lug-sails. Moreover, because the sails were fastened to strong bamboo battens, they were easily raised and lowered, enhancing a vessel's manoeuvrability before most winds. Even inland, shipping was progressive. The Song Chinese knew how to build paddle-boats capable of transporting 800 men.

Western Liao pressurize Jin on China's northern frontiers, skirmishing between Song and Jin forces commences.

1161 A Song army, under the command of Yue Fei, advances to the Huai River, recapturing some territories. Whilst the Prince of Hailing is campaigning, a cousin seizes the Jin throne. The Prince is murdered, and the new Jin emperor, **Shizong**, concludes a treaty with the Song. Shizong attempts to restore Jürchen custom among his people, but with limited effect. Even his son declines to learn the Jürchen language.

1162 Song Gaozong abdicates in favour of his adopted son Zhao Bozong, a descendant of the Northern Song emperor Taizu. At the **Battle of Caishi**, the Jin are heavily defeated by Yue Fei, and the Huai River becomes the effective frontier between the two empires. But when – against the new emperor **Xiaozong**'s orders – Yue Fei continues fighting, he is recalled to Hangzhou and executed.

During **Xiaozong**'s reign, the diminished Song empire recovers its prosperity and Hangzhou surpasses Kaifeng as a centre of wealth. Denied the northern trading routes, Chinese merchants develop seaborne trade with Japan, Korea, Southeast Asia, Malabar and the Persian Gulf.

1178 In the south, **Zhu Xi** establishes the 'School of the Way', a private academy dedicated to **neo-Confucian** and anti-pacifist principles. 'Filial piety', according to Zhu, implies a duty to reconquer territories lost to the Jin.

1187 The former emperor Gaozong dies after a 25-year retirement among concubines and artists.

1189 Import and export duties provide Xiaozong's government with revenues amounting to 65,000,000 strings of cash.

In the north, Jin Shizong is succeeded by his grandson the **Emperor Zhangzhong**, who restores Chinese custom.

Zhu Xi: Neo-Confucian Master (1130–1200)

Wary of the harm caused by aristocrats and eunuchs, the Song depended on the bureaucracy more than any previous dynasty. Because the tradition of the bureaucracy was Confucian, it follows that the Song polity too was Confucian in its dominant complexion. The **Confucianism** that emerged, however, was different from the Confucianism of Confucius. From the 11th century, scholars strove to transform a body of disparate archaic writings into a consistent world view. The lasting synthesis was achieved by **Zhu Xi**.

Although by the mid-12th century there were thirteen prescribed classics, Zhu focused on just four of them: the *Analects*; **Mencius**; the *Daxue* (**'Classic of Filial Piety'**); and the *Zhongyang* ('Doctrine of the Mean'), itself a synthesis of various compendia of *li* ('laws'). In his *Commentaries* of 1189 he retained some aspects of Confucian teaching, but abandoned others, replacing ancient rites and supernatural forces with an abstract moral standard he called the 'Supreme Ultimate'. Following Mencius, Zhu held that human nature is innately good, while allowing man's goodness may become obscured like 'a pearl dropped in muddy water'. To preserve his virtue, man must follow the 'golden mean'. He should neither succumb to myriad temptations of the flesh, nor pursue a subjective path of self-restraint of the sort recommended by some Buddhist sects.

But while Buddhism is disparaged, Zhu's philosophy is more syncretic than his polemics suggest. He allows *yin-yang* and the 'Five Elements' as mechanisms through which the Supreme Ultimate manifests itself, and Daoism proposes that the study of nature (*ge wu*) is fundamental to an understanding of humanity. Vilified during his lifetime because of his sympathy for the policies of Wang Anshi, Zhu was a 'sleeping dragon' who achieved only minor office. But posthumously, his interpretation of Confucius became the prevailing orthodoxy until the 18th century and beyond.

1190 Song Xiaozong abdicates in favour of his son, the **Emperor Guangzong**, but continues to guide, and sometimes meddle in, the affairs of state.

1192 Guangzong's empress Li proposes that their second son **Zhou Kuo** be made heir apparent. To Guangzong's chagrin, this is opposed by Xiaozong. As father and son quarrel, the court is factionalized.

1194 Zhou Kuo and his grandfather are reconciled on the latter's deathbed. In the north, the **Yellow River** alters course, exiting into the sea south of the Shandong peninsula. Flooding continues for thirty years, crippling the Jin economy.

1195 As senior minister Zhao Ruyu and the Dowager-empress Wu press for Zhou Kuo's succession, Guangzong abdicates on the grounds of ill health. As the amiable, but weak-minded, **Emperor Ningzong**, Zhou is perennially vulnerable to female influence. Early in his reign, his first empress **Han**, backed by the 'war' party, persuades him to disgrace Zhao Ruyu and appoint her militarist brother **Han Tuozhuo** senior minister. Hostilities against Jin resume.

1200 The **Mongol** leader Ong Khan – imposing his authority on a spread of nomadic tribes, including the Turkic Tartars – begins forging an army capable of long-range and lucrative raids. But although the Jin are discomfited, Han Tuozhuo fails to win back further territories for the Song.

1206 At the "tent city" Karakoram, Ong Khan is displaced as leader of the Mongols by Temujin, always known by his Persian name **Genghis Khan** ('Universal King'). Establishing the Great Khanate, and subjugating Tibet and the kingdoms of the Tarim Basin, Genghis embarks on a series of conquests that will outstrip the exploits of Alexander the Great.

1207 Song Ninzong is persuaded by his concubine **Yang** to execute Han Tuozhuo, on the grounds of his fruitless campaigns against the Jin. His lacquered head is sent as atonement to the Jin court.

Ningzong divorces Han's sister, and Yang becomes empress. Yang's brother **Yang Zishan** is appointed senior minister, alongside the chancellor Shi Miyuan. Empress Yang's greater ambitions, however, will be thwarted by the early deaths of her male offspring.

1209 Genghis Khan conquers the **Uighur** nation.

1210 Having destroyed a Jin army of 70,000, the Mongol horde sacks **Yanjing**, massacring its inhabitants.

1211 Jin, itself now driven south, re-establishes its government at Kaifeng.

1213 Genghis ravages China's northern plains until Jin agrees to buy him off with silk and gold.

1214 The Song, apprehending Jin's plight, withhold their annual tribute, weakening Jin's capacity to resist Genghis.

1215 Genghis treats northern China to a second display of wanton carnage and seizure. Shortly, however, he turns his attentions westwards, and for a decade China is spared further onslaught.

1223 Genghis returns to Karakoram, where he is beguiled by a Daoist sage, Chang Chun. Daoist monks within Genghis's territories are exempted from taxation.

1224 Genghis campaigns against **Xi Xia**.

1225 After Shi Miyuan fabricates an edict deposing the emperor's chosen heir Zhao Hong, Ninzong is succeeded by a descendant of Song Taizu, Zhao Yuju, the **Emperor Lizong**. Despite the proliferation of governmental regulations, the southern empire continues to prosper.

1226 Genghis overruns Xi Xia, which ceases to exist as a state. Such is the destruction perpetrated that the once prosperous northwestern region of China is permanently blighted. Wounded, Genghis is dissuaded from pursuing a similar strategy against Jin by his Khitanese adviser **Yelu Chucai**, who argues that a preservationist policy will yield greater returns. Yelu also encourages Genghis to create a civilian administration with a Central Secretariat, headed by Yelu himself.

1227 Genghis Khan dies and his territories are divided amongst his four sons.

Following the death of his conservative chancellor Shi Miyuan, Song Lizong posthumously elevates the neo-Confucian philosopher Zhu Xi to the rank of Duke.

> **“** My descendants will dress in gold and eat the finest meats and ride the finest horses and possess the finest women. But they will forget the man who gave them all these things. **”**
>
> Genghis Khan on his death bed

1229 Ogedai, asserting supremacy over his brothers, is elected **Great Khan** of the Mongols by a council of tribal chieftains. Although Ogedai retains Yelu Chucai's services, he displays scant aptitude for civil affairs. Rather, Ogedai resumes Genghis's campaigns of pillage and conquest.

The Jin emperor urges Lizong to form an anti-Mongol alliance, declaring 'We are to you as the lips are to the teeth; when the lips are gone the teeth will feel the cold.'

1232 Lizong enters an alliance with the Mongols against the Jin, supplying infantry to fight alongside the nomads' cavalry. In a combined military operation, Kaifeng is besieged and sacked. But heeding Yelu Chucai's advice, Ogedai spares its inhabitants.

> Among the weapons of the defenders was the heaven-shaking thunder-crash bomb. This consisted of gunpowder packed into an iron vessel. When the fuse was ignited and the projectile fired a thunderous explosion ensued which could be heard thirty miles away. All the surrounding vegetation was burned, and armour pierced by shrapnel. To protect themselves from Jin soldiers firing down on them the Mongols covered themselves and their trenches with cowhides, and dug fox-holes. So the Jin began lowering their bombs by iron chains, and detonating them when they reached the ground. As a result men and cowhides alike were blown to pieces, no trace of them remaining.

from the *Jin shu* (dynastic history of the Jin),
describing the siege of Kaifeng in 1232

1234 As Jin is subsumed within the Mongol empire, the last Jin emperor commits suicide. Immediately, Ogedai begins preparing for the conquest of his Song 'allies'. Instead of driving south, however, he campaigns in Vietnam, Yunnan and Sichuan from bases in Tibet. Resistance offered by the Vietnamese and the Yunnanese kingdom of Dali, as well as Ogedai's decision to campaign in Europe, earn the Song respite.

1237 Zhu Xi's writings are incorporated among the prescribed texts of the imperial examinations. He and other neo-Confucians are deified as sages in shrines throughout southern China.

1242 Ogedai's death, probably from alcohol poisoning, causes a dramatic suspension of Mongol aggression, which has now spread to Poland and Hungary. As Mongol chieftains debate the succession, their armies are withdrawn from all theatres of war.

Gunpowder

Gunpowder was the product of a centuries-long quest for the elixir of life. Among the substances Daoist alchemists experimented with were **saltpetre** (potassium nitrate, aka 'Chinese snow') and **sulphur**, which they had learned to purify. What they didn't know was that saltpetre releases oxygen when ignited, providing a fast-breeding incubator for any other combustible contained with it. The two were first mixed for military purposes in the 10th century, to make a slow fuse for a 'flame-thrower' using 'Greek Fire' (a prototype of napalm). It was then discovered that by increasing the proportion of saltpetre in an enclosed container, a far more potent admixture was achieved. From these humble beginnings the face of war was forever changed. During the 11th century, the Chinese rapidly developed a new arsenal of weapons: bombs, grenades, exploding arrows, rockets and mines; and a little later cannons and mortars. By 1040, when the first recipe for gunpowder was printed, it had become standard issue to Chinese artillerymen. In the 13th century **fireworks** were created, but so too was the first **handgun** (dating from 1288). In the same century, knowledge of gunpowder reached Europe. Its first recorded use in a Western battle was at Crecy, by the English against the French in 1346.

1245 In the wake of the Mongol invasions, the Franciscan friar **John Plano de Carpini** sets out on a two-year mission to China sponsored by Pope Innocent IV, but progresses no further than Karakoram.

1251 Genghis's grandson **Mongke** is elected Great Khan. Under his rule, the Mongols once again pursue war in all directions.

1253 The Mongol assault on China's southwestern frontiers is resumed in a six-year campaign under the leadership of Mongke's brother **Kublai**.

1254 William of Rubruck, an emissary of the French king Louis IX, is received on Christmas Day by Mongke at Karakoram. His reports tell of several Europeans employed by the Great Khan, as well as Syrian Nestorians.

1257 In Vietnam, the Mongols occupy the area surrounding Hanoi.

1259 The death of Mongke again leads to the fourfold, and this time permanent, division of the Mongol empire amongst his heirs. In the west the khanates of Chagatai, Ilkhan and the Golden Horde are established.

1260 Kublai becomes leader of the **eastern Mongols**, simultaneously proclaiming himself Great Khan. The master of northern China, among other territories, he moves his capital southwards from Karakoram to **Shangdu** ('Xanadu'), and imposes colonial rule through a Central Secretariat. Although his military remains strongly Mongol, Kublai appoints many western Asians, among them Persians, Arabs and some Muscovites, to senior administrative posts, preferring such 'foreigners' to either his own kind or native Chinese.

In **religion** he is strongly influenced by the Tibetan lama 'Phags-pa, a relative of the leaders of the new 'Yellow Robe' sect whose patriarchs will establish a succession of Dalai Lamas as the temporal, as well as spiritual rulers, of Tibet itself. 'Phags-pa is given temporal authority over Tibet, as well as spiritual authority over all Buddhists within Kublai's domains. Buddhist monks are granted exemption from taxes and corvee labour.

In Constantinople, the Venetian merchants Niccolo and Maffeo Polo set out on the first of two journeys to China.

1265 Song Lizong is succeeded by his nephew, the **Emperor Duzong**. Despite a strict Confucian upbringing, Duzong proves an effete and impractical ruler inclined to leave government to his ministers during a time of burgeoning crisis wrought principally by mounting Mongol pressure.

Kublai's capture of a Song fleet marks the beginning of an effective Mongol navy. To meet this challenge, taxes are raised to levels that generate social discontent.

1266 Kublai appoints Moslem architects to construct the strongly fortified **'Tartar City'** at **Beijing**, known variously under Mongol rule as Khanbalik and Dadu; but although the buildings include an imposing palace, Mongol princes continue to sleep in their traditional *yurts* (felt tents).

The Persian astronomer **Jamal al-Din** is persuaded by Kublai to reside at Khanbalik and reform the Chinese calender.

Needham's List: Chinese Science

Printing, gunpowder and the magnetic compass have long been acknowledged Chinese innovations. The true scope of Chinese ingenuity, however, only emerged with the pioneering research of the English embryologist **Dr Joseph Needham**. In 1946 Needham began his thirteen-volume *Science and Civilisation in China* – a forceful corrective to Western technological suprematism. In field after field, Needham showed that the Chinese once led the world. Their inventions and discoveries included: the iron ploughshare (6th century BC), sunspots, cast iron, the double-action piston, the kite (4th century BC), the collar-harness (3rd century BC), the rotary winnowing-fan, the seed drill, steel, circulation of the blood, the parachute, endocrinology (2nd century BC), the armillary ring, deep drilling for salt and gas, the belt-drive, the wheelbarrow, the sliding callipers, decimal fractions (1st century BC), the square-pallet chain pump, the suspension bridge, the stern rudder (1st century AD), the seismograph, tear gas (2nd century), the fishing reel, the metal stirrup, porcelain (3rd century), the umbrella, chess (4th century), the paddle boat (5th century), solar wind (6th century),

1267 Kublai moves his capital to Beijing. Shangdu, however, is retained as his summer capital, to which his entire court is obliged to make an annual six-week trek.

1268 Now in possession of four fleets, Kublai blockades Song ports on the Han, Yangzi and Pearl Rivers. The city of **Xiangyang**, regarded as the 'gateway' to southern China, falls to Mongol forces after a lengthy siege.

1270 Kublai proclaims a new dynasty, the **Yuan** (meaning 'origin'), and himself the 'Emperor of China'.

In Shanxi, **Guo Shoujing** (1231–1314) constructs a bronze 'Simplified Instrument', an advanced armillary sphere with a perfect central ring measuring 6ft in diameter. Encouraged by Kublai, Guo builds some 27 astronomical

the segmental bridge (7th century), the mechanical clock (8th century), playing cards (9th century), immunology and phosphorescent paint (10th century).

Inevitably, some of Needham's conclusions have been challenged in their detail, but his thesis that China was materially creative in a way no other nation was until the Industrial Revolution stands. Such creativity also happened irrespective of prevailing political circumstance. But Needham's work raises important questions. Why did Chinese science level out after the Song dynasty, the high point of Chinese material culture? And why did the Chinese not progress to discover modern science? The usual answer is that Chinese technology largely evolved among Doaist experimenters away from the centre of power, and hence resources; and that the neo-Confucian orthodoxy set in place by the Song inhibited further development. This, however, neglects the character of Western experimentation from Copernicus onwards. If modern science is grounded in the formulation and application of mathematical axioms, it was the non-Euclidean character of Chinese science that inhibited the 'break through'.

towers, the world's first network of observatories.

1273 A Song fleet is destroyed at **Jiaoshan** on the Yellow River by mixed Mongol land and naval forces.

1274 Duzong's death at the age of 34 leads to the accession of his 4-year-old son, the **Emperor Gongzong**. The **Dowager-empress Xie**, widow of the emperor Lizong, is appointed regent.

In the north, Kublai Khan makes his first attempt to conquer **Japan**, but his fleet is driven back by storms.

1275 According to his *Travels*, **Marco Polo** enters northern China in company of his father Niccolo to begin a sixteen-year sojourn.

1276 Following crushing victories in the Yangzi delta, the Mongol general **Bayan** attacks and enters **Hangzhou**. The Song court, including Gongzong, is taken prisoner and dispatched to Shangdu. Two of Gongzong's younger half-brothers, however, are secreted in Fuzhou. The elder, the 8-year-old **Zhao Shi**, is declared Emperor (**Duanzong**), but is forced to flee further south to Guangzhou.

1278 Roger Bacon's manuscript *Opus Maius* contains the earliest surviving reference to gunpowder in a Western source. Many of his ideas are from Chinese science, by way of Moslem and other Middle Eastern alchemists.

1279 As the Mongols capture Guangzhou, the remnant Song court puts to sea. Duanzong nearly drowns in a storm and he dies a few weeks later. His half-brother Zhao Bing is made Emperor, shortly before the climactic **Battle of Yaishan** in the estuary of the Pearl River. After hundreds of Song ships are sunk or captured, the **Emperor Bingdi**'s stripling body is found washed ashore. The Dowager-empress **Yang** escapes, but now learning the fate of her son Duanzong, throws herself into the South China Sea, to become later venerated as its goddess.

6
The Yuan (Mongol) Dynasty
1279–1368

In 1259 the **Mongol empire** stretched from Moscow to the Indus, from the Mediterranean to the Sea of Japan. The whole of central Asia, and more, belonged to the Great Khan **Mongke**. But Mongke's death in the same year marked the beginning of a hesitation in Mongol expansionism. Although Kublai Khan added the Southern Song empire to the catalogue of Mongol conquests, Mongke's division of the Mongol empire among four heirs set in motion discrete and eventually competing histories. Above the Black and Caspian seas was the Khanate of the **Golden Horde**; below, the **Ilkhanate**. Centred on the Hindu Kush was the Khanate of **Chagatai**. Even so, the 'eastern' domains that fell to Kublai were vast. They included – as well as northern China – **Mongolia**, **Manchuria** and, more tenuously, **Tibet**.

Ironically, modern China's claims over Tibet, a sparsely populated country of high plateaux and yet higher mountains, date from its own conquest by an alien people. But although the **Yuan dynasty** – from its inception in 1270 to its final defeat by the Ming in 1368 – lasted less than a century, and never lost the character of a military occupation, it left an abiding impression, and not just upon China's own territorial ambitions. The simple fact of Mongol rule over the whole of the steppe corridor revived the **Silk Roads**. Samarkand emerged as a major entrepôt in a trans-Eurasian trading system. Through it and similar dusty cities, notably

Bokhara, came a steady trickle of Europeans, among them several Franciscan emissaries and, perhaps, **Marco Polo**. Others, whose names are lost, served Genghis Khan's eastern successors as specialist craftsmen.

This perhaps was the true beginning of China's eventual and calamitous exposure to Western powers. It was at this time that the legend of **'fabulous Cathay'** – soon to propel Columbus and Magellan across the oceans – took hold. Ironically, without the magnetic compass and stern rudder (both Chinese inventions) European shipping would have remained confined to European waters. There would have been no United States. But the Mongols were not just mid-wives to the dissemination of Chinese culture. They added to the Chinese landscape. While the most visible expression of their endeavours is Beijing's **'Tartar City'**, their reorganization of the empire into larger administrative units prefigured today's provinces. They extended the Grand Canal, and built a network of straight highroads that outmatched anything accomplished by the Han or Tang.

The Yuan dynasty also imposed crippling taxes: equivalent perhaps to forty percent of China's Gross National Product. And they gave little in return. Because of a natural bias among Chinese historians against any kind of foreign usurpation, the health of Chinese society under Mongol rule remains unclear. On the one hand, it extended religious tolerance. In Gansu, especially, **Islam** bedded down. Chinese **'blue-and-white' ceramics** came into being, and **Chinese theatre** was born. On the other, the Yuan failed to enlist the enthusiasm of the scholar-gentry class. Overall, China's population declined by perhaps a third. How large a part plague, tuberculosis and famine played in this shrinkage has become contentious, as has the extent to which Chinese households evaded registration. Nonetheless, as the political narrative insists, the Yuan were never popular. Once their formidable

A Yuan dynasty 'blue-and-white' porcelain dish decorated with a continuous peony encircling lotus plants.

military energy was dissipated in a quagmire of despotic luxury and unwanted administrative responsibility, the Mongols' game was up. Losing touch with their warrior rationale, they succumbed to the subtler resilience of what was still the world's premier civilization.

1279 Assuming power over the whole of China, **Kublai Khan** (aka the Emperor Shizu) suspends imperial examinations and places government under his own and his military commanders' supervision. To the dismay of Chinese scholars, some **Moslems** are appointed to key civilian posts. Further, Kublai classifies his subjects into four categories of descending worth: Mongols; such 'helpful foreigners' as Persians and Moslem Arabs; 'northern' Chinese, including remnants of the Jin, Khitan and Tangut peoples; and 'southern Chinese', ie the former subjects of the Song empire. Confucian temples, however, are allowed to remain open, scholars are exempted from taxation, and some Confucian rites are performed at Kublai's court.

Denied the opportunity of attaining high position under **Yuan** rule, the scholar–gentry increasingly turn to estate management and the practice of medicine.

The **Grand Canal** is extended, connecting **Khanbalik** (Beijing) itself to Hangzhou.

1281 Kublai's favourite consort **Queen Chabi** dies. To allay his grief, Kublai attempts a second invasion of **Japan**, but again his fleet is defeated by storms. His armies are more successful in the southwest, where Mongol suzerainty over **Vietnam** is imposed.

1285 Following the death of Kublai's eldest son by Chabi, Kublai's personality becomes progressively morose.

1287 The Franciscan friar **John of Montecorvino** – sent to China by Pope Nicholas IV, partly with an eye to converting Nestorians to Catholicism – is received by Kublai, and is permitted to stay until his death in 1328.

The Mongols

"To conquer one's enemy is the supreme pleasure," said Genghis Khan: "to pursue him, to seize his property, to watch his family weep, to ride his horses, and to enjoy his wives and daughters." In the 13th century, a small nomadic people from the upper tributaries of the **Amur River** caused havoc throughout Eurasia, threatening civilization everywhere with destruction. How this came about puzzles historians. Archeologists have established that a lowering of temperatures by three or four degrees so disturbed the pastures of nomadic herders that a migration of some or other sort was inevitable. But this scarcely explains the peculiarly virulent form it took.

Conventionally, it is asserted that the **Mongols**, armed with scimitars and bows made of yak-horn and bamboo, had exceptional skills in group horsemanship, honed by long centuries of hunting and fighting in close-knit packs. But that must also have been true of other steppe peoples, for example the Tartars (with whom the Mongols are often confused). What seems to have happened is that the Mongol leadership, but especially **Genghis Khan**, realized the military potential of a widely diffused, but common steppe culture at a time of increased hardship. Classically, Genghis reorganized ad hoc defensive formations into offensive cohorts based, like the Roman legions, on tens, hundreds and thousands. Critically, he replaced clan loyalty by loyalty to the horde itself, at the officer level. Through these means, he overcame his neighbours, then bonded them into an invincible army with a shared ethos of pillage and plunder.

All men were raised as warriors. Any other occupation was deemed demeaning. The fruits of more-productive societies were theirs for the taking. In their conquest of China, they speedily adapted to **naval warfare** and the use of **gunpowder**. The modern artillery regiment is essentially a Mongol sophistication. But what the Mongols lacked was political cohesion. Too much depended on the prowess of their leaders. Upon their death, power was dissipated by internecine feuds; and they were unable to govern any large territory without the civilian skills of others.

Kublai Khan 1215–1294

The master of northern China from 1260, and of the whole of China from 1279, **Kublai Khan** was the product of a mixed inheritance. From his grandfather Genghis, his father Tolui, and his eldest brother Mongke he derived a typically Mongol thirst for military adventure – 'ancestral voices prophesying war', in Coleridge's phrase. From his Nestorian mother, however, – the talented **Sorghaghtani Beki** – he acquired a more rounded attitude toward the exigencies of power. Into her third and favourite son, whom she raised on Chinese soil, Sorghaghtani inculcated a respect for learning, religious toleration and Yelu Chucai's advocacy that China would yield greater returns if left intact.

Accordingly, having won the eastern domains of a partitioned Mongol empire after a bloody contest with his younger brother Ariq Boke, Kublai repaired some at least of the damage inflicted by his predecessors on the Yellow River plains. **Queen Chabi**, too, broadened Kublai's mind, introducing him to the intricacies of Tibetan Buddhism as personified by the lama **'Phags-pa**, and reconciling his steppe instincts to the functional necessity of a settled peasantry.

But there were limits to Kublai's impressionability. As well as southern China, Kublai coveted Vietnam, Burma and Japan. Having taken the Song empire, rather than use native Chinese administrators, he imposed a colonial regime sustained by the imported skills of, amongst others, Persians, Turks and Moslem Arabs entirely dependent on his patronage. There was, therefore, a hollowness to the cosmopolitanism he seemingly espoused. And by 1279, Kublai was already well passed his prime. Although he survived into his eightieth year, gout became his only steadfast companion. His feet clad in slippers of cured Korean fish-skin, he could no more than spectate the great hunts in which, as a youth, he'd shone, from the vantage of a litter kept aloft by four great elephants.

An idealized portrait of Kublai Khan, the Mongol warlord who became a famous Chinese emperor.

1289 The Mongol conquest of **Vietnam** is dashed at the Second Battle of Bach Dang River, where Vietnamese forces employ tactics identical to those of 939 against a Mongol fleet.

1290 A census conducted by the Central Secretariat indicates the **population** of China has fallen back to **60 million**. However, a disinclination by many Chinese to register their households, and non-compliance by some provincial officials, suggests a figure around 80 million is more accurate.

1292 A Mongol fleet reaches **Java**, but no conquest is attempted.

1294 Following his death, probably as a result of extreme obesity, Kublai's body is carried back to the Mongolian steppes where it is buried in an unmarked grave. He is succeeded by his grandson **Temur Oljeitu** (aka Chenzong), who continues Kublai's style of strong, but conciliatory, government over the Chinese.

As more members of the Mongol imperial household adopt Chinese custom, a rift develops between the Sinicized and non-Sinicized courtiers.

1295 The conversion of the western Mongol **Ilkhanate** to **Islam** profoundly alters the religious and ideological geography of central Asia. The eastern Mongols, however, remain eclectic in their faith, combining native shamanism with Tibetan Buddhism, Daoism and other beliefs.

c.1300 An estimated half-million Chinese are enrolled in **Buddhist monasteries**, the majority to take advantage of tax exemptions granted Buddhist monks by the Yuan dynasty. In southern China, especially, Buddhist institutions help preserve Chinese learning and culture. The Mongol occupation also stimulates the activities of early **secret societies**, among them the White Lotus Sect.

1307 The death of **Temur Oljeitu** sparks a succession crisis, contested principally among his nephews.

1308 Khaishan (aka Wuzong), brought up as a warrior leader outside China, becomes the third Yuan emperor. During his brief reign, government is made to suffer on account of his extreme impulses. Butchers are appointed ministers, and the amount of paper money in circulation is tripled.

1311 Khaishan is succeeded by his brother **Ayurbarwada** (aka Renzong). Educated by Chinese scholars, he dismisses Khaishan's ministers and reverses his policies.

1313 In a bid to win the support of the scholar-gentry, Ayurbarwada restores **imperial examinations**, although native Chinese are still barred from high office.

Wang Zhen – having crafted his own moveable type, containing 60,000 characters – publishes the *Nong Shu* ('Book of Agriculture'), an illustrated digest of Chinese farming techniques drawn from sources dating back 1000 years and more.

In the west, the Khanate of the **Golden Horde** converts to **Islam**.

1315 The promised imperial examinations are held. While knowledge of the neo-Confucian commentaries is made mandatory, non-Chinese candidates are offered a greatly simplified syllabus. Of the 300 degrees awarded, less than half are conferred on Chinese subjects.

1321 Ayurbarwada is succeeded by his eldest son **Shidebala** (aka Yingzong). Aged 18, Shidebala is no match for his grandmother, the dowager-empress Targi. With the chief minister Temudur, she campaigns tirelessly against the "Chinese" faction.

1322 When Temudur dies, the Chinese faction, rallying around the Chinese-educated emperor, succeed in overturning his appointees. Moslems are persecuted.

1323 Shidebala is assassinated by a group of Mongol princes whose stipends he has reduced. The steppe warrior **Yesun**

Marco Polo 1254–1324

A great traveller, or an even greater imposter? The man who for centuries was famed for having single-handedly 'discovered' China has of late come in for serious debunking. Some experts doubt whether **Marco Polo** even set foot in 'fabulous Cathay'. The son of a Venetian merchant who had already journeyed at least as far as Karakoram, by his own account, given in his *Travels*, Marco spent seventeen years in the service of **Kublai Khan**. Improbably, he tells us that he was present at the siege of Xiangyang in 1275 – two years before he set out from Europe – and that he was for a while Governor of Yangzhou – an appointment unnoticed by Chinese annals. He also fails to observe such obvious Chinese phenomena as the Great Wall, printing, foot-binding or tea.

Conversely, the *Travels* are brimful with details which, at the time, can only have been gathered first-hand. Polo describes graphically the many cities laid waste by Mongol aggression. His descriptions of both Mongol and Chinese custom are generally accurate, if somewhat inflated. Paper money, state granaries, the Grand Canal, Kublai's prodigious hunting parties, porcelain, deep-sea junks and the spittoon all figure in his narrative. Polo also gives us vivid portraits of other countries equally unknown to his readers at the time, among them Siam and Burma. His picture of Tibet as a land of musk, enchanters and many hawks rings strangely true. If he did merely concoct a fabric of other travellers' tales gleaned on lesser wanderings, then Polo had an exceptional memory.

The real problem is that Polo did not write his *Travels*, but recounted them to a known 'romancer', **Rusticello of Pisa**, while languishing in a Genoese jail in 1298. None of the extant texts can be considered incorrupt, and there may be parts missing. No doubt Polo, known by his contemporaries as 'Il Milione' (Big Mouth) did exaggerate his usefulness to Kublai Khan, but his gainsayers have been less quick to question the credentials of his amanuensis: a professional hack who must have wanted to turn a good story into an incomparable yarn.

Temur (aka Taiding), a grandson of Kublai Khan, is enthroned. Swiftly, however, Yesun Temur ousts the regicides, replacing them with ministers chosen from amongst his own followers. The prohibitions against Moslems are lifted, and both Moslem and Nestorian clerics are exempted from taxation.

Elsewhere, the former Song emperor **Gongzong**, having been sent to Tibet by Kublai to study as a monk, commits suicide. According to legend, Gongzong is the father of the last Yuan emperor Toghon Temur.

1325 As resentment against the Mongol occupation of China grows, the first bands of **peasant rebels** form. While the Yuan will be ousted by a massive popular uprising, at first such groups are merely intent on pillage, seldom distinguishing between Mongol and Chinese targets.

1328 Yesun Temur is succeeded by his cousin **Tugh Temur** (aka Wenzong), a supporter of the pro-Chinese faction.

1329 Tugh Temur abdicates in favour of his older brother **Khoshila** (aka Mingzong), but resumes the throne when Khoshila is assassinated. He assigns the responsibilities of government to two unpopular ministers, Bayan and El Temur. As a result of their strong-armed policies, unrest spreads among Mongol courtiers as well as among the emperor's Chinese subjects.

1331 An unidentified epidemic ravages Hubei province, killing over half its population.

1332 Tugh Temur is succeeded by Khoshila's youngest son **Irinjibal**, excluded from the official roster of Chinese emperors.

1333 Within two months of his accession, Irinjibal dies, and is succeeded by his elder brother, the 13-year-old **Toghon Temur** (aka Shundi). The minister Bayan is retained as chancellor, and his draconian anti-Chinese policies are extended. Chinese subjects are forbidden to carry arms, and many of their chattels are arbitrarily confiscated. Bayan is equally unsparing toward his Mongol rivals, and factionalism quickly turns to armed revolt. District by district, province by province, government collapses, the more so as flood defences in the Yellow River plains are abandoned, resulting in severe famine. Toghon, meanwhile, turns his back on the world, to indulge in esoteric Tibetan Buddhist rituals designed to accommodate his prolific sexual appetites.

1335 The Moslem traveller **Ibn Battuta** arrives in China. His written account will rival Marco Polo's in the Arab world.

1337 Beginning of the **Great Bubonic Plague** which will devastate Eurasia. Entering China from the steppes, it is possible that fleas trapped inside Chinese silk take the plague to Mediterranean ports. China itself suffers less severely than other nations.

The Yam

The Mongol empire expanded, more rapidly than any other, in an age when distance and time were still synonymous; but in relative terms the Mongols were masters of lightning communication. From Genghis Khan onwards they instituted a system of straight roads and **post-stations** known as the **Yam**, at first centred on **Karakoram**, and built by the forced labour of the vanquished. At 25-mile intervals, fortified stations provided fresh mounts, food and shelter. Wearing bells to announce his approach, a skilled courier could change mount at the gallop, and a relay could cover 250 miles in a single day. Riders wore *a paiza* (medallion) on their chest, authenticating their status. In due course, the Yam was introduced into China, centred on **Khanbalik**. Some 1400 staging posts were built, with a complement of 50,000 horses and 6000 boats, for crossing rivers. The dynamic backbone of the Mongol occupation, the Yam may be compared with the Great Wall as a means of ensuring security and intelligence.

1339 John of Marignola heads a third Franciscan mission to China, sponsored by Pope Benedict XII. He stays fourteen years, establishes a church, but departs when he senses the Yuan dynasty cannot last.

1340 Discontent with Mongol rule fuels rebellion in all parts of China. Peasants and scholars make common cause against their perceived oppressors. Bayan is toppled, but his successor ministers fail to restore order.

1344 When the Yellow River bursts its banks, the court decides to take no action. While millions will die of starvation and disease as a result, millions more become committed to rebellion.

1351 Belatedly, the government orders repairs to Yellow River flood defences; but by paying a conscripted workforce in valueless paper money it only encourages discontent.

1352 Zhu Yuanzhang, a low-born Buddhist mendicant, joins a rebel force west of Nanjing under the command of **Guo Zixing**. Immediately, Zhu demonstrates unusual qualities of leadership. Marrying Guo's daughter Ma, he becomes second-in-command of Guo's forces.

1353 Zhu captures the strategic stronghold of Chuzhou in Anhui province from its Mongol stewards.

1355 On Guo Zixing's death, Zhu assumes command of his rebel army. While seeking further military victories, Zhu attracts talented civilians to his camp. With their help, he projects himself as a national leader.

1356 Zhu captures **Nanjing**, and installs a Chinese administration. Although he proclaims himself the Duke of Wu, he acknowledges the claims of a Song pretender, **Han Lin-er**, to the imperial throne. He is hampered from conducting further campaigns against the Mongols by the rivalry of other Chinese leaders, among them **Chen Youliang**, the self-proclaimed 'Han' emperor with a large following in Hubei, and **Zhang Shicheng**, effectively the master of Jiangsu.

1363 Zhu kills Chen after a three-day naval battle on Boyang Lake.

1364 Zhu resumes his harassment of Mongol strongholds.

1367 In an 'accident', probably contrived by Zhu, Han Liner drowns when his boat capsizes on the Yangzi River. Shortly afterwards, Zhu captures and executes Zhang Shicheng. As Zhu prepares to attack the Mongols in their northern strongholds, other rebel warlords either submit to his authority or are eliminated.

1368 Proclaiming the **Ming** (meaning 'Brilliant') dynasty, and giving himself the regnal title **Hongwu** ('Vastly Martial'), Zhu sends his armies north under the command of Xu Da and Chang Yuchun. The Mongol armies, wanting effective leadership, often retreat without fighting.

In September Toghon Temur flees to Karakoram, where, two years later, he will die. Zhu's forces enter Beijing, and the bulk of China returns to Chinese rule.

The 'eastern' Mongols, however, divide into two groups: the **Oirats** and the **Khalkas**. When not distracted by internal schisms each will pose a threat to Chinese security.

7
The Ming Dynasty

1368–1644

Modelled on its Tang and Song predecessors the **Ming dynasty** was finally unable to learn from the past. Its political narrative is a sorry kaleidoscope of all the forces and failings that had bedevilled previous attempts to establish a 'ten thousand generation' imperium, as though China were indeed condemned to endlessly repeat the 'dynastic cycle' of rebirth, degeneration and overthrow. Dowager-empresses, court factions, disputed successions, weak emperors, self-serving mandarins, natural catastrophe, economic mismanagement, military shortcomings, peasant unrest and eunuch greed all played a part in a long drawn-out decay. Only this time around, the very context of Chinese history underwent a sea-change.

It was during the Ming period that **Europeans** began colonizing the Americas. They also began exploring eastern waters: first the Portuguese, then the Dutch and Spanish, then the English. Inevitably, they were drawn to the Chinese coast, to Chinese ports and to such commodities as silk, porcelain and tea. For the first time, truly **global trading networks** were established. What happened in and around Malacca, Manilla and Guangzhou (Canton) could affect, within a matter of months, what happened in Lisbon, Madrid, Amsterdam and London.

Seaborne mercantile activity meshed with national economic interest to dictate political and military strategy, often to deadly effect. From a Chinese perspective, this burden was apparent from the earliest contacts with European sailors. Portuguese adventurers, especially – nourished on a diet of Catholic suprematism that regarded the 'heathen' as expendable – but also their Dutch and English counterparts, thought nothing of murdering their way to riches. Small wonder that the Ming government, more used to the gentler behaviour of Arab, Indian and Annamese merchants, sought to exclude the 'red-haired' barbarians. But trade being trade, and profit being profit, China's own and mainly southern merchants had other thoughts. Eagerly exchanging Chinese produce for Hispanic American (as also Japanese) silver, they inspired, at the end of the 16th century, an extraordinary and inflationary economic boom that further destabilized Ming rule.

Insofar as the Ming court had a coherent plan, then it tended toward the rigid perpetuation of an **agrarian Middle Kingdom**. The founding **Hongwu** emperor, having driven out the Mongols, sought to control every aspect of China's external as well as internal relations. To give himself leverage over his northern and western neighbours, he made Chinese exports an imperial monopoly. No silk or tea or porcelain could be traded with Persians, Arabs, Uighurs or the Mongol and Jürchen remnants except within the framework of the imperial 'tribute' system.

Simultaneously, Hongwu revived the **examination system** for entry into the civil service along Song lines – neo-Confucian, and open to all. Between 1384 and 1498 over fifty percent of successful candidates came from families with no previous office-holders. But unlike the Song, Hongwu cared little for the opinions of his ministers. His reconstituted China was run as a populist autocracy, even though he also rewarded his sons and followers with hereditary provincial governorships that soon coalesced into the sort of entrenched elite Hongwu himself distrusted.

In the wake of Hongwu's efforts, the **Yongle emperor** (1403–24) reasserted Chinese regional hegemony, sponsoring the **oceanic voyages** of **Zheng He**, which could have led, but didn't, to a Chinese maritime capability equal to the European challenge. After Zheng's death, however, and after the Zhengtong emperor's capture by Mongols in 1449, the court became progressively introspective, for all its guarded welcome of a handful of scientifically savvy Jesuits. If Beijing's **Forbidden City** is the peculiar glory of Ming might, it is also the emblem of the dynasty's calamitous detachment. Having abandoned industrious Nanjing as their capital, and with their backs to the Great Wall, the Ming emperors closed their eyes to new realities. In the long-reigned **Wanli emperor** (1573–1620), the dynasty attained perfect despotic stasis. Long before it was unravelled by the West, China succumbed to the **Manchu**.

Note: Before the Ming dynasty Chinese emperors are known by their posthumous 'temple names', eg Gaodi ('High Emperor') or 'Yuanzong' ('Profound Ancestor'). From Ming onwards, emperors are known by their 'reign titles', used during their lifetimes.

1368 Zhu Yuanzhang, now the **Hongwu** emperor, deliberately blends elements of Tang and Song dynastic government. Sumptuary laws require Tang-style costumes to be worn at court. Imposing his sometimes cruel authority, Hongwu limits the powers of his ministers while awarding hereditary governorships to his sons. Refortified, **Nanjing** is retained as Hongwu's capital, encouraging further migration from the north. The peasantry is revitalized by offering it lands for resettlement laid waste by the **Mongols**. Campaigning against the Mongols and some remaining pockets of indigenous resistance continues.

1369 Ming forces destroy the Mongol 'summer capital' **Shangdu**.

1370 The 'eastern' Mongols are driven back into their original homelands. **Tamerlaine the Great**, a Turkic adventurer operating out of Samarkand, begins carving out a personal empire at the expense of the western Mongols that will also contain the spread of Islam.

1371 Chinese rebels in Sichuan are defeated by Ming forces.

1372 Xu Da leads a Chinese army across the Gobi desert, razes **Karakoram** and pushes as far north as the Yablonoi mountains in Siberia.

1376 10,000 bureaucrats are purged as Hongwu orders an anti-corruption campaign.

1380 Hongwu abolishes the post of prime minister (sometimes called chancellor) and assumes direct personal control of higher government. A further 30,000 officials are purged.

1381 Ming forces oust a remnant Mongol garrison from **Yunnan**, which is now integrated with the empire. Hongwu institutes a register of every household in China, listing its primary occupation. Such occupations are deemed permanent, although in practice this stipulation is evaded by hired labour and other devices.

1382 Hongwu creates the 'Embroidered Brocade Guard', a **secret police** detailed to inform the emperor on the activities of his officials. Hongwu also begins using palace **eunuchs** to carry through his policies.

1384 The **imperial examinations** are restored with a simplified neo-Confucian curriculum. When southern candidates prove disproportionately successful, the government insists on a quota of passes from the north.

1385 Thousands of officials are executed after the Censorate discovers that imperial grain revenues are going astray.

1387 Ming forces overcome the last remaining rebels in the south and southwest, completing the reconquest of all of China. From now on, Hongwu concentrates on reviving China's status as the effective regional power. **Envoys** are sent to neighbouring states, including Korea and Vietnam, to remind local rulers of their 'vassal' status and request 'tribute'. Nanjing becomes a centre for Eastern learning.

To maximize agrarian tax revenues, Hongwu orders a **register of land-holdings**. Because taxes are fixed 'for all time', in the long term this measure proves countereffective as expenditure and inflation rise.

1391 Ming forces take the Central Asian city of **Hami**; but as southern shipping routes displace the Silk Roads as the main trade conduit, no effort is made to recolonize 'Chinese Turkestan'.

1393 Hongwu orders the deaths of some 15,000 officials for insubordination.

1395 Tamerlaine imprisons Chinese emissaries to Samarkand when they present letters addressing him as an imperial vassal.

1398 The Hongwu emperor dies and is buried in a relatively simple tomb. 38 concubines are immolated with him. He is succeeded by his scholarly grandson, the **Jianwen** emperor.

1399 As Jianwen and his ministers endeavour to curb the powers of royal governors by recalling, and sometimes imprisoning or executing them, Hongwu's fourth son **Zhu Di**, Prince of Yan, launches a rebellion that sparks a devastating four-year civil war.

1402 Jianwen disappears, perhaps burned to death, as Zhu's forces capture and sack Nanjing.

The Hongwu Emperor 1328–98

Like Liu Bang, the founder of the Han dynasty, **Zhu Yuanzhang** came from peasant stock. That he learned to write was down to misfortune. At the age of 16, his entire family died of famine. Like thousands of others, he enrolled at a **Buddhist monastery**, simply to survive. Eight years later, with anti-Yuan activity surging in the Yangzi delta, he joined Guo Zixing's bandit rebels. His subsequent rise to a position of leadership was meteoric. China had once again produced a hero equally at home on the battlefield and in the council chamber. His capture of **Nanjing** was the turning point in his emergence as a national figure. Nor, having vanquished the Yuan and established the Ming dynasty, did his drive diminish.

Taking the reign-title **Hongwu** ('Vastly Marshal'), for thirty years, he oversaw every aspect of China's government. He revived and expanded **district and provincial schools** in order to exploit the best available talent. He pursued the Mongols into their own territories, and pushed China's northeastern frontier back into **Manchuria**. His envoys easily persuaded such lesser states as **Korea** to resume their 'tributary' status. Yet his rule was also despotic, at times resembling the ousted khans. His ministers were there to carry out his orders, not to advise on policy, and Hongwu thought nothing of ordering the deaths of thousands of 'disloyal' officials. In Nanjing, public floggings of even senior ministers were routine. Conversely, he protected the **peasantry** from which he had come, giving smallholders tax concessions to help rebuild their livelihoods. They, and not the merchant class, were the lifeblood of Hongwu's China.

1403 Zhu Di proclaims himself Emperor, assuming the reign title **Yongle** ('Eternal Joy'). He eliminates his former enemies and anyone associated with them, and reduces the powers of the hereditary princes. During his reign, Yongle oversees the full resurgence of a strong, unified and expansionist China while personally commanding continuing campaigns against the Mongols and other northern enemies. China extends its hold over southern Manchuria, still mainly inhabited by the Jürchen. Yongle's armies also reassert a Chinese presence in Annam (northern **Vietnam**). As paper money disappears, Yongle's government exploits its monopoly in mining **silver**, but the silver available in China is never sufficient to meet demand, and illicit trade with silver-rich **Japan** is therefore stimulated.

1404 In December, **Tamerlaine** assembles a force of 200,000 and marches east to add China to his conquests.

1405 Tamerlaine dies before entering Chinese territory, and his army withdraws.

For the first and only time, Japan agrees to become a Chinese 'tributary' state.

An imperial fleet, commanded by the eunuch **Zheng He**, sets out on the first of seven expeditions designed to impress Chinese power on the peoples and nations of southeastern and southern Asia. The first three (1405–11) reach Sri Lanka, Sumatra and Java.

Yongle establishes a College of Interpreters under the aegis of the Ministry of War to house and instruct envoys from other nations. A College of Translators is instituted to process foreign documents.

1407 Yongle decides to move his capital to **Beijing**, where work begins on a new imperial palace.

1410 Yongle leads the first of four campaigns against the **Mongols**; others follow in 1414, 1422 and 1444.

1411 Japan rescinds its tributary status. From this point onwards, **Japanese piracy** becomes a serious problem off China's coast.

1413 Zheng He begins a second series of maritime expeditions. Continuing until 1422, these include the mouth of the Red Sea and the east coast of Africa.

The imposing Temple of Heaven, built in Beijing around 1420, combines Chinese astrological values in both its exterior and interior.

Chen Cheng sets out across the Gobi desert on a two-year overland mission to repair relations with the **Timurid empire**, gather intelligence and impose Chinese influence on lesser Central Asian kingdoms.

1418 Chen reaches Herat, where he acknowledges the 'equal status' of Tamerlaine's Timurid heir Shahrukh.

1420 In Beijing, construction work on the **Temple of Heaven** begins. Yongle establishes the **Eastern Depot**, an imperial intelligence service staffed by eunuchs.

1421 Yongle formally declares **Beijing** his capital.

1424 Yongle dies, and is buried alongside the empress Xu and sixteen concubines in an imposing mausoleum. He is succeeded by his eldest son, the corpulent, but humanitarian, **Hongxi** emperor.

1425 Hongxi dies within a year of his succession. His eldest son succeeds as the **Xuande** emperor. Sharing power with his mother the Dowager-empress **Zhang**, appointed regent, Xuande establishes peace on China's northern frontiers. During his reign, the **Grand Secretariat** is revived as an effective instrument of government, and there is imperial encouragement for the arts. Conversely, the palace eunuchs are allowed to reassert political influence.

1426 Twelve years of insurgency in **Vietnam** culminate in Chinese humiliation at the battle of Tot Dong. The victor, Le Loi, establishes his own Chinese-style imperial dynasty with a capital at Hanoi.

In Beijing, the creation of a court school for **eunuchs** bodes ill for the currently harmonious relations between the throne and the bureaucracy. Leading eunuchs are appointed to military commands.

1431 The last of the great Ming naval expeditions under **Zheng He** sets sail. During a two-year voyage, Zheng

The Yongle Emperor 1403–24

The fourth of the founding Hongwu emperor's 26 sons, **Zhu Di** was most like his father, both in temperament and skills. Born in 1360, from an early age he displayed soldierly talent, and in 1380 was rewarded with the strategic military governorship of Beijing. Year-in, year-out, he conducted campaigns against the Mongols, taking the fight to China's most feared enemy. When the throne passed to Hongwu's grandson, Zhu Di decided to displace his nephew. After a protracted civil war he duly became emperor, and during his reign the Ming dynasty attained its maximum prestige.

Yongle's many accomplishments included a comprehensive refurbishment of the **Grand Canal**, and, through the Moslem eunuch Zheng He, the creation of a world-class **navy**. Japan was persuaded to join China's other neighbours as a tributary state, and northern Vietnam was briefly subjected to direct Chinese rule. A more permanent legacy was Yongle's choice of **Beijing** as his capital. While this made sense in terms of his personal provenance, and the need to continuously monitor the nomadic peoples of the steppe, it also gave China a seat of government far removed from what had already become the hub of its cultural and commercial activities. By involving palace eunuchs in the execution of his policies, Yongle also failed to enhance the authority of his appointed ministers. Rather, he groomed a hand-picked body of younger bureaucrats to supply him with a Yuan-style 'Grand Secretariat'. By seeking the company of Daoist sages and Tibetan lamas he emphasized the gap between the throne and China's traditional Confucian administrators.

visits Jeddah on the eastern coast of (modern) Saudi Arabia.

1435 Xuande is succeeded by his eldest son, the 8-year-old **Zhengtong** emperor. Reappointed regent, the Dowager-empress Zhang continues to provide China with firm, but fair, government.

1442 As the **Oirat Mongols** begin harrying the Chinese border Dowager-empress Zhang dies.

1443 Zhengtong, isolated from the outside world by court protocol, falls under the spell of his favourite eunuch **Wang Zhen**.

Zheng He (Cheng Ho) c.1370–1433

That China's foremost navigator was a eunuch was central to the eventual outcome of his extraordinary voyages. **Zheng He**'s successes were so resented by the Confucian outer court that any attempt to build upon them was firmly quashed. Born in Yunnan during the Mongol occupation, the boy Ma He was raised a Moslem. At the age of 10, he was captured by Chinese forces, castrated, and enlisted as an orderly in the Chinese army. In 1390, he fell under the command of the **Prince of Yan**.

The future Yongle emperor, impressed by Ma's abilities, gave him the Chinese name Zheng and promoted him to a junior command. Fifteen years later, Zheng was in charge of the **imperial navy**, and embarked on the first of seven unprecedentedly ambitious maritime expeditions. Setting sail with 27,000 men – including a full complement of doctors, clerks and interpreters, as well as sailors and soldiers aboard some 300 junks – Zheng canvassed all the ports of **Southeast Asia**. Between 1409 and 1433, he captained similar armadas that reached – as well as **Timor** in the east – the **Red Sea** and the **African coast** as far south as Malindi.

Yet the purpose of these costly adventures was neither trade nor military conquest. Rather, it was to show the Chinese flag to as many nations as possible, although a subsidiary function was to 'police' colonies of expatriate Chinese merchants wherever they had established themselves — indicating that already by the early 15th century the Chinese diaspora was under way. Regularly, Zheng returned with envoys and princes from far-off lands, volunteering, or cajoled into, nominal submission to the Son of Heaven. He also returned, to the astonishment of the court, with such exotic beasts as the giraffe. But while his missions extended the empire's tribute system, following his death, long-range maritime activity contracted sharply, so that by the time **Vasco da Gama** rounded the Cape in 1498, few, if any, Chinese vessels ventured beyond the Straits of Malacca.

1445 Publication of he *Dao zang* (Daoist canon) in 5000 uniform fascicles.

1449 Wang Zhen persuades Zhengtong to lead a punitive expedition against Oirat Mongols, numbering 500,000 men. To the chagrin of the Ming military, Zhengtong appoints Wang commander-in-chief. In the ensuing calamity, the retreating Chinese army is annihilated at Huai Lai. Zhengtong is taken prisoner. Rather than press home his advantage, Esen Khan, leader of the Oirat, withdraws to Mongolia with his captive.

1450 Amidst an unwillingness to pay an exorbitant ransom demanded by Esen Khan, Zhengtong's brother Zhu Qiyu is enthroned by ministers as the **Jingtai** emperor. Vital repairs to Beijing's defences are undertaken, and a Mongol army beaten off.

As a result of renewed Mongol aggression, it is decided to rebuild strategic segments of the **Great Wall**, covering the original stamped earth structure with brick. It is these non-continuous sections that are known to modernity.

Subsequently, Zhengtong is released, but Jingtai imprisons him in the inner recesses of the Forbidden City.

1454 The Oirat Mongols cease to threaten China when their confederation is thrown into confusion by the assassination of Esen Khan. The security of China's northwestern borders, however, is soon undermined by a resurgence of **Uighur** strength, and by the creation of the strong Mongol **Turfan** state under the leadership of Yunus Khan – threats ultimately contained only by the emergence of equally strong Uzbek, Kazakh and Kirghiz nations further west.

1457 As Jingtai is taken ill, Zhengtong is restored to the throne, now taking the reign title **Tianshun**. Jingtai is strangled, and his body denied space in the imperial burial

The Tribute System

That other rulers should pay **homage** to the 'Son of Heaven' was not just an expression of Chinese suprematism, as sometimes supposed by Western commentators, but an integral part of a flexible style of foreign relations that had its origins in the Former Han dynasty, and which sought to substitute dialogue for belligerence. When push came to shove, China was prepared to acknowledge the 'equal status' of a genuinely rival power. As the empire grew, so too did border problems multiply. Simply because China as a civilization was unmatched by any of its neighbours, it became a target for military opportunists.

The trick was to neutralize potential enemies through diplomacy and bring them within the imperial pale: to establish a *pax Sinica*, no less. Out of these considerations arose the **'tribute system'**, practised by the Tang and Song, but taken to its limits by the early Ming. In essence, a foreign ruler paid homage to China by sending envoys to its court. These envoys, kowtowing to the emperor, presented him with 'tribute'. In return, such envoys themselves received gifts, including special seals of office, ceremonial robes, and the promise of Chinese protection in the event of attack. Of the elements involved, however, **economic exchange** was, or became, the most important, allowing each party to acquire goods it needed or desired. Thus, Chinese gifts might include silk, porcelain and tea, while a steppe ruler's tribute included horses or jade. Quite often, the 'value' of Chinese gifts exceeded that of the tribute. In effect, China bought security on its borders while potentially hostile leaders acquired the prestige and some of the luxuries of being a part of the Chinese orb.

grounds. There follows a purge in which Tianshun rids himself of many foes and supporters alike. The emperor issues edicts outlawing Mongol custom, and takes steps to protect an imperial monopoly in selected porcelains.

1464 Tianshun is succeeded by his feeble eldest son, the **Chenghua** emperor. Government is placed in the hands of a twelve-strong council of regency, which works diligently to restore public order and confidence. The military is strengthened by the revival of a well-drilled palace guard, and performs well against Mongol and Jürchen incursions.

Chenghua, meanwhile, falls under the sway of his nurse-concubine **Wan Guifei**, who persuades him to depose his empress Wu. But, failing to provide Chenghua with an heir, Wan begins murdering boys born to other concubines. With the aid of two senior eunuchs, Liang Fang and Wang Zhi, she embarks on systematic embezzlement and exploitation that will net the three conspirators untold quantities of wealth. Every office is put up for sale, and the empire's resources are used to 'reward' lesser collaborators.

1475 To Wan Guifei's disbelief, an heir materializes in the shape of the boy **Zhu Yutang**, conceived five years earlier by an imperial chambermaid, but secreted for his safety by the deposed empress Wu. Zhu's mother Ji, originally recruited from a southern minority by palace officials, is murdered by Wan, but Zhu himself is left unmolested.

1477 All official records of the voyages of the eunuch Zheng He are destroyed by Confucian bureaucrats.

1480 The **Khalkas** eastern Mongols begin incursions against Chinese territory.

1487 Upon Chenghua's death, Zhu Yutang succeeds as the **Hongzhi** emperor. The youthful ruler shows his mettle by removing Liang Fang and other corrupt eunuchs from his court, and by demoting thousands of those who have purchased their offices. By advocating Confucian values, avoiding wars and personally maintaining a low profile, Hongzhi is able to restore respect for the Ming dynasty.

1498 The Portuguese seafarer **Vasco da Gama** rounds the Cape of Good Hope, opening the way for European penetration of the Indian Ocean and beyond.

Beijing (Peking) and The Forbidden City

Less than forty miles from the Great Wall, **Beijing** seems an unlikely site for China's second longest-serving capital (after Xian/Changan). Nonetheless, it was where Yongli transferred his government in 1407. Fourteen years later, the **Forbidden City** – housing imperial palaces, audience chambers and numerous other buildings – was completed. Such is its grandeur it is truly difficult to conceive any emperor not wishing to reside within its massive walls. Covering 250 acres, it is laid out on the traditional north–south grid plan, but incorporates several ornamental lakes and gardens, some of them inherited from the Mongol city Khanbalik. The names of the successive gates and halls speak for themselves: Supreme Harmony, Perfect Harmony, Preserving Harmony, and then the two imperial palaces, Heavenly Purity and Earthly Tranquillity. The Ming, such nomenclature tells us, intended to last. Nor is the fabric of the Forbidden City anything other than impressive. High walls, yellow tiled roofs and cascading marble terraces combine to form commanding perspectives, while snaking through this assemblage is an artificial river fed by the Western Hills. And yet the **Forbidden City** is only a small part of the metropolis constructed by the Ming.

Surrounding it was the far larger **Imperial City**, home to hundreds of thousands of officials, soldiers and eunuchs; and to the south of this is the equally extensive **Outer City**, where the commonalty lived, but also containing the **Temple of Heaven**, another ambitious Ming construction. Within a few decades, the population of Beijing reached three million, and has grown ever since. In 1949, the Communists confirmed Beijing's status as China's premier city – as indeed well they might: for Beijing's overwhelming ethos is one of jealous power locked within unfathomable recesses.

1505 Hongzhi's early death leads to the accession of his 15-year-old son, the **Zhengde** emperor. Lacking his father's sense of purpose, Zhengde alarms the Grand Secretariat by his antics. These include trading in the market as a

The first main courtyard of the Forbidden City, dominated by the Meridian Gate and constructed during the 15th century.

merchant and inviting wrestlers and other circus performers into the palace. Quickly, he falls prey to the wiles of his chief eunuch **Liu Jin**.

1506 Tiring of the obedient charms of his palace harem, Zhengde begins visiting Beijing's many brothels. He is also drawn toward the mystic abstractions of Tibetan Buddhism.

1510 A revolt aimed at toppling Zhengde, and led by a hereditary prince-governor in Ningxia, is suppressed, but the emperor is forced to concede the corruption of Liu Jin, whose personal wealth is revealed to stand at 36 million pounds of gold and silver.

In **Sichuan**, endemic **banditry**, generally a sign of popular discontent, proves harder to quell. Zhengde – now casting himself in the role of military leader – adopts 127 junior officers as his 'sons' and begins drilling his eunuchs in Beijing's imperial parks.

1511 Having established the 'Cape route', the **Portuguese** take control of the Straits of Malacca, linking the Indian and western Pacific oceans – a seizure that marks the advent of European seafarers in East Asian waters. Malacca itself remains an international entrepôt, and its expatriate Chinese merchant community permitted to stay.

1516 Unusually, for a Chinese artist, **Zhou Chen** paints a series of portraits, known as 'Beggars and Street Characters', of destitutes observed in the streets of Suzhou, the centre of Ming silk manufacture.

1517 Zhengde begins two years of 'campaigns' along the quiescent northern frontiers with an 'army' dressed in silk uniforms. Portuguese ships enter Chinese waters for the first time.

1520 Appointing himself High Commander, Zhengde journeys down the Grand Canal with a flamboyant entourage.

Critical officials are publicly flogged.

In Nanjing, the emperor outlaws the keeping of pigs, on the grounds they share the same homophone (*zhu*) as his family name.

1521 Within weeks of reaching Beijing, Zhengde's barge sinks. He dies having contracted an illness from the Grand Canal's waters. Zhu Houcong, a grandson of Chenghua, ascends the throne as the **Jiajing** emperor. Aged 14, he elevates his branch of the Zhu family by styling his mother **Jiang** Dowager-empress. Under her guidance, Jiajing purges the eunuchry. Attaining manhood, however, Jiajing is largely content to leave government to the devices of his ministers. These include the **Single Whip** tax reform, aggregating smaller levies into a single lump-sum payment.

Ferdinand Magellan, a Portuguese navigator in Spanish employ, "discovers" the Philippines, thus paving the way for a trans-Pacific trade after further expeditions by Garcia de Loaisa (1525) and Alvaro de Saavedra (1527). China will derive several new crops from the **Americas**, including sweet potatoes, peanuts and tobacco.

1522 In an attempt to force his way up the Pearl River toward Guangzhou, the Portuguese seafarer Alphonso de Mello is repulsed by Chinese arms. Portuguese prisoners are executed as pirates.

In the same year, the **Romance of the Three Kingdoms** is published (see p.117).

1528 Jiajing's empress Chen dies after the emperor's violence toward her induces a miscarriage. '

1529 Death of the philosopher **Wang Yangming**.

1534 Jiajing divorces his second empress Zhang.

Wang Yangming 1472–1529

The only notable philosopher of the Ming period, **Wang Yangming** was born in Zhejiang province, the son of a high-ranking minister. As a youth, he was an accomplished archer and a keen Daoist. Entering the civil service in 1499, he quickly gained a reputation as a military theorist, but in 1506 was disgraced after championing a fellow official against a powerful eunuch. Ordered by the emperor to receive forty strokes of the bamboo, imprisoned, and then banished to Guizhou, it was during his exile that Wang questioned the assumptions underlying the orthodox **neo-Confucianism** of Zhu Xi (see p.201). Rehabilitated in 1511, his career culminated in the governorship of Jiangxi. In his official capacities, Wang successfully combated ethnic insurgency and the rebellion of a disaffected prince.

He is best remembered, however, for the ideas contained in his *Chuanxi li* ('Introduction to Practical Living'). Rejecting Zhu's formalism, Wang argued that true knowledge is inward. The world is to be known through introspection, not by over-familiarity with the classics or by the objective study of phenomena. Wang stressed the unity of thought and action. While not gainsaying Confucian ideals, he posited that the only way to understand, say, filial piety is to practice it. Infants and children are naturally virtuous, therefore much may be learned by contemplating them. Inevitably, Wang's brand of romantic existentialism excited the opprobrium of the intellectual establishment, and he was not acknowledged as a sage until 1584. In the 18th century, he was again censured for encouraging individualism. But perhaps because of a Daoist element in his thought he has never been short of followers.

1539 To further enhance his branch of the Zhu family, Jiajing upgrades his parents' burial place at Zhongxian in Hubei into an imperial mausoleum.

1540 From about this time, raids by **Japanese pirates** on China's southeastern coasts intensify.

1542 Either on their own initiative, or acting on behalf of some unidentified party, **eighteen imperial concubines** attempt to strangle Jiajing in his bedchamber. When Fang, one of the eighteen, raises the alarm, her colleagues are apprehended and executed. Fang is pardoned, and soon becomes Jiajing's third empress.

Having resolved internal differences among the eastern Mongols, **Altan Khan** launches a devastating raid against northern China, killing an estimated 200,000.

Portuguese traders who have established themselves at the Zhejiang port of **Ningbo**, expand their 'colony' to 3000 men.

1544 The Portuguese are expelled from Ningbo after they begin constructing a fort.

c.1545 Publication of *The Classic of Lu Ban*. A vademecum for builders and carpenters it embodies many of the principles of *feng shui* – a divinatory system for establishing 'correct' procedures when siting a house and making other kinds of related decision.

1549 Portuguese traders are expelled from **Quanzhou** (aka Zayton, southern Fujian province) after attempting to found a colony. From now on, they and other European interlopers are known as 'Ocean Devils'.

1550 Altan Khan's forces lay siege to Beijing. When the city's defences hold, the Mongols withdraw.

1552 Unlike their Franciscan and Dominican predecessors, **Jesuit missionaries** are confined by the Chinese government to the **Macau** peninsula, in the mouth of the Pearl River (Guangdong province). **Francis Xavier**, head of the Jesuit and therefore Catholic mission to East Asia, dies there, having never set foot on the Chinese mainland.

1555 Japanese pirates venture as far up the Yangzi as Nanjing, and for ten weeks pillage without hindrance.

The Age of Porcelain

Landscape gardening, carved ivory and furniture design are each prized features of Ming culture. But the period is best known by its **porcelain**, particularly its **blue-and-white ware**. Although blue-and-white originated during the Yuan dynasty, when cobalt from Katanga in Africa was first imported through the Middle East, Ming blue-and-white is generally regarded as a ceramic high-point, to the extent that the **'Ming Vase'** has become synony-mous with auction-house fever. Even contemporaneously, the value of Chinese porcelain exceeded that of any other export commodity weight-for-weight.

The lead was taken by the first Ming emperors, who patronized an imperial porcelain factory at **Jingdezhen** in Jiangxi. Crucially, Jingdezhen-ware was used as a status gift in the complex inter-state exchanges that underpinned the 'tribute system'. But as much was manufactured for domestic use. In 1433, 433,000 matching pieces were ordered for the **Forbidden City**. Nor did Jingdezhen restrict itself to blue-and-white. As the factory evolved into a highly-skilled industrial complex, experiments with many other glazes were made; and although blue-and-white is esteemed for its decorative inventiveness, some of the most sat-isfying Ming porcelains are non-blue monochromes.

1557 Despite their previous unruly behaviour, and follow-ing pressure from southern Chinese merchants, Portuguese traders are permitted to establish a colony at **Macau**, albeit under strict government supervision. This founding of a European bridgehead on Chinese soil presages a profound shift in global economic and cultural relations.

1560 Several thousand Japanese pirates land in Fujian and for several months freely loot the province's towns and cities.

1567 Jiajing is succeeded by his eldest son, the **Longqing** emperor. Interested only in his private pleasures, Longqing entrusts government to his minister **Zhang Zhuzheng**.

Zhang rids the palace of Daoists, contains Japanese piracy, and in 1571 persuades Altan Khan to become China's 'vassal'.

1570 Probable publication date of the *Xiyouji* ('Journey to the West', aka 'Monkey'), a fantastic novel based on the travels of Xuan Zang.

1572 The founding of **Manilla** (modern capital of the Philippines) as a Spanish Pacific entrepôt initiates a commercial boom in Guangzhou and other southeastern seaports. Chinese luxuries are exchanged for **Mexican silver dollars**, which now become a 'hard' currency inside China.

1573 Longqing is succeeded by his senior surviving son, the **Wanli** emperor. During his 47-year reign the economy generates levels of wealth not seen since the heyday of the Song dynasty.

The 'Wanli Period' is also an age of literary and artistic enterprise. None of its successes, however, can be attributed to the emperor himself. Only rarely will he display any interest in government.

1575 For the first time, and only on specified dates, Portuguese merchants are permitted to travel up the Pearl River from Macau to Guangzhou.

1577 Altan Khan is converted to Tibetan Buddhism by a Yellow Sect lama whom he grants the title **Dalai Lama**. The Dalai Lama's two predecessors are similarly honoured in retrospect. Despite the arcane rules surrounding the Dalai Lama's reincarnation, Altan Khan's great-grandson will be identified as the fourth Dalai Lama (1588).

1583 In the far northeast, **Nurhaci** (b. 1559) becomes leader of the **Jürchen** people, presaging their national revival.

The Chinese Novel

During the Ming period Chinese poetry ossified into mannered pastiche. Nor did other established literary genres fare much better. As though to compensate this falling-off, the **Chinese novel** was not only born, but exhibited what in retrospect seems an astonishing range of style, competence and subject matter. There were some precedents. During Tang times, some scholars composed short stories. During Song times, professional storytellers attracted large audiences on street corners. To help them memorize their plots, 'libretti' were prepared and sometimes printed, called *huapen*. But it was during the late 15th and 16th centuries that the novel proper emerged fully fledged.

Two of the earliest examples are also two of the finest: the ***Romance of the Three Kingdoms*** (see p.117); and ***Shuihu zhuan***, translated by Pearl S Buck as *All Men Are Brothers*, but better known as *The Water Margin*. In the last of these, the exploits of **Song Jiang**, a known Shandong bandit leader, and his 108 seemingly lawless companions, are celebrated to the hilt, as officials are lampooned for their cupidity and bad faith. History, real or imagined, likewise inspired **Wu Chengen**'s *Xiyouji*, based on the Tang monk Xuan Zang's travels to India in search of Buddhist texts. The central character of Wu's phantasmagoric fiction, however, is Monkey, an irrepressible animal sage. Trans-culturally, the result is a collision between Don Quixote and Walt Disney.

But Ming fiction, feeling its way toward realism, also addressed the present. The late 16th century *Jin Ping Mei* (translated by Clement Egerton as *The Golden Lotus*) by **Wang Shizhen** is an extended narrative of relationships within a provincial family. Sexually explicit, Wang offers a sensitive portrayal of his womenfolk. A more blatantly erotic novel is **Li Yu**'s *The Before Midnight Scholar*, published in 1640. Yet scarcely anything is known about the authors of these and other Ming novels. Scorned by the scholar-gentry, but belonging to the same class, Ming novelists preferred anonymity and pseudonymity, for all that they deliberately wrote in demotic *baihua* Chinese.

The Jesuit **Matteo Ricci** crosses from Macau to the Chinese mainland and begins missionary work.

1584 Matteo Ricci's *Mappa Mundi* ('Map of the World') is printed in China. A significant advance on Chinese cartography, it indicates to the court that the Jesuit order may be of practical use.

1589 Following the death of his chief minister Zhang Zhuzheng, Wanli withdraws from public life. In a system where the imperial seal is a requisite for action, much important business goes unattended. Vacancies within the bureaucracy are left unfilled, and both the judiciary and the military are hampered from fulfilling their obligations.

1592 China responds to the Japanese invasion of Korea by initiating a ruinously expensive and ultimately futile five-year war to 'protect' its vassal state.

1594 In a rare intervention, Wanli authorizes heavy taxes on shops, boats and other means of trade in an attempt to fund China's war with Japan. Collected, and sometimes embezzled, by **eunuchs**, often with violence, such taxes alienate many of China's middling subjects.

1598 Shogun Hideyoshi's death leads to the withdrawal of Japanese forces from Korea.

Tang Xianzu's classic drama *The Peony Pavilion* is first staged in Beijing.

The Jesuit Matteo Ricci visits Beijing to present his doctrines to the court. Despite bureaucratic misgivings, Ricci is permitted to stay in the capital until his death in 1610.

1599 As China's imperial government becomes gridlocked by Wanli's reluctance to perform his responsibilities, **insurgency** breaks out in the south.

1600 China's **population** exceeds **150 million**. Improvements in diet, and the universal popularity of

Matteo Ricci 1552–1610

Sanctioned by the papacy in 1540, Ignatius Loyola's **Society of Jesus** furnished the Catholic Church with an intellectual elite to combat the 'heresies' of the European Protestant Reformation. But perhaps because so many early Jesuits were drawn from the seafaring Iberian peninsula, there was, from the outset, an emphasis on apostolic missions to distant lands still in the process of being discovered. Thus, from 1540 until his death in 1552, the Spaniard **Francis Xavier** worked to establish an eastern church, visiting India, the spice islands and Japan. But although from the middle of the century Jesuits were permitted to reside at Macau, it befell the Italian **Matteo Ricci** to become the first Jesuit to enter China proper. No one could have been better suited to the task.

Having studied under the mathematician Christopher Clavicus (chief architect of the Gregorian calender) Ricci arrived in **Macau** in 1582. In 1583, he was allowed into **Guangdong province**. A year later, he published his impressive *Mappa Mundi*, or 'Great Map of Ten Thousand Countries', guaranteed to impress Chinese officialdom. It was another eighteen years, however, before he was authorized to visit **Beijing**, where he remained until his death. By then, he had written several books in Chinese. Some presented Catholic doctrine in terms compatible with Chinese culture, others conveyed elements of Western science and technology.

A gifted linguist, he possessed silken social skills, securing him the friendship of princes and scholars alike. In every way, he personified Jesuit strategy: missionary work combined with 'modern' learning and a personal diplomacy aimed at high places. **Adam Schell von Bell** and **John Schneck**, Ricci's successors in Beijing, further advanced Jesuit prestige by reforming the Chinese calender. They also introduced the **telescope**, one of many Western inventions that entered China under the Jesuit umbrella. But a century later, the missionaries' endeavours to ingratiate themselves upon their Chinese hosts by any means backfired. Their accommodation of Chinese ancestor-worship angered the Vatican, fomenting the **Rites Controversy** (see p.277).

marriage among the young, are two possible reasons for the increase.

1601 In the Yangzi city of Suzhou, silk-workers strike against low wages and high taxation. Further **strikes** occur at the imperial porcelain factory at Jingdezhen. Across southern China, workers grasp that they can articulate their grievances by withdrawing their labour.

1604 Senior bureaucrats and scholars form the **Donglin Society**, committed, in the first instance, to the restitution of 'orthodox' Confucian thought in the face of the 'heretic' Wang Yangming's individualistic philosophy (see p.246).

1611 The **Donglin Society** becomes politicized, opposing bureaucratic corruption and the power of the court eunuchs.

In the southern seas, the **Dutch East Indies Company** sets up a trading colony at Batavia (modern Jakarta). As silver is traded for pepper, spices and Chinese silk, Amsterdam emerges as a world bullion capital.

1616 Renouncing his allegiance to China, the Jürchen leader **Nurhaci** declares himself 'khan' of a new **Jin dynasty**. Simultaneously, the term Jürchen is replaced by **Manchu**, designating the nation occupying the whole region of Manchuria.

1618 Nurhaci attacks Chinese and 'loyal' Jürchen settlements in a strategically important area to the east of the Liaodong River. As Chinese subjects are recruited into his administration, any of his soldiers caught looting are publicly punished. Strict sumptuary laws, however, oblige Chinese subjects to wear *queues* (pigtails) and shave the front part of their heads.

In **Beijing**, the arrival of Ivashko Petlin marks the first diplomatic contact with the Russian court of **Muscovy**.

1620 Following his father's death, Wanli's eldest son by the concubine Wang accedes to the throne. The **Taichang** emperor, however, reigns for only five weeks. Falling ill, he dies, allegedly poisoned by Wang's rival concubine Zheng. As his mentally unstable eldest son is enthroned as the **Tianqi** emperor, power accrues to the eunuch **Wei Zhongxian**, formerly an imperial butler. By creating a network of spies, Wei runs the court as a personal fiefdom, using Tianqi's timid compliance to rubber-stamp innumerable corruptions. The bureaucracy responds by promoting members of the Donglin Society to senior positions.

1621 The Manchu Jürchen leader Nurhaci seizes **Mukden** (modern Shenyang) and other key cities in Manchuria.

1622 The Ming general **Yuan Chonghuan** temporarily halts Jürchen encroachment.

In Macau, an attack by **Dutch colonizers** is beaten off by the Portuguese garrison.

The Dutch sail on to the island of **Taiwan** (Formosa), to found a trading colony called Zelandia.

1623 Nurhaci's aggression is further undermined when his Chinese subjects in Liaodong rebel. With much bloodshed on both sides, the uprising is eventually suppressed.

1624 Wei Zhongxian orders the deaths of senior members of the Donglin Society, known as the **Six Heroes**. As Wei makes himself dictator, the administration is purged of a further 700 Donglin supporters.

1625 Nurhaci brutally suppresses a second 'Chinese' uprising in Liaodong. Yuan Chonghuan counterattacks Manchu forces.

In the former imperial capital of Xian, the unearthing of the **Nestorian Tablet** assists Jesuit arguments about the compatibility of Christian and Chinese beliefs.

The Wanli Emperor r. 1573–1620

Wanli is China's one long-reigning emperor about whom nothing good may be said. He had as little to do with his responsibilities as was humanly possible. In thirty years, between 1590 and 1620, he met with his Grand Secretaries a mere five times. At a court hidebound by rigid protocol, officials and foreign envoys regularly kowtowed before an empty throne. When his mother Lishi died in 1614, he failed to attend her funeral. Because he could not be bothered to set his seal, in ministry after ministry, positions fell vacant. Worst hit was the **Censorate**, instituted for maintaining discipline within the bureaucracy. Wanli dissipated instead vast amounts of revenue on a life of private luxury and indolence. Wedding clothes for his many children became a main item in the national budget. Ministers who complained were flogged. Ministers who protested their punishment were flogged harder. Obese and bloody-minded, he ringed himself with 10,000 fawning eunuchs, whose idle hours were passed sequestering imperial revenues. Yet perhaps the most alarming aspect of Wanli's reign was that nothing was done to get rid him. If he himself lacked conscience, the rest of the system wanted resolution.

Nurhaci 1559–1626

Following the destruction of the Jürchen Jin empire by the Mongols in 1264, a gulf developed between the 'wild' forest-dwelling Jürchen of the Amur valley – who subsisted by hunting and fishing – and the sedentary town-dwelling Jürchen who lived on the plains close to China. These two groups might have devolved into separate peoples. To the east, however, in the Long White Mountains, was a third set of Jürchen, the **Jianzhou** clan. It was their hereditary khan, coming to power in 1583, who restored unity among the Jürchen at large.

Strong, intelligent and vastly ambitious, **Nurhaci** first defeated his four rival Jürchen khans, then prepared to challenge the Chinese empire itself, forging the **Manchu state** and many of its characteristic institutions. These included a written Manchu language, and from 1601, the distinctive **Manchu 'banners'**.

A banner was primarily a military unit, or belonging. There was a red banner and a blue banner, bordered or unbordered, and so forth, four to begin with, many more later, including 'Chinese banners' made up of those Chinese who had settled in Manchuria. But a Manchu banner was also a unit of social and fiscal administration. If Nurhaci's bannermen were enlisted in his armies, so too were their families. War widows and orphans enjoyed basic welfare. Brilliantly, these arrangements allowed the Jürchen to retain local identities within a larger loyalty framework. Equally, Nurhaci avoided antagonizing the Chinese empire prematurely, building instead a robust economy based on the export of furs and pearls. In this way, he galvanized a people long written off as an ineffectual threat. Thus, too, he is to be regarded as the real founder of the **Qing dynasty** that ruled China until 1912.

1626 Nurhaci's death generates a power struggle between his sons and nephews. His eighth son, **Hong Taiji**, emerges victorious. Hong reconstructs his court on a Chinese model, and introduces competitive examinations for administrative positions. By pursuing a conciliatory policy toward his Chinese subjects, he encourages defectors from the Ming regime.

1627 Sentenced to death on charges of corruption, Wei Zhongian commits suicide.

1628 Tianqi is succeeded by his conscientious, but ineffectual, younger brother, the **Chongzhen** emperor. The extent of administrative decay is exposed when tens of thousands of northern Chinese die of famine. Across China, **bandit groups** form, opposed to both the Ming regime at large, and to local mandarins. Yuan Chonghuan is given command of the empire's northeastern armies.

1629 Although successful against the Manchu Jürchen, Yuan alienates his senior officers by summarily executing a fellow general in a fit of jealousy.

1630 When a Manchu army reaches the outskirts of Beijing, Yuan is accused of forming an alliance with Hong Taiji. His body is cut into pieces in a city marketplace.

1635 Hong Taiji increases his manpower and resources by invading Mongolia. Eight Mongol 'banners' are added to the Manchu army after Mongol leaders renounce their allegiance to the Ming dynasty. In China itself, the spread of peasant unrest renders large parts of the country ungovernable. Rebel leaders stage a meeting at Rongyang (Henan province) to discuss co-operation against the Ming. Shortly afterwards, the Ming mausoleums outside Beijing are looted. Chongzhen dons mourning garb and orders the execution of the tombs' eunuch guardian. The tomb musicians, however – having fallen into rebel hands – become the cause of a rift between the two principal rebel leaders, Li Zicheng and Zhang Xianzhong, who return to their bases in Hubei and Sichuan respectively.

An imperial fleet operating from bases on the Shandong peninsula launches effective raids against Manchu coastal stations in Liaodong.

Chinese Theatre (Peking Opera)

The guardian spirit of Chinese theatre, known generically as **Peking Opera**, is the Tang emperor **Xuanzong**. Having one night dreamed of a troupe of heavenly dancers, he established an academy for the performing arts, called the Pear Garden after its location within Changan's imperial parks. But although Tang entertainments combined song and recitation with short scenes, and although elements of Chinese dramatics can be traced to shamanistic rites of archaic times, **Chinese theatre** as such emerged only during the **Yuan** and **Ming dynasties**. Essentially popular in its appeal – mixing spoken dialogue with arias and recitative, and always styled in the language of the people – it rapidly acquired enduring conventions.

Extravagant costumes identified a limited *personae dramatis*: the old man, the young hero, the pure virgin and the wily concubine being the most common stereotypes. As with Elizabethan theatre, female parts were played by men, and musicians sat on a

Figures from the Beijing Opera: Highly stylized costumes were matched by

square protruding stage. A typical night at the theatre lasted many hours. Hawkers moved among the audience as two or three plays were performed consecutively, with virtuoso turns withheld until late in the evening. Away from the stage, actors were regarded as inferiors, the first Ming emperor even going so far as to threaten to cut out the tongue of any official who consorted with them. The scholar-gentry class especially affected to despise the stage.

But if Chinese theatre remained rooted in entertaining melodramas up until the introduction of purely spoken drama in the 20th century, it served a real social purpose, allowing grandees, merchants, artisans and soldiers to mingle in the same space. From early on, it evolved discrete traditions, chief among them the boisterous **'northern' school**, and the more refined **'southern' school**. Strictly speaking, **'Peking Opera'** (*jing xi,* or 'capital play') was an offshoot of the latter and, in particular, the theatre of Suzhou. But early Western spectators, unversed in Chinese nuance, assumed all Chinese theatre was much the same.

equally stylized rules of composition and delivery.

In the same year, **English trading vessels**, belonging to the (London) East India Company, make their first appearance in southern Chinese waters.

Hong Taiji renames his 'Jin' dynasty the **Qing** ('Pure').

The Manchu Qing impose vassal status on Korea.

Hong Taiji, adding two Chinese 'banners' to his army, raids the lower Yellow River basin.

In the south, the English merchant seafarer **John Weddell** sails three ships up the Pearl River to Guangdong. Attempting to secure his objectives by force, Weddell is expelled from Chinese waters.

1638 The Ming government prohibits tobacco, but this does little to discourage the spread of smoking.

1639 The *Nong zheng quan shu* ('Complete Agricultural Management') by the Jesuit convert Xu Guangqi is published, introducing Chinese readers to Western crops and farming techniques.

1642 After an intermittent ten-year siege, the Chinese city of **Jinzhou**, south of the Daling River, falls to the Manchu. The strategic **Shanghaiguan Pass**, however, is held by the Ming general **Wu Sangui**. Behind him, the situation worsens. Floods and famines swell the ranks of peasant rebel groups as **Li Zicheng** – a one-time ironworker from Shaanxi – proves his potential as national leader.

In **Tibet**, the fifth Dalai Lama, nominally under Ming protection, asserts his temporal power and orders the construction of the Potala palace at Lhasa.

1643 The sudden death of Hong Taiji leads to the succession of his ninth son Fulin, aged 5. Actual power is exerted by **Dorgon**, the boy's uncle and regent.

1644 Li Zicheng marches across the northern plains toward **Beijing**. As he advances, so his army grows. In April, he enters the capital without opposition. Fortified by alcohol, the Emperor Chongzhen tells his palace women to kill themselves. Some obey, others do not. Cutting off the arms of one of his daughters, he kills another, then begins slaying his concubines. The following dawn, attended by a solitary eunuch, Chongzhen hangs himself on a locust tree behind the palace.

Aware that the Qing Manchu leader Dorgon is intent upon invasion, but fearing an attack by the Ming general Wu Sangui, Li Zicheng orders the breaching of Yellow River dikes at Kaifeng, then marches toward the Shanghaiguan Pass. Wu, pondering whether to side with Li against Dorgon, or with Dorgon against Li, decides on the latter course. According to legend, he resents Li for 'stealing' a favourite concubine. Wu abandons the Pass and marches toward Beijing. Li seizes and beheads Wu's father and on June 3 declares himself emperor. Dorgon passes freely through the Great Wall and, joining forces with Wu, enters Beijing on June 6. Putting Li to flight, he enthrones the Manchu boy-khan as the **Shunzhi** emperor and proclaims the **Qing dynasty**.

> ❝ Weak and of scant virtue I have offended Heaven. Because I allowed my ministers to mislead me rebels have taken my capital. I die too ashamed to meet my ancestors. My headdress removed, my hair hanging over my face, the rebels may quarter my body. Yet I pray no harm befalls my people. ❞
>
> The Chongzhen emperor's final words, inscribed on his sleeve.

8
The Qing (Manchu) Dynasty
1644–1912

For a generation after 1644, Ming loyalists offered resistance, but overcoming them enabled the **Manchu** to impose their authority not just on the south, but also on Taiwan; and in the 18th century the empire achieved its greatest extent. The Tarim basin was pacified, the Ili River valley to the north of the Tian Mountains brought under imperial control, and Tibet integrated as a protectorate. Burma and Siam joined Korea and Vietnam as tributary states. On the home front, too, the empire prospered. For a century, there was domestic peace. Scholarship entered a new phase of critical and encyclopedic ambition. As the economy grew, quality consumer goods became ever more abundant.

Yet however hard they strove, the Qing could never disguise the fact that theirs was an alien usurpation. Their power necessarily depended on intelligence, often in the form of 'secret' memorials to the throne. Manchu and Chinese custom remained separate, most visibly in the matters of foot-binding and the shaven heads and *queues* (pigtails) required of all ethnic Chinese males. 'Keep your hair and lose your head,' said popular sentiment, 'or lose your hair and keep your head.' However 'benevolent' their intentions, the Qing emperors ruled autocratically, putting too heavy a strain not just on their own individual efficacy, but also on the continuing abilities of the **Manchu 'banner' armies** to police a huge and populous terrain.

In the 19th century, entropy set in, on both counts. The

Manchu emperors and the bannermen lost their vim. But unlike the meltdown of previous dynasties, the Qing's presaged something more fundamental: the meltdown of the imperial system itself. As China's **population** accelerated out of hand – 200 million in 1750, in excess of 400 million by 1850 – the court in Beijing became increasingly remote, increasingly irrelevant. Sheer numbers placed unprecedented pressure on the land, always vulnerable to flooding and drought. But the unwillingness of the Qing to create new cities, or indeed undertake other kinds of large-scale works once two new summer palaces had been built, intensified the potential for both rural and urban revolt. The empire had long had an unruly underclass, but never on the same scale.

Against this background erupted the **Taiping** and **Nian rebellions**, as well as a series of regional uprisings: Moslems in Yunnan and the northwest, and the Miao in the south. That the Qing weathered these storms was a miracle achieved only with the financial and military help of **Western powers**. Yet those powers acted only in their own predatory interests, and it was their wider intervention in Chinese affairs that, for better or for worse, doomed dynasty and formal empire alike. Twelve years after the **Boxer Uprising** of 1900, the Qing ended as they had begun: with a boy-emperor on the throne, and the nation in turmoil.

The Shunzhi, Kangxi, Yongzhen and Qianlong Emperors 1644–1796

That the empire did survive another quarter of a millennium had much to do with a built-in veneration for the throne. What was the alternative after all? Until late in the 19th century, the very idea of a republic was unknown in China. All its immediate neighbours were, one way or another, autocratic monarchies. But that the Qing dynasty itself survived was another matter. Much must be credited to the skills of it's first four throne-holders, two of whom – **Kangxi** and **Qianlong** – reigned sixty years apiece, providing much needed stability at the top.

It also helped that the Manchu were not entirely new to the task of governing China. Their ethnic predecessors, the **Jürchen**, had ruled the Yellow River plains between 1126 and 1234. Indeed, prior to 1644, a part of the Manchurian population was Chinese, as were several Manchu institutions.

Despite the bald fact of military conquest, the Manchu offered China better management, and were tolerated as a result. Existing structures, far from being dismantled, were preserved, repaired and improved. The imperial examination system continued. From its inception, the Qing dynasty sought to govern with, and through, Chinese officials. The still vitally important **scholar-gentry class** was co-opted in, not frozen out. There were also **banners** made up of 'loyal' Chinese soldiers. To be sure, for many generations the highest positions were occupied solely by Manchu, and the 'new' territories in the west were reserved for Manchu exploitation. But the Kangxi emperor, especially, worked indefatigably to create at least an aura of fairness.

The Qing forsook the Ming preference for primogeniture. The best, not necessarily the eldest, son inherited the empire. Thus, Kangxi came to the throne, and thus did **Qianlong**, an emperor who seemed cast in the same illustrious mould as his grandfather. But as Qianlong aged, three untoward developments marred his reign. He allowed power to fall into the hands of **Heshen**, a favourite, who unscrupulously revived palace corruption. The **White Lotus rebellion**, while harbingering much greater regional revolts, was serious enough in itself. But the most telling damage was perhaps the most inadvertent. By snubbing an embassy sent from Britain, Qianlong hardened the rapacity of an emergent global superpower.

1644 The 6-year-old Fulin is enthroned as the **Shunzhi** emperor, inaugurating the **Qing Dynasty**.

Li Zicheng flees to Shanxi with the remnant of his rebel army.

Zhang Xianzhong withdraws his forces to Chengdu where he proclaims a despotic 'Great New Kingdom of the West'.

Ming loyalists (aka 'legitimists') begin regrouping south of the Huai River.

In **Beijing**, all Chinese subjects are expelled from the Imperial City. A 'Chinese city' rapidly forms south of this.

1645 A Manchu army occupies Shanxi in pursuit of Li Zicheng.

In Nanjing, **Prince Fu**, a grandson of the Wanli emperor, sets up a rival Ming court.

In May a second Manchu army invests Yangzhou. The city falls after a week-long artillery bombardment and its citizens are slaughtered. Fearing similar reprisals, Fu surrenders Nanjing and is sent to Beijing where he will die the following year.

Ming resistance continues under two other imperial princes at Fuzhou and Guangzhou. To help identify Ming loyalists, the Qing government begins enforcing **sumptuary laws** previously applied in Manchuria: Chinese males are required to wear queues and shave the front part of their heads. Chinese officials are also required to adopt Manchu dress (high collars and tight tunics). Foot-binding is forbidden among Manchu females, and it is decreed that only well-born Manchu daughters can become imperial concubines.

1646 Li Zicheng abandons Xian and marches east with his few remaining troops. In the summer he is surrounded on the border of Jiangxi province. Either he kills himself, or is killed by peasants. As Manchu forces advance southwards, Ming resistance at Fuzhou crumbles. The **Prince of Gui**, Wanli's last surviving grandson, proclaims himself Emperor at Zhaoqing, to the west of Guangzhou.

In Sichuan, Zhang Xianzhong burns Chengdu and marches eastwards, destroying everything in his path.

The Qing government holds **imperial examinations** based on the Ming curriculum. Of the 373 degrees awarded, most go to candidates from the Beijing area.

1647 Zhang Xianzhong is trapped and killed by Qing forces. Driven out of Zhaoqing, the Prince of Gui regroups in Guizhou, but the Ming Pretender's court is constantly harried.

Li Zicheng 1605–46

Born in Shaanxi, **Li Zicheng** worked in an iron factory and as a wine-store assistant before becoming a militiaman. When his unit mutinied in 1631, Li joined a group of mountain rebels, rapidly becoming their commander. A keen disciplinarian – he forbade his followers to loot – from 1639 Li began assembling a civilian administration to govern villages and counties he had seized. By 1644 his movement had gathered sufficient momentum to challenge for power. Self-styled 'the dashing general', he proclaimed a new dynasty, the **'Great Shun'**, and took Beijing, driving the last Ming emperor to suicide. His triumph, however, was short-lived. Expelled from the capital by Wu Sangui and the Manchu, Li spent his last months as a fugitive at the head of a dwindling band of increasingly querulous followers. One of a line of protean figures periodically thrown up by China's peasantry, Li may or may not have had the wherewithal to govern the empire, but Wu's treachery in allowing the Manchu to pass through the Great Wall assured him a place in the pantheon of Han Chinese heroes.

1648 In **Guangzhou**, officials are seized and killed in an anti-Qing uprising. Encouraged by this patriotism, Gui re-establishes his court at Zhaoqing, but divisions among his followers prevent him from taking further advantage.

1650 As anti-Qing resistance collapses in Guangdong, Gui is driven into Yunnan.

In Beijing, the regent **Dorgon** dies after a hunting accident. Swiftly, 13-year-old Shunzhi asserts his authority over a bickering court.

1652 **Tibet**'s fifth **Dalai Lama** pays homage to Shunzhi in Beijing at a time when the influence of his Gelugspa (Yellow Robe) sect is spreading into Nepal, Sikkim and Ladakh. In return, the emperor confirms the Dalai Lama's temporal and spiritual sovereignty in his own lands.

1659 Following a decade of warfare, the Qing government pacifies **Yunnan**.

1660 Seemingly strong-willed, Shunzhi first tries to kill himself, then offers to abdicate in order to become a Buddhist monk following the death of his favourite concubine Xiao Xian.

1661 Four months after Xiao's death, Shunzhi dies of smallpox. His 7-year-old third son, the **Kangxi** emperor, is enthroned. That Kangxi has survived smallpox in childhood is a strong factor in his favour. A four-man regency, dominated by the Manchu warrior **Oboi**, is appointed. The number and influence of palace eunuchs is reduced. Shunzhi's favourite, the Jesuit **Adam Schall von Bell**, is briefly imprisoned, and imperial revenues are boosted by a new regimen of taxes.

When **Dutch pirates** pillage the holy island of Pudushan in the Bay of Hangzhou, the regency reacts by limiting all trade with Western nations to Guangzhou, adumbrating what will become known as the **Canton System** (see pp.282–83). Equally anxious to curb illicit trade with **Taiwan**, Oboi orders the coastal population of Fujian

The Shunzhi Emperor 1638–61

Unlike China's previous dynasties, the **Qing** was not forged by a strongman who then declared himself emperor. At the time of his enthronement, **Shunzhi** was aged 6. The hard military work had been done by others of his Manchu clan, notably his grandfather **Nurhaci**, and his uncle **Dorgon**. But when Dorgon died in 1650, Shunzhi at once showed his mettle, obviating factionalism and the need for a further regency. Applying himself to the study of Chinese, he acquired a thirst for **Chan Buddhism** (see p.153). Whether his reign would have blossomed remains unfathomable. Conventionally, Shunzhi's infatuation with Xiao Xian so debilitated his strength that, following her death, he succumbed to smallpox, aged 22. By then, he had already demonstrated a dependence on others outside his familial circle. He had adopted the Jesuit **Johann Adam Schall von Bell** as his 'grandpa' and had reinstated the privileges of the palace eunuchs. The record suggests an interesting and intense young man struggling to maintain his depth.

province opposite Taiwan to remove twenty miles inland.

In the southwest, a Qing army commanded by Wu Sangui crosses into **Burma** in pursuit of the Prince of Gui. To avoid conflict, the Burmese ruler surrenders Gui into Qing hands.

1662 The **Prince of Gui** and his son are publicly strangled in Kunming (the capital of Yunnan). Qing mastery of the south, however, remains tenuous insofar as it is divided between three 'loyal' Chinese military governors, known as the **Three Feudatories** (*San fan*): Wu Sangui (Yunnan, Guizhou); Shang Kexi (Guangdong, eastern Guanxi); and Geng Jimao (Fujian). Not only do they retain imperial revenues, but they extort loyalty payments from Beijing in order to conduct bogus campaigns against nonexistent insurgents.

Zheng Chenggong – a Fujianese pirate-adventurer better known as **Koxinga** – captures the Dutch strongholds of Zeelandia and Provinitia in Taiwan. Although Koxinga dies in the same year, the Zheng family strengthens its control over the island, attracting thousands of Chinese to settle in trading communities based on a surplus of rice, salt and sugarcane.

A Dutch naval fleet commanded by **Balthasar Bort,** operating out of Batavia (modern Jakarta), defies Qing trading restrictions by forcing its way into ports on China's east coast.

In Beijing, the rehabilitated Jesuit Schall von Bell is appointed director of the Bureau of Astronomy.

1664 Although a Qing navy, armed with Jesuit-designed cannon, proves effective against Bort's Dutch marauders, an expeditionary force fails to dislodge the Zheng from Taiwan.

1669 Abetted by his grandmother and the palace guard, Kangxi topples his regents. Oboi, seized by wrestlers hiding behind the throne, is charged with corruption and imprisoned. He dies a year later.

1670 The Kangxi emperor issues his **'sacred edict'** (*Shengyu*), a sixteen-point manifesto of mainly Confucian 'kingship tenets' held up as a model for benevolent despotism.

1671 Shang Kexi hands over the military governorship of Guangdong to his son Shang Zhixin. Soon afterwards, Geng Jimao dies in Fujian, and his powers are assumed by his son Geng Jingzhong. Since neither governorship was intended to be hereditary, a challenge to Qing authority is implicit in both these developments.

1673 In December Wu Sangui renounces his loyalty to the Qing. Proclaiming a new 'Zhou dynasty', and drawing on the support of southern Chinese resentful of Manchu rule, he marches his army into Hunan. Wherever he passes,

Chinese men are urged to cut their queues to demonstrate their loyalty to a "Chinese" cause.

1674 The **War of the Feudatories** is widened when Geng Jingzhong declares independence in Fujian and occupies much of Zhejiang province. Kangxi takes personal command of Qing forces arraigned against the *San fan*.

1675 In the far west, the partly Mongol and Tibetan Buddhist **Zungar** people begin a five-year expansion under their leader **Galdan**. Pushing eastwards, Galdan's forces capture Kashgar, Turfan and Hami.

1676 Shang Zhixin joins the other two feudatories in revolt. As Qing forces struggle to contain Wu Sangui and Geng Jingzhong, Shang marches into Jiangxi. The three warlords fail to co-ordinate their campaigns, however. Geng breaks ranks and surrenders to the Manchu.

1677 Shang in turn surrenders, having argued with Wu Sangui about rank and appointments.

1678 Wu Sangui dies of dysentery. Shang and Geng are executed. Despite persistent pressure to banish the Portuguese from **Macau**, Kangxi allows them to stay after the gift of an African lion.

1679 In order to enlist the support of dissident scholars, the Kangxi emperor announces the compilation of an **official history** of the Ming dynasty. In a special examination, candidates are nominated at the provincial level, and the winners invited to join the writing team in Beijing.

1680 In the wake of the three feudatories, Manchu bannermen are garrisoned at strategic points throughout southern China.

1681 The Manchu conquest of China is completed when Wu Sangui's grandson commits suicide in Kunming after his small army is surrounded. The governorships of Yunnan, Guizhou and Guangdong are given to senior Manchu bannermen.

1683 Following the defeat of the Zheng family by Shi Lang in a sea battle among the Pescadore islands, Taiwan is incorporated within the Chinese empire as a 'district' of Fujian province. On the mainland, those moved inland in 1661 are permitted to return to their coastal dwellings.

In Manchuria, **Russian** soldiers and trappers begin raiding across the Amur River.

1685 Kangxi orders a retaliatory attack on a Russian 'outpost' at Albazin. Albazin falls, but is lost again to a force sent from the Russian garrison at Nerchensk. Throughout

---

Koxinga (1624–62)
and the House of Zheng

Zheng Cheng'gong, known as **Koxinga**, was the son of a wealthy Fujianese 'maritime adventurer' and a Japanese woman from Nagasaki. In 1644 he enrolled at the Imperial Academy in Nanjing, but with the overthrow of the Ming by the Qing he immediately threw in his lot with the Ming legitimists, combining insurrection with piracy. Establishing a stronghold at **Xiamen** (Amoy) in 1659, he took part in a campaign that saw rebel forces encamped outside Nanjing. Koxinga then turned his attention to **Taiwan**. Driving the Dutch out in 1661, he created a personal kingdom that was a magnet for disaffected Han Chinese. After his death, his son **Zheng Jing** continued Koxinga's 'Ming loyalist' wars up until 1681.

In retrospect, the chief legacy of the house of Zheng's resistance was an extension of the Manchu empire. Only by capturing Taiwan could the Zheng finally be suppressed. It is Koxinga, however, who has attracted most attention. Perceived in the West as a romantic pirate – on his ships he employed black slaves escaped from the Portuguese colony at **Macau** – in the East he has been the hero of many causes. In the 18th century, Japanese dramatist Chikamatsu extolled him as a 'sage king'; in the 20th, he was both a natural icon for Chiang Kaishek's Guomingdang, and a 'revolutionary martyr' for the Communists.

the next four years, continuous skirmishing between imperial and Russian units assumes the proportions of a war.

Peace between China and Russia is brokered by Jesuit intermediaries. The **Treaty of Nerchensk** cedes the Amur River watershed to the Qing. Russia further agrees not to assist the nascent Zungar empire. In return, China grants trading concessions and, unprecedentedly, the right of extradition.

1692 Partly as a reward for Jesuit diplomatic services, Kangxi issues an **edict of tolerance** with regard to the Christian religion. While this enables the Jesuits to expand their mission, in the long-run it encourages the **Rites Controversy** (see p.277).

c.1695 In mid-reign, Kangxi institutes a system of **secret palace memorials** whereby reports prepared by trusted servants, many of them eunuchs, on such matters as tax collection and the behaviour of individual officials, can be forwarded clandestinely to the throne. Only the emperor may break the seals on such documents, and use the vermillion ink with which his replies and comments are written.

1696 Kangxi leads an 80,000-strong mixed Manchu-Chinese army across the Gobi desert and decisively defeats the Zungar khan Galdan at the **Battle of Jab Modo**. Northern Mongolia and the city of Hami are added to the Chinese empire.

1699 *L'Amphithrite* – a vessel belonging to the Compagnie des Indes Orientales – initiates trading relations between **France** and China. A vogue for *chinoiserie* affects French taste, and with it French design, at the time enjoying cultural paramountcy in Europe. As well as some French Jesuits, *L'Amphithrite*'s passengers include the Italian artist **Giovanni Gheradini**, the first of several professional Western painters to attach themselves to the Qing court, including, from 1715, **Giuseppe Castiglione**.

1700 China's **population** reaches 120 million.

The Kangxi Emperor 1654–1722

No list of the world's great monarchs would pass muster without **Kangxi**'s inclusion. For half a century, he governed China with an undiminished appetite for detail. In old age, he annotated several hundred documents a day. As a younger man, he was an outstanding militarist. He faced down the **Three Feudatories**, and subjugated both **Taiwan** and **Tibet**. In an arduous campaign, he overcame the threat posed by the **Zungaria**, and he acted promptly to contain the expansion of the **Russian empire** on his northeastern borders. But by studying the Chinese classics and by perfecting his calligraphy Kangxi also acquired the aura of a 'sage ruler'. From 1677 onwards, he regularly convened a study group of leading scholars inside the Forbidden City. Out of this emerged what is sometimes called the **Confucian Revival**. In other ways, too, Kangxi was a determined patron of traditional **literature**, commissioning an array of encyclopedias and lexicons. Behind such encouragement, however, lay an acute understanding of statecraft. In as much as Confucianism was an ideology of 'filial' obedience tailored to the governing class, its promotion matched the interests of the Qing regime. He urged that the death penalty be used sparingly, and in a meet-the-people exercise, undertook six 'grand tours' of China. He lived frugally, and relished the Spartan camp-life associated with protracted summer hunts that rekindled links with his Manchu patrimony. The one blot on his reign was the delinquency of his chosen heir, **Yinreng**. But for the good of China Kangxi disavowed his firstborn.

1703 Kangxi orders a **summer palace** to be built at **Jehol** (Chengde), a place of natural beauty outside the Great Wall. By adding Tibetan-style temples, including a replica of Lhasa's Potala, Kangxi seeks to impress the Mongols and other potentially unruly northern 'barbarians' with the ordered might of the Qing empire.

In the same year, the *Quan Tang shi* is published, a comprehensive anthology of Tang poetry commissioned by the emperor.

The emperor Kangxi captured in old age by French artist Pierre Duflos.

> When we pass [beyond the Great Wall] for the summer visit to the Jehol palace, which has the reputation of being a cool place, we are still troubled by the heat. We think it must be far worse in Beijing. We are always mindful of the sufferings of our subjects. At the moment all under heaven is peaceful, the farmers and merchants are content. But we fear that the prisoners who are lying in prison, in chains or in the cangue, must be sick from the heat. When we think of them our heart is full of pity. We command therefore that all the prisoners in the capital be treated with great kindness. More ice shall be taken to the prisons. The number of their chains shall be diminished and those who bear the cangue shall be taken out of it. When the summer has passed the usual routine may be observed.

Kangxi, from Sven Hedin, *Jehol, City of Emperors* (1932)

1705 Maillard de Tournon, a papal envoy sent by Clement XI, arrives in Beijing to begin discussions with the emperor and his advisers in a bid to resolve issues of temporal and spiritual authority governing the Jesuits, known as the **Rites Controversy**.

1706 As 'talks' break down, Maillard de Tournon threatens to excommunicate all Christians in China adhering to Kangxi's insistence that ancestor-worship be sustained and that the emperor himself should be regarded as the head of the Catholic Church in China. In response, Kangxi expels those missionaries adhering to the papal line.

1708 Kangxi disgraces his eldest son and designated heir **Yinreng**, after secret memorials confirm a debauched lifestyle that includes the procurement of young boys for sexual pleasure. Yinreng is placed under house arrest and his associates imprisoned or executed.

The 'Rites' Controversy

Throughout the 17th century, **Jesuits** as well as other Catholic missionaries, made slow but steady headway in China, even though their converts never exceeded at most 0.1 percent of the population – a mean total compared with the inroads made by, for instance, Islam. For the Jesuits, however, quality meant more than quantity. What mattered was their position at the court, where they regularly supplied the senior staff at the Imperial Bureau of Astronomy, and acted as consultants in foreign affairs, notably with regard to Russia.

But Kangxi's 1692 edict granting Christianity 'tolerance' was deceptive. It was not, as some Fathers thought, a licence to pros-elytize, much less an admission of the 'truth' of Catholic dogma, and when **Pope Clement XI** sent an envoy to Beijing to enforce doctrinal adherence, two insoluble heads of contention were dragged to the surface. The Vatican would not allow any hint of **ancestor-worship** within services conducted in China; and it insisted on the **primacy of the pope** in spiritual affairs. These dogmas cut directly across the grain of Confucian culture and the authority of the emperor. There were other issues at stake besides: for example the **practice of concubinage**, as opposed to the Christian ideal of monogamy.

Kangxi's response was swift. Any missionary who adhered to the papal line was to be expelled forthwith. Many Jesuits chose to defy Rome, but for the remainder of the 18th century their pres-ence in China was restricted to Beijing, Guangzhou and Macau. Dominicans and Franciscans, on the other hand, left *en masse*, and it was not until the 19th century, and the advent of a Protestant evangelicalism prepared to flout imperial decrees, that the Christian conversion of China returned to the international agenda. What was not understood then, and what had not been understood before, was that the Chinese were spiritually self-suf-ficient, even though they lacked a state religion embracive of all classes.

1709 Yinreng is partially restored to favour.

1712 Yinreng, continuing his debaucheries, and perhaps plotting against his father, is rearrested and permanently barred from the succession. By not naming an alternative heir, Kangxi introduces unnecessary tensions into his court.

In an attempt to regularize **imperial revenues**, the emperor decrees fixed returns for given districts in place of capitation taxes. In the long-term, however, this encourages cupidity among provincial officials who squeeze the peasantry for extra profits.

1716 Kangxi orders the compilation of a new **Chinese lexicon**, the *Kangxi zidian*. 47,035 Chinese characters are classified in 214 groups according to their stem or radical – a practice that continues to the present day.

1720 Following the murder of the Dalai Lama, a disputed succession in **Tibet** persuades Kangxi to intervene directly. Armies sent from Sichuan and Gansu converge on Lhasa, and a new Dalai Lama amenable to Manchu influence is installed. Much of eastern Tibet is incorporated into **Xinghai province** while the remainder becomes a Chinese protectorate.

In **Taiwan**, a revolt led by Zhu Yigui is crushed within two months.

In Guangzhou, Chinese merchants seeking to exploit a rapidly expanding trade with England, Holland and other Western nations, form a cartel to fix prices. This, the *cohong*, becomes the cornerstone of the **Canton System** (see pp.282–83).

1721 The sixtieth anniversary of Kangxi's accession prompts 'spontaneous' celebrations throughout China. In Beijing the emperor hosts a banquet as part of a 'Festival of Old Men'. China's elderly are given handouts of silk and exempted from taxes.

> Like other Europeans the Russians, Dutch and Spanish succeed in whatever they determine to do. They are fearless, clever, and opportunistic. As long as I am alive China need not fear them. I respect them, they respect me and they do their best to serve me. The rulers of France and Portugal have sent me excellent subjects, skilled in the sciences and arts, and they benefited the empire. But should our government falter, should civil war break out, or should we be invaded by the Mongols, what then would become of our empire? The Europeans would do with China as they please.
>
> The Kangxi emperor, in a secret memorandum to his family and ministers written shortly before his death.

1722 The Kangxi emperor dies peacefully in December, but without having declared his heir. His forceful fourth son Yinzhen seizes the throne, as the **Yongzheng** emperor.

1723 Yongzheng secures his position by arresting those brothers, including Yinreng, likely to contest his enthronement. Each dies in prison. Conversely, Yongzheng's trusted younger brother **Yinxiang** is placed in charge of an audit office established to monitor the collection of imperial revenues.

In Suzhou, a **strike** by cotton processors is ruthlessly suppressed.

1726 For three years, ethnic insurgency – chiefly among the opium-growing **Miao** people – festers in Yunnan. As the uprisings are put down, the hill tribes are either slaughtered or coerced into registering their households with provincial authorities. To evade Manchu control, some begin migrating to the northern uplands of Burma, Siam (Thailand), Laos and Vietnam.

1727 A second **Sino-Russian treaty** is concluded at Kiakhta. While borders are again defined in China's favour, to the chagrin of the Jesuits the Russian Orthodox Church is permitted to establish a mission in Beijing. Kiakhta itself becomes an important entrepôt in a burgeoning Sino-Russian trade based on the exchange of tea and silk for furs.

1728 **Zeng Jing**, a young teacher, attempts to revive the writings of **Lu Liuliang**, a fiercely anti-Manchu 17th-century scholar, as a way of castigating Yongzheng as a usurper. Yongzheng orders Lu's body to be disinterred and dismembered, and all scholars employed by the state to take an oath of loyalty. Because of his youth, and to avoid making a martyr of him, Zeng is pardoned: a decision overturned by the succeeding Qianlong emperor, who will order Zeng's public execution by slicing.

In the same year 100 copies of the monumental *Gujin tushu jicheng* are printed, a 'Collection of Texts and Illustrations Old and New' in 10,000 chapters. Compiled by Chen Menglei and Jiang Tinxi, the work is ascribed to the Kangxi emperor.

1729 Faced by fresh **Zungar** hostilities, Yongzheng creates an 'inner cabinet' comprising himself, Yinxiang and two Grand Secretaries to secretly prepare a military counterattack. Concurrently, he establishes an equally secret Board of Military Finance. Out of these arrangements emerges the **Grand Council** of later Qing times. Memorials are submitted to the throne about the growing use of opium, but Yongzheng, persuaded of its medicinal properties, takes no action.

In Suzhou, a second strike by cotton workers is even more ruthlessly crushed.

1732 8000 men are lost when a Chinese army is defeated by the Zungars at Khobdo.

The Yongzheng Emperor 1722–1735

The most ruthless of the Qing emperors, **Yongzheng** made good his claim to the throne by disposing of all his brothers except the loyal Yinxiang. That Yongzheng placed Yinxiang in charge of the imperial audit office, however speaks volumes of the usurper's seriousness of purpose. Sharing his father's thirst for detail, Yongzheng worked long hours to eradicate bureaucratic corruption. To remove an incentive to dishonesty, he raised officials' salaries. He also alleviated the condition of China's outcast population, known as the 'mean people'. But overwhelmingly, the evidence suggests that Yongzheng was a control freak. He curbed the powers and status of his fellow Manchu princes, encouraged his provincial governors to submit secret reports on each other, personally edited the official history of his father's reign, and secreted the name of his designated heir in a sealed casket behind an ancestral tablet. Yongzheng's reign also saw increased migration of Han Chinese settlers into areas of China traditionally inhabited by ethnic minorities, notably Yunnan.

1735 Yongzheng dies in October, officially of natural causes, but rumours spread that he has been murdered by the daughter of a man he had previously ordered to be executed. The name of his chosen heir is discovered in a sealed box.

1736 Accession of the **Qianlong emperor**, Yongzheng's 25-year-old fourth son. For the first forty years of his reign, Qianlong maintains close personal supervision over government. Until 1750, however, he is 'assisted' by a four-man regency.

1739 Qianlong orders an annotated edition of the **standard dynastic histories** that will partially expose the bias of previous 'official' historians.

1741 The British Royal Navy commodore **George Anson** puts into Guangzhou with a fleet damaged by an encounter with Spanish men-of-war but is treated unsympathetically by government officials. Anson's subsequently published account of events – as well as underlining the need for a British military base in the Far East – stimulates anti-Chinese feeling in London.

1746 Ethnic minorities in western **Sichuan** begin a thirty-year insurgency against Manchu rule.

1747 Qianlong commissions Jesuit designers and architects to create a new summer palace – the *Yuanmingyuan* – to the immediate northwest of Beijing. Combining Chinese and European styles, this will survive as a showpiece of Manchu 'cultivation' until its destruction in 1860.

In the far west, Ahmad Shah Durrani forges a strong state in Afghanistan that blocks further Chinese expansion beyond the Tianshan mountain range.

The 'Canton' System

Although **Guangzhou** (Canton) on the Pearl River had been southern China's busiest port for a thousand years, it was only between 1720 and 1759 that the legendary, and for some infamous, **'Canton System'** fell into place. The government imposed measures designed to regulate trade with the West, and make it self-policing. Chinese merchants in Guangzhou, having formed a guild (the *cohong*) amongst themselves, were made responsible for the behaviour of their 'red-haired' clients. They were also required to make sizeable annual payments to the imperial treasury, and were overseen by an official known as the *hoppo*, responsible not to any ministry in Beijing, but to the local Governor-General.

At most times, the *cohong* had between ten and a dozen members. Some went bankrupt, but most made fortunes. On their side, Western traders were permitted to buy such core commodities as silk and tea only at Guangzhou, and only between the months of October and May. An area of the river foreshore outside the city walls was reserved for their use. There they could lease, but not own, **factory-warehouses**, of which there were between

1750 Dispensing with his regents, Qianlong assumes absolute authority. For the next thirty years the empire pursues assertive policies vis-à-vis its neighbours and attains its maximum extent.

1751 Tibet's incorporation within the empire is formalized after a military expedition enforces Chinese suzerainty. From this point, an *amban* appointed by the emperor will monitor and supervise Tibetan affairs.

1754 In a move that combines self-regulation with legal liability, the *cohong* (merchant guild) of Guangzhou is ordered to stand surety for its Western trading partners.

1759 Following Zunghar insurgency in the western Tarim Basin, an army led by the Manchu bannerman **Zhaohui**

fifteen and twenty. Both women and firearms were prohibited. Europeans committing offences were liable to Chinese law, and Chinese subjects were forbidden to teach Europeans their language on pain of death – of small consequence, since the Portuguese already possessed Macau as a colony, and here many Europeans resided 'out of season'.

What did hurt was the steady suspicion of price-fixing by the *cohong*, and the fact that the Chinese appeared to want relatively few Western commodities. For decades, vast quantities of silver, mined either in South America or in Japan, poured into China. To overcome this imbalance, the **British East India Company** and others developed the **country trade**, buying rice and other products, including **opium**, the Chinese did want from its neighbours, and then shipping them to Guangzhou. But although opium helped equalize profitability, the 'Canton System' was seen in the West as a restrictive practice determined by a despotic regime. As 'free trade' evolved between nations in the 19th century, so the use of force against China became more likely.

Cinnabar lacquer snuff bottle, 1720–1820.

reasserts Chinese rule in territories to the immediate east of the Pamir mountains.

In a unilateral bid to expand British trade, **Captain James Flint** of the East India Company sails his seventy-tonne armed trader *Success* into the northern port of Tianjin and attempts to present his compliments to the emperor. When his ship is wrecked on its way back to Guangzhou, Flint is seized and imprisoned. The emperor issues an edict reaffirming the limitation of Western trade to Guangzhou.

1760 As Manchu control of what will become **Xinjiang** province is consolidated, Zhaohui establishes a 20,000-strong garrison at **Ili**. When Zhaoji returns to Beijing as an unprecedented honour he is met outside Beijing by the emperor. Xinjiang, with its mainly Moslem population, is conceived, however, as a Manchu preserve, with few ethnic Chinese being allowed to settle within its boundaries.

1762 The capture of Manilla by the British East India Company marks the beginning of the continuous presence of **British sea-power** in Far Eastern waters.

An official census puts China's **population** at 200 million.

1765 An uprising by **Turkic Moslems** in Ili suggests that China's control over its western territories is still tenuous.

Qianlong's second empress, Ula Nara, retires to a monastery, his first empress having died in 1738.

1768 Qianlong is persuaded that sorcerers – by cutting off his Chinese subjects' pigtails – are creating a potentially lethal army of rebellious automatons. Many are tortured to extract confessions before Qianlong acknowledges he has been misguided by unreliable officials.

In the same year, the *Rulin Waishi* ('Unofficial Lives of the Scholars') is published, a novel written circa 1750 satirizing the conduct of impoverished Confucian scholar-gentry.

c.1770 Rogue English merchants begin exchanging **opium** grown in India and Afghanistan for tea, silk and other commodities. Soon adopted by the East India Company, this extension of the **'country trade'** becomes the primary mechanism for turning China's export surplus into a corrosive deficit.

1774 Wang Lun, a herbalist and martial arts exponent, foments an anti-Manchu uprising around the city of Linqing (Shandong province). Although the small-scale revolt is harshly suppressed by Manchu bannermen, because of Wang's links with the (Buddhist) **White Lotus Sect**, his revolt is seen as a significant watershed in the involvement of **'secret societies'** in Chinese politics. The uprising coincides with the onset of a fifteen-year **literary inquisition** ordered by Qianlong and directed against pub-

The Qianlong Emperor 1711–99

Like all the early Manchu emperors, Qianlong was more at home on horseback than on the throne.

As **Qianlong's** reign ripened, so it slackened. Unless his abdication of 1795 be taken at face value, he was China's longest-serving emperor. Between his accession in 1735 and 1750, government held an even course as Qianlong shared decision-making with a group of regents nominated by his father. For the next thirty years, he ruled alone. It was during this period that **'Chinese**

lications critical of the Qing dynasty. 2320 books are completely banned, and 345 subjected to partial censorship.

1775 In the fortieth year of his reign, Qianlong succumbs to the charm of a young Manchu guards officer, **Heshen**. Heshen is appointed to key positions within the imperial household, and then in the Grand Council. In control of both Beijing's military and imperial revenues, he shamelessly enriches himself at the throne's expense.

In **Vietnam**, thousands of Chinese are massacred in Gia Dinh (Saigon) as a nationalist rebellion led by the **Tay Son** brothers spreads.

Turkestan' was effectively pacified, leading to the creation of China's largest province, today called **Xinjiang**, and virtually eradicating the centuries-old threat of nomadic invasion. But campaigns in Mongolia, the west, and the southwest drained the imperial coffers, a situation exacerbated by the rise to power, after 1780, of Qianlong's grasping favourite, Heshen. If to the outside world – including commentators caught up in the European Enlightenment – Qianlong appeared a near-impossible example of benevolent monarchism, inside China the cracks were beginning to show. **Corruption** among provincial officials was on the increase, and the government failed to improve its income by tapping into the empire's busy, thriving economy. On the surface it seemed a vibrant culture: the last great age perhaps of the Chinese arts, even though nothing particularly new was added to the repertoire. But if, like Kangxi, Qianlong was an eager patron of Confucian scholarship, he also revived **literary censorship**. Again like Kangxi, he was a keen archer, and hunted to within two years of his death; but he was less diligent as a ruler. His artistic afternoons were spent painting and writing poems. Of the latter, some 40,000 are ascribed to his pen. Over six feet tall, he was an imposing figure, and legend claims that, as an 8-year old, he confronted a bear with perfect equanimity.

THE QING EMPIRE

N

• Ürümqi

• Kashgar

NEW TERRITORIES
(XINJIANG)

• Dunhuang
Jiayugang

• Khotan

QINGHAI

Xining •

TIBET

• Lhasa

B R I T I S H
E M P I R E

Kunming •

YUNNAN

— Extent of Qing empire
--- Provincial/territorial boundaries

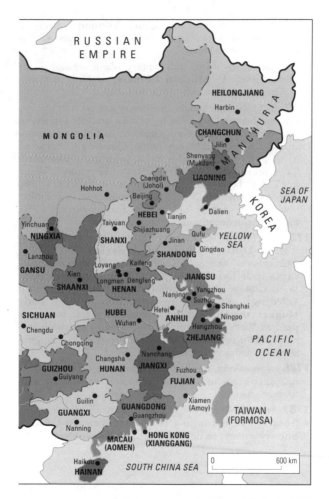

RUSSIAN
EMPIRE

MONGOLIA

HEILONGJIANG
Harbin

CHANGCHUN
Jilin

Shenyang
(Mukden)

LIAONING

Chengde
(Johol)

Hohhot

Beijing

HEBEI   Tianjin

Dalien

MANCHURIA

SEA OF
JAPAN

KOREA

Yinchuan

NINGXIA

Taiyuan

Shijiazhuang

SHANXI

Jinan

YELLOW
SEA

Lanzhou

SHANDONG

Qingdao

Qufu

GANSU

Loyang   Kaifeng

Xian

SHAANXI

Longmen Dengfeng

HENAN

JIANGSU

Nanjing

Yangzhou

Suzhou

SICHUAN

HUBEI

Hetei

ANHUI

Shanghai

Ningpo

Chengdu

Wuhan

Chongqing

ZHEJIANG

Hangzhou

PACIFIC
OCEAN

Changsha

Nanchang

GUIZHOU

HUNAN

JIANGXI

Guiyang

Fuzhou

FUJIAN

Guilin

GUANGDONG

Xiamen
(Amoy)

TAIWAN
(FORMOSA)

GUANGXI

Guangzhou

Nanning

MACAU
(AOMEN)

HONG KONG
(XIANGGANG)

Haikou

HAINAN

SOUTH CHINA SEA

0   600 km

1776 After prolonged campaigning, **Yunnan** is pacified. From now on, increasing numbers of Han Chinese settlers migrate to the province.

1781 Inspired by a late 18th-century Islamic revival in the west, a revolt by **Moslem Chinese**, or Hui, in Gansu province, is suppressed by Manchu forces.

1782 As Qianlong's literary inquisition gathers momentum, private libraries are raided by officials and the owners of 'anti-Manchu' publications punished. To define an acceptable and permanent literary canon, Qianlong orders seven hand-copied sets of the *Si ku quan shu* ('Complete Collection of the **Four Treasuries** of Literature'), begun in 1772, to be placed in China's principal libraries. 79,000 chapters arranged in 36,275 volumes contain the complete texts of 3400 works and extracts from a further 6780, together with accompanying commentaries.

1784 *The Empress of China*, a trading vessel from the newly formed **United States of America**, anchors at Guangzhou. Joining the Canton System, American merchants trade furs and North American ginseng for traditional Chinese commodities. When a Chinese subject is killed by a salute fired from the English vessel **Lady Hughes**, the Governor of Guangzhou threatens to suspend all Western trade unless the offending gunner is surrendered for execution. After tense negotiations, the gunner is handed over and publicly strangled.

1786 In Shandong, the **Eight Trigrams** sect mounts a second anti-Manchu uprising intimately connected with 'secret societies'.

1787 Anti-Manchu revolt spreads to **Taiwan** where settlers from Fujian belonging to the **Heaven and Earth Society** attempt to dislodge Manchu officials.

1788 In Vietnam, as the nationalist Tay Son rebellion gains its objectives, the Tonkinese emperor Le seeks sanctuary in Guangxi. Immediately agreeing to restore his 'vassal' to his throne, Qianlong dispatches an army to Hanoi.

1790 Qianlong's tenth daughter is given in marriage to Heshen's son. In Vietnam, during Tet (New Year Festival), 4000 Chinese troops are slaughtered. When the Tay Son rebels offer to accept Qianlong as their suzerain overlord, the emperor reverses his policy and the deposed Le is abandoned.

The minority **Yao** people attempt an uprising in Guangxi province, and Nepal stages an invasion of southern Tibet.

1791 Posthumous publication of Cao Xueqin's *Hongloumeng* (**'Dream of the Red Chamber'**), widely regarded as China's finest novel.

Dream of the Red Chamber

The *Hongloumeng*, written by **Cao Xueqin** (1715–63) and translated variously as *The Story of the Stone* and *Dream of the Red Chamber*, stands beside the much earlier Japanese *Tale of Genjii* as a supreme example of Eastern fiction. Combining eroticism, humour, pathos, the supernatural and tragedy, its huge canvas is episodic rather than linear. If it has a central character, then that is **Jia Baoyu**, the talented, headstrong, but ultimately doomed, heir of a family that, attached to the fringes of court society, has seen better days – much like Cao's own Nanjing relatives. Jia Baoyu, though, is but one among many characters, each given his or her own space within the overall framework. Each character, too, rises above conventional stereotyping to become an acute individual portrait. Even so, the manifold demands of Confucian clan-life are always present. Set in the Kangxi period, the *Hongloumeng* is nevertheless a powerful tale of decay, and in its exhaustive exploration of the tensions between ethos and personality, furnishes an exemplary elegy of the empire itself.

The Macartney Mission of 1793

The London **East India Company**, despite its official monopoly in the Anglo-Chinese tea trade, felt perennially stymied by the Canton System. In a bid to lift restrictions, and open new ports for its vessels, it financed two missions which, backed by George III, sallied forth as full-blown embassies. While the first never reached China, the second was headed by **Earl George Macartney** of Lissanoure, a distinguished career diplomat. Macartney headed straight for Tianjin, and then made his way upriver to Beijing, bringing with him a large cargo of mainly newfangled scientific gifts for Qianlong.

After a tiresome wrangle over whether Macartney should 'kow-tow' before the emperor (ie bow three times and touch the ground nine times with his head) an audience was granted on September 14, in the grounds of the old summer palace at **Jehol**. In the event, Macartney was permitted to kneel on one knee. An imperial rescript, however, addressed to King George, rejecting every one of Britain's requests, had already been drafted. In words that stung Macartney to the quick, and later goaded his compatriots to obtain the concessions sought by direct action, the emperor declared: 'As your Ambassador can see for himself, we possess all things. I set no value on objects strange or ingenious, and have no use for your country's manufactures.'

Formally, therefore, the embassy was an abject failure. But as a fact-finding mission, much was achieved. Macartney was allowed to return down the **Grand Canal**, and from this journey a greatly improved understanding of China was gleaned, including its military weakness. Macartney's team also collected specimens of the **tea-plant** that seeded the first plantations in British India. While much has been made of both sides' supposed intransigence, Macartney's visit was a vital passage in East–West relations.

1792 After a costly campaign, Nepalese forces are expelled from Tibet. **Nepal** itself is coerced into becoming a Chinese tributary, a status retained until 1908.

1793 Despite being granted an audience with Qianlong, **Lord Macartney** – representing the British monarch George III on a diplomatic mission to Beijing funded by the East India Company – fails to gain trading concessions for his compatriots.

1795 Qianlong 'abdicates' on the pretext of not wishing to reign longer than his esteemed grandfather Kangxi.

The nine-year **White Lotus Rebellion** begins in the borders between Hubei and Shaanxi provinces.

The Jiaqing, Daoguang, Xianfeng and Tongzhi Emperors 1796–1875

Lord Macartney described China as 'an old, crazy, first-rate man-of-war, which a fortunate succession of able and vigilant officers has continued to keep afloat'. In the century that followed, nearly everything that could go wrong did go wrong. Both on the peripheries, among the non-Han peoples inhabiting the frontiers, and in the heartlands, revolt festered. But if anti-Manchu feeling culminated in the awesome **Taiping Rebellion** of the 1850s, an equal threat came from much further afield.

Political reform and the Industrial Revolution created in

Europe compact, dynamic and competitive states that sought fulfilment through the acquisition of far-off colonies. One by one, they eyed the Chinese prize. The Qing resisted, but failed to grasp the signal importance of sea power. In command of the oceans, it was the bullying English who unlocked the empire, unscrupulously using **opium** as the key.

In the wake of war, and the 1842 **Treaty of Nanjing**, other nations piled in, the United States and then Japan among them. In a series of 'unequal treaties', China surrendered its effective autonomy without quite becoming any one power's colony. Instead, there arose the novelty of the treaty ports and their 'foreign concessions', governed by Western law, not Chinese custom.

Such large-scale intervention bequeathed a legacy of **'anti-imperialism'** that in the 20th century provided Marxism with a fertile seed-bed. Yet, as Macartney's comment intuited, the fault lay equally with China's own imperialism. It was not a small boat that was going under, but a ship of the very greatest magnitude; and the Qing emperors, like their Ming and other predecessors, sat 'facing south' on their thrones, immobile in their splendour, and fatally insensitive to change.

Although by 1800, the empire's population had swollen to 300 million, there was no commensurate expansion either of government, or in the numbers of what today would be called stakeholders. Degrees awarded in the imperial examinations did not increase, nor did imperial revenues. But if China was inward-looking, that was because there was little perceived need for it to be anything other that that. In the past, the chief danger had always come from the northern and western 'barbarians'. Perhaps because they were themselves northerners, the **Manchu** allowed both the object and the style of their foreign relations to remain focused on **Central Asia**.

Even so, left to its own devices, the empire might well have continued to evolve at its own gradual pace. A vast surplus of cheap labour obviated the need for machines. There existed an empire-wide credit-system and flow of goods, and southern merchant guilds provided a mechanism for moderate capital investment. But Western ambition, Western inventiveness and ultimately Western politics, were not to be gainsaid. Although the Qing survived the shock of the Taiping, the dynasty's inherited and cherished anachronisms were unlikely to grant more than a temporary respite.

1796 Although Qianlong abdicates in favour of his 36-year-old fifth son, the **Jiaqing** emperor, power continues to be wielded by the outgoing emperor's favourite **Heshen**, and by Qianlong himself.

1799 Qianlong's death enables Jiaqing to move against Heshen, who is stripped of his appointments and 'persuaded' to commit suicide. Heshen's colossal and mainly ill-gotten wealth is shared by the emperor with three surviving brothers. Having been brought up by Confucian scholars, Jiaqing exhibits a willingness to work, but lacks the will to surmount the internal and external threats of his reign. Even as he assumes power, the **White Lotus Rebellion** spreads to Sichuan and Henan provinces.

1800 The **population** of China reaches an estimated 300 million.

As annual British imports of Chinese **tea** pass ten million kilograms, Jiaqing issues fresh edicts outlawing the purchase of **opium** from Western merchants in Guangzhou. He fails, however, to create an effective navy, and English traders sell opium in smaller ports under the cover of their superior cannon. At the same time, **Vietnamese pirates** begin operating off China's southern coast.

The White Lotus Rebellion

The first truly serious, but inadequately organized, indigenous uprising the Qing had to face once the Ming legitimists had been quashed in the 17th century was the **White Lotus Rebellion** of 1795–1804. The *Bailian jiao* – a semi-secret sect that combined Buddhism with worship of the 'Eternal Unborn Mother' – had existed since the 13th century, but only became politicized with the overthrow of the Ming in 1644. At the end of the 18th century, it exploited peasant discontent aroused by the rapacity of the Heshen clique, in 1795 provoking revolt in the mountainous areas of **Shanxi**, **Hubei** and **Sichuan** provinces. At first, this took the form of resistance to tax collectors, then the building of stockades, and finally assaults on Manchu positions. It promised its followers both the restoration of the Ming, and the advent of a reborn Buddha. That it lasted nine years was due to its mountain character, and to government inaction. Monies earmarked for combating the White Lotus 'army' were sequestered by Heshen and his associates. Only after Heshen's demise was the rebellion finally crushed, by mainly Chinese militias. But although the Emperor Jiaqing may be given credit for taking more earnest action than his father, little attempt was made to examine the root causes of sedition, which, fifty years later, fuelled the **Taiping**.

1804 The nine-year White Lotus Rebellion is finally suppressed after many of its followers are rounded up, given military training, and persuaded to combat the sect as paid militiamen.

1805 Seven Chinese pirates form a confederation to work the South China Sea. The group is closely bonded by mutual sharing of women and homosexuality. With links to Fujian's secret societies, its de facto leader is **Shi Yang**, a former prostitute and the owner of a gambling den in Guangzhou.

1807 'Eastern' **Tibetans** in Xinghai province stage a short-lived uprising.

1811 The part-Buddhist, part-millenarian **Heavenly Principle Sect** launches a three-year revolt in southwest Shandong province.

1813 Led by **Lin Qing**, the **Eight Trigrams** – an anti-Manchu sect espousing belief in the Eternal Unborn Mother – takes control of villages in Hebei. In October sect members, disguised as pedlars, attempt to enter the Forbidden City. Although some succeed, the imperial intelligence network is ready for them and most are cut down. Lin is publicly executed by slicing. Jianqing issues edicts banning the use of **opium**, but the effect of these is counter-productive. Corrupt officials, merchants and organized crime syndicates (**triads**) co-operate to expand opium addiction.

1816 The London East India Company dispatches a fresh trade mission to Beijing headed by **Lord Amherst**. When Amherst requests time to consider an order to kowtow before the emperor he is immediately expelled from China. Coupled with the Macartney mission of 1793, this stiffens British determination to open up the China market by any means.

1817 China experiences its first known outbreak of **cholera**, a scourge that particularly affects eastern seaboard ports for decades to come.

In the far west, an anti-Manchu 'holy war,' aimed at recovering Kashgar in the Tarim Basin, is proclaimed by **Jahangir**, supposedly a descendant of the Prophet Mohammed.

1820 Jiajing dies of heatstroke at the 'old' summer palace at Jehol.

Li Ruzhen publishes his novel *Flowers in the Mirror*, in which contemporary genteel society is satirized by gender reversal.

1821 Jiajing is succeeded by his second son Min Ning. Like

The Imperial Examination System

A key to the empire's longevity was one of its most widely admired features: an effective bureaucracy. But how was such a machine to be staffed? From the Han dynasty onwards, future officials were trained by **state-sponsored colleges**. As these expanded, so too did the concept of **written examinations**. The Tang, Song and Ming dynasties each added their own refinements. By Qing times, the examinations had evolved into an awesome sequence of hurdles and pitfalls. To stand any chance of success, the would-be candidate had to commit nine 'classics' to memory. Ahead of him lay tests at district and prefectural levels. If he passed these, he was qualified as a 'licentiate' to sit examinations at the provincial, capital and palace levels. As few as one in a thousand made it to the highest grade, but success in Beijing guaranteed lucrative employment. For those who failed, the mere fact of having been a licentiate was sufficient to secure a job as a teacher.

As the syllabus at every level was narrowly **Confucian**, the system inculcated a common ethos, as well as supposedly searching out the best minds. But its very success made it inflexible. The '**eight-legged essay**', in particular – a 'by numbers' requirement for answering set questions introduced in 1487 – militated against originality. There was also a persistent temptation to raise revenues by selling lower and middle degrees. During the reign of **Daoguang**, in particular, rich merchants, although traditionally excluded from China's elite, discovered they could buy their sons' way in. Thereafter, the imperial examinations fell into increasing disrepute, and their abolition – achieved under duress in 1905 – was high on the agenda of reformers and republicans alike.

his father, the **Daoguang** emperor is decent, parsimonious and ultimately ineffectual. He fails to tackle China's growing **opium** problem, and allows the **Grand Canal** to fall into disrepair, generating unemployment and unrest in the heart of China.

In Guangzhou, when a crewman aboard the American vessel **Emily** kills a local woman by dropping a pot into her small boat, the Chinese threaten to suspend all trade with the United States unless the man is handed over for execution. The *Emily*'s master, fearful that his cargo of opium will be exposed, complies.

1825 Illicit opium imports push China's **trade balance** into the red.

Tea

The Coca-Cola of pre-modern times, **tea** was appreciated and used in China, first as a medicine, then as a beverage, from perhaps the 4th century BC. From late Ming, it made its way to **Europe**, where its use enjoyed a similar evolution, particularly in **Britain**. In London, the first tea-shop opened in 1657, but it was only from around 1720 that, among the English upper classes, it became fashionable, immortalized by the poet **Alexander Pope**'s satiric couplet apropos Queen Anne: 'Here thou, great ANNA! Whom three realms obey,/Dost sometimes counsel take – and sometimes Tea.'

Like a similar vogue for Chinese porcelain, Chinese tea satisfied the cravings of a feminized high culture hankering after French taste. Given such a premium, it's small wonder that the British government imposed exorbitant duties on its import, which was in any case the monopoly of the **East India Company**. But when other continental traders, notably the Ostend Company, began smuggling tea into Britain, the government abolished tea duties in 1784. From this point onwards, tea's social remit expanded. Particularly in England's industrialized northern cities, it became popular among the working class. By 1867 tea accounted for 67 percent of China's exports. But how was it to be paid for, given the savvy cupidity of Guangzhou's tea-merchants? One answer was to grow tea less expensively in India. Another was to create a rival export commodity with even greater 'therapeutic' properties: opium.

1826 To improve grain supplies to Beijing and other northern cities, the minister He Changling proposes the creation of an improved seagoing **merchant navy**, but his plans are blocked by vested interests controlling the Grand Canal.

In the west, Jahangir succeeds in temporarily driving Qing garrisons out of the Tarim Basin.

1827 A 22,000-strong army led by Yang Fang retakes Kashgaria. Jahangir is captured and sent for execution to Beijing.

He Changling's collected works, offering 'constructive criticism' of the Qing regime, are published; but while his advice is taken seriously by scholars, it is ignored by the throne.

1834 In order to promote domestic competition, the British government revokes the East India Company's trade monopoly in the Far East. As a result, more opium enters Chinese markets. **Lord Napier** is dispatched to superintend British merchants at Guangzhou. Demanding to meet Guangzhou's Governor-General, Napier sails a squadron of gunboats up the Pearl River. Only his death from malaria prevents a major incident.

1836 As **Protestant missionaries**, evading Manchu laws, begin making ground in southern China, Daoguang orders the seizure of all Christian literature in Chinese hands.

1838 After a four-year debate with his ministers, Daoguang rejects the argument that **opium use** should be legalized as the surest way of containing Western predation. Instead, he issues edicts banning the trade in opium, and sends **Lin Zexu** to Guangzhou as an imperial commissioner with special powers to enforce compliance.

1839 Lin Zexu orders opium users in Guangzhou to surrender their supplies and pipes within two months, and

> **"** I am told that in your own country opium smoking is forbidden under severe penalties. This means you are aware of how harmful it is. But better than to forbid the smoking of it would be to forbid the sale of it and, better still, to forbid the production of it, which is the only way of cleansing the contamination at its source. So long as you do not take it yourselves, but continue to make it and tempt the people of China to buy it, you will be showing yourselves careful of your own lives, but careless of the lives of other people, indifferent in your greed for gain to the harm you do to others; such conduct is repugnant to human feeling and at variance with the Way of Heaven. **"**
>
> Lin Zexu, in a letter to Queen Victoria, 1839

foreign traders to hand over their opium cargoes, including those held offshore in warehouse vessels, without compensation. British and other Western merchants refuse to comply, arguing that they are merely the handlers of others' goods. To force the issue, Lin requests the surrender of **Lancelot Dent**, a leading English merchant, on March 24. When Dent is withheld, Lin announces a complete cessation of trade. 350 Western merchants are surrounded in their factories. In May, 20,000 chests, containing three million pounds of opium, are handed over to Lin and emptied into the sea. All but sixteen of the Western merchants are permitted to leave Guangzhou. In response, the British foreign secretary Lord Palmerston triggers the **Opium War** by ordering a fleet of twenty ships and 4000 troops to south China. Lin, meanwhile, arrests many Chinese addicts, and forcibly clears Macau of foreign opium traders. As the price of opium soars, the British superintendent **Charles Elliott** establishes an alternative trading base on the barren island of **Hong Kong**.

A group of Western factories at Guangzhou (Canton) before they were destroyed by fire in 1822.

1840 In June a British fleet, commanded by Elliott's cousin **George Elliott**, arrives in the mouth of the Pearl River. Leaving four warships to blockade Guangzhou, Admiral Elliott takes the main body of his forces up the Chinese coast. In July, having seized Zhoushan, he establishes control over the Yangzi delta. He then sails further north, and invests the mouth of the Bai He River, threatening Tianjin and Beijing itself. In August talks commence with the Manchu spokesman **Qishan**, who persuades Elliott to return to Guangzhou for further negotiations. Immediately afterwards, Qishan replaces Lin Zexu, who is relieved of his duties.

The Opium War

Even though its immediate cause was the Chinese government's attempts to crack down on the import, sale and use of opium, the **Opium War** of 1839–42 was the culmination of longstanding foreign grievances against the **'Canton System'** (see pp.282–83). Because by 1839 it had the largest stake in the 'China trade', **Britain** took the lead in forcing China to open up its markets. In a compelling display of gunboat diplomacy, the Qing were pressured into authorizing four new **treaty ports**, in addition to Guangzhou. And that was just the beginning of a process that, over sixty years, saw the transformation of China's seaboard into a Western preserve. But while Western companies brought with them many of the accoutrements of modern civilization – including steamships, railways and telegraph wires – Britain's 'victory' left a lasting shadow. From the late 18th century, the **East India Company** had used opium to pay for Chinese commodities in full knowledge of its narcotic consequences. Particularly after 1820, opium sales in China soared, as it found takers in eunuch and even official circles. But it was not just the individual smoker who suffered. Between 1820 and 1830, the amount of **silver** leaving China quadrupled, damaging the entire economy. Moreover, opium had infiltrated the military, leaving China's defences vulnerable to attack. Nor did Western traders ease off selling opium to China once its free-trade objectives were realized. Hong Kong-based **Jardine and Matheson** and other companies simply enlarged the market by flooding it. By 1867 opium accounted for fifty percent of China's imports, and the figure continued to rise. Opium dens proliferated in every city, and it was not until the advent of Mao Zedong's communist government in 1949 that the drug was finally removed from the everyday Chinese scene.

1841 George Elliott and Qishan agree terms in Guangzhou. Hong Kong island is ceded in perpetuity to Britain, a $6 million 'indemnity' is offered by the Chinese and the 'Canton trade' allowed to resume. Qishan, however, is adjudged to have exceeded his authority by Daoguang and is dismissed. Simultaneously, Daoguang decrees that the costs of the treaty be borne by southern officials, and by those living in the southern seaports. Elliott is dismissed by Palmerston for having failed to secure better terms and replaced by **Sir Henry Pottinger**, who seizes Guangzhou, then repeats Elliott's strategy by moving his fleet into the Yangzi delta.

1842 After awaiting reinforcements from India, Pottinger resumes his campaign. Shanghai is taken in June, and Zhenjiang in July. But instead of sailing north, Pottinger lays siege to Nanjing. Outgunned, the Manchu surrender, and on August 29 the **Treaty of Nanjing** is signed, ratified by Daoguang in September, and by Queen Victoria in December. Qishan's concessions of the previous year are confirmed. In addition, five cities are opened to trade: Guangzhou, Fuzhou, Xiamen, Ningbo and Shanghai, with consular and residential rights for the British in each. The *cohong* system is abolished, and the British are permitted to trade with whoever they please. War reparations are increased to $410 million, and by inference, the opium trade allowed to continue.

1843 In a supplement to the Treaty of Nanjing, 'reasonable' tariffs are fixed on tea, silk, cottons and other commodities, allowing the Chinese government to derive revenues from foreign trade, although still no mention is made of opium. In an all-important eighth article, Britain is accorded **most favoured nation** status, meaning no other nation will be granted more favourable terms.

1844 President Tyler of the **USA** sends **Caleb Cushing** to China to negotiate trade and diplomatic terms similar to those secured by Britain. Fearing further military humiliation, the Qing government responds positively. Talks in Macau between Cushing and Qiying (the Manchu governor-general of Guangzhou) result in the **Treaty of Wanghia**. The terms of the Treaty of Nanjing are extended to give American **missionaries** the right to work in China, and to establish schools and hospitals. Critically, the right of **legal extra-territoriality** is also granted. In October **France** concludes a similar treaty. Other Western nations will follow suit.

Extra-Territoriality and the Chinese Legal System

One of the hazards for foreigners trading in China were the perceived inadequacies of its **legal system**. There was no such thing as due judicial process. From the Qin dynasty onwards, the throne periodically issued a **legal code**. This defined wrongful behaviour, and set out a tariff of punishments. There were no courts as such, however, and few procedural rules. The law was administered autocratically instead, by **mandarins** hearing both criminal and civil cases in their official dwelling, the *yamen*. Such magistrates had the power of summary execution. They could also commute imprisonment and corporeal punishment into cash payments. Being a magistrate was, therefore, a lucrative calling, and corruption was rife. The only means of appeal was to petition the emperor, but that too was an expensive recourse that meant bribing officials and eunuchs. Redress was beyond the means of most families.

The Chinese legal system enshrined the interests of the governing class in a haze of Confucianism. **Westerners**, used to the relative impartiality of an at least nominally independent judiciary, baulked at the prospect of Chinese justice. The *Lady Hughes* and *Emily* incidents of 1784 and 1821 furnished vivid examples of the want of the rule of law, and it was a major breakthrough when the **USA** established the principle of **legal extra-territoriality** in 1844. From now on, Western subjects were to be tried in Western courts for any alleged wrongdoing in China. Such courts were instituted in the national concessions created inside the **treaty ports**, notably **Shanghai**. The same courts could also try Chinese subjects living inside the concessions.

1850 The Daoguang emperor dies. Aware of his shortcomings as a ruler, he leaves behind instructions for the distribution of his robes amongst his officials.

China's **population** reaches an estimated 420 million. Food and land shortages, and the accretion of an urban underclass, are now important factors in the spread of anti-Manchu sentiment.

In March **Hong Xiuquan** – the messianic leader of an armed neo-Christian sect called the **Society of God Worshippers** that has already built up a sizeable following around Thistle Mountain in Guangxi – effectively issues a challenge to Manchu rule when he proclaims a 'Heavenly Kingdom'. The sect, renamed the *Taiping Tianguo* ('Heavenly Kingdom of Great Peace'), but usually abbreviated to the **Taiping**, will furnish the bloodiest revolt of the Qing period, accounting overall for perhaps 20 million lives.

In December government troops are sent to crush the Taiping and capture Hong Xiuquan.

1851 Daoguang is succeeded by his fourth son, the **Xianfeng** emperor, a timid ruler who spends much of his reign secreted in the two imperial summer palaces.

On January 1 Manchu forces are defeated by the Taiping at Jintian.

On January 11 Hong Xiuquan proclaims himself Heavenly King. As the government prepares to send a much larger army, Hong abandons his base area, leading his followers first eastwards to the mountainous border between Guangxi and Guangdong provinces, and then northwards toward Yongan. As the Taiping army swells to 60,000, Yongan falls to the rebels. Entering the city, Hong treats its citizens fairly within the framework of an outwardly egalitarian, but disciplined, social order that he now institutes in an urban setting for the first time.

The Nian 1851–68

The **Nian Rebellion** was more a symptom of a breakdown in law and order than a concerted attempt to overthrow the Qing. In the borderlands between Shandong, Anhui, Jiangsu and Henan provinces an age-old practice of female infanticide had produced a surplus male population, so there was no shortage of soldier-bandits when conditions deteriorated. The decay of the Grand Canal and a cycle of Yellow River floods were the immediate causes of increased levels of outlaw activity that in 1851 coalesced into a distinctive uprising. Its leader, insofar as there was one, was **Zhang Luoxing**, an Anhui landlord who was a known salt smuggler, and who had connections with several secret societies, including the Heaven and Earth Society. Typically, the Nian conducted looting and kidnapping raids out of 'safe' bases, and it is doubted whether their combined numbers ever exceeded 50,000. For seventeen years, however, they terrorized a Chinese heartland. In the 1930s their tactics were fondly recalled by Communist commanders. The word itself, Nian, refers to mobile guerilla groups, as well as torches made from twisted paper used in nighttime raids.

In the same year, a second revolt, known as the **Nian Rebellion**, breaks out in the borderlands between Anhui, Shandong, Jiangsu and Henan provinces. Although this lasts seventeen years, unlike the Taiping, the Nian are made up mainly of bandits and other opportunists with some connections to China's secret societies.

1852 As the Manchu military noose around Yangan tightens, Hong Xiuquan marches his followers into the countryside in April in search of 'the promised land'. 2000 Taiping troops are killed in a rearguard action, but shortly afterwards, 5000 Qing troops are massacred in a mined mountain pass. Hong attacks but fails to take Guilin, but in May captures Xingan. In June the Taiping storm Quanzhou. When Hong's deputy Feng Yunshan is fatally wounded by a sniper Quanzhou's citizens are butchered. In the autumn Hong attempts to take Changsha, but abandons Hunan when a court official, **Zeng Guofan**, begins organizing the provincial militia into an effective defence. Instead, Hong moves eastwards down the Yangzi. In December he takes Yuezhou, on the Dongting Lake. Vast quantities of guns and ammunition, as well as 5000 boats, fall into Taiping hands.

1853 On January 12 Wuchang and its great wealth falls to Hong Xiuquan, giving him control of the middle Yangzi. On February 10 the main body of the Taiping army leaves Wuchang, advancing rapidly eastwards. After a short siege **Nanjing** itself succumbs to the rebels. On March 29 Hong enters the inner citadel escorted by 32 consorts dressed in imperial yellow. 40,000 Manchus, including women and children, and Nanjing's small Catholic population are massacred. Buddhist and Daoist temples are destroyed, and orders promulgated for the execution of prostitutes, adulterers, homosexuals and other 'reprobates'. As the Taiping regimen is imposed, Hong begins adopting imperial habits. Surrounding himself with concubines, he takes to wearing a crown while planning further campaigns. Yangzhou is annexed in April, but in May a 40,000-strong army sent northwards toward Beijing flounders. In September an attempt to capture Shanghai is frustrated by a coalition between Manchu and militia forces, and a disinclination among Shanghai's secret societies to parley with the Taiping.

In Nanjing, a rift develops between Hong and his 'East King', **Yang Xiuqing**. In favour of restoring Chinese custom, Yang undermines Hong's authority by proclaiming himself 'God's cypher'.

In the south, Hong's 'Wing King' **Shi Dakai** joins forces with triad organizations to bring Guangdong province briefly under Taiping control. The city of Nanchang, however, is relieved by the sudden appearance of Zeng Guofan and his militia army.

1854 The Taiping 'northern expedition' army is annihilated by Manchu forces after it is trapped on mud-flats created by diverting part of the Grand Canal into a dry riverbed.

The **Western powers**, meanwhile, apply pressure for further trade concessions. International tension rises as Beijing refuses to consider British, French and American demands.

In Guizhou, a third rebellion breaks out among the **Miao** minority people, lasting until 1872.

1855 As Hong Xiuquan's 'court' continues to factionalize, a stalemate between Taiping and government forces prevails in the Yangzi delta. Elsewhere, however, the Nian rebellion draws fresh recruits when the **Yellow River** bursts its banks.

Moslems in **Yunnan** – aggravated by high land taxes and disputes over gold- and silver-mining rights – begin a revolt that will continue until 1873.

A 'Kingdom of the Pacified South' is proclaimed at Dali, its leader, **Du Wenxiu**, styling himself 'Sultan Suleiman'. It is, however, a good year for **Shanghai**, which is spared disorder and becomes the preferred port for many Western traders.

Hong Xiuquan 1814–64

Born in rural Guangdong, **Hong Xiuquan** was raised to pursue a government career. But although he passed the district examinations, he failed, in all four attempts, at the provincial level. It was while sitting the provincial exams in Guangzhou in 1836 that Hong was given some Bible tracts written by a Christian convert, **Liang Afar**. Two years later, during the course of a fever, he had a dream in which an old man and his son ('Elder Brother') harangued Hong to go forth and exterminate devils. Only in 1843, however, did the slow-learning Hong put two and two together. Rereading Liang's tracts, he grasped that the old man was God, his son Christ, and therefore Hong himself a younger son of God.

Wielding a big devil-slaying sword, Hong set about preaching his version of Christianity. In 1844 he was dismissed from a teaching post after breaking the school's Confucian tablets. But as a preacher he was charismatic. Among the many followers he attracted was a cousin, **Feng Yunshan**, who had the organizational skills Hong lacked. After a brief return to Guangzhou – where he took a course in private Bible studies from Isaacher Roberts, an American Southern Baptist – Hong joined Feng on Thistle Mountain. Together they forged the **Society of God Worshippers**, with Hong himself at the centre of an idiosyncratic understanding of the Old Testament.

Out of these unlikely beginnings the full misery of the **Taiping** was launched. Hong's latent mania became manifest at Nanjing, once he had proclaimed himself Heavenly Emperor. Insisting on abstention for others, he surrounded himself with 88 'consorts', and rifled bad scriptural translations for references to himself. Disavowed by Western missionaries, Hong nonetheless offered millions of 'ordinary' Chinese a forceful repudiation of a regime long passed its sell-by date. In an obscure, but compelling, way his message connected to an unvoiced faith in the ancient 'Mandate of Heaven'.

1856 Yang Xiuqing increases his following among the Taiping by gaining important victories over Qing forces in the Yangzi delta.

In September Hong Xiuquan, nervous for his own position, orders the deaths of Yang and hundreds of his supporters. Shi Dakai withdraws from Hong's court to set up a rival Taiping government in Sichuan.

In the north, the Nian rebels adopt the Manchu banner system to promote discipline among their ranks.

In the south, when government officials stop and search the Hong Kong-registered vessel *The Arrow* in the Pearl River, the British mount a military reprisal, sparking the **Arrow War**.

1857 In January a plot to poison all non-Chinese residents of Hong Kong is uncovered, and traced to the 'Alum' Chinese bakery.

In December British naval ships commanded by **Lord Elgin** sail into the Pearl River estuary after a Chinese mob sets fire to the Western factories.

1858 When Qing officials refuse to negotiate, Elgin shells Guangzhou. The Governor-General of Guangdong and Guangxi provinces is seized and shipped to Calcutta. In October Elgin moves his fleet to Shanghai, and in November sails up the Yangzi toward Wuchang. Passing Nanjing, Elgin's fleet comes under Taiping fire. Elgin returns fire, causing substantial damage to Taiping batteries.

Elgin's naval task force progresses northwards to Tianjin. The strategic Dagu Forts are taken, and in June the Qing government concedes the **Treaty of Tianjin**. Travel restrictions inside China are lifted, a British embassy is permitted in Beijing, and ten new treaty ports, including (putatively) Nanjing, are opened. Christian missionaries are to be given official protection, and, by agreeing fixed tariffs, the import of opium is effectively legalized. The same benefits are rapidly extended to other Western powers, in line with the 'most favoured nation' system. While the treaty is perceived as a humiliation by Chinese officials, it clears the way for foreign 'assistance' in the Manchu struggle against the still powerful Taiping.

1859 **Hong Rengan**, a relative of Hong Xiuquan, travels from Hong Kong to Nanjing to persuade the Taiping leader to liberalize his regime by introducing Western banking and transport systems. His failure helps harden the case against Hong Xiuquan in foreign circles. However, when the Qing administration reneges on its promise to allow Western embassies in Beijing, intergovernmental tensions revive. The British, supported by the French, attack the Dagu Forts for a second time, but fail to capture them.

1860 When several members of a British negotiating party are seized and killed, Lord Elgin responds strongly. In October a combined British and French force attacks and enters Beijing. The Yuanming yuan summer palace is looted and destroyed. Xianfeng having fled to Jehol, Elgin negotiates the **Treaty of Beijing** with the emperor's brother Prince Gong.

The Treaty of Tianjin is confirmed, and new clauses added. Tianjin is opened as a treaty port, and **Kowloon**, adjacent to Hong Kong, is leased to the British until 1997. The Chinese undertake to pay substantial reparations, and to lift travel restrictions on Chinese subjects seeking employment overseas, thus swelling the ranks of 'coolie' labour gangs in the Americas and British colonies in Australia.

A Taiping army, commanded by **Li Xiucheng**, takes Suzhou and prepares an assault on Shanghai. A Qing counterattack is badly mauled outside Nanjing.

1861 Xianfeng dies at Jehol aged 30, the victim of palsy and a debauched lifestyle. To cope with China's increasingly complicated international relations, the Qing government reluctantly opens a Foreign Affairs office, the *Zongli yamen*, in Beijing – in reality, a committee of the Grand Council.

In September Zeng Guofan launches a concerted campaign against Taiping positions in the Yangzi delta. Anqing is captured, depriving Nanjing of vital supplies.

1862 After a bitter court wrangle, Xianfeng's concubine **Cixi** (aka Xiao Qin) – supported by Prince Gong and the dowager-empress Xiaochen – enthrones her 6-year-old son, the **Tonghzi** emperor, while assuming the title dowager-empress for herself. Although Cixi rapidly emerges as China's most powerful figure, immediate policies are determined by Gong, a reformist anxious to enlist the co-operation of the Western powers, and a supporter of the 'modernizing' general Zeng Guofan. Revolt spreads to the northwest, however.

In **Gansu**, after a dispute about the price of bamboo poles, inter-communal tension between Hui Moslems and Han Chinese flares into open fighting. The **Moslems**, encouraged by 'New Islamic Teaching', launch attacks against Xian and Tongzhou. Driven back into Gansu, their continuing revolt challenges Manchu control for ten years.

In Yunnan, Moslem rebels occupy Kunming, but are swiftly expelled. Zeng Guofan makes further headway against the Taiping as he begins the encirclement of Nanjing.

1863 Aided first by the American **Frederick Ward** of Salem, and then by the British **Charles Gordon** (aka 'Chinese' Gordon and 'Gordon of Khartoum'), Zeng Guofan and his subordinate **Li Hongzhang** forge the **'Ever Victorious Army'**, initially for the defence of Shanghai. Drilled to Western standards, and armed with Western rifles supplied by Shanghai gun-runners, the EVA emerges as the most effective weapon against the Taiping.

In May the Taiping commander Li Xiucheng, abandoning a campaign in Anhui province, suffers a severe defeat as he tries to recross the Yangzi.

The Taiping

What the **Taiping** offered its followers – who included a smatter-
ing of landlords as well as rural and urban poor – was a radically
different, yet divinely sanctioned, alternative to the existing imperial and mandarin matrix. For a decade, rebel and government
forces battled for control of the **Yangzi delta**. Amid harrowing
scenes of civilian massacre, 600 cities were taken and retaken by
the opposing sides. Despite its **messianic Christian veneer**,
however, the 'Heavenly Kingdom of Great Peace' contained no

'Chinese' Gordon directing an assault on Suzhou in 1863 during the suppression of the Taiping Rebellion.

term that was not in some way familiar to the demotic Chinese mind. Its strongest feature – and the one that has most attracted the attention of communist historians – was its apparent **egalitarianism**.

Particularly in cities, the Taiping instituted a regimen that made no distinction in status. The leadership aside, all Taiping citizens, including women, were equal. Land was redistributed equitably, and surplus produce requisitioned by communal granaries. There were stringent prohibitions against adultery and prostitution, males and females were segregated, and conjugal rights regulated. But so long as the Taiping 'revolution' stood some chance of success, such collectivist abstentions were morally uplifting. Critically, the Taiping also mastered the art of **military discipline**. Among its early converts were a body of miners who proved invaluable in siege warfare. Once a county or a town had been secured, then a system of conscription was applied. Every five households had to furnish a corporal, every 25 a sergeant.

Where the Taiping revolt failed was in political acumen. Helped in its initial stages by outlaws and secret societies, once established, it cut every kind of tie. Fiercely anti-Manchu, the Taiping became anti-foreign as well. Nor was any attempt made to co-ordinate strategy with other, contemporaneous uprisings, notably the Nian, and in the end the Taiping experiment collapsed around the megalomania of its arguably insane leader, **Hong Xiuquan**.

In Sichuan, Shi Dakai surrenders to the Qing. Despite assurances to the contrary, his 2000 soldiers are massacred, and Shi himself dismembered.

In December Suzhou is recaptured, and the final assault on Nanjing begins.

1864 The death of the Taiping leader Hong Xiuquan in June, either from illness or by suicide, heralds the collapse of the Taiping rebellion. As Zeng Guofan bombards Nanjing, thousands of its inhabitants choose suicide rather than surrender. Hong's son **Tiangui** manages to escape, but is apprehended in October and executed. After Nanjing falls, Zeng is ordered to fight against the Nian rebels.

Li Hongzhang urges that a Western scientific curriculum be added to the imperial examination syllabus, but his recommendations are rejected.

1865 Zeng Guofan's Nian campaigns are obstructed by a lack of co-operation from the governor-generals of the four affected provinces, and by the weariness of his troops. He also faces a challenge from his subordinate Li Hongzhang, who creates a fiercely loyal force modelled on Zeng's own 'Ever Victorious Army'. When Li demonstrates superior effectiveness in the field, he is appointed overall commander, and Zeng is demoted to the governorship of Liangjiang (comprising Anhui, Jiangxi and Jiangsu provinces).

1866 As the northwestern Moslem rebellion spreads, the government appoints **Zuo Zongtang** Governor-General of Gansu and Shaanxi provinces. At the last moment, however, Zuo – having proved his abilities against the Taiping – is ordered to divert his energies to assist Li Hongzhang against the Nian.

1868 Employing the tactics of attrition, Li Hongzhang destroys the last of the rebel bases in Shandong, bringing to an end the Nian rebellion. For this, he is rewarded with the title 'Grand Guardian of the Heir Apparent', even though there isn't one.

In November Zuo Zongtang, operating out of Xian, begins his campaigns against the northwestern Moslems. Instilling discipline into his troops, he selects as his principle target the most effective Moslem general and self-proclaimed prophet **Ma Hualong**.

Zeng Guofan 1811–72

A ranking official, **Zeng Guofan** took temporary retirement in 1852, following the death of his mother. Thus, he found himself at home when the **Taiping rebellion** spread to his native Hunan. His response was twofold. He personally took charge of the local militia to defend his and his neighbours' property, and in doing so he consciously copied Western techniques of military training. In due course, he created the **'Ever Victorious Army'** and, with some Western assistance, defeated the Taiping. In Chinese history he is credited with overcoming a dangerous foe, and for being the first to understand the urgency of military modernization. As pertinent as these achievements are, however, the bald fact remains that he was Chinese. Not since the Three Feudatories had such military power been vested in a non-Manchu. While this was largely a matter of necessity, he opened the way for other Chinese strongmen, notably his two subordinates **Li Hongzhang** (see p.326) and **Zuo Zongtang**. Cynics suggest that, even though all three remained loyal to the throne, Zeng set the pattern for the resurgence of the Chinese warlord, a type that fairly wrecked the 1912 Republic.

1869 The opening of the **Suez Canal** by the British revives the old Asian coastal trade routes. As Guangzhou and other southern Chinese ports recover from the depredations of the Taiping rebellion, China as a whole enters a period of economic growth.

1871 Zuo Zongtang storms Ma Hualong's fortified headquarters at Jinjibao in Ningxia. Ma is taken prisoner and publicly sliced to death. Zuo begins a pacification programme that will introduce many new Han Chinese settlements into the affected territory.

1872 Dowager-empress **Cixi** arranges the marriage of her son the Tongzhi emperor to **Alute**, the daughter of a leading Manchu family.

Li Hongzhang − working to achieve modernization through private adventure-capitalism − founds the **China Merchants Steamship Company**. With Li's support, Yung Wing, the first Chinese national to graduate from an American University (Yale, 1854), sets up a programme to send further Chinese students to the USA. With missionary support, the '**Hartford project**' benefits 120 Chinese before its closure in 1881.

1873 Tongzhi celebrates his coming of age by receiving foreign ambassadors in an elaborate ceremony during which they are not required to kowtow before the throne. The event, however, is stage-managed by Cixi, who retains her grip on power by encouraging her son in his dissolute vices.

The Moslem rebellion in Yunnan is ended when Dali is captured and Du Wenxiu is executed. Increased Chinese migration to Yunnan accelerates non-Chinese emigration to the countries of Southeast Asia.

In the northwest, Moslem insurgency is finally broken by Zuo Zongtang. In Xinjiang, however, other Moslem groups begin their own insurgency.

1874 Tongzhi, already infected with syphilis, contracts smallpox and dies after an apparent recovery. Rumours suggest that his mother Cixi − fearful of the growing influence of his empress Alute − has administered poison.

The Guangxu and Puyi Emperors 1875–1912

During the reigns of the two last emperors, the **Western powers** continued making deep inroads into China. Many more cities were opened up as treaty ports, both on the eastern seaboard and in the riverine interior. But now a new power entered the ring. At first **Japan** flexed her muscles in

Korea, then stunned the world by defeating Russia in Manchuria. But while Japan posed the biggest long-term threat, many dissidents felt that post–Meiji Restoration Japan provided an appropriate model for China to follow; and indeed the revolution that overthrew the Manchu Qing was in part fomented by Chinese students and expatriates living in Tokyo.

It was not just a dynasty that tottered toward collapse as the 20th century beckoned, but an entire political culture. With over 400 million ethnically diverse mouths to feed, China was the most populous nation on earth, yet it was still governed for the benefit of a narrow elite whose active membership perhaps never numbered more than 10,000. Worse, from a majority Han perspective, the ruling **Manchu house** was foreign. So when the famine-stricken empire, regularly humiliated by other nations, was plunged into a series of crippling wars, it is small wonder that the edifice disintegrated.

The **later Qing** were always a step behind. The case for reform was sometimes aired, but more often spurned. The defining moment came with the **Boxer Uprising** of 1900, a seizure second only to the Taiping Rebellion in magnitude. A seemingly spontaneous and deeply xenophobic revolt in the northern heartlands, aimed primarily against Christians and foreign control, was allowed to get out of hand. **Cixi**, the dowager-empress who ruled China in her nephew's name, dithered, then let the Boxers have their way, with disastrous consequences.

Such reforms as the Court countenanced in the wake of the Boxers served only to impair what remained of its authority. Power devolved rapidly away from the centre, and the end came when the provinces united against **Beijing**. The Qing were smashed, and with the Qing the imperial system itself. Yet, looked at as a whole, this turbulent period

The Dowager-Empress Cixi
(Tz'u-His) 1835–1908

The 'old Buddha', as **Cixi** came to be known, was the daughter of an impoverished Manchu civil servant. Recruited as a junior concubine for the Xianfeng emperor, she bore his only son, the **Tongzhi** emperor. Aided by Xianfeng's brother Prince Gong, she imposed her personal authority as dowager-empress on a court riddled with corruption. Nor was her power diminished when her son attained his majority in 1873, and it is likely she devised his death in 1874. Beforehand, she had arranged for her younger sister to marry another of Xianfeng's brothers, Prince Jun, promising them their firstborn son would succeed Tongzhi. **Guangxu** was duly enthroned in 1875 and Cixi continued to rule from 'behind the curtain'.

From 1884, she bolstered her position by assembling around her a clique of reactionary conservatives. The greatest challenge to her authority came in the wake of China's 1895 defeat by **Japan**. Guangxu, breaking loose from her control, attempted wholesale reform. Abetted by senior army commanders, however, Cixi reasserted herself, and although the **Boxer Uprising** forced her hand politically, she retained power until 1908 when, a day before her own death, she allegedly poisoned the emperor. Certainly, she is known to have ordered the drowning of a royal favourite, the **Pearl Concubine**, in 1900, and was probably behind her fellow dowager-empress Xiaochen's death in 1881. Much given to slapping, scratching and beating her attendants, she depended on the loyalty of her eunuchs. Universally condemned as a *grand guignol* tyrant, the collapse of imperial China has been laid squarely at her door. A skilful manipulator, Cixi lacked the wherewithal to look beyond the only life she was accustomed to.

contained the seeds of regeneration. The intrusion of foreigners into China's teeming eastern cities brought the products of the Industrial Revolution as well as fresh ideas. The last decades of the 19th century witnessed the emergence of an often outspoken press, as well as innumerable foreign

The dowager-empress Cixi – detail from a photograph taken in 1903.

books published in translation. By the century-end railways, steamboats, telegraph wires and engineered weapons were familiar to many Chinese. But what had first to be resolved was whether modernization served the national interest, or whether, as conservatives and some rebels believed, the two were antithetical.

1875 Flouting protocols governing the imperial succession, the Dowager-Empress **Cixi** installs her 4-year-old nephew on the imperial throne as the **Guangxu** emperor. His mother is Cixi's sister, formerly married to Xianfeng's brother. Cixi's coup so consolidates her power that Guangxu's reign is considered as an extension of her own.

1876 **Zuo Zongtang** is given command against **Yakub Beg** in Kashgaria in the far west, and authorized to finance his army by raising foreign loans.

Korea is forced into signing the **Treaty of Kanghwa** with **Japan**, marking the beginning of Japan's envelopment of "the hermit kingdom".

Following the murder of Augustus Raymond Margary, a British diplomat, in Yunnan in 1875, China is pressured into signing the **Chefoo Agreement**, opening Yichang, Wuhu, Wenzhou and Beihai as treaty ports.

The first, foreign-built **railway** in China, between Shanghai and Wusong, is bought by Shanghai's Governor-General and destroyed. **Li Hongzhang**, however, establishes a modern coal-mine outside Tianjin, partly to supply fuel for his growing steamship company.

1877 Zuo Zongtang crushes Kashgarian independence by defeating Yakub Beg, who commits suicide in May.

1878 The first modern cotton mill, founded by Li Hongzhang, is opened in Shanghai.

1879 Japan annexes the **Ryukyu Islands**, previously regarded as a Chinese tributary territory.

The Chinese Diaspora

From the early 14th century, Chinese traders established settlements beyond the confines of the empire, first in **Southeast Asia**, notably at Malacca, then further afield. From the 1840s onwards, emigration assumed a different, mass-scale pattern. Driven by famine, civil strife and the allure of supposed riches, hundreds of thousands of Chinese set out from Fujian, Guangdong and other southern provinces for the **Americas**, the **Carribean**, **Africa**, **Australia** and **Europe** – a diaspora made possible by steam-powered shipping and unscrupulous intermediaries.

For most Chinese, however, life as a 'coolie' on foreign plantations or in foreign factories was little better than it had been at home. For those who survived, it took two or three generations to establish themselves as citizens. By 1880, an estimated 100,000 were spread across the United States – in New York there were already Chinese laundries. From the time of the **Californian Gold Rush** (1848–49) America was seen as the 'golden mountain'. But in 1882, the first of several US anti-Chinese race laws was passed, suspending further immigration by labourers for ten years. In 1888 the automatic right of re-entry for those who had already settled was abrogated. A series of Chinatown riots and "*tong*" wars between secret societies had given the Chinese community a bad name – a prejudice later reinforced by the *Fu Man Chu* novels of the English thriller-writer Sax Romer.

The growing prosperity of some overseas Chinese, however, often based on the restaurant trade, provided an important source of funds for political dissidence. Sun Yat-sen's long campaign for a republic received vital donations from abroad. And the trend continues. After 1949, the USA in particular became a source of material and ideological sustenance for those fleeing or opposing **communism**. Post-1976, the West has become an important means of higher education, particularly for the children of ranking Party officials. Some have returned to China, others have not. Either way, this secondary diaspora is a vital cog in the mechanism that currently sees China embarked on a course of technological catch-up.

1880 Li Hongzhang establishes an arsenal at Tianjin capable of manufacturing bullets and shells for imported Remington and Krupp guns and howitzers.

1881 The death of Tongzhi's widow Xiaochen, removes a potential rival to Cixi, who now 'rules supreme'.

The **Treaty of St Petersburg**, – concluded after several years' wrangling – establishes demarcation lines between Chinese and Russian interests in Central Asia.

In Shanghai, the foreign concessions are linked by China's first **telephone lines**.

1882 Having begun their conquest of **Vietnam** in 1853, the **French** take Hanoi and Haiphong. To protect its 'vassal' state, China sends troops into Tonkin, but these withdraw before engaging the enemy.

In the **USA**, Congress passes the first of a series of laws excluding further immigration of Chinese labourers.

> ❝ In addition to the 53 million ounces of silver we spend on foreign cottons, we buy such items of ordinary use as heavy silk, satins, woolens, fine silks, gauze, and felt; umbrellas, lamps, paint, suitcases and satchels; chinaware, toothbrushes, tooth-powder, soap and lamp-oil. Among comestibles we buy coffee, Philippine and Havana cigars, cigarettes and rolling paper, snuff, and liquor; ha, dried meats, cake candy; and salt; and medicines -- liquid, pills, powders – as well as dried and fresh fruit. We also buy coal, iron, lead, copper, tin, and other materials; wooden utensils, clocks, watches, sun-dials, thermometers, barometers, electric lamps, plumbing accessories, mirrors, photographic plates, and other amusing or ingenious gadgets. As more households get them, more people want them, so that they have reached as far as Xinjiang and Tibet. ❞
>
> The 'second memorial' of Kang Yuwei to the imperial throne, 1895

1884 Continuing French incursions into northern Vietnam precipitate the **Sino-French War**. A Chinese fleet is destroyed at Fuzhou (Fujian province).

Following Zuo Zongtang's defeat of Yakub Beg in 1877, the vast western province of Xinjiang is formally incorporated into the Chinese empire, although resistance to Chinese rule by the Moslem **Uighur** peoples continues.

1885 The French blockade Taiwan. In June a Sino-French Treaty ends hostilities. Vietnam becomes a French protectorate.

In **Shanghai**, the Polytechnic Institute is opened to teach Western technology to Chinese students.

1887 Guangxu comes of age, but continues under the tutelage of his aunt Cixi.

1888 The **Yuanmingyuan** (new summer palace), is restored, following its pillage by Anglo-French forces in 1860. Much of its funding has been siphoned by Cixi from monies earmarked for the modernization of China's navy. Of particular expense is a **marble boat** on the palace's ornamental lake.

1890 Chongqing, in Sichuan, is opened as a treaty port, reflecting the inland advance of Western interests.

1894 When King Kojong of **Korea** requests military assistance from China against rebels in May, Japan sends an army into Seoul and on July 21 installs a puppet government. On August 1 China and **Japan** declare war on each other. China is swiftly defeated on land and sea. In October Japanese troops advance into Manchuria. In December a second Japanese army occupies Lushun (Port Arthur). Despite these incursions, China's southern armies remain uninvolved. In the same year the republican **Dr Sun Yat-sen** sets up his first anti-Manchu association – the *Xing Zhong hui*, or 'Society for the Revival of China'.

Li Hongzhang 1823–1901

Sometimes called the 'Bismarck of the East', and the most impressive of the late Qing statesmen, **Li Hongzhang** was a 'self-strengthening' modernizer who stopped short of political reform. In 1862 he became acting governor of Jiangsu and played a key role in the suppression of the **Taiping Rebellion**, establishing up-to-date arsenals in Shanghai and Nanjing, and working closely with 'Chinese' Gordon. In 1870 he was rewarded with the governorship of the capital province **Hebei** (then Chihli). He was also appointed **Superintendent of Trade** in northern China, and masterminded many military and civil projects that called for an understanding of Western technology. He created naval dockyards at Lushun, a modern mint, a steam-powered merchant fleet, China's first successful **railway line** and a telegraph system that linked inland cities with the seaboard treaty ports. Trusted alike by the court and by foreigners, he was frequently called on to conduct sensitive negotiations – a second career that lasted from the Margary Affair of 1876 to the Boxer protocols of 1901. Whilst negotiating the **Treaty of Shimonoseki** in 1895 he was wounded in the face by an assassin's bullet – an incident he used to soften Japan's demands. Equally skilled at amassing a personal fortune, Li died the richest man in China.

1895 In January Japanese troops advance into Shandong and seize defences at Weihaiwei. In April the Sino-Japanese War is concluded by the **Treaty of Shimonoseki**, negotiated by Li Hongzhang. China is obliged to pay substantial indemnities, to abandon its tributary interest in Korea, and to cede Taiwan, as well as the Pescadores, to Japan. The Japanese, claiming 'most favoured nation' status, are permitted to build factories in any treaty port. Some European powers take advantage of China's humiliation to wring further concessions. In response to defeat, young radicals start 'Revive China' and 'Self-Strengthening' associations, adopting the slogan *ti-yong* – an abbreviated form

Photo portrait of Li Hongzhang, the richest and most powerful
politician-entrepreneur of late 19th century China.

> It is a well-known fact that in ancient times countries were destroyed by the might of other countries. But today countries are ruined by foreign trade, a thing which is overlooked by everybody. When a country is conquered by the armed forces of another country, it perishes but its people remain; when a country is destroyed by trade, its people perish together with it. That is the danger now facing China.
>
> The 'third memorial' of Kang Yuwei to the Imperial Throne, 1896

of the proposition that while Chinese learning should remain the *essence* (*ti*), Western learning should be embraced for its *practical use* (*yong*). At the imperial examinations, 1300 scholars – primed by **Kang Yuwei** and **Liang Qichao** – present Guangxu with a 'Letter of Ten Thousand Words' urging immediate reform.

In October a plot by **Sun Yat-sen** to instal a republican government in Guangzhou is foiled. Many members of the *Xing Zhong hui* are killed or jailed. Sun flees to the USA.

Disregarding Cixi, Guangxu begins taking an earnest interest in Kang and his fellow 'progressives'.

1896 **Sun Yat-sen** is kidnapped in London by Qing agents and held at the Chinese legation, but is released after the intervention of Dr James Cantlie, Sun's supervisor from his days in Hong Kong as a medical student. As a result, Chinese opposition to Qing-Manchu autocracy gains worldwide publicity. Observing at first hand the side-effects of British industrialization, Sun begins to incorporate socialist principles into his republican doctrine, creating a gulf between himself and such 'constitutional' reformers as **Kang Yuwei**.

In the same year, **Robert Hart**, as Commissioner of Customs, reorganizes the Chinese postal service, and construction begins on Li Hongzhang's Beijing–Tianjin railway.

1897 Sun Yat-sen fails to gain immediate support among the large expatriate Chinese community in Tokyo and Yokohama, and encounters hostility from the 'Protect the Emperor Society', established by Kang Yuwei and Liang Qichao.

In November, when two German Catholic missionaries are murdered in western Shandong, **Germany** responds by occupying **Qingdao**. Resentment at foreign interference begins focusing on Christian missionaries and their Chinese converts.

In Shandong, floods followed by drought are attributed to the meddling of 'foreign devils' whose tall churches 'block the sky'. Shasi, Sanshui, Suzhou and Hangzhou become treaty ports.

1898 In a **'scramble for concessions'** foreign powers continue to take advantage of China's weakness. **Russia** is granted a 25-year lease on **Lushun**, and on June 1 **Britain** wins a 99-year lease on the 'New Territories' adjacent to Hong Kong. Other concessions are gained by Germany and France.

On June 11 Guangxu responds to Kang Yuwei and Liang Qichao by initiating the **'Hundred Days' Reform'**. In a comprehensive overhaul of the education system, schools are ordered to offer Western as well as Chinese syllabuses. Provincial authorities are instructed to establish technical institutes. Army drill is to be westernized, and there is to be a new navy. Kang and Liang are given senior court positions.

In the summer, flooding in Shandong displaces over a million people. As anti-Christian sentiment intensifies, a demotic 'secret' society – the 'Righteous and Harmonious Fists', or **Boxers** – begins making its presence felt.

On September 21 **Cixi** – claiming that French and British influence lie behind Guangxu's reforms – places the emperor under arrest and annuls his edicts. Kang and Liang flee abroad. Other reformers are imprisoned or executed. By 1906 some 15,000 'progressive intellectuals' will have relocated to Japan.

1899 The 'patriotic' Boxer movement gains momentum, particularly among peasants and artisans in Shandong, Shanxi and Shaanxi. At first Cixi, fearing an anti-Manchu revolt, is alarmed, but then decides she can use Boxer activities as a lever against foreign domination. Prince Duan, known for his Boxer sympathies, is appointed head of the *Zhongli yamen* (foreign affairs bureau).

Kang Yuwei 1858–1927

An outstanding classical scholar, **Kang** was born into a scholar-gentry family in Guangdong. In 1897 he published his seminal work, *Confucius the Reformer*, arguing that far from being an inflexible lawgiver, the Great Sage understood and even desired change. By then, Kang had already embarked on his own political mission. In 1895 he had been the principal mover behind a student memorial to the throne urging reform. He also submitted a series of individual **memorials**. In 1898 – in the wake of China's defeat by Japan – the emperor responded to the progressives by instituting the 'Hundred Days' Reform'.

Although catapulted to high rank, Kang's aspirations were quickly dashed by Cixi's counter-coup, and until 1914 he lived in exile. Nor, having set out a programme of constitutional monarchism, could he support **Sun Yat-sen**'s revolutionary republicanism. Notebooks unpublished during his life reveal an unusually wide-ranging mind that grappled with, among other chimera, the idea of a global government. Always concerned with technological as well as literary subject matters, he championed *ti-yong*, a synthesis between Chinese learning and Western technology first proposed by Zhang Zhidong (1837–1909).

Railway concessions are granted to Russians in Manchuria and Germans in Shandong.

1900 Cixi and the Grand Council ignore Western demands to suppress the Boxer 'uprising'. Boxer bands, moving northwards, enter Beijing and Tianjin, and the German Minister and the Chancellor of the Japanese legation are assassinated. Throughout northern China, Christian missionaries and their families are attacked. In the worst massacre, 42 are killed at Taiyuan, having been promised protection by the Governor of Shanxi. In all, 200 foreigners are murdered. Railways, railway stations and telegraph lines are also vandalized as the movement expresses its anti-modernization character.

The **'Eight Great Powers'** (Britain, France, Germany, the USA, Russia, Austro-Hungary, Italy and Japan) respond by acting in close concert for the first and only time. On June 19 a combined expeditionary force captures the **Dagu Forts** outside Tianjin. On the same day, the court demands the withdrawal of all foreign legations from the capital. When the legations refuse, Boxer insurgents lay siege to them, unimpeded by imperial guards.

On June 21 an imperial edict declares war on all eight powers. On August 14, 20,000 allied troops under British command enter **Beijing** and relieve the legations. As Cixi takes flight with Guangxu – disguised as peasants in a cart – Western soldiers loot Beijing. The Forbidden City becomes the expeditionary army's headquarters.

Russia overruns most of **Manchuria**, setting up a future conflict with Japan.

In October Sun Yat-sen's followers attempt revolution for the second time at Huizhou in Guangdong, but are crushed by provincial authorities. Before 1911 there are seven further attempts at a republican coup.

The Boxers

The **Boxers** (or *Yihe chuan*, The Righteous and Harmonious Fists) are shrouded in imponderables. Why, at a time of widespread resentment toward the ruling Manchu, did a powerful grass-roots movement driven by the slogan *'Support the Qing, destroy the foreigner'* well up seemingly spontaneously from the most oppressed tiers of society? Yet the movement, made up over-whelmingly of peasants and labourers, manifested disparate ele-ments. Folk superstition was matched by rituals derived from China's secret societies. Nationalism blended with an unthinking repudiation of modern technology. The discipline of a partly invented martial art was traduced by the thrust of a diffident pitchfork.

First detected in Shandong in 1898, the Boxers spread rapidly along the **Yellow River**. Somewhere behind them was a leader-ship that has never been satisfactorily identified. By the spring of 1900, they roamed unopposed through **Shaanxi**, **Shanxi**, **Henan** and **Hebei**, directing their violence primarily against **Christians**. The ancient gods of China had been slighted. Now they must be avenged. Female adherents were sorted into two kinds: 'Cooking Pot Lanterns' catered for the Boxers' alimentary needs; but teenage 'Shining Red Lanterns' strove to reclaim the Chinese male from the clutches of his 'convert' wife. Notorious among the latter was **'Lotus' Huang**, a prostitute turned seer. Thus replen-ished, Boxer men, believing themselves occultly invulnerable to Western bullets, paraded in their coloured turbans and crimson leggings, casting fear throughout the countryside, then in Beijing. Not for the first time, an eruption of the irrational shook the Chinese nation to its core. In their style, their agenda, and the way they were manipulated by the court, the Boxers foreshadowed Mao Zedong's Cultural Revolution.

1901 In April a 'Bureau of Government Affairs' is estab-lished to consider reforms. The *Zhongli yamen* is replaced by a Ministry of Foreign Affairs. On September 7 a rem-nant administration in Beijing signs humiliating **protocols**

Western revenge: The decapitated heads of Boxer rebels strung on a city wall. An illustration in *Le Petit Journal*.

with the Eight Powers. An indemnity of US$333 million is levied against China, in theory tying up much of its revenue until 1941. The Dagu Forts are razed, and the foreign occupation of many northern cities authorised. Pro-Boxer officials are executed, 'obliged' to commit suicide, demoted or exiled.

1901 also sees the creation of the **New Army**, based on Li Hongzhang's earlier modernization of the Beiyang (North China) Army. Thirty-six divisions are placed strategically throughout the empire under the control of a central commission. But as these replace the old Manchu banners, they are widely infiltrated by republican sympathizers at the officer level.

1902 Cixi and the emperor return to Beijing. The dowager-empress officially receives foreign envoys, and then their wives, inside the Forbidden City. Reluctantly, she accepts the need for reform, but fails to introduce the sweeping changes needed to save the throne.

Britain and Japan, meanwhile, conclude a treaty of mutual protection with regard to their interests in China and Korea.

An imperial rescript disowns **foot-binding**.

The first **automobiles** are shipped into Shanghai.

1903 An imperial edict encourages industry and commerce, raising the traditionally low status of merchants and businessmen.

The Revolutionary Army, written by 18-year-old **Zou Rong**, is published in Shanghai. A powerful and inflammatory tract advocating the overthrow of the Manchu, it becomes an inspiration for all revolutionaries, including Sun Yat-sen.

By remaining in the foreign concession at Shanghai, Zou escapes execution by the Qing, but dies two years later in a Western jail. In the same year, the Shanghai Chamber of Commerce is opened.

> **❝** I do not begrudge repeating over and over again that internally we are the slaves of the Manchus and suffering from their tyranny. Externally we are being harassed by the Powers, and we are doubly enslaved. The reason why our sacred Han race, descendants of the Yellow Emperor, should support revolutionary independence arises precisely from the question of whether our race will go under and be exterminated. **❞**
>
> Zou Rong, *The Revolutionary Army*, 1903. Trans. John Lust

1904 On February 8 Japan triggers the **Russo-Japanese War** by arbitrarily attacking a Russian naval squadron at Lushun. China remains neutral even though hostilities are conducted on Manchu territory.

In **Tibet**, a British expeditionary force led by Francis Younghusband reaches Lhasa, challenging Chinese suzerainty.

1905 In March 300,000 Russians are defeated by 150,000 Japanese at **Shenyang**, and in May a Russian fleet is defeated in the Tsushima Straits.

In August Sun Yat-sen founds the *Tongmen hui*, or **Revolutionary Alliance** in Tokyo, with Sun as its president and Huang Xing and Song Jiaoren as his deputies. Its manifesto sets out four aims for China: (1) The expulsion of the Manchus; (2) the restoration of 'Chinese' rule; (3) the creation of a republic; and (4) a redistribution of land among peasants.

In September the **Treaty of Portsmouth** (New Hampshire) – brokered by US President Theodore Roosevelt – concludes the Russo-Japanese War. Russia's rights in Manchuria are ceded to Japan, which also gains new rights in Korea.

In December the court sends a mission of inquiry to Britain, France and other 'modern nations' to determine an appropriate constitution for China. The mission will nominate Japan's as the appropriate model.

The **imperial examination system** is abolished, signalling the demise of the scholar–gentry class.

There is a **boycott of American goods** in protest at Congress's refusal to repeal the anti-Chinese race laws of 1882–94.

1906 Zhang Yitang is sent to **Lhasa** to reassert Chinese suzerainty over Tibet.

Railways

The social, economic and military impact of emergent **rail transport systems** in the 19th century can hardly be overstated. But while by 1896 Japan had 2300 miles of track already laid, China could boast only 370. To many, railways were another means of foreign encroachment, unnecessary in view of China's highly developed system of waterways. The first line to be constructed – outside of Shanghai in 1877 – was bought by the Governor and dismantled. A second start was made by **Li Hongzhang**, but it was not until after China's defeat by Japan that the Qing acceded to Western demands for railway concessions. The Russians in Manchuria, the Germans in Shandong and the French in Yunnan went quickly to work, and so by 1906 there were close on 4000 track-miles.

But because of their foreign ownership, China's new railways were politically contentious. Taking matters into their own hands, Chinese entrepreneurs launched a **'railways rights recovery'** movement. Shareholding syndicates began buying up the concessions. But in 1910 the government, lured by the prospect of immense profits, decided the railways should be nationalized. In May, 1911 a decree offered incomplete compensation. To make matters worse, the Qing borrowed US$50 million from a British-American bank to finance its liabilities, further alienating a business class that, crucially, controlled many of China's new provincial assemblies. For all its socialist ideals, the **1911 revolution** was made possible by China's capitalists.

In September the court proclaims its intention to draft a new **constitution**, but without specifying any date.

On September 20 an imperial edict outlaws the production and use of opium. This, however, alienates those profiting from the opium industry, and sets up a rapport between criminal triads and revolutionaries.

The first Chinese translation of **Communist Manifesto** is published.

> ❝ Since one of the principles of our revolution is equality, we intend to establish a republic when we succeed in overthrowing the Manchu regime. In a republic all citizens will have the right to participate in the government, the president of the republic will be elected by the people, and the parliament will have deputies elected by and responsible to their respective constituents. A constitution of the Chinese Republic will then be formulated to be observed by all Chinese. Anyone who entertains the thought of becoming an emperor will be crushed without mercy. ❞
>
> from a Proclamation issued by Sun Yat-sen's *Tongmeng hui*, 1907

1908 In August the court agrees to draft proposals for a constitutional monarchy. The creation of a **national assembly** is accepted in principle, but with many limitations to its powers. Further, a nine-year 'period of transition' is stipulated, ruling out the possibility of any parliament before 1917. Elected local and **provincial assemblies**, however, are established immediately. The combined effect of these resolutions is to decentralize political initiative.

On November 14 **Guangxu** dies aged 37. The following day **Cixi** dies aged 73. In accordance with Cixi's dying wishes, Guangxu's 2-year-old nephew is nominated heir to the throne, as the **Puyi** emperor. A Council of Regency composed of 'vainglorious Manchu princes' assumes the reins of government.

Electric trams are first introduced in Shanghai.

1909 In June elections to the new provincial assemblies are held, albeit on a 'wealth and education' suffrage so narrow that less than 0.6 percent of China's population is eligible to vote. In October, at a self-convened pan-provincial congress, the assemblies' representatives vote to petition the Court for an immediate national assembly. The Court agrees on condition it nominates half its 200 members.

1910 In April the Council of Regency formally proclaims China's sovereignty over Tibet, and the French **Yunnan-Vietnam railway**, linking Kunming to Hanoi, is completed. Korea, meanwhile, is reduced to the status of a Japanese colony. **Yuan Shikai**, commander of the Beiyang (Northern) Army, and credited with having prevented the spread of Boxerism into southern China, is relieved of his post by a government apprehensive of his popularity. In the autumn heavy floods create famine in many areas. On October 3 the **National Assembly** convenes. It petitions the court for a new parliament based on a wider suffrage.

1911 Faced by a budgetary deficit, the government increases **taxation** on tea, salt, wine, tobacco and other commodities.

In April Huang Xing attempts a republican uprising in Guangzhou. Student revolutionaries returning from Japan are seized and executed.

In May the government proclaims the nationalization of China's largely foreign-owned **railways**. But as Chinese entrepreneurs have also invested in the railways, through **'railway rights recovery societies'**, and provisions to partially indemnify private investors are applied unevenly between provinces, China's emergent business class is alienated. Sichuan's business-dominated provincial assem-

Missionaries

That the Chinese are somehow immune to alien indoctrination is contradicted by the spread of Buddhism during the first millennium, and by the adoption of Marxism-Leninism in the 20th century. **Christianity**, however, never fared so well, except in such anomalous pockets as Hong Kong, Macau and Taiwan, despite a good start by the Jesuits in the 17th century. But in the 19th century, as Qing control waned, so evangelical Protestantism waxed, supported by the **London Missionary Society** (founded in 1795), the **China Inland Mission** (1866) and other international bodies.

From 1807, when **Robert Morrison**, working undercover as an employee of the British East India Company, began proselytizing in Guangzhou, a new breed of missionary regularly ran the gauntlet of government opposition. Many were **congregationalists**, belonging to smaller rather than established churches, among them Methodists, Baptists and Unitarians. Unlike the Jesuits, these sought followers among the destitute, and in 1844 the United States 'persuaded' the Chinese government to both tolerate and protect its missionaries throughout the empire.

The Confucian scholar-gentry, however, remained hostile, as did many rural communities. In quite separate ways, both the pseudo-Christian Taiping Rebellion and the overtly antagonistic Boxer Uprising rendered the missionaries' task all but impossible. Yet slowly they became associated with three goods the Chinese did not have: modern medicine, modern education and a version of democracy. While conversion-rates remained meagre, by opening dispensaries, schools and later colleges, the missionaries gradually overcame prejudice. In the early 20th century, their activities expanded steadily; but then first the Japanese invasion, then Communism put an end to missionaryism. While under Mao Zedong Christianity was proscribed, a post-Mao revival, closely monitored by the state, has been extremely modest.

bly sanctions mass anti-government demonstrations. In Hubei officers of the New Army pledge their support for the Revolutionary Alliance.

On September 7 Zhao Erfeung, the Governor of Sichuan, sends troops against railway rights demonstrators, killing thirty and prompting nationwide protests.

On October 9 revolutionaries who have taken refuge in the Russian Concession at Hankou (with Wuchang and Hanyang one of the three sub-cities of Wuhan) accidentally detonate a bomb. When Qing police move in to make arrests and summary executions on October 10, two battalions of the New Army mutiny and seize a munitions depot in Wuchang. This action, known as the **Wuchang Uprising**, ignites a general revolt.

On October 11 revolutionaries take control of Hanyang, and troops in Hankou mutiny on October 12. One after another, the provincial assembles declare their support for Sun Yat-sen. The Manchu regency, despite recalling **Yuan Shikai**, is paralysed. Troops sent south from Beijing by train are cut off north of the Yellow River. New Army commanders who have remained loyal distribute a twelve-point proposal. In desperation, the court accedes to most of their demands and on November 11 Yuan is ordered to form a cabinet pending the promulgation of a new constitution. Hankou and Hanyang are recaptured, but 'loyalist' forces are defeated outside **Nanjing**, which now becomes the centre of rebellion.

On December 29 **Sun Yat-sen**, having persuaded the British government to embargo any further loans to the Qing court, is elected Provisional President by a congress of delegates from sixteen provincial assemblies.

1912 On January 1 **The Republic of China** is proclaimed in Nanjing. As the revolution's success remains in doubt, particularly north of the Yellow River, Sun Yat-sen telegraphs Yuan Shikai, offering him the presidency if he will change sides. Yuan agrees. At the end of January, 44 Beiyang Army commanders urge the cabinet to accede to a republic. In return, the Nanjing government agrees that the imperial family should continue living inside the Forbidden City with an annual stipend of US$4 million.

On February 12 the boy-emperor Puyi's **abdication** is promulgated, ending an empire begun 2132 years before. Three days later, the Republican Senate confirms Yuan's appointment as Provisional President, pending nationwide elections.

In the new republic, the Chinese lunar calender is replaced by its Western counterpart.

> " It is now evident that the hearts of the majority of the people are in favour of a republican form of government: the provinces of the South were the first to espouse the cause, and the generals of the North have since pledged their support. From the preference of the people's hearts, the Will of Heaven can be discerned. How then could We bear to oppose the will of the millions for the glory of one Family? Therefore, observing the tendencies of the age on the one hand and studying the opinions of the people on the other, We and His Majesty the Emperor hereby vest the sovereignty in the People and decide in favour of a republican form of constitutional government. "
>
> Edict of Abdication, issued by the Dowager-empress Longyu on behalf of the Puyi Emperor, February 12, 1912

9
The Republic of China (ROC)

1912–1949

The **Republican Revolution** of 1911–12 abolished China's ancient imperial system but did little else to mend China's woes. Rather, it unleashed a sustained upheaval that – combined with an unprecedented succession of floods, drought and famine – accounted for the deaths of untold millions, and rendered the nation vulnerable to **Japanese aggression** in the 1930s. Nor could much be done in the interim about the entrenched interests of those Western powers that had wrung concessions from the Qing. **Sun Yat-sen**'s overwhelming weakness at the beginning of 1912 was military. In this respect, the Revolution – made possible only by the turn-coat intervention of **Yuan Shikai** – was fatally ill-prepared. Instead of using his muscle to cement a new order, Yuan rapidly suborned it. Claiming the Presidency as his fit reward, he sidelined Sun, then groomed himself for a restored throne.

Yuan was thwarted by a second revolt among the provinces. His example, however, encouraged the aspirations of other military commanders. The period between 1916 and 1928 is known as the **Warlord Years**. Each had his own army, style and objectives. While some were content to protect their turf by entering into usually short-lived alliances with rival warlords, others saw themselves as champions of whatever they conceived to be the national interest. The nett effect was to instill a culture of conflict. Only the treaty ports, under Western control, remained relatively quiescent.

But Sun Yat-sen was not a man to give up easily. Out of the ruins of his revolution he raised the **National Party**, or *Guomindang*, and in Guangzhou laid the foundations of a regime capable of taking on the warlords at their own game. It befell his successor, **Chiang Kaishek**, however, to implement the **Northern Expedition** that reunified most of China and made possible the **'Nanjing Decade'** (1927–37).

Even Chiang's strong-arm methods proved fallible. In the ideological, cultural and military free-for-all that followed 1912, a new configuration of revolutionary energies germinated. Sometimes abetted, and sometimes hindered, by the USSR, the **communists**, when not engaged in wasteful power-struggles among themselves, learned how to turn every setback to advantage. All but destroyed by Chiang in 1935, their steel was forged during the 'heroic' **Long March**, from Jiangxi to Shaanxi.

But the true making of the **Communist Party of China** (**CCP**) was the **Japanese occupation** of 1937–45. The Japanese, launching their assault on China from Manchuria, swiftly overpowered the Guomindang. Even with American help, from before the Pearl Harbor incident, Chiang was able to do little more than sustain the fact of resistance. Yet the Japanese, too, were unable to control the whole of China, and it was in these circumstances that the communists, mobilizing the peasantry, husbanded their growing strength while engaging in sufficient forays against the foreign invaders to encourage the Chinese at large to believe that their real salvation rested with them, and not the tainted Guomindang.

Following Japan's defeat by the Allies in 1945, China reverted to **civil war**. Possessing the more disciplined force, and implementing **Mao Zedong**'s concept of a 'people's war', the communists won. Like previous interregnums, the anarchic ROC had spawned fresh ideas and fresh initiatives.

As Chiang tested the possibilities of fascism, a new intelligentsia – educated either abroad or in colleges and universities sponsored mainly by American, and often Christian, organizations – grappled with the implications of democratic liberalism. But the war-management skills derived from Mao's adaptation of Marxism-Leninism proved finally invincible.

1912 In March the government of the **Republic of China (ROC)** promulgates a draft constitution, pending national elections at the end of the year. Already, however, **Sun Yat-sen** and President **Yuan Shikai** begin falling out as Yuan promotes his supporters to key positions.

The first in a series of multi-million-dollar loans is negotiated with Britain, France and other powers.

In April Yuan transfers the Republic's capital from Nanjing to **Beijing**, where a provisional Senate is convened.

On August 25, ahead of the national elections, Sun Yat-sen founds the **Guomingdang** (National Party).

In November Russia undertakes to promote Mongolian independence, following an ethnic uprising in Outer Mongolia.

In December the Guomingdang – in a campaign orchestrated by **Song Jiaoren** – gains a sweeping victory in the national elections. Suffrage, however, is limited to five percent of the population, based on education and wealth.

1913 On March 20 Song Jiaoren is assassinated, almost certainly at Yuan Shikai's bidding. When the bicameral National Assembly convenes in April, the Guomingdang majority endeavours to block a fresh loan of $25 million negotiated by Yuan with mainly British banks. Yuan responds in June by ordering his troops to surround the Assembly building in Beijing and expel Guomingdang members.

In July a **Second Revolution** begins when several provincial assemblies and city governors repudiate their allegiance to Yuan. Unrest spreads as new militias and revolutionary armies are formed. Yuan, however, moves swiftly to crush dissent, and on October 6 he is formally elected President of the Republic by a rump assembly. As the foreign powers signal their recognition of Yuan's government, the Guomingdang is outlawed and its members purged from provincial assemblies. A month later, Sun Yat-sen departs for Japan.

In November China concedes the 'autonomy' of **Outer Mongolia**.

1914 On January 10 Yuan replaces what remains of the National Assembly with a 'Political Council' staffed by close supporters. In February he issues orders dissolving China's provincial assemblies, and in May annuls the Provisional Constitution of 1912. Over the summer, he appoints loyal generals to provincial and city governorships.

As war breaks out in Europe, on August 6 Yuan proclaims Chinese neutrality, but as many of the contending nations have substantial interests in China, it can only be a matter of weeks before China too becomes involved. 150,000 Chinese will enlist in the British army, mainly as auxiliaries to combat Germany on the Western Front.

On August 23 Japan, taking advantage of European disunity, issues Germany with an ultimatum to withdraw from Japanese lease-held territory in Shandong.

In November, as Sun Yat-sen foments a **Third Revolution** from Tokyo, Japanese troops occupy Qingdao and Germany 'surrenders' its Shandong concessions.

In December, shortly after the appearance of new coins bearing Yuan's head, the ROC President decrees his term of office will run for ten years.

Yuan Shikai 1859–1916

A protégé of Li Hongzhang, **Yuan Shikai** was one of the few stars of the last years of the Manchu. He failed to win a degree under the imperial examination system, but quickly made his mark as a soldier, then as a diplomat serving in Korea. From 1901 he was military governor of the Beijing metropolitan area, and shortly afterwards was appointed a Grand Councillor. Like Li, he endeavoured to modernize the imperial army, while creating an effective police force to maintain order in China's increasingly turbulent cities. His politics, however, remained **conservative**.

Intensely loyal to Dowager-empress Cixi, in 1908 he was 'retired' by a court nervous of his prestige, then recalled as the tide of republicanism rose. As the commander of China's most disciplined force by late 1911, he held the trump card as the Qing dynasty unravelled. As first **President of the ROC**, however, he was more interested in reviving authoritarian government than in pandering to democratic and socialist sentiments, and by making the new cabinet answerable to himself rather than the National Assembly, he established a dictatorship. He may well have gotten away with it had not his vaulting ambition got the better of his undoubted pragmatism. By openly declaring his wish to become emperor, he plunged China back into civil war.

1915 In January **Japan** presents Yuan Shikai's government with **21 Demands**, designed to extend its influence and power inside China. After fraught negotiations – accompanied by widespread civil unrest and a boycott of Japanese goods – Yuan accedes to most of Japan's wishes, and a Sino-Japanese treaty is signed on May 25. Disturbances continue into the autumn as Yuan orchestrates a campaign for the 'restoration of the monarchy'.

In June severe flooding affects Anhui and other central provinces, and in July Hubei is plagued by locusts.

The first edition of the *Qingnian zazhi* ('Youth Magazine'), edited by Chen Duxiu, is published in

Yuan Shikai – the Republic of China's first president who sought to become an emperor himself.

Shanghai in September. Renamed *Xin Qingnian* ('New Youth Magazine') in 1916, this quickly establishes itself as a leading forum for 'progressive', then **communist** opinion.

In December, after Yuan proclaims his intention to become the first emperor of a new dynasty, several military governors revolt.

1916 As gubernatorial revolt against Yuan spreads, fighting erupts in many provinces. Industrial strikes become commonplace.

In March Yuan is forced to abandon his imperial ambition. The crisis still remains unresolved following Yuan's death, from uraemia on June 6. Although **Li Yuanhong** (1864–1928) – Yuan's chosen successor, declared President the following day – renounces monarchism and restores some of the Republic's institutions, his policies fail to assuage either the Guomindang, or those governors who, having tasted power under Yuan, turn to **warlordism**.

1917 As Britain supports Japan's claims in Shandong, a rift develops between Li Yuanhong and his military prime-minister **Duan Qirui** as to the merits of China's entering World War I as Germany's ally.

In March China severs relations with Germany.

In May Duan, having taken the Allied side, is removed from office. When Duan threatens reprisals a month later, Li requests **Zhang Xun**, the leader of a coalition of northern governors, to rid Beijing of Duan's supporters. Zhang enters the capital, and promptly restores the Qing monarchy. Li is pressured into dissolving the reconvened National Assembly, and on July 1 the 'last emperor' **Puyi** is returned to the throne.

On July 7 Zhang Xun's troops are routed by forces loyal to Duan Qirui. Reinstated as prime minister, Duan removes Puyi. Li Yuanhong is replaced as President by **Feng Guozhang**.

Dr Sun Yat-Sen 1866–1925

Revered by the communists and widely known as *guofu*, 'father of the nation', **Sun** was born into a poor Guangdong family. He emigrated to Hawaii as an adolescent and was educated by missionaries in democratic as well as Christian ideals. In 1886 he returned to China to attend medical school in Guangzhou, and continued his training in **Hong Kong**. His exposure to Western values focused his mind on political issues, and in 1894 he offered his services to Li Hongzhang. Spurned, Sun dedicated himself to the overthrow of both the Qing and the imperial system, spending many years fundraising in the United States, Europe, Japan and Southeast Asia.

In 1895 he returned to Tokyo, to set up a first republican association, and in 1905 he established the *Tongmen hui* (Revolutionary Alliance). It was this umbrella of dissident groups that achieved Sun's aims in 1911 and 1912. Through it, Sun promulgated the three main strands of his political philosophy: nationalism, democracy and the people's welfare. He also encouraged women activists. In Asia, such ideas branded him a liability. He was paid off by the Japanese government in 1907, and expelled the following year from French Indochina.

Sun learned of the **Wuchang Uprising** in a newspaper while in Colorado. Returning to China, he secured the ousting of the Qing by yielding the presidency to **Yuan Shikai**. Within months, the two leaders were at loggerheads. To consolidate his position, Sun concentrated on building the **Guomingdang**. By the time of his death in 1925 he had seemingly established the party's ascendancy, but his appointment of **Chiang Kaishek** as chief-of-staff exposed China to both further feuding and betrayal. While Chiang's promotion might be seen as a fatal error of judgement, more realistically, it reflected the stranglehold exercised over Chinese politics by the '**secret**' **societies**. In 1904 Sun himself had been initiated into a Hawaiian triad, and he was permanently indebted to Charlie Soong, a triad heavyweight one of whose daughters, Qing-ling, Sun bigamously married in 1914.

Sun Yat-Sen, the leading ideologue of Chinese republicanism and founder of the Guomiangdang or National Party.

China formally declares war on Germany on August 14.

Returning from five years overseas, **Sun Yat-sen** declares a rival ROC government in **Guangzhou**, also opposed to Germany, on September 10.

In October conflict between Guangzhou and Beijing escalates into open war. As widespread flooding occurs in the north, Duan orders his troops south. In the same month the Bolshevik 'October Revolution' in Russia suggests new, more radical, solutions to old problems.

1918 The northern army splits into three principal factions: Anfu, loyal to Duan Qirui; Zhili, commanded chiefly by **Wu Peifu**; and the 'Fengtian/Manchurian Clique', led by **Feng Yuxiang** and **Zhang Zuolin**.

In May, in the south, a newly convened National Assembly in Guangzhou reorganizes the 'Military Government', redistributing some of Sun Yat-sen's powers among a committee of seven commanders who also turn to warlordism.

In November north–south hostilities end as a ceasefire is signed, prompted in part by the cessation of war in Europe. While China is ostensibly partitioned, in reality it is fragmented, as regional commanders defy the orders of both Guangzhou and Beijing.

Earlier in the year, radical opinion is incensed by Beijing's decision to commit Chinese troops to Japan's attempts to protect its interests against Russia – a policy continued by **Xu Shichang**, who is elected President in Beijing in October. Duan resigns as prime minister. At Beijing University a pro-Bolshevik study-group chaired by **Li Dazhao**, and attended by **Mao Zedong**, considers whether mobilizing China peasantry might not be the best means of fostering revolution.

1919 In March Lenin founds the **Communist International** (**Comintern**) in Moscow, geared to promoting communist revolution around the world.

On April 30, despite Chinese objections, the **Versailles Peace Conference** (convened by the Great Powers to resolve differences arising out of World War I) accedes to Japan's demands for the transfer of German interests in Shandong to itself. News of this humiliation sparks nationwide protests. On May 4 3000 students from Beijing University and other colleges gather at the Gate of Heavenly Peace (**Tiananmen**). Prevented from entering the Imperial City, they march toward the foreign legations, then divert to the residence of the Minister of Communication – Cao Rulin – who has previously negotiated substantial loans from the Japanese government. A group of students set fire to his house. The Chinese Minister to Japan, Zhang Zhiongxiang, is also assaulted. Thirty students are arrested, one dying in hospital shortly after. As the **May Fourth Movement** ignites, student riots occur in many cities.

On May 19 a co-ordinated general strike by students begins, again in Beijing, where on June 3 the police make many more arrests. On June 5 sympathetic strikes organized by business interests and workers begin in Shanghai, then spread to Wuhan, Tianjin and Jinan. On June 10 the Beijing government dismisses Cao Rulin and Zhang Zhongxiang. On June 12 final demonstrations are held in Shanghai and other cities to mark the students' 'victory'.

The Treaty of Versailles is signed by the major powers, though not by China, on June 28.

On October 10 Sun Yat-sen relaunches his National Party, still known as the Guomingdang.

1920 In the north, warlord tensions erupt into civil war, with the Zhili and Fengtian factions combining against Duan Qirui.

In May, the **Communist Party of China** (**CCP**), headed by Chen Duxiu and backed by the Comintern, is secretly inaugurated at a girl's school in the French

Concession of Shanghai. Communist cells are quickly implanted in other cities.

In June, Sun Yat-sen disavows the Military Government in Guangzhou following an unresolved power-struggle within its leadership. At the end of the month Beijing takes China into the newly created **League of Nations**.

1921 In May Sun's authority is revived when he is elected Extraordinary President of the **Second Guangzhou Regime**, constructed to replace the dissolved Military Government.

In July the **CCP** holds its First Congress in Shanghai. Thirteen Chinese delegates (including Mao Zedong) representing sixty members are joined by 'Maring' (H Sneevliet) from the USSR, representing the Comintern. Chaired by Zhang Guotao, Congress appoints Chen Duxiu as Party Secretary-General. Although Mao Zedong is excluded from the Central Committee, he shortly becomes Secretary of the CCP's Hunan branch. After hastily removing to a boat on a lake for security reasons, Congress formulates two main policies: (1) the CCP should involve itself in and promote all labour movements; and (2), in line with Soviet strategy, it should co-operate with the Guomingdang.

1922 In the north, the Zhili faction, under the command of Wu Peifu, wars with Zhang Zuolin. Zhang is driven back into Manchuria as Wu establishes control over Beijing.

In February Sun Yat-sen begins planning a **Northern Expedition** against the northern warlords to reunite the country, but his strategy is undermined by factionalizing inside the Guomingdang.

In May Peng Pai organizes the **Haifeng Federation of Peasant Unions**, the first of many communist peasant movements, in southern Guangzhou.

In July the Second Congress of the CCP formally affiliates itself with the Comintern.

On August 9 Sun Yat-sen flees Guangzhou after his palace comes under fire from a former supporter, Chen Jiongming. In Shanghai he co-opts the communist leader Chen Duxiu onto a committee set up to advise on the reorganization of the Guomingdang.

In **Beijing**, as female education spreads, a **Women's Rights League** holds its first meetings.

1923 In January, advised by the Comitern, Sun Yat-sen persuades the Guomingdang to adopt a **revised constitution**

The Warlords

Although he had appointed most of them, **Yuan Shikai** got short shrift from the Republic's military governors when he made known his intention of becoming emperor toward the end of 1915. **Cai Ao**, the governor of Yunnan, sped to Beijing, overtly to pursue a courtesan, but in fact to plot with others against the President. The conspiracy exposed, Cai proclaimed Yunnan's 'independence', and for three months ran Yuan's forces ragged in the southwest. Other governors followed suit.

All-told, there were around 200 **warlords**. Some had 'official' status, others did not. Some were professional soldiers, others mere bandits. Many had connections with the triad underworld. The most colourful was **Zhang Zongchang**, governor of Shandong. Known as the 'Dog-meat General', he had a personal guard of 4000 White Russians, as well as a Russian harem. But whatever their individual characters, for ten years the warlords reduced the Chinese landscape to constant warfare. The most powerful was the fiercely anti-communist **Wu Peifu**, who controlled the Yellow River plains. But even Wu was vulnerable if the two other northern big men, **Feng Yuxiang** and **Zhang Zoulin**, combined against him. Feng (known as the 'Christian warlord' after baptizing his troops with a fire-hose) controlled the northwest from his base in Shaanxi, while Zhang (and later his son Zhang Yuelin, the 'Young Marshal') had command of Manchuria. But warlordism was also as prevalent in the south, and obstructed Sun Yat-sen's Guangzhou-based republic.

based on his three principles of Nation, Democracy and Welfare. In the same month mercenaries hired by Sun retake Guangzhou. On January 26 Sun signs a joint communiqué with the Soviet representative, Adolphe Joffe, thus gaining some international recognition for his Guangzhou government. The USSR agrees to support the Guomingdang in its effort to reunify China while conceding that China is not yet 'ready' for a socialist revolution.

In February Sun returns to Guangzhou as self-styled 'generalissimo' of the restored regime. In the north a strike by rail-workers on the Beijing–Hankou line is savagely crushed by Wu Peifu.

In March Sun appoints **Chiang Kaishek** (in Pin-yin **Jiang Jieshi**) as his Chief-of-Staff. Michael Borodin, a Comintern emissary, is given the title 'formal adviser'. Fighting against Chen Jiongming and other southern warlords continues, but with Russian help Sun strengthens his army.

In June the Third Congress of the CCP confirms its support for the Guomingdang, adopting Lenin's **'bloc within'** strategy.

1924 In January the Guomingdang holds its first Congress in Guangzhou. It commits itself to the defeat of warlordism and imperialism, and invites 'mass participation' by peasants and workers. Three members of the CCP, including Li Dazhao, are elected to the Guomingdang's Central Executive. Mao Zedong – now a member of the CCP Central Committee – is named as an alternate member. When the Congress closes, Sun establishes the **Whampoa Military Academy**. Chiang Kaishek is appointed commandant, and Borodin organizes Soviet trainers.

In the north, the 'Second Zhili-Manchurian War' erupts. Wu Peifu suffers defeat after his ally Feng Yuxiang switches sides.

In May the Beijing government signs a Sino–Soviet agreement. On November 26, however, a People's Republic, independent of China, but closely controlled by the USSR, is proclaimed in (Outer) **Mongolia**.

Toward the end of the year, as Feng Yuxiang consolidates his control of the north, the Guomingdang prepare to relaunch the 'Northern Expedition'. The former Emperor Puyi, meanwhile, expelled from the Imperial Palace by Feng, seeks refuge in the Japanese legation.

1925 In a year marked by military and civil turbulence, severe famine in Sichuan accounts for three million lives. Warfare continues between the northern warlords, and the Guomingdang is embroiled in an 'Eastern Expedition' against its southern opponents.

As the industrial strike, often orchestrated by communists, becomes a main weapon of 'proletarian' discontent, students take to the streets in all China's larger cities to protest against the abuses of government and the continuing presence of foreign powers. Such disruptions coalesce into a nationwide movement following the **May Thirtieth Incident**, when British troops open fire on students in Shanghai.

The death of **Sun Yat-sen** from cancer in Beijing on March 12 heralds a shift away from socialist policies by the Guomingdang, which proclaims a 'national' government in Guangzhou on July 1.

In August Chiang Kaishek gains outright command of the Guomingdang's **New Revolutionary Army**.

In November members of the Guomingdang executive known as the **Western Hills Clique** determine at a meeting held outside Beijing to purge their party of communists. **Wang Jingwei** is singled out as the individual most responsible for communist 'infiltration'.

The Triads

Thanks to the predominantly urban Chinese diaspora, the **triads** are probably the world's biggest **criminal fraternity**, however loosely interlinked. Experts disagree as to their origin, however. Throughout imperial times many different kinds of society were formed, some of them within the law, some outside, ranging from religious sects, clan associations, trade and merchant guilds to martial arts academies, blood brotherhoods and bandit gangs. Authoritarian government, particularly by the 'alien' Mongols and Manchu, was a powerful spur to secrecy and mutuality. In triad folklore, the early **White Lotus Society** (see p.296) loom large, as do the **warrior-monks of Shaolin**. It was probably the Qing attempt to outlaw and then tax opium that created the decisive impetus, however.

By the 1920s, amid the turmoil of the early republic, racketeering of every kind was commonplace. Strongest in Shanghai, where 'Big-eared' Du Yuehsheng's **Green Gang** ruled the roost, the triads also controlled other cities, with Hong Kong and Macau providing safe havens for their most wanted members. Sun Yat-sen and Chiang Kaishek both had underworld connections, and both were married to daughters of a known 'big man', **Charlie Soong**. Yet the Soong family was equally involved in 'straight' banking. Because of *guanxi* – the Chinese tradition of personal networking and indebtedness – any attempt to distinguish between legitimate and illegitimate business practice was futile. Similarly, whether Chiang's persecution of communists from 1926 was politically motivated, or foisted upon him by Shanghai's "families", remains unclear.

After 1949 triads were suppressed on the mainland by the CCP, although today's illegal **emigration scams** run by 'snake-heads' in Fujian and a resurgence of **narcotics-trading** show the triads are back in force.

1926 In January the second Guomingdang Congress rejects the Western Hills Clique's anti-communist recommendations as unconstitutional, and both Li Dazhou and Wang

Jingwei are re-elected to the Central Executive Committee.

In the north, Feng Yuxiang is driven out of Beijing after Wu Peifu forms an alliance with Zhang Zuolin.

On March 20, in the **Zhongshan Incident**, Chiang Kaishek – having remained aloof from Guomingdang infighting – seizes a gunboat anchored close to the Whampoa Academy, and arrests its captain, Li Zhilong, a known communist, and possible participant in a plot to remove Chiang. Fifty other communists are also seized. Chiang proclaims martial law in Guangzhou and disarms guards protecting the Guomingdang's Soviet advisers. Anticipating his own arrest, Wang Jingwei flees abroad. Some Russian militarists' services are retained, however, as Chiang also purges right-wing members of the party.

In July Chiang orders the **Northern Expedition** to commence, and becomes Chairman of the Guomingdang Central Executive Committee. The communists, taking orders from Moscow, declare their support for Chiang's 'anti-warlord' and 'anti-imperialist' campaign. Although Wu Peifu and other northern warlords offer resistance, by winter, Chiang's armies are in control of Hunan, Hubei, Jiangxi and Fujian provinces.

1927 On January 1 the Guomingdang capital is transferred from Guangzhou to **Wuhan**. As Chiang Kaishek's Northern Expedition prospers, Nanjing falls on March 24. 'Chinese' Shanghai – where a CCP-led workers' movement is being suppressed by rival warlords – capitulates soon afterwards. Communist relief, however, is short-lived. On April 12 Chiang orders a purge of CCP members living in the city. On April 13, when the communists orchestrate mass protests and strikes, Chiang's troops open fire, killing at least 100 protestors. In the ensuing **'white terror'**, thousands more are eliminated by police and army sweeps, but also by the Green Gang triad. Even so, at

Moscow's bidding, the CCP continues its uneasy alliance with the Guomingdang.

On April 18 Nanjing is declared capital of the Republic, inaugurating **The Nanjing Decade**. At the fifth Guomingdang congress, held in Hankou, the party is threatened with fissure when the communists announce they will withdraw their support for the reunification campaign unless Wang Jingwei, returned from abroad, is reinstated in the Guomingdang leadership. While Chiang vows to destroy his 'Wuhan rivals', Wang begins distancing himself from the communists.

In May, Japanese troops seize Jinan from Guomingdang control in order to protect its interests in Shandong.

In June the northern warlord **Feng Yuxiang** throws in his lot with Chiang, and persuades Wang Jingwei to counter communist influence within the Guomingdang. On June 23 Wang moves to suppress the General Trades Union in Wuhan. Meanwhile, Chiang's troops take both Beijing and Tianjin. Although fighting against individual warlords continues, China is largely reunified.

In July Wang pursues his campaign against labour organizations throughout Hubei, and persecutes CCP members. As the anti-communist drive spreads, Borodin and other Soviet advisers leave China. With the Guomingdang–CCP alliance in tatters, the communists stage an uprising at **Nanchang** (Jiangxi province) on August 1. Although this signals the 'birth' of the **Red Army**, the revolt is crushed within days. Chen Duxiu is censured at an emergency meeting of the CCP Central Committee and Qu Qibai is elected Party Secretary-General in his stead.

In September Mao Zedong stirs peasant revolts in Hunan, known as the **Autumn Harvest Uprising**. When these fail, Mao too is censured for pursuing tactics contrary to those recommended by the Comintern. Peng Pai, meanwhile, sets up the first Chinese soviet in **Lufeng**, in southern Guangdong. Shortly afterwards, a second soviet is established at nearby Haipheng. Mao's standing is partially restored when a communist-backed urban uprising known as the **Guangzhou Commune** also fails. Several thousand peasants and workers are eliminated in the subsequent Guomingdang crackdown.

On December 14 Chiang Kaishek's government breaks off diplomatic relations with the Soviet Union.

1928 Peng Pai's Lufeng and Haipheng soviets are crushed by the Guomingdang in March.

On June 4 the former warlord **Zhang Zuelin** dies when his train is blown up by Japanese extremists angered by his alliance with Chiang Kaishek. Notwithstanding, Zhang's son, Zhang Xueling, pledges the loyalty of the northeastern provinces to the Guomingdang. Nominally the whole of China comes under Chiang's rule.

In Moscow, **Joseph Stalin** states that the CCP should seek to oust the Guomingdang. As the Red Army, bolstered by Whampoa-trained officers, gathers strength, skirmishing between the two sides proliferates.

Driven out of Hunan, Mao Zedong, together with **Zhu De**, begins constructing a communist **'base area'** in the Jinggang mountains of Jiangxi. Other base areas are established elsewhere.

On October 10 Chiang is formally acknowledged Chairman of the National Government.

1929 In January Chiang stages a **'National Reorganization and Demobilization Conference'**, attended by Feng Yuxiang and other 'loyal warlords'. The Republic's armies are reduced to less than one million. As the communists' Jingganshan base expands, however, Chiang devises a costly strategy of **'encirclement'**.

In Shanghai and other cities, workers' unions are smashed, and many of their leaders killed. **Li Lisan** urges dramatic

Shanghai

Shanghai was made by the Taiping Rebellion, when the seizure of Nanjing forced Western traders to develop an alternative Yangzi port. By 1860 there were more ships going in and out of Shanghai than London. By the 1920s it had become the fifth biggest city in the world. Divided into three sections – the **International Settlement**, dominated by the British, a separate French Concession, and the sprawling Chinese Municipality – it was the centre of both China's domestic and foreign commerce. It was also the country's first truly modern industrial city, with an emphasis on garment manufacture. There was a racecourse, countless hotels, dance halls, cinemas and colonial clubs – famously a notice on one of Shanghai's parks advised 'No Dogs! And No Chinese!'

But if the waterfront Bund, with its banks and merchant houses, was China's concrete interface with the global trading community, Shanghai was also, as Chiang Kaishek remarked, a 'sink of iniquity'. As well as prostitution, the triads organized protection rackets and trafficked narcotics. More soberly, Shanghai was a centre of political intrigue, and where the Communist Party first incubated. Shanghai's presses, too, enriched every shade of readership. But the circus ended in 1937. Greater Shanghai fell to the Japanese, and had to wait forty years before being revived by **Deng Xiaoping**'s reforms. Today, dubbed the world's largest building site, it again challenges Beijing as China's premier conurbation.

reprisals against the Guomingdang, including the storming of key cities by the Red Army. Mao, Zhu De and other communist leaders advocate a more gradual policy of building up strength in rural areas.

1930 Swayed by Li Lisan and by Moscow, the CCP orchestrates a spate of strikes and urban uprisings across China but these are easily suppressed by the Guomingdang. Only in Changsha is communist control established for more than a few days. But when Changsha is recaptured, Li's

Shanghai during the 1920s: A view of the Bund that doubled as the city's main commercial avenue and a waterfront promenade.

strategy is discredited. The Guomindang itself, meanwhile, splits asunder.

In May Chiang's authority is challenged by an alliance comprising Feng Yuxiang, Yan Xishan and Wang Jingmei. 200,000 die in the ensuing civil war.

Aided by Zhang Xueliang, Chiang defeats his adversaries in October, and consolidates his power over the nationalist alliance.

In December the smouldering power-struggle within the CCP comes to a head with the **'Fujian Incident'**, when troops loyal to Li mutiny against Mao. Mao responds by executing 2000 fellow communists as 'traitors'.

In another year of famine, affecting Shanxi and Gansu, an estimated 4,000,000 Chinese die of hunger and disease.

1931 A group of Chinese communists, known as the **'28 Bolsheviks'**, return from training in Moscow and take control of the CCP, sometimes eliminating their rivals.

In July, 100 million are made homeless when the Yangzi bursts its banks at Hankou.

As Chiang Kaishek continues his 'encirclement' of communist base areas, on September 18, in an unprovoked attack, Japanese troops seize a Chinese barracks outside Shenyang (Mukden) in the far northeast. The **'Mukden Incident'** leads to the Japanese occupation of the whole of **Manchuria** inside of two months.

In November an 'All China Soviet Congress' convened by Mao Zedong at Ruijin in Jiangxi issues a 'national' constitution together with land and labour laws that presage a coming 'class-struggle' by denying rights and freedoms to landlords, bureaucrats, the gentry, monks and industrialists. In the Jiangxi base area, wealthier landowners are dispossessed.

1932 At the end of January a combined Japanese naval and army force occupies outer Shanghai.

Lu Xun 1881–1936

1912 prompted a literary renaissance. A generation of talented novelists, essayists and poets abandoned classical Chinese – incomprehensible to anyone not educated under the now defunct Confucian examination system – in favour of the 'vernacular', everyday Chinese as it was actually used and spoken. Such writers included Ding Ling, Lu Xiaoman, Mao Dun, Hu Yepin, Ba Jin, Shen Congwen and Lao She. Their work, radical in its intent, and sometimes self-consciously modernist, looked to Japanese and Western models for inspiration. But the giant in the swell was **Lu Xun**.

A member of the scholar-gentry class, Lu carried over a teasing, but also bitter, refinement into his use of the demotic. As a boy in Zhejiang, he saw his grandfather disgraced for embezzlement, and his father die of opium addiction. Studying first to become a military engineer in Nanjing, then a doctor in Tokyo, Lu turned author after being struck by the seeming unconcern on the faces of Chinese bystanders in a photograph of an execution. His aim was to revive his compatriots' humanity, and with it their self-esteem. His means, however, were satirical. In *Ah Q Zhengzhuan* ('The True Story of Ah Q'), the best-known of his stories, Lu depicts a simpleton whose look-on-the-bright-side mentality makes him a permanent underdog. Following its publication in 1925, **'Ah Q-ism'** became a catchphrase, both for China's abject surrender to foreign powers, and its sufferance of warlordism.

Yet from that date, Lu turned to the *zawen*, or literary essay, abandoning fiction. He also gravitated toward communism, although he never joined the Party that later venerated him. Had he lived on, it is highly conceivable that his Swiftian sense of injustice would have punched some holes in monolithic Maoism sooner or later. 'In China,' Lu commented wryly, 'it is the old who write obituaries of the young'.

In March Japan renames Manchuria **Manchukuo**, declaring it a separate state. The former emperor Puyi is installed as 'Chief Executive', and Changchun made its capital.

Unable to respond militarily, Chiang Kaishek concludes peace terms apropos Shanghai in May, freeing up his forces to resume their campaign against the communists.

In the summer the 'Fourth Encirclement' is launched against the Jiangxi base area, which now straddles the Fujian border. Mao Zedong – recommending that Guomingdang troops be deliberately drawn into communist-controlled territory – loses favour with his colleagues.

In October Zhang Guotao establishes a new communist base area in Sichuan.

1933 Japan withdraws from the League of Nations after it refuses to recognize Manchukuo.

In April the USSR calls for a united Chinese front against Japan's 'imperialism'. Speaking in Fuzhou, Chiang Kaishek dismisses the Japanese as 'dwarf-pirates', signalling his intent to continue hostilities against 'Jiangxi's local pirates'.

By the terms of a truce signed on May 31,China cedes its interests in Manchuria to Japan. Japan, however, continues to mount incursions from Manchuria. In Fujian, the governor Chen Mingshu – dismayed at Chiang's pusilanimity – declares independence under the banner of a 'People's Revolutionary Government'. Unsupported by the CCP, Chen's rebellion is crushed by Guomingdang forces.

From July, Chiang launches his fifth and largest encirclement campaign against the Jiangxi soviet. His tactics include moving peasants into controlled 'safe' villages, building new roads for the use of military convoys and erecting chains of defensive-offensive blockhouses. Without effective artillery, the communists are severely pressed.

1934 As Chiang's forces begin prevailing against the Jiangxi base area, Mao Zedong conducts a **'rectification programme'** against 'counter-revolutionaries'. As thousands are executed some speak of a 'red terror'.

Attempting to seize the ideological initiative, on February 19, Chiang promotes a **'New Life'** movement designed to instil values of public loyalty and family virtue.

On March 1 the puppet Puyi is proclaimed Emperor of Manchukuo by Japan.

The Long March

Faced with annihilation by the Guomingdang, in October 1935 the largest of the communist armies was evacuated from the largest communist 'base area', under the command of **Zhu De**. A year later, 7000 survivors out of an initial 100,000 arrived in **Shaanxi**, to set up a new soviet. Many had died in battle, and as many died of hunger, frostbite, disease and sheer fatigue. Such losses were nothing short of a military calamity. Yet the **Long March** was rapidly enshrined as the central episode in Chinese communism's triumphalist mythology, compared by some to the biblical exodus of Israel out of Egypt.

The 6000-mile slog, detouring past Kunming in the southwest, had traversed every kind of terrain in every kind of weather under almost continuous Guomingdang harassment. Had Chiang Kaishek not had the Japanese to contend with as well, he may well have mopped up the remnants. But although the march was attended by feats of unambiguous heroism, including the taking of an iron suspension bridge under enemy fire, its true significance was political. When the March began, the CCP was still dominated by the 'returned Bolsheviks' of 1931. When it ended, **Mao Zedong** was firmly at the helm. The decisive moment occurred at **Zunyi**, in January 1936, when at an impromptu meeting of a decimated Politburo, Mao imposed his authority. Quickly, he assembled around him nearly all the names associated with the Communist Revolution: Zhu De himself, Zhou Enlai, Lin Biao, Chen Yun, Liu Shaoqi, even the young Deng Xiaoping. With the support of these comrades, Mao was able to resist a challenge to his leadership from the 'Muscovite' Zhang Guotao.

In October the Guomingdang government adopts a **new draft constitution**, allowing for the reintroduction of limited democracy. On October 16, to avoid entrapment by Guomingdang forces, Zhu De leads the communists' 'First Front Army' westwards through enemy lines on what will become the first leg of the **Long March**.

On November 10 Guomingdang troops enter Ruijin, bringing the Fifth Encirclement Campaign to a hollow conclusion.

1935 In the second week of January, at a crisis meeting held at **Zunyi** in Guizhou, Mao Zedong, supported by Zhu De, rubbishes CCP strategy, attacking the Comintern agent Otto Braun and the leader of the 'Chinese Bolsheviks' Bo Gu. Urging that the Party's priority should be to resist Japan, Mao calls for the greatly damaged Red Army to proceed northwards. Winning over Zhou Enlai, Mao wins the debate, and with it de facto leadership of the Party, which henceforward abides by his strategy of building support among the peasantry.

More immediately, Mao decides to take the First Army to northern Sichuan to meet up with the Fourth, commanded by Zhang Guotao, a CCP founder member. To evade Guomingdang forces, a long detour is made via Yunnan. In June the two armies rendezvous, but divide again when Mao and Zhang, a supporter of the Bolshevik line, fall out.

On August 1 the CCP issues an 'Appeal to Fellow-countrymen to Resist Japan and for National Salvation'.

On October 20 what remains of Mao's army reaches northern Shaanxi, where a small base area already exists, bringing to an end the 6000-mile Long March. Communist efforts now focus on creating a main Chinese soviet in the northwest. Throughout the year, floods devastate both the Yellow and Yangzi river basins.

1936 As the USSR concludes a mutual defence treaty with the newly formed People's Republic of Mongolia, Japan tries to lure Chiang Kaishek into an anti-communist pact. Out of these circumstances is born the **Xian Incident** of December 12. Having travelled to the Shaanxi capital to co-ordinate an offensive against the communist base area, Chiang is arrested by his former ally Zhang Xueliang, whose Manchurian army has been ear-marked for Chiang's proposed 'Northwest Bandit Suppression' campaign. Zhang demands that Chiang make the expulsion of the Japanese his priority and form a united front with the CCP. Zhou Enlai flies into Xian to broker an agreement. Chiang accepts Zhang's terms and on December 25 he returns to Nanjing with Zhang, whom he promptly imprisons for treason. Chiang does abide by the terms of the Xian agreement, however.

The CCP moves its headquarters to **Yanan** (Shaanxi), which becomes the centre of Communism in China, attracting artists and intellectuals as well as fighters. Between the beginning of 1937 and the spring of 1945 membership of the CCP grows from approximately 40,000 to around 1,200,000.

1937 All-out war between China and Japan is triggered by the **Marco Polo Bridge Incident** on July 7, when Japanese troops conduct a nighttime attack on Wanping, a township close to Beijing. Mao Zedong immediately offers Chiang Kaishek the Red Army's unconditional support against the 'invaders'. The Japanese take Beijing and bomb Tianjin.

In August Japan assaults Shanghai, taking the Chinese city, and in September begins bombing Nanjing, now abandoned as the Republic's capital in favour of Wuhan.

In Shanxi, communist troops commanded by **Lin Biao** defeat a Japanese force at Pingxinguan, but in December Nanjing falls to General Iwane Matsui. In the subsequent atrocities, known as the **Rape of Nanjing**, over 200,000 Chinese civilians are massacred.

Lin Biao, Mao Zedong and Chou en Lai – three leaders of the communist revolution, pictured here together in 1971.

1938 As the Sino-Japanese War spreads, Japan bombs many Chinese cities, including Guangzhou, and Hitler announces Germany's recognition of Manchukuo.

Despite incurring heavy losses at Taierzhuang (Shandong) in March, and the deliberate breaching of Yellow River dykes in July, Japanese forces capture China's coastal ports one by one.

In October, first Guangzhou, then Wuhan falls. Chiang Kaishek retreats with his government to the **Chongqing** (Sichuan), where he is able to receive war-supplies from, amongst other nations, the USA. Japanese forces are also less successful in the northwest, where communist units adopt hit-and-run guerilla tactics.

Zhang Guotao, having failed to oust Mao Zedong as communist leader, defects to the Guomingdang.

The Rape of Nanjing (Nanking) 1937–38

Japan's army in China had as its slogan 'Loot all! Burn all! Kill all!' Entering a city abandoned by Chiang Kaishek and its defending officers, its troops perpetrated a slaughter that stands out even among the dismal catalogue of 20th-century atrocities. All told, up to 300,000 Chinese were butchered, the majority of them non-combatants, but also 80,000 disarmed soldiers. All the usual cruelties were present: gang rape, genital mutilation, sexual enslavement and torture. Their hands tied behind their backs, victims were used for 'bayonet practice'. Just as disturbing was the way in which the 'rape' was initially celebrated by Tokyo's newspapers. Japanese officers, bragging the numbers they had killed, were congratulated. Only an outcry by the world press persuaded the Japanese government to censor such reports. Later on it claimed that Nanjing had been 'fabricated' by the Chinese.

But the killings, attested by survivors on both sides, continued, and the final tally would have been far higher but for the 'International Safety Zone'. The leading protector of the Chinese was the German **John Rabe**, an employee of Siemens, and also, curiously, a member of the Nazi Party. In 1947 **General Iwane Matsui** was hanged by the International War Crimes Tribunal. It has been suggested he took the rap for Emperor Hirohito's brother Prince Asaka, a senior commander in Nanjing. But the USA, too, has been tarred. Anxious to use Japan as a buffer against communism after the wars, American officials 'overlooked' what had happened, even though the Japanese had sunk one of their ships, the USS *Panay*, as it ferried Western fugitives along the Yangzi.

On November 3 Japan's Prime Minister, Prince Konoe Fumimaro, proposes a **'co-prosperity region'** for East Asia which he invites the Chinese government to join. Chiang refuses, but others, notably Wang Jingwei, comply.

1939 The southern island of Hainan falls to Japan in February.

In May Japanese planes bomb Chongqing, killing thousands. Japanese troops also combat Soviet forces in Mongolia.

On June 1 Wang Jingwei arrives in Tokyo to discuss the creation of a puppet Chinese government in the manner of Manchukuo. Throughout the month, fighting occurs between Guomindang and communist forces in Hebei. The 'united front' is further damaged by Chiang's promulgation of 'Measures Restricting the Activities of Alien Parties'.

In July, in order to safeguard its interests in Tianjin, Britain adopts a policy of neutrality toward Japan. Notwithstanding, in August Japanese warships blockade Hong Kong.

World War II commences on September 3, when Britain and France declare war on Germany. In October Guomindang forces successfully defend Changsha, but in November the Japanese take Nanning (Guangxi). Tensions between the Guomindang and CCP escalate.

1940 Mao Zedong orchestrates rallies to denounce Wang Jingwen's collaboration with Japan. Despite this, on March 30, a pro-Japanese **puppet government** headed by Wang is instituted at **Nanjing**. Instantly recognized by Germany, it is repudiated by the United States, while Britain and France, mindful of their wider Far Eastern interests, turn a blind eye. On November 30 Wang's government cedes most of its powers to Japan. In December the communist **Hundred Regiments Offensive** undermines Japan's control of northern China.

1941 In January the strained alliance between the Guomindang and the CCP is shattered by the **Southern Anhui Incident**, when nationalist forces attack units of the communist New Fourth Army.

In August a group of 'volunteer' Americans led by Claire Chennault is absorbed into Chiang's army.

In October Guomingdang forces withstand a second attempt by the Japanese to take Changsha. Nationalist morale is further bolstered when the United States enters both the 'Pacific' war and World War II after the surprise bombing of **Pearl Harbor** (Hawaii) by Japan on December 7. Japan interns citizens of Allied countries unable to escape occupied China.

On December 9 the Guomingdang government declares war against Germany and Italy.

1942 To strengthen discipline, Mao Zedong launches a draconian 'rectification programme' amongst cadres and troops in his Shaanxi base area.

On January 15 a third attempt by the Japanese to take Changsha is repulsed by Guomingdang forces.

In February US Congress approves $500 million in aid to the nationalist Chinese. Chiang Kaishek, assuming supreme command after the **Burma Road** is opened as a supply line, sets up a 'Price Stabilization Fund' in an unsuccessful attempt to check runaway inflation in Chonqing.

In March US promises of assistance to the Guomingdang are confirmed as **Joseph Stillwell** is appointed Chief-of-Staff in the 'China theatre'.

In May Mao adumbrates his theory that all art and literature embodies class struggle and should follow the 'mass line'. Some writers in Yanan are persecuted.

In the summer, Japan completes its conquest of Southeast Asia and cuts the Burma Road. Allied supplies to the Guomingdang are instead airlifted from India, on a route known as **'the Hump'**.

1943 In January Wang Jingwei's government declares war on Britain and the USA. Chiang Kaishek signs treaties with the same two countries by which the principle of extraterritoriality is abolished and both powers relinquish their Chinese concessions, excluding Hong Kong.

In March Mao becomes **Chairman** of the CCP Central Committee.

In December Chiang joins Franklin D Roosevelt and Winston Churchill at the **Cairo Conference**, where it is agreed Manchuria and Taiwan will return to Chinese rule once the Axis is defeated.

1944 In April, Chinese resistance collapses in the Yellow River plains as Japan launches its massive **'Ichigo'** offensive in a final push to secure all China. On June 18

Chiang Kaishek (Jiang Jieshi) 1887–1975

The son of a Zhejiang salt-merchant, **Chiang Kaishek** progressed from small-time hoodlum in his youth to President of the ROC and founder of modern **Taiwan**. Between 1906 and 1911 he trained as a soldier, mostly in Japan, and participated in the Republican Revolution, but in 1916 reverted to his former ways by becoming a **Green Gang** triad member. In 1918 he joined the Guomingdang,

An inflationary Chinese banknote from 1931 bearing the head of Chiang Kaishek (Jiang Jieshi).

Changsha falls, giving Japan control of an unbroken rail-link between Korea and Vietnam.

In July US military personnel visit Yanan to reconnoitre the possibility of collaboration with the Red Army. American airplanes for the first time bomb Japanese targets inside China.

In the same month Guomingdang delegates attend the **Bretton Woods Conference**, organized by the United Nations. China is named a future 'director' of the proposed World Bank.

and in 1923 spent several months in Moscow observing the Bolshevik Red Army.

As Sun Yat-sen now understood, only by making itself strong militarily could the Guomingdang attain its goals. With Russian help the **Whampoa Military Academy** was established, with Chiang as its 'commandant' – an appointment that transformed the Guomingdang's fortunes, but also its character. Inheriting Sun's mantle, Chiang increasingly played the role of dictator. The three obstacles to power were the warlords, the communists and Japan. Against the first Chiang prevailed brilliantly; against the second only temporarily; and against the third hardly at all. His decision to crush the **CCP** first, and only then fight the Japanese, was a strategic blunder. Under Chiang's leadership the Guomingdang became a corrupt city-based administrative apparatus. If inflation soared, that was partly because he never quite severed his underworld connections.

In 1932, launching an elite security corps called the **Blue Shirts**, he seemed most like an oriental Mussolini. Once the Japanese had withdrawn, he was easily outmanoeuvred by Mao Zedong. Yet post-1949 he resuscitated the ROC on the island of Taiwan, serving as the President of a compact, illiberal but economically dynamic state until his death. Known simply as 'CK' to his admirers, Chiang's limited talents were suited to a smaller stage.

In October Roosevelt replaces Stillwell with **Albert Wedemeyer** as Chief-of-Staff in China after Stillwell and Chiang quarrel. Wang Jingwei dies in Japan.

1945 In January **Moslem Uighurs** proclaim a republic in Xinjiang.

At the **Yalta Conference** in February, Roosevelt gives Stalin free reign in Manchuria in return for co-operation against Japan.

Facsimile of Mao's poem *Loushan Pass* written in the poet's

In June Guomingdang delegates sign up to the United Nations Charter in San Francisco.

On August 14, following the atomic bombing of Hiroshima and Nagasaki, Japan surrenders to the Allies, and the Pacific War ends. A 'Treaty of Friendship and Alliance' is signed between Guomingdang China and the Soviet Union in Moscow. Later the same month Mao Zedong, Zhou Enlai and US envoy **Patrick Hurley** travel

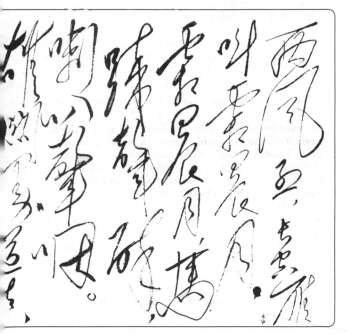

uniquely anarchic handwriting.

to Chongqing for discussions on a 'coalition' government with the Nationalists.

In November **George C Marshall** replaces Hurley as the US Congress presses for reconciliation between China's two main parties. Chiang, however, would rather fight Mao, and on November 25 students at the Southwest Associated University in Kunming stage demonstrations to protest Chiang's 'civil war' strategy.

1946 In January Marshall persuades the CCP and Guomingdang to participate in a 'political consultation' at Chongqing, but deadlock is reached over how to integrate the two armies.

In March Soviet troops begin withdrawing from Manchuria in such a way as to facilitate their replacement by Chinese communists.

In May Chiang returns his capital to Nanjing.

On June 16 Chiang launches his first attacks against communist positions.

In November Chiang convenes a **National Constitutional Assembly**, from which the communists are excluded. On December 25 the assembly recommends universal suffrage and the secret ballot. Such is the Guomingdang's capacity for economic mismanagement, however, that many Chinese refuse to be taken in by such assurances.

1947 Guomingdang forces take Yanan as the communists prepare a major counteroffensive. On May 4, in remembrance of 1919, students and workers demonstrate in Shanghai against inflation and food shortages. As other cities respond, the protest movement, orchestrated by the communists, sweeps across China.

On May 13 the **communist counteroffensive** begins in the northeast.

People's War

That the communists succeeded in gaining power was as much due to their style of warfare as their political acumen. Although care was taken to build up conventional forces, known first as the Red Army, then the People's Liberation Army, two other interrelated components were of equal strategic importance: **guerilla warfare**, and what Mao called **'people's war'**. Although communist tactics evolved collectively, it was Mao who gave them classic expression. 'The ability to run away is the essence of the guerilla', 'Revolutionary war is an anti-toxin which not only eliminates the enemy's poison but purges us of our own filth', 'To get rid of the gun we must first grasp it in our own hands', and 'Without a people's army the people have nothing' are among the maxims that set him close to Sunzi as a theorist.

Most effective was his analogy of the revolutionary as a fish swimming in a sea that is the people, bound together and disciplined by a common ideology. Armed struggle was as much about attaining Utopia as defeating the enemy. The communists also made a point of paying for whatever supplies they took. Such principles, though, were born of necessity. Communists had little access to modern weapons other than by seizure, and they therefore had to create alternative strengths. Packaged, these found a ready market in peasant-heavy Third World countries after 1945, most spectacularly in **Vietnam**, but also as far away as Angola and El Salvador.

On October 10 the CCP calls for a nationwide revolution to overthrow the Guomingdang.

1948 Communist forces, now called the **PLA (People's Liberation Army)** score decisive victories in northern China. Although the Guomingdang are now clearly out-matched, in April the US Congress grants $338 million to the Nationalist government.

On August 19 Chiang, finally enjoying the title President of China, attempts to check runaway inflation by issuing

'Financial and Economic Emergency Discipline Regulations'.

> **❝** Political scientists have analysed the common view of 'democracy' held by China's whole reform generation from Liang Qichao and Yen Fu right through to Mao and Deng. In this view inherited from optimistic (man-is-educable) Confucianism, good government rests on a natural harmony of interest between the ruler and all individuals, the people. Both seek the welfare of the state ('national wealth, strong military') because the enlightened Confucian-trained individual recognizes that social order will make his life livable while disorder will endanger it. In this state-centred view every individual should develop his abilities and so contribute more to the common good. The proper individual therefore goes along with, fits in, and pulls his weight, and this is 'democracy'. Antisocial anti-collectivists are, as Mao put it, not part of 'the people'. An 'I-will-be-heard' contention against authority is fundamentally immoral. **❞**
>
> J.K. Fairbank, *The Great Chinese Revolution 1800–1985*

1949 The capture of Beijing by communist forces on January 31 heralds the beginning of the end of the Guomingdang. Nanjing falls on April 23 and Shanghai on May 27.

On October 1, at a rally in Tiananmen Square, Mao proclaims the **People's Republic**.

On December 2 Chiang Kaishek escapes by air to Taiwan, where he sets up a rival, albeit far smaller, nationalist Republic.

10
The Rule of Mao Zedong

1949–1976

The advent of the **People's Republic** was widely welcomed in China, by some with revolutionary joy, by others with relief. At last the wars were over. And the new regime, broadly modelled on, and at first materially supported by, the Soviet Union, made a creditable start. Although remnants of the **Guomingdang** continued to operate out of remote bases – notably along the borders with Burma and Vietnam – and although separatist movements in Xinjiang and Tibet especially presented long-term military and political problems, peace returned to China's heartlands. Many of the government's new laws were progressive. An ambitious programme of agrarian reform created a long overdue redistribution of rural wealth. In the cities, the CCP demonstrated its moral confidence, ridding the streets of their gangs, prostitutes and opium dens. Women, in particular, were offered a better deal, their equal status and right to divorce codified in a new family law. And for a while, despite a foreclosure on private enterprise, the economy improved. Year on year, between 1950 and 1957, grain production and industrial output rose, albeit from a low base.

Rapidly, too, China re-established itself as a regional power, succouring fellow communist regimes in both Vietnam and Korea. But then the Revolution turned sour, through a series of mass-campaigns that went savagely awry: **collectivization**, the **Hundred Flowers Movement**, the **Great Leap Forward**, 'socialist education', and, most familiarly, the **Cultural Revolution** of 1966, that ended only with the death of **Mao Zedong** ten years later.

Without question, Mao was primarily responsible for these disasters. After 1949 his position inside China, and inside the monolithic Party he had helped forge, was near unassailable. Those who did challenge him were either eliminated or marginalized with consummate skill. He was the traditional strongman who had pulled China back from the brink of disintegration and achieved the miracle of reunification. His character was correspondingly complex. The socialist crusader was a firm admirer of the tyrannical First Emperor, **Qin Shihuangdi**. Instead of using victory to create a compact in which the different elements of Chinese society could bind together, Mao continued revolutionaryism as though victory were still to be won. At times it seemed he really did nurture an egalitarian vision; at other times he behaved like a traditional despot. His China was both robustly isolationist, and determined to strut the world stage, his rapprochement with the USA in 1972 being just one of many breathtaking policy somersaults.

Perhaps what stuck in Mao's craw the most was any sense of indebtedness to the **USSR**. Certainly, the grotesque excesses of his rule were the product of a desire to out-perform his Russian mentors. And so tens of millions died, for the sake of preserving one man in power.

1949 Following Mao's proclamation of the **People's Republic of China (PRC)** a communist government – sometimes called the 'the one party state', and modelled on the Soviet system – is established in **Beijing**, with Mao adding the title Chairman of the State to his party chairmanship. **Zhou Enlai** is appointed Premier as well as Foreign Minister.

In principle, the leadership of the new power pyramid is

answerable to a mass base, but in practice the effect is always reversed. A **Central Committee** of between 100 and 300 members is 'elected' by a National Congress, at which the entire Party membership is represented. Out of the Central Committee is drawn a **Politburo** of around fifteen members which meets weekly, and from this is extrapolated a smaller **Standing Committee**, comprising China's top leaders.

A Party Secretariat, however, ensures that the outcome of every Party election is predetermined according to the leadership's wishes. Overall, this structure is replicated at provincial and country levels, so that throughout China no distinction exists between Party, Legislature and Executive, or indeed Judiciary. The armed forces, too, are maintained under close CCP control. As in early imperial times, officials are placed in a hierarchy of 24 grades, and rewarded accordingly.

In December Mao visits Moscow, to express solidarity with **Stalin**, whose economic as well as political support he needs. By also supporting the communist Viet Minh war against France in Vietnam, Mao hardens **Cold War** divisions.

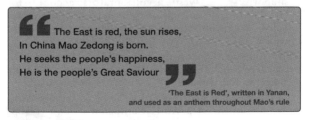

" The East is red, the sun rises,
In China Mao Zedong is born.
He seeks the people's happiness,
He is the people's Great Saviour "

'The East is Red', written in Yanan,
and used as an anthem throughout Mao's rule

1950 On January 14 a Sino-Soviet friendship treaty is signed by Zhou Enlai in Moscow.

In April Guomingdang resistance on the southern island

of Hainan is crushed. On April 30 a new **Family Law**, granting unprecedented rights to women, is promulgated. Within weeks, a million divorce petitions are submitted to 'people's committees'.

On June 25 the **Korean War** begins as the communist North Korean leader Kim Il Sung, with the covert approval of Stalin, launches an attack on South Korea. On June 27 the USA declares its support for South Korea and Syngman Rhee, and moves its Seventh Fleet into the Taiwan Straits, inhibiting a planned assault on **Taiwan** by the PRC.

On September 30 South Korean, American and other UN forces advance into North Korea. On October 19 units of the PLA cross the **Yalu River** into Korea as 'Chinese People's Volunteers'. On November 25, under the command of Peng Dehuai, China inflicts heavy losses on US forces commanded by Douglas MacArthur. Stalin however, fearful of US reprisals, wavers in his support for Mao's initiative. The Chinese themselves will also sustain heavy casualties, due to a combination of wasteful 'human wave' battle tactics, poor supply lines and freezing weather.

At home, a nationwide purge of former Guomingdang supporters and 'Western collaborators' accounts for 700,000 lives. Hundreds of thousands of landlords are killed. 'Bourgeois intellectuals' are subjected to 'thought reform'.

1951 Although Communist forces take the South Korean capital of Seoul, the Korean War devolves into a stalemate along the 38th parallel.

In China, Mao induces a climate of panic through 'mass line' campaigns. A **3 Antis Campaign** (against corruption, waste and over-bureaucratization) is followed by a **5 Antis Campaign** (against bribery, tax evasion, fraud embezzlement and the leaking of secrets), used as a catchall to reduce China's business class. As the CCP continues

Unbowed by critics in the Party, Mao Zedong rides the wave of the Cultural Revolution in 1966.

Mao Zedong 1893–1976

A giant not just of the Chinese but also the world stage, **Mao** was born in Shaoshan village, Hunan, the son of a small-time grain profiteer whom Mao claimed he 'learned to hate'. Educated locally, Mao trained as a teacher, but was drawn toward revolutionary politics from his late teens. In 1918 he worked as an assistant to the librarian of Beijing University, Li Dazhao, who introduced Mao to both Marxism and anarchism. Two years later, Mao came to the attention of **Chen Duxiu**, the founder of the CCP, and from then on was intimately involved with the Party's growth, both in Hunan and nationally.

The road to personal ascendancy, however, was twisted: Mao was demoted at least six times, mainly for insisting that a communist revolution would only succeed if China's peasantry, not its urban proletariat, were mobilized. Such setbacks honed Mao's political skills: he became adept at seeing off his rivals, among them Zhang Guotao and Liu Shaoqi. But it was his genius as a polemicist that enabled him, from 1936, to dictate Party ideology, to the extent that '**Mao Zedong Thought**' became embedded in the PRC's constitution. By manipulating such concepts as 'right opportunism' and 'left deviationism', Mao could destroy whomever he pleased even among fellow communists.

Behind such manoeuvres, however, lay a serious purpose. Mao's vision of a socialist China was dynamic. 'Class struggle' was not a one-off event, but a continuous process articulated by recurrent 'mass-line' campaigns directed against any kind of recidivism. Since antagonistic 'contradictions' were a necessary aspect of political life, Mao's philosophy was deeply anti-Utopian, as evidenced in the culminating **Cultural Revolution** of 1966. Yet as time passed, Mao's supreme gamesmanship focused on the perpetuation of his own prestige – a characterization supported by the undignified details of his later private life, when innumerable young women supplied his couch – and his reign was finally marked by contempt for everything and everybody, not least China's hallowed peasantry.

to eliminate landlords and 'intellectuals', the state internal security apparatus is steadily augmented.

In October PLA forces reassert Chinese control over **Tibet**. The youthful fourteenth Dalai Lama (Tenzin Gyatso b. 1935) becomes a Chinese puppet ruler.

1952 As the communists' initial **land reform** programme is completed – with the elimination of landlords and 'rich peasants', and despite opposition from **Liu Shaoqi** – Mao begins **rural collectivization** with the first agricultural co-operatives. A Soviet-style '5 Year Plan' is adopted for economic growth, with an emphasis on the rapid development of heavy industry on the back of an anticipated rise in grain production. Smaller private enterprises as survive are coerced into 'partnership' with the state.

1953 With the closure of grain markets, a state monopoly in agricultural produce is established. As grain quotas for the cities and the military are fixed at artificially low prices, and the obligatory formation of co-operatives spreads, the protests of farmers in Guangdong and other southern provinces spill over into violence. The revolt, however, is swiftly and brutally suppressed. 'The peasants want freedom,' Mao tells an aide, 'but we want socialism.'

On July 27 fighting in Korea ends as an armistice is signed at Panmunjon. In the Yangzi delta there is heavy flooding. According to a national census, China's **population** rises to 582,600,000. To promote further growth, the PRC abandons birth control programmes.

1954 In February Mao purges the Politburo to assert his authority and the 'socialist' line.

In April Zhou Enlai attends the **Geneva Conference**, convened to resolve conflicts in Indochina. As the talks begin, the Chinese-backed Viet Minh destroy a French super-garrison at Dienbienhphu. As a result **Vietnam**, like Korea, is partitioned North and South, 'communist' and 'free'. South Vietnam falls under American protection, as does, increasingly, the 'renegade' Chinese republic in Taiwan.

In September the First National People's Congress adopts a **National Constitution**.

In November Mao initiates a 'rectification' programme against writers, scholars and college teachers.

1955 Mao's purge of the intellectuals intensifies with the public denunciation and imprisonment of the writer Hu Feng.

In April Zhou Enlai signs China's agreement to the principle of 'peaceful co-existence' among 'non-aligned countries' at the **Bandung Conference** in Indonesia.

In the summer Mao presses for 'full collectivization' in the countryside – sometimes called the **Little Leap Forward**. Individual land-ownership is abolished, and peasants are allowed only small personal plots to raise vegetables and small animals. From October the size of individual co-operatives is expanded, to between 200 and 300 families. In December Mao declares that the eradication of all private business is official state policy.

1956 The first fissure in the Sino-Soviet axis forms when **Nikita Khrushchev** denounces Stalin as a 'brutal psychopath' at the 20th Soviet Party Congress on February 25. Khrushchev is censured for 'revisionism' by the *People's Daily* in Beijing, and Mao adopts the formula that Stalin was 'three parts bad, but seven parts good'. Despite this, in order to stimulate debate about socialist ends and means, and perhaps to woo back overseas Chinese, in April Mao devises the slogan 'Let a hundred flowers bloom, let a hundred schools of thought contend.' Wary of recent persecutions, however, China's intellectuals are slow to respond.

At the 8th CCP Congress in September – after Mao announces he will soon resign as Chairman of the

Republic in favour of Liu Shaoqi – a power struggle emerges as Liu, supported by **Deng Xiaoping**, attempts to limit Mao's powers. References to 'Mao Thought' are deleted from the Constitution. Mao reacts by demoting two of Liu's backers, Luo Ruiqing and Wang Dongxing.

By December, the collectivization of China's 400 million peasants is all but complete. 1956 also sees the introduction of 'internal passports', preventing further urban migration, and the creation of a **space agency**.

1957 In April the **Hundred Flowers Movement** finally gets off the ground after Mao appears to support freedom of expression among writers and artists. In May, however, his initiative gets out of hand as more and more 'flowers' speak out against his regime's 'malevolent tyranny'. Taxes are withheld and strikes called. Mao and other leaders are attacked, and at Beijing University calls for multiparty elections are posted on a 'democracy wall'. Mao's response is draconian.

On June 8 he launches an **Anti-Rightist Campaign**, co-ordinated by Deng Xiaoping, as a result of which 520,000 urban dwellers are rusticated for 'reform through labour'. Retrospectively, Mao justifies the Hundred Flowers campaign as a means of "coaxing snakes out of their holes, then striking against them".

In October, as Russia launches its *Sputnik* space satellite, Mao launches an ecologically ill-considered **Four Pests** campaign (against rats, flies, sparrows and mosquitos) to accelerate China's economic performance.

At a **Conference of World Communist Parties** held in Moscow in November Mao declares that China will overtake Britain 'within fifteen years'. Khrushchev agrees to aid a Chinese nuclear weapons programme. Accordingly, the 'Ninth Academy of Science' is established on Lake Koko Nor in Qinghai.

> Mao had an almost mystical faith in the role of the leader. He never doubted that his leadership, and only his leadership, would save and transform China. He was China's Stalin, and everyone knew it. He shared the popular perception that he was the country's messiah. Khrushchev's attack against Stalin forced Mao to be defensive, threatened to undermine his rule, and called his own leadership into question. For Mao to agree to the attack against Stalin was to admit that attacks against himself were permissable as well. This he could never allow. In 1953, after Stalin's death, Mao had welcomed Khrushchev's assumption of Soviet leadership. Following his attack on Stalin, though, Mao turned bitterly hostile, convinced that the new Soviet leader had violated a fundamental tenet of revolutionary morality – that of unswerving loyalty.
>
> Zhisui Li, *The Private Life of Chairman Mao* (1994)

1958 Mao tours the provinces, formulating the **Great Leap Forward** intended to propel China into fast-track industrialization and modernization. This is launched from May onwards, with the support of Liu Shaoqi and other senior leaders. At its heart is the further collectivization of the peasantry into 'people's communes', each consisting of 30,000 members and providing its own medical and welfare services. Rapidly, 24,000 such communes replace the 750,000-odd recently established co-operatives. All personal plots and livestock ownership are banned, meals are to be taken communally, and sleep is rationed at six hours every two days.

In September orders are issued for every commune (urban now as well as rural) to set up 'backyard' blast furnaces to bolster steel production. Throughout China, utensils and other metal objects are smelted in makeshift ovens. As a result, labour is diverted from the fields, and grain yields plummet. Since food is requisitioned as tax for the cities, severe shortages affect the countryside and many provinces experience famine. As coal and wood supplies dwindle, peasants burn their furniture to keep the furnaces going. Although a first tractor plant comes on line, its Russian-designed machines are of scant use to Chinese agriculture.

On May 1 China's first **television** service is inaugurated by the state.

In July Khrushchev – anxious to maintain communist-bloc solidarity, and aware that China is preparing to attack **Taiwan** – secretly visits Beijing for talks with Mao. Mao receives him beside a swimming pool wearing only trunks. Despite Khrushchev's concerns about provoking the USA, China launches a bombardment of the Taiwanese island of Qemoy on August 23. Washington sends a war-fleet armed with nuclear weapons into Taiwanese waters. Asked whether he is worried about a nuclear attack, Mao replies that a few million deaths would be of little consequence compared with an opportunity to 'permanently resolve east–west differences'. For several weeks, international tensions run high, until, lacking Soviet support, the PRC scales down, then terminates its military activity.

1959 As the Great Leap Forward takes hold, peasants begin dying in their millions.

In March an uprising in **Tibet** is ruthlessly suppressed. The Dalai Lama flees to India, where he sets up a politically damaging government-in-exile. Tibet itself is subjected to close Chinese rule from this point as its considerable mineral resources are tapped for the benefit of the PRC.

In April the Second National People's Congress affirms Mao's resignation as Chairman of the Republic and Liu Shaoqi's appointment in his place.

The Great Leap Forward 1958–61

Interest in Maoist China has concentrated on the shambles of the **Cultural Revolution** (see p.400), perhaps because it targeted city-dwellers and the 'educated' elite. Numerically, the **Great Leap Forward** was the greater catastrophe, claiming some thirty million lives. A combination of policies inspired by Mao's determination to rival the USSR brought ruination to the countryside. To produce greater yields, farmers – already robbed of individual incentive by collectivization – were instructed to abandon traditional methods and adopt 'close planting, deep ploughing'. As a result, **grain yields** plummeted.

But because of the quota system, collectives were obliged to send the same amounts of grain to China's cities as in previous years. Further, the landscape was denuded by the intensive use of wood to feed useless **'backyard' steel furnaces**. Nor did DIY irrigation projects help. By 1960 even rats were dying of starvation, and cannibalism was widely reported. Yet local officials colluded in the experiment by submitting false returns, so that even Mao had no idea he had created the world's greatest man-made famine. At least, though, he had his scapegoats when the truth came out.

In August, at a meeting of the Central Committee in Lushan, **Peng Dehuai** – reporting the effects of the Great Leap Forward – makes an unequivocal attack on both the policy and its instigator. Mao denounces Peng and his supporters, and threatens to 'take to the hills' to found a new revolutionary army if opposition to himself continues. Mao's anger is aggravated by Khrushchev's decision to suspend Soviet nuclear-arms co-operation, and his declared 'neutrality' vis-à-vis Taiwan.

In September Peng is replaced as Defence Minister by **Lin Biao** as Mao launches a campaign against 'right opportunists'. Thousands of senior and middle-ranking cadres undergo 'struggle sessions' and are dismissed from their posts.

The year's grain harvest falls short of its 375 million tonnes target by 200 million tonnes. There are severe droughts in the north, and flooding in the south. In Beijing trees are stripped of their bark for food.

> ❝ During a gathering at a friend's house in the neighbouring village [in Anhui], I heard horror stories of villagers who had exchanged babies to eat. I pitied them all. Who had made these parents live to taste, inconceivably, of human flesh mixed with parental tears? By this time, I was able to discern clearly the face of the executioner, whose like would only come along 'once in several centuries in the whole world and once in several millennia in China' – and his name was Mao Zedong. ❞
>
> The dissident Wei Jingsheng, in the *New York Times*, 1980

1960 By the end of the year, the Great Leap Forward will have caused an estimated thirty million deaths. Anhui, Shandong and Henan are worst-hit.

In June Khrushchev denounces Mao as an 'ultra-leftist'. The Chinese *People's Daily* denounces Khrushchev as a 'bourgeois revisionist'. In July the withdrawal of Soviet advisers from China seals the **Sino–Soviet split**. In some western provinces, as well as in Tibet, armed rebellions flare against CCP rule.

In September the Central Committee issues guidelines for 'Adjustment, Consolidation, Strengthening and Uplift', signalling the end of the Great Leap Forward.

1961 To effect relief, grain supplies are imported from Canada and Australia. As the failure of Mao's policies is acknowledged in the highest circles, Liu Shaoqi, supported by Deng Xiaoping, openly challenges Mao's authority. Notwithstanding, many middle and lower ranking cadres are purged for failing to implement his policies. As reconstruction begins, communes are scaled down. Peasants are once again permitted to husband small personal plots.

In Beijing, the Vice-Mayor **Wu Han** writes and produces *Hai Rui Dismissed From Office*, an historical drama that contains a veiled attack on Mao's treatment of Peng Dehuai.

1962 At a **'7000 Cadre Conference'** held in the capital, Mao is criticized by **Peng Zhen**, Beijing's mayor, and privately censured by Liu Shaoqi. In response, Mao makes a rare self-criticism, and withdraws to Hangzhou, leaving Liu, Zhou Enlai and Deng Xiaoping in charge of China's affairs. Between them they effect a partial rapprochement with the USSR.

In July Mao returns to Beijing unannounced. Supported by Lin Biao and other 'hard-liners', he at once sets about reclaiming lost ground with a fresh campaign against 'right revisionists'. In September he uses his platform at an enlarged Central Committee meeting to emphasize the value of 'class struggle' and identify 'ideological enemies'. Some ministers loyal to Liu are purged.

In the same month a six-week border war with **India** erupts as 30,000 Chinese troops attack Indian installations, partly in retaliation for India's accommodation of the Dalai Lama. Tibet's second highest authority, the previously amenable Panchen Lama, is imprisoned for nine years after he submits a report to Mao detailing his country's ills since 1959.

Mao's fourth wife, **Jiang Qing**, appears in public for the first time when, alongside her husband, she welcomes President Sukarno of Indonesia to Beijing.

1963 Mao's vendetta against the 'Liu Shaoqi clique' gathers momentum as he launches a **Socialist Education** campaign. Work teams are sent from cities to the countryside to root out local corruption, but also to learn 'socialist' values at first-hand by working in the fields. The campaign is backed by the publication of a diary supposedly written by **Lei Feng**, a soldier-peasant killed the previous year. 'Lei Fengism' is promoted by Lin Biao as unswerving devotion to the 'true' (ie Maoist) cause. Lin's propaganda efforts are strengthened in May, when he publishes *Quotations from Mao Zedong*, aka **'The Little Red Book'**. An anthology of Mao's sayings originally intended for use in the PLA, it is soon distributed throughout China's population. Concurrently, Jiang Qing launches scathing attacks on Liu, Deng and other 'rightists'.

Some sayings of Chairman Mao

'A revolution is not a dinner party, or writing an essay, or painting a picture, or doing embroidery; it cannot be so refined, so leisurely and gentle, so temperate, kind, courteous, restrained and magnanimous. A revolution is an insurrection, an act of violence by which one class overthrows another.' (1927)

'Everything reactionary is the same; if you don't hit it, it won't fall. This is also like sweeping the floor; as a rule, where the broom does not reach, the dust will not vanish of itself.' (1945)

'The atom bomb is a paper tiger which the US reactionaries use to scare people. It looks terrible, but in fact it isn't.' (1946)

'After the enemies with guns have been wiped out, there will be enemies without guns; they are bound to struggle desperately against us, and we must never regard these enemies lightly.' (1949)

'Classes struggle, some classes triumph, others are eliminated. Such is history, such is the history of civilisation for thousands of years.' (1949)

from *Quotations from Chairman Mao Tse-tung*, Beijing 1966

1964 In June Jiang Qing attempts a 'Cultural Rectification' campaign, but is blocked by Peng Zhen.

In September Liu Shaoqi sends his own workteams into the countryside as a counter to Mao's Socialist Education initiative.

On December 26, at a Beijing banquet held to mark his 71st birthday, Mao speaks of a need to move against 'power-holders within the Party taking the capitalist road'.

1965 In February Mao sends Jiang Qing to Shanghai to encourage the journalist **Yao Wenyuan** to write an article attacking Wu Han's play *Hai Rui Dismissed from Office*. Having been vetted by Mao, Yao's essay is published in Shanghai on November 10, and reprinted in the *People's Daily* on November 30. By targeting Wu, Mao is also targeting his immediate boss Peng Zhen, and by extension Peng's ally Liu Shaoqi.

1966 In February Jiang Qing is appointed to the PLA's Cultural Affairs Department. From this platform she denounces Peng Zhen's attempts to brush aside Yao Wenyuan's attack on Wu Han. On May 16 Peng Zhen is dismissed, and a Central Cultural Revolutionary Committee, dominated by Jiang, is formed without reference to the Politburo. This, and a 'May 16 Circular' sent to Central Committee members, are conventionally deemed the start of the **Great Proletarian Cultural Revolution**. Yao publishes a further essay indirectly indicting Liu Shaoqi, and student unrest, fomented by Mao's supporters, begins at Beijing University, then spreads to other colleges.

At Qinghua University, the term **Red Guard** is coined when a militant student group undertakes to defend Mao against 'rightist' teachers. To quell the unrest, Liu sends in work squads, but these are immediately branded 'black groups' by the students, who now employ violent methods against their opponents. Teachers are 'struggled

Liu Shaoqi 1898–1969

Like Mao, **Liu Shaoqi** was the son of a prosperous Hunanese peasant. In 1921 he was among a small handful selected to study at Moscow's University of the Toilers of the East. Between 1922 and 1935 he demonstrated organizational talents of a high calibre, helping build the CCP into an effective political body. In Yanan, he belonged to Mao's inner circle, and wrote *How To Be A Good Communist*. Cautious by nature, but unwavering in his commitment to communist ideals, Liu played the role of anchor-man in the 1949 regime. Yet this was his undoing.

Sometimes willing to put a dampener on Mao's personal ambitions – 'The perfect leader does not exist' he said – he nonetheless rose to become titular **Head of State** in 1959. As such, he was a natural magnet for Mao's critics within the Party. As Mao's policies floundered, so the number of such critics swelled, and by 1963 Liu was positioned to challenge for power, but his failure to apply the knock-out punch cemented his fall. Arguably, the Cultural Revolution was conceived to remove the 'Liu Shaoqi reactionary clique'. In any event, Liu became its biggest scalp. Stripped first of his offices, then of his Party membership, he died ignominiously in Kaifeng, denied treatment for cancer.

against' (verbally abused) in open sessions, and kicked and beaten, often to death. Liu urgently requests Mao to return to Beijing from his summer residence in Hangzhou to resolve the crisis, but for two months Mao watches events unfold from the sidelines.

On July 16, however, in a propaganda coup designed to exhibit his personal virility, Mao 'swims the Yangzi', and two days later enters Beijing. Jiang leads a mass rally at Beijing Normal University, calling for further student action.

On August 5 Mao's 'big character' poster 'Bombard the Headquarters' authorizes Red Guard attacks on officials and official institutions. On August 8 Liu Shaoqi is demoted to eighth place in the Party rankings, and Lin Biao is elevated to second. On August 18 the first of many **mass rallies** extolling Mao and Mao Zedong Thought is held in Tiananmen Square as a campaign against the **Four Olds** (thought, culture, customs and practice) is launched.

In October, Liu and Deng are widely reviled for attempting to revive 'capitalist dictatorship'. The following month workers are encouraged to form **revolutionary units** in their workplaces in emulation of the students. In every city teachers and officials are either killed or driven to suicide.

> At the beginning of the rally [of August 18, 1966] Mao was given a Red Guard armband by a little girl. He allowed her to slip it over her left sleeve and up his arm. He stood beside her for a while, then when the girl told him her name was Bin Bin, which means 'gentle and polite', Mao turned to her and said, 'Apply Violence!' The girl Red Guard immediately changed her name to Yao Wu, which means 'apply violence'. This is the only known direct order given by Mao to a Red Guard, and his words travelled across the vastness of China like a thunderbolt.
>
> Anhua Gao, *To the Edge of the Sky* (2000)

1967 In January the Cultural Revolution achieves its greatest turbulence as Red Guards run rampant. In Shanghai, a workers' coalition, headed by Wang Hongwen, seizes control, setting up a 'revolutionary committee' that is quickly copied in other towns and cities, replacing existing 'people's committees'. On January 3, Red Guards enter the Zhongnanhai (CCP headquarters precinct) in Beijing and subject Liu Shaoqi to a 'struggle session'. In Nanjing, cadets seize senior officers at a PLA barracks.

In February (the **'February Countercurrent'**) conservative leaders criticize the Cultural Revolution. Army units occupy some colleges and other sites in an attempt to restore order even as unrest spreads inside the PLA itself.

In April Lin Biao forbids the PLA to act against 'radicals'. Students, meanwhile, begin factionalizing, with open warfare between 'rebels' and 'party loyalists'. PLA militia units side with the former against the latter.

In July Liu is again publicly humiliated, as is Deng Xiaoping.

In August both leaders are placed under house arrest after Liu 'resigns' as Head of State.

In September, fearing that the Cultural Revolution has overreached itself, Mao authorizes PLA units to open fire on radicals in 'self-defence'. The Red Guards continue their persecution of individual civilians.

1968 As the PLA becomes more heavily involved, the Cultural Revolution alters direction. Revolutionary committees, largely comprising armymen, take control of schools, colleges, factories and urban administrations.

In July Mao appeals to the students of Qinghai University to stop forming factions. Those who dissent are removed to the countryside to be 're-educated' by the peasants. By December this becomes a general policy: up to 10 million Red Guards are made to live and labour indefinitely in remote co-operatives. Most colleges cease to function.

In October Liu is expelled from the Communist Party as the Central Committee confirms Lin Biao's status as Mao's approved successor. Deng is stripped of office, but not expelled.

1969 In March, following border incidents, fighting breaks out between Chinese and Russian troops for control of Zhenbao Island on the Ussuri River. Hostilities continue throughout the spring and summer as Mao whips up anti-Soviet hysteria. In Beijing, a vast underground complex of nuclear shelters is built.

The Cultural Revolution 1966–76

An extraordinary experiment in anarchic totalitarianism, the **Great Proletarian Cultural Revolution** destroyed the lives of millions. Having gagged China's intellectual community with the Anti-Rightist Campaign, and mauled the peasantry with the Great Leap Forward, Mao turned his attention on his own Party, and its huge enrolment of urban cadres, at a time when his authority was challenged by Liu Shaoqi and other ministers.

His chosen instrument was China's youth. Growing up in a repressive state, they needed something to hate. Suddenly, Party membership and Party loyalty meant nothing. First teachers, then middling officials, and finally Politburo members were subjected to often lethal harassment. Not only were victims' ideological purity called to account, but also their family backgrounds. Any whiff of a 'bourgeois' connection, however remote, was sufficient to incur humiliation. Men and women were dragged from their homes, paraded through the streets in dunces' hats, then denounced in violent 'struggle sessions'.

Directly, the Cultural Revolution claimed a million lives, indirectly many more. It was also attended by nationwide iconoclasm. Books were burned, ancient monuments pillaged. In its second phase, however, Mao unleashed the **PLA**. Now it was the young Red Guards themselves who suffered. An entire 'lost generation' of students was banished to the deep countryside, along with their professors and many doctors. All of a piece with Mao's belief in perpetual revolution, the Cultural Revolution's spurious glamour was felt as far away as Europe, where in 1968 students in Paris and other cities attempted a downthrow of their own. Like Che Guevara, Mao was idolized by some as a transcendent saint.

In April two-thirds of the 1500 delegates attending the Ninth CCP Congress are armymen. A newly 'elected' Politburo is similarly dominated by the PLA and the Cultural Revolution Group. Mao is acclaimed 'supreme leader' as Zhou Enlai slips down Party rankings.

In September, as a Sino-Soviet ceasefire is signed, China carries out its first **nuclear test**. Deng leaves Beijing for the relative safety of Jiangxi. On November 12 Liu dies of cancer in a Kaifeng bank vault.

1970 As the Cultural Revolution dissipates, and Mao puts out tentative feelers toward a Sino-American rapprochement, differences between Lin Biao and Jiang Qing surface. When Lin presses to become Chairman of the Republic, he is criticized by Mao at a Central Committee meeting in Lushan.

In December Mao and Zhou Enlai launch a campaign against Lin's close supporter Chen Boda.

1971 In March, Lin Biao's son **Lin Liguo** begins plotting Mao's assassination with fellow airforce officers to safeguard his father. In the same month **'ping-pong diplomacy'** is born when an American table-tennis team competing in Nagoya (Japan) expresses a desire to visit China. The team is at once invited to Beijing and lavishly received by Mao in the Great Hall of the People.

On July 9 US Secretary of State **Henry Kissinger** makes the first of two clandestine visits. Over the summer Mao, as Chairman of the Military Commission, begins removing Lin's supporters from senior army posts.

On September 13, during an apparent security alert, Lin Liguo persuades his father to board a Trident jet at Beidaihe. When it becomes clear that his plot has been discovered, the airplane, instead of flying to Guangzhou, heads north and crashes in Soviet Mongolia, having apparently run out of fuel, killing all on board.

On October 15 the PRC is admitted to the **United Nations**. The Taiwanese Republic of China loses its seat.

In December all Lin's supporters are stripped of their civil and military posts.

Lin Biao 1907–71

Where Liu Shaoqi lacked final ambition, **Lin Biao** was made of it. The son of a cloth manufacturer, Lin engaged in revolutionary politics from his late teens. In 1925 he enrolled at the Whampoa Military Academy, then attached himself to the Communist commander Zhu De. Both during the Long March and against the Japanese in Shaanxi he displayed outstanding military leadership.

Despite a lifelong addiction to morphine acquired while convalescing from wounds, after 1945 he again demonstrated fine generalship against the Guomindang in Manchuria. Victories earned high office post-1949. In 1959 he replaced Peng Dehuai as Defence Minister. In the ensuing political infighting he sided unambiguously with Mao, assuring him of the PLA's support during the Cultural Revolution.

His crime against Mao, however, was his impatience. Unwisely, he openly pressed to become Chairman of the Republic, in Liu's wake. The tussle that followed was a tragicomedy of mutual paranoia. Mao feared Lin was out to usurp his throne; Lin feared Mao had him marked for disgrace. Nor did it help that Lin finally fell out with the venomous Jiang Qing. Just when he became privy to his son's conspiracy to assassinate Mao remains unclear. In the event, he allowed himself to imagine the worst, and so boarded the ill-starred Trident. Hearing of his death, Mao resorted to an old proverb: 'If it is going to rain, or mother-in-law wants to re-marry, heaven itself is powerless to intervene.'

1972 Following Lin Biao's death, Mao pursues a divide-and-rule policy against the Politburo. To balance the influence of Jiang Qing's Cultural Revolution faction, he directs Zhou Enlai to rehabilitate previously purged ministers, among them Luo Ruiqing.

On February 21 US President **Richard Nixon** arrives in Beijing at the start of a state visit that marks a watershed in geopolitical relations, formalized in the 'Shanghai Communiqué'. As the USA winds down its involvement in **Vietnam**, so Mao seeks a superpower relationship to counter the USSR's increasing influence in Hanoi and other Asian capitals. Reconciliation with the West is underlined in September with a further state visit by the Japanese prime minister Tanaka Kakauei.

1973 In March Deng Xiaoping is rehabilitated, to work alongside Zhou Enlai. In August, however, Jiang Qing, Zhang Chunqiao, Yao Wenyuan and Wang Hongwen, later known as the **Gang of Four**, are appointed to the Politburo, and in September Wang is designated Mao's approved successor. As a **Criticize Confucius and Criticize Lin Biao** campaign makes headway, it seems that the Jiang Qing radicals have the upper hand.

1974 Jiang overplays her hand when she extends her attacks to Zhou Enlai. Deng takes over the management of foreign affairs from Zhou and in April outlines Mao's 'Three Worlds Theory' at the UN Assembly. From this is derived the concept of the **Third World** as a geopolitical power-block. As Mao's enthusiasm for Wang Hongwen wanes, Deng becomes sole Deputy Premier, Vice-Chairman of the CCP and Chief of Staff of the Military Commission.

1975 At a Central Committee meeting in January tensions between the Gang of Four and the Deng-Zhou faction erupt in open feuding. Jiang attempts to have Deng's promotions overruled, but Deng, protected by a now bedridden Mao, is able to introduce a package of modest economic reforms.

1976 Zhou Enlai dies on January 8. **Hua Guofeng**, a 'neutral' low-profile Hunanese minister, and Mao's latest choice as successor, is appointed premier in his place.

At a mass-memorial for Zhou held in Tiananmen Square on April 5, tens of thousands of mourners are violently dispersed after they protest the influence of the Gang of Four. Two days later Deng is held responsible for the

Jiang Qing, sometimes known as Madame Mao, pictured during the course of her trial in 1981.

Zhou Enlai 1898–1976

Always the acceptable face of Chinese communism, **Zhou Enlai** alone among the leadership came from a genteel background. He studied in Japan, and then in France. Enrolled in the CCP in 1922, two years later, in line with the Comintern's 'bloc within' strategy, he became political director of the Guomingdang's crack Whampoa Military Academy. Subsequently, many Guomingdang officers defected to the nascent Red Army. During the Long March, Zhou was instrumental in securing Mao's leadership, even though the two men had often differed. Thereafter, Zhou played a main role in both the military and political evolution of the Party, and in 1949 became the PRC's premier – a post he retained until his death, despite fluctuations in his Party ranking.

During the Cultural Revolution he gained a reputation for fearlessly protecting friends and colleagues, among them Deng Xiaoping, and for generally endeavouring to moderate Mao's policies. Equally, he was admired abroad for his silken diplomacy, and helped persuade **Henry Kissinger** to visit Beijing, paving the way for Nixon's visit of 1972. His last years, however, were clouded by factional unpleasantness, due mainly to Jiang Qing's acrimonious envy. In part, the 1973 'Criticize Confucius, Criticize Lin Biao' campaign was directed against himself. Yet Zhou had the last laugh. The demonstrations at his memorial service in Tiananmen Square sent out an unambiguous message that the **Gang of Four** were only to be tolerated on Mao's moribund sufferance.

Tiananmen Incident and stripped of his posts. Evading Jiang, he flees to Guangzhou.

On May 11 and June 26 Mao suffers heart-attacks.

On July 28 an earthquake kills 700,000 in the northern industrial city of **Tangshan**.

In the early hours of September 9 Mao dies in Beijing.

On October 6, in a move co-ordinated by Hua Guofeng, Politburo member Ye Jianying and security supremo Wang

Dongxing, the Gang of Four are placed under arrest and Hua's authority as CCP Chairman is confirmed. As the Cultural Revolution peters out, those banished to the countryside from 1968 return to their city homes.

Jiang Qing 1913–91

An actress by temperament as well as by profession, Shandong-born **Jiang Qing** found her feet in Shanghai in the early 1930s, playing, among other roles, Nora in Ibsen's *A Doll's House*. A member of the CCP from 1933, she may also have been a Guomingdang double-agent, and was married at least twice before making tracks for the Communist base-camp at Yanan. There she married Mao. Aware of her murky past, Mao's comrades insisted she play no part in politics. During the 1950s she took to her bed, estranged from her husband and suffering a series of mainly psychosomatic illnesses, but came to prominence once Mao decided he could deploy her against Liu Shaoqi. Out of these circumstances was hatched the Cultural Revolution.

Making up for lost time, Jiang seized her opportunity with focused malevolence, waging war on Mao's supposed enemies, and instituting a terror of intolerance. Her reform of the Peking Opera reduced China's dramatic repertoire to just eight revolutionary musicals. But having set her up, Mao reined her in again, branding Jiang and her three closest associates the 'Gang of Four' in 1974. During her show-trial in 1980–81, the 'mad empress' screamed abuse at her accusers while claiming she had been nothing more than Mao's 'mad dog'. Spared execution, she remained in prison, where eventually she hanged herself.

11
China since 1976

Mao's death in 1976 presented his successors with a problem. The Party needed a new direction, not so much to retain the people's support, as to reclaim it. Impressively, it was **Deng Xiaoping** who provided hopeful solutions. His maths may have been awry, but by conceding that Mao had been 'seventy percent right, thirty percent wrong' – just as Mao once said Stalin was 'three parts wrong but seven parts right' – he furnished a face-saving formula whereby China could begin to come to terms with its immediate past.

But Deng's strategy was more than a public relations exercise. His project was to transform the economy by making private enterprise integral to recovery. Out of the blue, he proclaimed that 'To get rich is glorious'. Simultaneously, he promoted joint ventures with foreign companies, and a score of high-tech research centres. From the mid-1980s, China's space programme was sufficiently advanced to be sending Australian and Brazilian communications satellites into orbit. For a while the world was agog. Deng seemed to defy the system that had moulded him. Yet, as **Tiananmen Square** brought home in 1989, there were limits to the 'Deng Reforms'. Democratization in the Western sense wasn't, and never had been, on the cards. It was against the Party's interests.

The situation in China has grown more complex since. Deng's successor **Jiang Zemin** elected to continue Deng's 'open door' policy toward foreign investment while maintaining an authoritarian stance apropos political freedom and rights. By 2000 China had attracted a staggering US$350 billion dollars of inward investment, much of it from the USA, Japan and Europe. Yet despite such success, the fabric of government looks increasingly strained, and there are doubts about the solvency of the country's less than fully independent commercial banks, obliged to prop up **moribund state-owned enterprises** with the savings of individual depositers. Most China watchers concur that corruption is rife, among both provincial and central Party cadres. Too many of China's new nightclubs and other sundown enterprises are owned by Politburo members' children, while directives that the armed forces should in part earn their own keep by developing 'business interests' have led to massive smuggling scams that deprive the government of legitimate revenues.

On the streets of China's now vibrant cities, **criminal gangs**, too, have reappeared. Periodically, the government cracks down on crime and corruption, but increasingly this looks like selective window-dressing. Meanwhile, as private enterprise takes over from state provision, education and healthcare programmes in many provinces are verging on collapse.

To get rich is indeed glorious, but only for the rich. The urban glitz that greets China's contemporary visitors in Beijing, Shanghai or Guangzhou masks an awesome social divide. Out in the sticks, a billion peasants remain tied to land they can lease but cannot own. Nor are they allowed to travel at will inside their country. And if, for the bulk of China's population, life remains hard, then for China's ethnic minorities the prospects are even grimmer. Not only in **Tibet** and **Xinjiang**, but also in Yunnan, Guizhou, Sichuan, Gansu and Inner Mongolia conditions for non-Han Chinese are adverse.

Even so, the urban minority that now has Western living standards within its grasp is bigger than the whole population of the USA; and for as long as the economy holds up, the newly enriched are unlikely to press for sweeping reform. But against this prognosis there are at least some contraindications. The more corrupt government becomes, the more dissidents will be listened to. It is also the case that government is fighting a losing battle against the Internet and other means of absorbing information and values from an outside world dominated, for better or for worse, by the ideals of Western liberalism.

The mysterious, changing, yet innately Chinese, **Falun Gong** movement of the 1990s may or may not presage upheaval. In China tomorrow anything may happen, but when it does, it is likely to reflect the abiding conundrum: How can such a large, populous and diversely talented nation-empire necessarily act in its own best interests?

1977 **Deng Xiaoping** is restored to his 1974 offices, making him second in power only to Hua Guofeng. Seeking to appoint 'experts where experts are needed', he combats waste and corruption in government programmes.

1978 Over the summer Deng pursues the **Four Modernizations** (originally proposed by Zhou Enlai): of agriculture, industry, defence and science. The mass importation of particularly Western technology and machinery begins. Many of those purged during the Cultural Revolution are rehabilitated.

In the countryside, as communes and co-operatives are abandoned, a **'household contract'** system allows farmers to grow and sell their own produce in free markets. Also in charge of foreign affairs, Deng achieves 'normalization' in relations with the USA, although Washington insists on its right to sell arms to **Taiwan**. The Coca-Cola Corporation is admitted into the Chinese market.

In Beijing, radical students begin a new **'Democracy Wall'** movement (aka the 'Beijing Spring') by posting criticisms of Mao Zedong and the Gang of Four, and calling for improved rights and freedoms.

1979 In January, touting China's new "open door" policy, Deng tours the USA.

In February China launches an ill-fated punitive expedition against **Vietnam** after Vietnam invades China's client-state Cambodia.

In March, as the Democracy Wall movement spreads, Deng links economic development with the continuation of a one-party socialist state. **Wei Jingsheng** and other dissidents are arrested. In October they are put on trial and given heavy prison sentences.

In December the Democracy Wall is closed. As China's population reaches 900 million, the PRC introduces a **'one couple one child'** policy. Female infanticide and enforced abortion become commonplace, but China's peasantry, dependent on the labour of its children, generally evades this law.

> **"** Freedom of speech of the individual citizen must be based on the four basic principles of insisting on the socialist road, the dictatorship of the proletariat, the leadership of the Party, and Marxism-Leninism-Mao Zedong thought. The citizen has only the freedom to support these principles, and not the freedom to oppose them. **"**
>
> The State Prosecutor, at the trial of Wei Jingsheng, October 1979

1980 In March, backed by a majority of the Politburo, Deng ousts Hua Guofeng's supporters from the same body. To further economic growth, he initiates **'Special Economic Zones'**, beginning with Shenzhen, adjacent to Hong Kong, offering tax concessions to foreign investors.

Vietnam

In the wake of World War II, the CCP aided **Ho Chi Minh**'s Viet Minh government in its struggle against French colonial rule. The climactic victory of Dienbienphu, secured with Chinese artillery, secured a communist regime in North Vietnam, and Beijing continued to support Hanoi during its war of reunification against Saigon begun in 1959. But as the **USA**'s defence of South Vietnam stiffened from 1963, so Hanoi increasingly looked to Moscow for material support. Beijing, meanwhile, swung the other way.

Anxious to create a Sino-American entente to counter Soviet prestige, but also to undermine Taiwan, **Mao** allowed geopolitical calculations to trump socialist solidarity. 'I don't have a broom long enough to reach Taiwan,' he rebuked North Vietnam's Pham Van Dong in 1973, 'and you don't have a broom long enough to reach Saigon.' Notwithstanding, Saigon fell to Hanoi in April 1975. In the same month, communist regimes were also established in **Cambodia** and **Laos**. While Soviet influence prevailed in a reunified Vietnam, Chinese influence prevailed in its Indochinese neighbours. But then in 1978, after repeated Khmer Rouge incursions, Vietnam invaded Cambodia. China responded with a disastrous punitive expedition in 1979. Its tactics ill-considered, the PLA was forced to retreat, sustaining heavy casualties. Since then – territorial disputes about the tiny Spratley and Paracel islands aside – Chinese initiatives in Indochina have been restricted to the diplomatic and economic.

As many factories open under Taiwanese, Korean, Japanese and Western management, critics will regard the SEZs as a throwback to the Treaty Ports of the 19th century. The three-month trial of the **Gang of Four** begins in November.

1981 In January Jiang Qing and Zhang Chunqiao are given suspended death sentences, later commuted to life imprisonment.

In June, Hua Guofeng 'retires', leaving Deng Xiaoping

'**paramount leader**'. Deng slashes China's military budget by 25 percent as the PLA is depoliticized. Over the next fifteen years, China's GNP grows an average 9.8 percent per annum.

1982 Deng further promotes economic reform under the slogan 'Socialism with Chinese characteristics' as his close supporter **Hu Yaobang** is elected CCP General Secretary. A state visit by British prime minister Margaret Thatcher initiates negotiations about **Hong Kong**, due to return to Chinese rule in 1997.

1983 As gangsterism returns to Chinese cities, thousands are executed during an anti-crime drive. A companion campaign against 'spiritual pollution', aimed at political dissidents, is also pursued by Deng's government.

1984 To rejuvenate the CCP, Deng institutes a mandatory retirement age for all officials other than Politburo members. Over the next two years, 1.5 million 'veterans' leave their jobs on full-pay.

In April China launches a first **communications satellite** into space.

On September 26 China and Britain agree terms on the handover of Hong Kong. By a 'one country, two systems' provision from 1997, Hong Kong will enjoy a high level of self-government as an SAR (Special Administrative Region). Meanwhile, China's grain harvest achieves a record 400 million tonnes, even though many peasants have switched to raising cash crops to maximize personal profits.

1985 With inflation running at nine percent, China's economy shows signs of overheating. In Beijing and other cities students protest against the import of mainly Japanese manufactured goods.

1986 As conservatives urge an economic slowdown, 'liberals' argue for even more rapid modernization. **Feng**

Tibet and Xinjiang

China's repute as the world's last surviving colonial empire is validated by its continuing maltreatment of the peoples inhabiting its vast western territories. **Tibet**'s ambiguous status as a dependency was resolved in 1951 when 80,000 PLA troops staged an invasion from the east. A further show of force in 1959 drove the theocratic **Dalai Lama** into exile in India. Since then, a determined but militarily feeble Tibetan independence movement has been regularly suppressed. Just as regularly, the Dalai Lama (awarded the Nobel Peace Prize in 1989) has evoked international sympathy for the plight of his people. A similar persecution of the **Moslem populations** of Xinjiang (Uighurs, Kazakhs, Kirghiz and Chinese Hui) has attracted rather less publicity. Uighur attempts to establish an independent state of East Turkistan have been consistently thwarted.

While historically, Chinese occupation of both territories is 'justified' on the grounds of strategic security, genocidal policies have undermined China's international standing. It is unlikely, however, that the PRC will relax its hold on either Tibet or Xinjiang. Both offer *Lebensraum* for Han Chinese settlers, and both are mineral rich. Tibetan uranium, especially, is vital for China's nuclear weapons programme, while Xinjiang's desert landscape affords ideal nuclear testing grounds, as well as sites for China's teeming *laogai*, or prison labour camps. Nor does the international community have the will to protect human rights when such action would jeopardize burgeoning commercial relations between powerful Western states and China itself.

Lizhi, an astrophysicist at the Chinese University of Science and Technology, calls for 'democracy and human rights'. In December Feng's challenge is taken up by students in Shanghai and other cities. The government responds with a renewed campaign against dissidents.

1987 Hu Yaobang is blamed by Deng for political unrest and removed from office. He is replaced as CCP General

Secretary, however, by the 'liberal' **Zhao Ziyang** – a move balanced by the appointment of the hard-liner **Li Peng** as premier. In October Deng begins relinquishing his many official positions. But while soon his only title will be 'Chairman of the Chinese Bridge Association', he does not abandon actual power.

> "Democracy can develop only gradually, and we cannot copy Western systems. If we did, that would only make a mess of everything. Our socialist construction can only be carried out under leadership, in an orderly way and in an environment of stability and unity. That's why I lay such emphasis on the need for high ideals and strict discipline. Bourgeois liberalization would plunge the country into turmoil once more. Bourgeois liberalization means the rejection of the party's leadership; there would be nothing to unite our one billion people, and the party itself would lose all power to fight."
>
> Deng Xiaoping, *Fundamental Issues in Present-Day China* (1987)

1988 As **inflation** hits twenty percent, panic buying of food and consumer goods grips many cities.

In October a section of the Great Wall is swathed in out-size bandages by dissident artists eager to proclaim 'China's infirmity'. After an absence of 23 years, ranks and insignia are restored to the PLA, now dressed in uniforms reputedly designed by the French couturier Pièrre Cardin.

1989 In March Feng Lizhi calls for the release of China's many political prisoners to mark the approaching 70th anniversary of the May 4 Movement.

It is the death on April 15 of Hu Yaobang, now perceived as an arch liberal, however that sparks widespread demands for reform. A small body of students camp out in Beijing's **Tiananmen Square**, ahead of Hu's memorial service on April 23. By April 27 the number of demonstrators has grown to 50,000, among them many workers. Although Li Peng opts for a strong response, Zhao Ziyang argues in favour of dialogue with the protestors. In the face of government indecision the demonstration swells, spilling over into nearby streets.

On May 13 student leaders begin a hunger-strike, two days ahead of the Russian leader **Mikhail Gorbachev**'s arrival on a state visit.

On May 17 the PRC's leadership convenes at Deng's residence and, swayed by Li, determines to forcibly end the demonstration. Next day Zhao apologizes to the protestors. Stripped of his office, he is replaced as General Secretary by **Jiang Zemin**.

On May 20 martial law is imposed in Beijing, but it is several days before army units are moved into the city's outskirts, and several more before they are persuaded to act against their own people.

On June 3 the PLA begins emptying Beijing's streets, and in the early hours of June 4 deploys tanks to clear Tiananmen Square. Estimates of those killed, including some soldiers as well as students, workers and other civilians, range between 700 and 3000. In the ensuing months, government security forces hunt down those regarded as the 'ringleaders' of the 'Tiananmen Square incident'. Similar episodes, unreported in the international press, occur in other cities.

1989 is also marked by a renewed and brutal suppression of political opposition in **Tibet**.

1990 Limited collectivization is reintroduced into some rural areas to create economically efficient 'super-farms'. **McDonald's**, the US hamburger restaurant chain, opens its first outlets in China.

Tiananmen Square 1989

By 1989 China had become a multigrievance society. As some Chinese prospered, others suffered from the contraction of state-run industries and a declining provision of welfare. Increased commercial and cultural links with the West, and a partial liberalization of China's domestic media, had exposed city-dwellers to new ideas and lifestyles. Among the young, the age of jeans and pop music had arrived. Even so, the explosion of dissent that occurred in **Tiananmen Square** was not just, or even mainly, a clamour for Western-style democracy, despite the best efforts of the Western media to portray it as such.

Student leaders condemned the 'new capitalism', while the large contingent of workers were most concerned with real pay levels at a time of rampant inflation. Because of these complexities, the government dithered, split between the hard-liner **Li Peng**, and the liberal reformist **Zhao Ziyang**. It did not help the situation that the protest coincided with a state visit, designed to repair Sino-Russian relations, by Mikhail Gorbachev, the apostle of glasnost and perestroika. Suddenly, China was under the gaze of the international media as never before. But there is scant evidence to suppose that the infamous 'crackdown', once ordered, was ordered reluctantly. Deng, Li and their associates acted to preserve the hegemony of the Party. For a while afterwards, the PRC became a pariah state. But economic self-interest, and the need to enlist China's support on the UN Security Council for their war against Saddam Hussein in 1992, meant that the USA and its Western allies were soon ready to forgive and forget, although 'Tiananmen '89' remains talismanic among human and political rights activists.

In December, inauguration of the Shanghai Security Exchange heralds the beginning of a stock-market system.

1992 Aged 88, Deng tours central and southern China to generate support for renewed economic reforms. In October the fourteenth CCP Congress endorses Deng's

At the climax of the Tiananmen Square protests, a statue of the Goddess of Democracy raises the torch of liberty in the face of Mao Zedong.

policies against hardliners seeking a return to state planning. The first **stock market** proper is opened in Guangzhou, and China's biggest Special Economic Zone is launched at Pudong in the suburbs of Shanghai.

Deng Xiaoping 1904–97

The architect of China's post-1976 reconstruction, and the son of a Sichuan farmer, **Deng Xiaoping** spent six years studying in France. Recruited by the communists in 1925, he played an integral part in the CCP's rise to power. During the **Long March**, he edited the mimeographed *Red Star* army newspaper, and from 1948 commanded the army that took Shanghai. In 1951 he masterminded the PRC's occupation of Tibet, and was rewarded with a vice-premiership in 1952.

In the tortuous years ahead, only his friendship with Zhou Enlai enabled him to survive the enmity of Lin Biao, Jiang Qing and other ultrahardliners. During the Cultural Revolution, Deng was vilified as 'Number Two Capitalist Roader', just behind Liu Shaoqi. But while Liu paid the ultimate penalty for his opposition to Mao, Deng was merely exiled to Nanchang, where he spent several years working at a tractor repair plant. Rehabilitated in 1973, by early 1975 he seemed most likely to succeed Mao. But in 1976 he was again ostracized, and it was not until 1981 that Deng emerged as China's unequivocal 'paramount leader'.

Able to bend a demoralized government to his will, he pushed for technological modernization and economic liberalization. Having recourse to a Sichuanese proverb, he cheekily proclaimed: 'It doesn't matter if the cat is black or white, so long as it catches the mouse.' But having gained the West's admiration, he promptly lost it by his knee-jerk response to **Tiananmen Square**. Viewed within the context of Chinese history, however, Deng belongs squarely among the great consolidators and constructivists. That he eschewed the vanities of power in favour of unremitting hard work is also to his credit.

1993 As television sets become commonplace, private satellite dishes are outlawed to minimize the impact of foreign broadcasting.

1995 As Deng slips into a permanent coma, Jiang Zemin, Chairman of the Military Commission as well as Party General Secretary, assumes full power. After years of discussion, work begins on the **Three Gorges Dam Project**, the world's largest hydroelectric enterprise. In the coming decade, a 350-mile-long reservoir will be created between Chongqing and Yichang on the upper Yangzi, yielding increased power capacity and flood control. Its critics claim environmental damage, the displacement of 1.3 million people, the destruction of a premier scenic beauty, and the embezzlement of funds by contractors and local officials.

1996 A 'Strike Hard' anti-crime campaign leads to the execution of 4000 offenders, in most cases following only minimal judicial proceedings. Fresh anti-migrant laws are enacted to limit urban drift.

In **Taiwan**, the first free elections for the Presidency and National Assembly generate fresh tensions with the mainland. The PRC stages military and naval exercises in Fujian, firing missiles into the Taiwan Straits, but a military strike is ruled out after the USA moves a battle fleet into Taiwanese waters.

In the same year China becomes the world's largest garment exporter – a trade valued at US$38 billion.

1997 Deng dies on February 19.

At midnight on June 30, Jiang Zemin presides over a ceremony marking the return of **Hong Kong** and associated territories to Chinese rule. The last British Governor, Chris Patten weeps as he boards the royal yacht *Britannia*. A democratically elected multi party Legislative Council is replaced by an appointed council, but in other respects Hong Kong's 'freedoms' are left intact as China seeks to convince Taiwan it has nothing to fear from mainland rule.

The PRC, meanwhile, gamely refuses to devalue the yuan despite feeling the effects of a pan-East Asian recession, and in so doing attracts further inward investment from global capital markets. While ninety percent of Chinese households now own a television, seventy percent lack hot water.

A 'Law on Lawyers' for the first time permits those accused under Chinese criminal law to engage a defence counsel, but the 'rule of law' as adumbrated by the UN Universal Declaration of Human Rights remains a distant prospect.

1998 Zhu Rongji, a former Mayor of Shanghai and loyal supporter of Jiang, replaces Li Peng as prime minister. Negotiations for the PRC's eventual membership of the **World Trade Organization** commence.

Across China, an estimated 300,000 cases of HIV infection are reported by the World Health Organization.

1999 The government begins persecuting the esoteric **Falun Gong** movement after 15,000 of its members stage a rally in Tiananmen Square on April 27.

In Washington, the Cox Report implicates Chinese agents in the theft of US nuclear secrets.

Severe flooding in central China leads to several thousand deaths.

Jiang and Boris Yeltsin conclude a Sino-Russian 'anti-Nato' pact at Kishkek in Kirghistan.

On October 1 carefully choreographed celebrations mark the 50th anniversary of the PRC.

On November 15 China and the USA reach a preliminary agreement regarding China's entry into the World Trade Organization.

Jiang Zemin b. 1926

The PRC's 'third generation leader', **Jiang Zemin** is perceived as a politically conservative technocrat who, unlike Mao and Deng, had no first-hand experience of military affairs prior to becoming party leader in 1989. Under his rule, the PLA has played a conspicuously reduced role. Conversely, the People's Armed Police and other 'security' services have been greatly expanded. Born in Yangzhou, Jiang trained as an engineer in Nanjing and joined the Party in 1946. Somewhat fortuitously, he became manager of the American-owned popsicle factory where he was working when the communists took Shanghai in 1947. Subsequently, he pursued a career that combined industrial with political management.

Ostracized during the Cultural Revolution, he became **Mayor of Shanghai** in 1985 after overseeing sensitive electronics and space-rocket projects. In 1987 he became party chief in the same city, and a member of the Politburo. His promotion to **General Secretary** of the CCP during the **Tiananmen Square** crisis took most observers by surprise. In April, however, he had faced down students in Shanghai, and he was conveniently distanced from factional infighting in Beijing.

Throughout the 1990s, Jiang extended Deng's mix of economic opportunism and authoritarian government. On the world stage, he has won affection by his willingness to sing folk and music-hall songs in a variety of languages. His critics, however, recall how when Jiang himself was a student he joined anti-Guomingdang demonstrations demanding democratic reform; and how in Shanghai, as well as gaining the nickname 'Flowerpot', he was known as a 'velvet-covered needle'.

On December 20 **Macau** reverts to Chinese administration after 450 years of Portuguese rule. Its many casinos remain open, but its criminal gangs are suppressed.

2000 In January 1200 government agents are sent to Fujian province to counter **corruption** among officials.

On February 21 the State Council releases a paper ahead of fresh elections in Taiwan stating that the PRC will consider 'all possible drastic measures including force' if Taiwan refuses to negotiate its 'reunification' with the mainland.

In November China launches and recovers its first **unmanned spacecraft**, ahead of manned space flights by the year 2005.

In December, relations with Taiwan ease as the way is paved for 'direct' commercial air and shipping links.

In an attempt to control dissemination of 'subversive' information through the **Internet**, the PRC promulgates largely ineffectual laws to regulate Websites.

2001 China's **population** is estimated at 1.34 billion – over a fifth of the world's total. Of this, about one billion are peasants, materially and educationally backward. Only two percent of Chinese can expect tertiary education, and up to a third live below the poverty line as defined by the World Bank. Average per capita income is less than US$250. Other agencies point to endemic **pollution**, the hidden **insolvency** of many industries part or fully owned by the state, the persistent use of **torture**, and the arbitrary detention of up to four million individuals in **labour camps**. Conversely, China's economic growth rate, running at about eight percent of its annual GNP, continues to outpace that of any other major nation, and 2001 saw important advances in China's international standing.

In July Jiang Zemin visits Moscow and signs a **Sino-Russian friendship treaty** with Vladimir Putin; and Beijing is named as the host city for the **2008 Olympic Games**.

In the wake of Al-Qaida's attack on **New York City** on September 11, Sino-American relations are repaired following a rupture caused by the forced landing of an American spy plane on Hainan island earlier in the year.

Falun Gong

Described variously as a personal health regimen, a religious sect, an evil cult and a front for political opposition, **Falun Gong** originated in 1992, one among several groups purporting to revive **Daoist** meditative breathing techniques known as *qigong*. Falun Gong, however, is overlaid with **Buddhist** precepts: its disciplines can 'move' the 'Great Wheel of Dharma'. Its doctrines, spread by publications, videos, the Internet and by word-of-mouth, are summarized in the formula *zhen shan ren* – 'truth, goodness, forbearance'.

Its founder, **Li Hongzhi**, born in Manchuria in 1952, served in the PLA as a trumpeter. That he has resided in the USA since 1998 has exacerbated the suspicions of a government paranoid about any mass movement not controlled by itself, especially one that apparently appeals to a broad cross-section of society. Since April 1999, Falun Gong has been energetically suppressed, on the grounds that its esoteric self-healing message is damaging to public health, for all that public healthcare programmes are also conspicuously failing. Reportedly, 10,000 adherents have been detained in prison camps, with 100 or more custodial deaths resulting from maltreatment.

For their part, Falun Gong members make a habit of meditating in such public arenas as Tiananmen Square while insisting on their right to private devotion. Inevitably, comparisons are drawn with the White Lotus, Taiping and Boxer insurgencies of the 19th century. For the PRC, the danger is that by overreacting it will turn Falun Gong into the threat it perceives.

Since China, the USA and Russia each have a vested interest in combating the spread of Islamic fundamentalism and terrorism in Central Asia, a rare state of accord pertains between the three powers.

In November, the PRC is admitted into the **WTO**, on the understanding that its domestic markets will become fully open to international competition in 2005. Western media coverage of China, however, remains focused on such issues as institutionalized corruption, the Taiwan question, Falun Gong and government efforts to control access to and use of the Internet.

During 2001, it is also officially conceded that the spread of HIV infection inside China is far greater than hitherto acknowledged in official statistics.

Books

Books

The existing literature on Chinese history would require a lifetime to absorb. The excellent *Cambridge History of Ancient China*'s bibliography alone lists some 2000 items. As some of the better books about China are out of print, access to a good library is first base for any serious interest in the subject. That said, the titles that follow should not be impossible to find. Whenever a book is in print, the UK publisher is given first in each listing, followed by the publisher in the US – unless the title is available in one country only, in which case we have specified which country, or is published by the same company in both territories, in which case only the publisher is specified.

General History

S.A.M. Adshead *China in World History* (Macmillan). Having the temerity to compare the Chinese with other major civilisations yields a hugely ambitious, sometimes inaccurate, but always stimulating overview. Now in its third edition.

Cambridge History of China (Cambridge University Press). This monument of scholarship in fifteen volumes provides the fullest, if highly academic, survey of Chinese history post-221 BC. First began publication in 1979.

John King Fairbank *China: A New History* (Harvard University Press). Good single-volume histories of China are scarce, but Fairbank's seasoned outline is commended.

Valerie Hansen *The Open Empire: A History of China to 1600* (W.W. Norton). This companion volume to Spence's *The Search for Modern China* is readable, but weak on political narrative.

Morris Rossabi *China and Inner Asia: from 1368 to the Present Day* (Thames & Hudson o/p). Rossabi explores China's ongoing struggle against its 'barbarian' neighbours.

Jonathan Spence *The Search for Modern China* (W.W. Norton). Written by the doyen of contemporary Sinologists, this fine book combines cultural and literary insights in its examination of Chinese history since 1644. Now in its second edition.

Culture and Science

C.P. Fitzgerald *China: A Short Cultural History* (Westview Press; Holt, Reinhart & Winston). Fitzgerald's 1954 work may have little time for anything post-Ming, but his judgements about most of what went before remain as sure-footed as they are elegant.

Andrew J. Nathan and Robert S. Ross *The Great Wall of China and the Empty Fortress* (W.W. Norton). This re-assessment of China's supposedly xenophobic foreign relations is both convincing and timely.

Joseph Needham *Science and Civilisation in China* (Cambridge University Press). Needham's great labour in thirteen volumes is justly regarded as a watershed study of Chinese science and technology, as well as a model investigation of mainly ancient and medieval mechanics. Robert Temple's *The Genius of China: 3000 Years of Science, Discovery and Invention* (Prion Books; Touchstone) furnishes a somewhat breathless, but authorised, precis of Needham's magnum opus.

Laurence Sickman and Alexander Soper *The Art and Architecture of China* (Yale). First published in 1968 and now in its third edition, this is a dated, but still sound, single-volume introduction to its subject-matter.

Jonathan Spence *The Chan's Great Continent: China in Western Minds* (Penguin; W.W. Norton). Spence reviews the shifting responses of Western writers to China from Marco Polo to Italo Calvino.

Joanna Waley-Cohen *The Sextants of Beijing* (W.W. Norton). The author argues plausibly that the Chinese have been more open to foreign innovation than is usually acknowledged.

Ancient China

Elizabeth Wayland Barber *The Mummies of Ürümchi* (W.W. Norton). A sensible, but imaginative account of the recent discovery of Caucasian remains in the Tarim Basin.

Michael Loewe and Edward L. Shaughnessy (eds.) *Cambridge History of Ancient China* (Cambridge University Press). This weighty 'companion volume' to the *Cambridge History of China* is a state-of-the-art 'introduction' to the conundrums and complexities of the historical and archeological records, and a must for the serious student.

Jessica Rawson *Ancient China: Art and Archaeology* (British Museum Publications). Published over two decades ago, and now showing its age, Rawson's nicely compacted summary is still as good as any a starting point.

Jessica Rawson (ed.) *Mysteries of Ancient China* (British Museum Publications; Braziller). A richly illustrated guide to the archeology and material artefacts

Imperial China: from 221 BC to 1644

Hans Bielenstein *The Bureaucracy of Han Times* (Cambridge Univeristy Press o/p). Beneath the grey surface of this seminal structural analysis of imperial government in its formative period, lurks a riot of hyperbolic Chinese nomenclature.

Woodbridge Bingham *The Founding of the T'ang Dynasty* (Baltimore o/p; Octagon). In its time (1941), this fascinating scholarly monograph set new standards for Chinese studies.

Arthur Cotterell *The First Emperor of China* (Macmillan o/p; Holt

Rinehart o/p). While the definitive study of the Terracotta Army has yet to be written, this provides a genial introduction to Qin Shihuangdi and his world-class folly.

Michael Loewe *The Pride That Was China* (Sidgwick & Jackson; St Martin's Press). Loewe has nothing but contempt for everything post-Ming, but knows his way around the early dynasties as well as any other scholar.

Robert Marshall *Storm from the East: from Genghis Khan to Khublai Khan* (University of California Press). Based on a BBC TV series, this is an unscholarly but reader-friendly introduction to the Mongols.

Ann Paludan *Chronicle of the Chinese Emperors* (Thames & Hudson). Good on the basics, handsomely illustrated, but unevenly written.

Edwin G. Pulleyblank *The Background of the Rebellion of An Lu-Shan* (Oxford University Press o/p). First published in 1955, Pulleyblank questions the prejudices surrounding the supposed destroyer of the Tang imperium.

The Qing Dynasty 1644–1912

Peter Fleming *The Siege at Peking* (Oxford University Press). Detailing the end of the Boxer rebellion, Fleming's often reprinted study (first published in 1958) is quintessentially a colonial narrative, however well-worked.

Christopher Hibbert *The Dragon Wakes: China and the West 1793–1911* (Longman o/p). A cultured narrative of the impact of Western acquisitiveness and Western assertiveness on the Middle Kingdom.

Colin Mackerras (with Robert Chan) *Modern China: A Chronology from 1842 to the Present* (Thames & Hudson o/p). This month-by-month chronology is short on overview, but particularly useful for students of the later Qing who have the patience to combat its byzantine layout.

Aubrey Singer *The Lion and the Dragon* (Barrie & Jenkins). Singer lovingly re-tells the story of Earl Macartney's ill-fated trade mission of 1793.

Jonathan Spence *God's Chinese Son: The Taiping Heavenly Kingdom of Hong Xiuquan* (HarperCollins; W.W. Norton). Of the many accounts of the Taiping Rebellion this is the most widely available, and also the most probing.

Jonathan Spence *Treason by the Book* (Penguin). By brilliantly reconstructing an illusory conspiracy during the Yongzheng emperor's reign, Spence reveals the extent and workings of the Manchu secret service.

Arthur Waley *The Opium War Through Chinese Eyes* (Stanford University Press). Waley's 1958 classic still serves as an exemplary antidote against any temptation to write Chinese history without reference to Chinese sources.

Twentieth Century China

Jasper Becker *Hungry Ghosts: China's Secret Famine* (John Murray; Henry Holt). Becker relentlessly uncovers the debacle of the Great Leap Forward after the communists had established power.

Martin Booth *The Dragon Syndicates: The Global Phenomenon of the Triads* (Bantam; Carroll & Graf). A well-documented, but overly alarmist investigation of organised crime Chinese-style.

Fox Butterfield *China: Alive in the Bitter Sea* (Random House). While every reporter wants to add his or her fevered grote's worth, Butterfield's intimate portrayal of Chinese society in the immediate wake of the Cultural Revolution survives the test of time.

Jung Chan *Wild Swans: Three Daughters of China* (Flamingo; Anchor). One of the first 'personal' memoirs to present a view of the Cultural Revolution from the inside, this is a vital read, although other expatriate memoirs deserve attention, notably Anhua Gao's *To the Edge of the Sky* (Viking).

Iris Chang *The Rape of Nanking: The Forgotten Holocaust of World War II* (Penguin; Basic Books). Chang's exposé of what the Japanese did in Nanjing in 1937 is as disturbing as it is full-frontal.

John King Fairbank *The Great Chinese Revolution 1800–1985* (HarperCollins). Fairbank offers a compelling and hard-edged political analysis of the traumas underlying China's transition from feudal empire to neo-modern state.

Max Hastings *The Korean War* (Pan; Touchstone). One of the best war reporters around delivers a superbly engrossing military and political reconstruction of a conflict that nearly sparked World War III.

Adrian Levy and Cathy Scott-Clark *The Stone of Heaven: The Secret of Imperial Green Trade* (Phoenix; Little, Brown & Co). Two journalists harrowingly reveal how the Chinese and increasingly international appetite for jade underwrites the worst excesses of the military regime in Myanmar/Burma. Their understanding of less recent Chinese history, however, is factually and interpretatively inadequate.

Roderick Macfarquar *The Origins of the Cultural Revolution* (Oxford University Press; Columbia University Press). Macfarquar's huge, three-volume work, written over three decades, is the indispensable source for those seriously interested in possibly the 20th century's most bizarre ideological contortion.

Andrew J. Nathan and Perry Link (eds.) *The Tiananmen Papers* (Little, Brown & Co; Public Affairs). Consciously echoing the *Pentagon Papers* that helped end the American war in Vietnam, this purports to spill the beans on those who ordered the brutal 1989 crackdown.

Harrison Salisbury *The Long March: The Untold Story* (McGraw-Hill). Unlike the Guomingdang, Salisbury succeeds in capturing The Red Army in its legendary retreat from Jiangxi to Shanxi.

Tsering Shakya *The Dragon in the Land of Snows: A History of Modern Tibet Since 1947* (Pimlico; Columbia University Press). A pro-Tibetan, but disciplined, assessment of the effects of Chinese rule where it is least welcomed.

Edgar Snow *Red Star Over China* (Bantam; Grove Press). Containing extended interviews with Mao Zedong before he acceded to power, this famous book, written in 1937 by a sympathetic American, was largely responsible for the mystique of the early Chinese communists as perceived in the West.

Jonathan Spence *The Gate of Heavenly Peace: The Chinese and their Rebellion* (Viking). Spence covers much the same ground as Fairbank (see above), but from a cultural (and often literary) perspective.

Dick Wilson *China's Revolutionary War* (Weidenfeld; St. Martin's Press). Written by a seasoned China-hand, this is a usefully concise political and military introduction to the protracted struggle between the communists and the Guomingdang for ultimate power.

Justin Wintle *The Viet Nam Wars* (Weidenfeld; St. Martin's Press). As well as clarifying China's backing for Ho Chi Minh's communists in their struggle against the French, the author summarises the subsequent rupture between the two states apropos Cambodia.

Francis Wood *No Dogs and Not Many Chinese: Treaty Port Life in China 1843–1943* (John Murray; Trafalgar Square). A wide-ranging and mainly anecdotal history of the Western experience inside China.

Contemporary China

Jasper Becker *The Chinese* (John Murray; The Free Press). Having dished up the dirt on the Great Leap Forward, Becker seeks to uncover the true extent of corruption and governmental desuetude under the current regime.

Graham Hutchings *Modern China: A Companion to a Rising Power* (Penguin). A journalist's bulky *vade mecum* to the contemporary scene.

David Leffman, Simon Lewis and Jeremy Atiyah *China: The Rough Guide* (Rough Guides). Now in its second edition, this provides a mine of valuable information about China today, its provinces, cities and historic sites.

Joe Studwell *The China Dream: The Elusive Quest for the Greatest Untapped Market on Earth* (Profile Books; Publishers Group West). By far and away the most informative analysis of China's economy since the Deng Xiao Ping reforms, and of the West's frenzied attempts to take the proffered bait.

The CIA's **cia.gov/cia/publications/factbook/geoc/ch.html** is a surprisingly visitable website. Amnesty International's **amnesty.org:COUNTRIESàCHINA** highlights human rights violations. The fairest English language press coverage of China is probably the *New York Times*, freely accessible on **partners.nytimes.com**.

Biographies

Edward Behr *The Last Emperor* (Macdonald & Co; Bantam Doubleday). Closely related to Bertolucci's film epic of the same title, Behr's biography of the unfortunate Puyi underscores the frailty of all monarchies.

Richard Evans *Deng Xiaoping and the Making of Modern China* (Penguin). Hardly definitive, this early appraisal by a former UK ambassador to Beijing is nonetheless rewarding as a first-base fix on Deng's still underrated achievement.

Bruce Gilley *Tiger on the Brink: Jiang Zemin and China's New Elite* (University of California Press). Gilley is candid about Jiang's foibles, but misses out on the man's formidable politicking.

Zhisui Li *The Private Life of Chairman Mao: The Memoirs of Mao's Personal Physician* (Arrow; Random House). Li's is probably the most intimate portrait of a tyrant ever penned outside fiction, and certainly the most grotesquely entertaining.

Harold Z. Schiffrin *Sun Yat-sen: Reluctant Revolutionary* (Little, Brown & Co). Lives of Sun are usually as muddled as they are partisan, but this one rises above the pack.

Philip Short *Mao: A Life* (Hodder; Owl Books). An immaculately well-researched chronicle of Mao's dogged rise to power and his imperious continuance therein.

Ross Terrill *White-Boned Demon: A Biography of Madame Mao Zedong* (Stanford University Press). The best account of Jiang Qing and the Gang of Four to date.

Arthur Waley *The Life and Times of Po Chü-i* (Allen & Unwin (UK) o/p) and *The Poetry and Career of Li Po* (Unwin Hyman o/p). Waley's are beautifully sensitive and learned studies of two outstanding Tang poets first published in 1949 and 1950 respectively.

Marina Warner *The Dragon Empress* (Vintage; Trafalgar Square). Of the many books about that perfect vamp the Dowager-empress Cixi and her eunuch court, this is the most evocative, and also the most literary.

Burton Watson *Ssu-ma Ch'ien: Grand Historian of China* (Columbia Univeristy Press o/p). Sima Qian, the Han scholar who more than any other shaped Chinese historiography, is sympathetically and intelligently brought back to life in this 1958 volume. In 1962 Watson also translated Sima Qian's history, as *Records of the Grand Historian of China* (Columbia University Press, 2 vols.).

Literary classics in translation

In all cases the translations of Chinese classics from which quotations are derived in the main body of this book are recommended. Details of these will be found in the 'Notes and Acknowledgements' section. Other translations that have not been quoted but which merit particular mention are:

The Book of Songs (Shi jing) (Grove Press). China's oldest and most important poetry collection was skillfully rendered into English by Arthur Waley in 1937, the master of verse translation.

Wu Cheng-en *Monkey* (Penguin). If you're looking for a medieval cult novel full of the sort of acrobatic imagery that makes *Crouching Tiger, Sleeping Dragon* the film it is, then read Waley's translation completed in 1942.

I Ching or Book of Changes (Yijing) (Routledge). Of the many attempts to translate the *Book of Changes*, this 1951 English version by Cary F. Barnes of Richard Wilhelm's translation, with its full textual commentaries, has the most appeal.

Cao Xueqin *Story of the Stone (aka The Dream of the Red Chamber)* (Penguin). David Hawkes's fastidious 1975 translation of China's greatest, and also longest novel in five volumes (see p.291) is an achievement in itself.

Lu Xun *AhQ and Others: Selected Stories of Lusin* (Greenwood Press o/p). Translated by Chi-chen Wang in 1941, the teasing simplicity of Lu Xun's stories (see p.365) makes it hard to understand why China's leading early 20th-century writer has yet to be fully appreciated in the West.

index

a

b

m

n